CW01066601

Women in Asia Publication Series

WOMEN IN ASIA

WOMEN IN ASIA

Tradition, modernity and globalisation

Louise Edwards & Mina Roces

Routledge
Taylor & Francis Group

LONDON AND NEW YORK

First published 2000 by Allen & Unwin

Published 2020 by Routledge
2 Park Square, Milton Park, Abingdon, Oxon OX14 4RN
605 Third Avenue, New York, NY 10017

First issued in hardback 2021

Routledge is an imprint of the Taylor & Francis Group, an informa business

National Library of Australia
Cataloguing-in-Publication entry:

Women in Asia: tradition, modernity and globalisation.

Bibliography.
Includes index.
ISBN 1 86508 318 6.

1. Women—Asia, Southeastern. 2. Women—East Asia. 3. Women—India.
4. Sex role—Asia, Southeastern. 5. Sex role—East Asia. 6. Sex role—India.
I. Edwards, Louise. II. Roces, Mina, 1959– . III. Title. (Series: Women in
Asia publication series).

305.42095

ISBN 13: 978-0-367-72010-0 (hbk)
ISBN 13: 978-1-86508-318-6 (pbk)

Contents

Notes on contributors ix
List of tables xii
Acknowledgements xiii

1. **Contesting gender narratives, 1970–2000** 1
   Mina Roces & Louise Edwards
    The development narrative and globalisation 6
    'Being women' in Asia 1970–2000 10
    Focus on the Asian woman: 1970–2000 and beyond 12
    References 15

2. **Becoming modern in Malaysia: women at the end of the twentieth century** 16
   Maila Stivens
    The new Malaysia 17
    Class, state and gender in the new Malaysia 20
    Family and domesticity 25
    Rural women 28
    Politics, religion and nation 30
    Conclusion 32
    Notes 32
    References and recommended readings 34

3. **The status of women in a patriarchal state: the case of Singapore** 39
   Jasmine Chan
    Changes in women's lives 40
    The patriarchal state and women's status 43
    The women's movement in Singapore 52
    Conclusion 54
    Notes 55
    References and recommended readings 55

4. **Women in the People's Republic of China: new challenges to the grand gender narrative** 59
   Louise Edwards
    Building China's socialist modernity 60
    Dismantling socialism and consequences for women 63
    Representatives of women: the Women's Federation 64
    Politics in the communist state 68
    Problems in paid employment 70
    Women and population control 73

Educating the modern Chinese woman 77
Intellectualising feminism and academic work 79
Conclusion 81
References and recommended readings 82

5. **Diversity and the status of women: the Indian experience** 85
Ruchira Ganguly-Scrase
Male/Female sex ratio 86
Literacy 87
Labour force participation 87
Cultural constructions of gender and sexuality 88
Activities of the women's movement 90
Communalisation of gender identity 98
Communalism and feminist scholarship 103
Towards the future 104
Conclusion 107
Notes 107
References and recommended readings 108

6. **Negotiating modernities: Filipino women 1970-2000** 112
Mina Roces
Women and power/women and politics 115
Women activists 120
Women and labour 124
Legislation and women's status 132
Cultural constructions of women 133
Conclusion 134
Notes 135
References and recommended readings 135

7. **Indonesian Women—from *Orde Baru* to *Reformasi*** 139
Kathryn Robinson
The gender order of the New Order 141
Gender diversity in Indonesia 142
Marriage Law 146
New Order social policy 148
Economic policies 150
Political representation 154
Sexuality and personal freedom 156
New definitions of gender difference 159
Political violence and women 160
Conclusion 163
References and recommended readings 165

8. **Rhetoric or reality?: contesting definitions of women in Korea**
    Sasha Hampson   170
        Changing Korean families: the resilience of Confucianism   171
        Women creating the 'economic miracle'   176
        Education for social mobility   179
        Women's participation in politics and government   181
        The Korean women's movement   182
        Sexual and domestic violence   184
        Conclusion   186
        References and recommended readings   186

9. **Breaking the patriarchal paradigm: Chinese women in Hong Kong**
    C.Tang, W.T. Au, Y.P. Chung and H.Y. Ngo   188
        Population and demographics   190
        Education   191
        Employment and income   192
        Political participation   196
        Perceptions of gender equality and the persistence of stereotypes   197
        Violence against women   198
        Hong Kong's women's movement   201
        Conclusion   204
        References and recommended readings   204

10. **Being women in Japan 1970-2000**   208
    Elise K. Tipton
        The home: women's domain?   209
        The paid workplace: separate and unequal   214
        Women in the public arena   217
        Women as subject and object in the world of popular culture   221
        Conclusion   225
        References and recommended readings   226

11. **Women in Taiwan: linking economic prosperity and women's progress**
    Lan-hung Nora Chiang   229
        Women and family planning   230
        Women's educational attainment   232
        The economic achievements of women in Taiwan   235
        Political and social participation   239
        Conclusion   242
        References and recommended readings   244

12. Exploring women's status in contemporary Thailand   247
Bhassorn Limanonda
     Cultural values and gender equity   248
     Official policies on women: the evolution of strategic plans   251
     Reproduction, sexuality and the changing demographic profile   253
     Education and employment   255
     Women's status in the family   259
     Conclusion   261
     References and recommended readings   261

13. Militarism, civil war and women's status: a Burma case study   265
Janell Mills
     Women in monarchic Burma: pre-1886   267
     Women in the colonial period (1886–1948)   270
     Women in independent Burma: parliamentary period
        (1948–62)   271
     Women in the first period of military rule (1962–88)   272
     Women in Burma after 1988   276
     Conclusion   286
     References and recommended readings   287

14. Re-gendering Vietnam: from militant to market socialism   291
Esta Ungar
     The pre-1973 period   292
     The 1973–1986 period: peace and socialism   295
     The period since 1986: economic liberalisation   307
     References and recommended readings   314

Index   318
World Wide Web addresses on women in Asia   324

Notes on contributors

Jasmine Shariff Chan holds a PhD in Sociology from Yale University. She teaches in the Department of Sociology at the National University of Singapore. Her current research interests are feminist theorising and methodologies, sociology of law, and the state. She is always interested in feminist strategies, an interest that grew out of her PhD dissertation on feminism and gender bias in the American courts. She is presently working on feminist discourses and the authoritarian state, with particular emphasis on the Southeast Asian region. Recent motherhood also played an important role in putting a new perspective on many issues, personal and professional!

Lan-hung Nora Chiang is Professor of Geography at National Taiwan University. She received her PhD from the University of Hawaii and her MA from Indiana University. She has been the Director of the Population Studies Centre and President of the ROC Population Association. Her current research projects include China's township industries and migrants, and recent Taiwan immigrants to Australia. She is the Co-ordinator of the Interdisciplinary Group of Australia Studies at National Taiwan University.

Louise Edwards teaches Asian Studies at Australian Catholic University. A PhD graduate from Griffith University, her publications include *Men and Women in Qing China* (1994), *Recreating the Literary Canon* (1995) and *Censored by Confucius* (1996) (with Kam Louie) as well as numerous articles. Her research interests include the women's suffrage movement in China during the first half of the twentieth century, Chinese literature and the intellectual history of China. She is currently secretary of the Asian Studies Association of Australia and Councillor of the Chinese Studies Association of Australia.

Ruchira Ganguly-Scrase holds a PhD in Anthropology from the University of Melbourne. She teaches sociology and anthropology at Charles Sturt University. Her research interests include gender relations in India, globalisation and cultural politics of minorities. Currently she is working on a project that examines the impact of globalisation and economic liberalisation in India. She has published a number of articles on women's work, ethnographic method and economic reform in India. Her forthcoming book is titled *Global Issues, Local Contexts: The Rabi Das of Bengal.*

Sasha Hampson lived in Seoul between 1993–98 and studied at Yonsei University. Her Masters thesis focussed on the Korean comfort women and Sex Workers in US military base in Korea. Through her research she became involved with several women's organisations such as the Asian Women's Centre for Culture and Theology, the Korean Council for Women Drafted for Military Sexual Slavery by Japan and Saewoomto.

Bhassorn Limanonda is associate professor in the College of Population Studies at Chulalongkorn University. She was awarded a PhD in Sociology-Demography from Brown University USA. From 1988–92 and 1996–97 she was Director of the Institute for Population Studies at Chulalongkorn University. Her major research interests are marriage, family, women, AIDS and reproductive health.

Dr **Janell Mills** is a graduate of the Universities of Queensland and London and an Honorary Research Associate in Economic History at the University of Sydney. She studied at the School of Oriental and African Studies in London for her doctorate on 19th century Burmese history and has written a number of articles on Burma.

Kathryn Robinson is an anthropologist who has worked mainly in South Sulawesi, Indonesia. Her research has been concerned with aspects of contemporary women's social participation in Indonesia, including women's political activism, the relation of women to government programs, and international female labour migration. She has published extensively on the Soroako nickel mine, on Sulawesi traditional architecture and has, with Mukhlis Paeni edited a series of books on the anthropology of South Sulawesi. Her major publications include *Stepchildren of Progress: The Political Economy of Development in an Indonesian Mining Town* (1986), and *Living Through Histories: Culture, History and Social Life in South Sulawesi* (1998) (with Mukhlis Paini). Currently, she is Senior Fellow and Head of Department in Anthropology, Research School of Pacific and Asian Studies at the Australian National University.

A PhD graduate from The University of Michigan, **Mina Roces** teaches history at the University of New South Wales in Australia. She is the author of *Women, Power and Kinship Politics: Female Power in Post-War Philippines* (1998), and *Kinship Politics in Post-War Philippines: The Lopez Family, 1945–2000*, (forthcoming). Her articles have also appeared in a number of journals including: *Modern Asian Studies, Asian Studies Review, Public Policy, Lila: Asia Pacific Women's Studies Journal*, and *Moussons*. Current research interests include post-war Philippines (particularly kinship politics), gender and power in twentieth century Philippines, contesting definitions of Filipino identity in the twentieth century, technocrats and politics, and Filipino migrants in Australia.

Maila Stivens did postgraduate work in Anthropology at Sydney University and at the London School of Economics. She has carried out research on middle class kinship in Sydney, on gender, 'matriliny' and development in Negeri Sembilan, Malaysia, on modernity, work and family among the new Malay middle classes and on the 'Asian Family' and Asian Values. She has taught Anthropology at University College London and is now Director of Women's Studies at the University of Melbourne. Her most recent main publications include *Matriliny and Modernity: Sexual Politics and Social Change in Rural Malaysia* (1996); a co-edited volume, with Krishna Sén, *Gender and Power in Affluent Asia* (1998), and a co-edited volume *Human Rights and Gender Politics* (2000, in press).

Catherine So-kum Tang is an Associate Professor in Psychology and Director of the Gender Research Programme at Chinese University of Hong Kong. Professor **Winton Wing-tung Au** is an Assistant Professor in Psychology, Professor **Ngo Hang Yue** is an Associate Professor in the Department of Management and Professor **Chung Yue Ping** is Professor and Dean of the Faculty of Education. The authors are all members of the Gender Research Programme at the Hong Kong Institute of Asia-Pacific Studies, The Chinese University of Hong Kong. They have collaborated on a number of gender-related projects such as gender equality, equal opportunity, violence against women and women's health in Hong Kong.

Elise K. Tipton teaches Japanese history in the Department of Japanese and Korean Studies at the University of Sydney, Australia. Her current research projects include the history of the Japanese birth control movement and the café in modern Japanese urban life. Recently, she has edited *Society and the State in Interwar Japan* (1997) and co-edited *Being Modern in Japan: Culture and Society from the 1910s to the 1930s* (2000).

Esta Ungar is a full-time lecturer in History at the University of Western Australia. Her primary research area involves history and development in Asian socialist countries with particular reference to land and gender issues. She also has overseas aid project experience under a number of international (UNDP, UNFPA) and local donor agencies (International Women's Development Agency, Quaker Service Australia). She took her PhD degree at Cornell University and originally specialised in Vietnamese and Chinese history and the formation of the state in fifteenth-century Vietnam.

List of tables

Malaysia

Table 2.1   Percentages of total number of male and
female workers employed in primary, secondary
and tertiary industries, 1970–90   21

Table 2.2   Occupational structure   22

Table 2.3   Female students as percentage of enrolment
by level and stream of education, 1970–90   25

Taiwan

Table 11.1   Educational attainment of population
aged 6 and over   233

Table 11.2   Students of colleges in National Taiwan
University by sex, 1997   234

Table 11.3   Industry of employed persons in Taiwan
area by sex   236

Table 11.4   Labour force participation rates in Taiwan
by sex   237

Vietnam

Table 14.1   Women in government national level   297

Table 14.2   Women in government provincial level   297

Table 14.3   Women in government district level   297

Table 14.4   Women in government local level   297

Table 14.5   Women in state leadership positions   298

Table 14.6   Women in Communist Party positions
at the national, provincial and local levels   299

Table 14.7   Widowed males and females by age cohort
in 1989   311

Table 14.8   School attendance by sex for children
age 10 and above in 1989   312

Acknowledgements

The Women's Caucus of the Asian Studies Association of Australia has been an important source of support for women in Asian Studies and for those working on women and gender in Asia in particular. The completion of this volume owes a great deal to the members of the Caucus who variously participated in conferences, contributed to the newsletter and served on the ASAA Council. Of particular significance has been the support of Beverley Hooper and Susan Blackburn. Over the past few years Bev and Sue have been friends and mentors for innumerable women in the field and our thanks go to them.

The continuing value of the ASAA in providing the location for productive interactions between academics and students working across the entire Asian region and within a wide range of disciplines is indisputable. John Butcher and John McKay, as Publications Officers for the ASAA have been instrumental in ensuring that the four ASAA Publications Series continue to thrive and we would like to thank John Butcher in particular for his help in smoothing the progress of this volume.

We would also like to thank the publishing team at Allen & Unwin for their help and support in the production of this book. Patrick Gallagher, Bridie Henehan and Rebecca Kaiser have provided invaluable advice and support.

Finally, Mina and I would like to make a special 'thank you' to the contributing authors of the various chapters. Each completed her chapter quickly and expertly and, in the course of our many conversations across the ether, made this project thoroughly enjoyable.

Louise Edwards,
Brisbane

Mina Roces,
Sydney

1999

1 Contesting gender narratives, 1970–2000

Mina Roces & Louise Edwards

University of New South Wales

Australian Catholic University

Modernisation is not gender neutral. In the modernisation process women are 'developed' differently, often inadvertently, from men. Similarly, women participate in development projects with objectives that often differ from those of men. By actively creating 'modernity' in this era of rapid globalisation, women in Asia are establishing dynamic new conceptions of contemporary cultural practice for their various nations, regions or communities. So diverse are the pictures and experiences of modernity that it is more fruitful to explore the multiple modernities of Asian women, or in Maila Stivens' terms, their 'divergent modernities' (Stivens 1998, p. 10). The development project of the close of the twentieth century provided new opportunities for women in the Asian region, but it also posed new dangers. This volume addresses the manner in which the 'woman question' has interacted with the dominant national discourses of 'development', 'globalisation', and 'modernisation' in a range of country case-studies. Recent social changes in women's place in society, often expressed as 'progress towards modernity', are untangled in recognition that not all change is 'progress' and not all 'modernity' enhances women's status.

The three decades 1970–2000 have seen this development project increase in speed and intensity. Development has been the mantra for government decisions and international aid programs. The results in the Asian region are impressive, wealth has been produced and life has improved for millions of people. The chapters in this book explore the ways in which these programs changed the lives of women in the region and the manner in which women have mobilised development and globalisation for their own national feminist causes. In this sense, the divergent modernities we are speaking of are in many ways shaped by women themselves who as agents of change have harnessed the power of the development narrative for their own ends. How have women in Asia engaged with the development and modernisation projects to create a new, modern Asian woman? How have they negotiated for a diversification in the traits of the iconic modern woman so invoked in the nationalist discourse? How do women in Asia use the narratives of globalisation—development and modernity—to create new possibilities and expand their opportunities? What is the Asian counterpart of the modern woman at the end of the twentieth century?

Women have taken up the development narrative to promote women's rights, status and value within the utopian vision of modernising the nation. The development of women, these activists have stressed, is crucial to the development of the nation. To harness the energies of all the people, women must also be developed—but, they argue, in ways that reflect the special needs of women. Engagement with the devil that is 'development' provides the opportunity for furthering women's rights and improving women's status. Part of this process involves exposing 'development' as a masculinist project, but it also allows scope for challenging the oppression of women by the equally masculinist traditional cultural practices. By employing the utopian vision of a modern state, women activists are able to dismantle aspects of the 'traditional' woman that maintained male dominance in the household and public life for centuries. Narratives of modernity provide the discursive tools for unravelling traditions and creating new national female identities.

If indeed it is more accurate to speak of 'divergent modernities' and multiple modernities, can we argue then that we must also speak of multiple gender narratives within single Asian societies? Up until the first half of the twentieth century it was more common to have one official gender narrative that was clearly hegemonic in a specific Asian cultural context. In most cases women were seen to be wives and mothers or as 'bearers of sons'. Although there may have been hidden pockets of resistance to the overarching narrative, they have never been able to seriously contest the official grand paradigm. In the last thirty years of the twentieth century however, new gender narratives have emerged which have begun to challenge the traditional one-dimensional definition of woman. Part of the legacy of modernisation, globalisation (including the globalisation of Western liberal feminism and of Third World feminisms), and 'development' has been the laying of foundations for negotiating new cultural constructions for women. But the new configurations have not merely replaced traditional discourses on gender. Instead, contesting gender narratives compete for supremacy. The 'modern' Asian woman embodies the complexities, contradictions and ambivalences that shaped Asian women in the last thirty years as they grappled with confronting multiple and divergent modernities. For example, Wan Azizah Wan Ismail is a political activist transformed into the voice of the *reformasi* movement (reform movement) in Malaysia. But she is also a traditional woman; a doctor of medicine who ceased practising medicine to fulfil her role as wife and mother. At the same time, she is clearly perceived to be the alter-ego of her husband Anwar Ibrahim (Prime Minister Mahathir's political rival). Her identity is also expressed in the trope of the Islamic revivalist movement—she wears the veil. But because the veil is alien to traditional Malay culture (Ong 1990), it resonates a form of non-Western *modernity* while reinforcing women's agency (Stivens this volume).

The tension between one official gender narrative and the other multiple gender narratives is one major theme that permeates the experiences of women between 1970–2000. In many instances the traditional patriarchal paradigm is being challenged by the 'development narrative' or by a feminist narrative. Such new paradigms come from the 'outside' as part of the globalised ideas of liberal feminism and human rights. Organisations such as the United Nations (UN) proposed international legislation regarding the promotion of women's rights, gender equality and women's empowerment—such as CEDAW (Convention on the Elimination of All Forms of Discrimination Against Women: 1979) and DEVAW (Declaration on Violence Against Women: 1993). The formation of the Asian Pacific Economic Co-operation (APEC) group in 1989 has also resulted in specific initiatives relating to women and economic structural change. If we view a model of tension between one hegemonic gender narrative versus multiple narratives trying to offset or challenge it, is there a danger then that the developmental model (including Western liberal feminism in its globalised form) may become the official gender narrative? Would it be problematic for women in Asia if this narrative of development (which also has masculinist overtones plus Western ideas of liberal feminism) became the hegemonic narrative replacing the traditional Asian gender discourse?

There is no doubt that development has benefited women though the advantages have not been unambiguous. In fact, women in Asia have made strategic use of the narrative to help increase their status and make gains in terms of political empowerment, increase in wages, addressing issues of rape and domestic violence, etc. But, Western feminism has also been viewed as disruptive and alien, challenging 'Asian values'. Asian women activists have been proactive in refocusing the arguments away from the perceived disjunction or foreign source of Western liberal feminism by stressing the 'nationalist' aspect of such feminist principles in liberating women for 'development'. Those invoking the development narrative for women's ends are mostly middle-class women rather than working class or poor women. It is middle-class women who have access to the institutional structures promoting modernisation. They eschew the confrontational approach for legislative reform. These are middle-class women working the 'middle-ground'—created by the poles marked by radical activists and government hacks.

Nationalism provides a cover of respectability within this strategic use of the development narrative for women's interests. Without the appeal to national development lobbying for equality in divorce rights, women's refuges, legislation against violence against women (VAW) or equal pay would ring of a Westernised and disruptive feminism. The important function that women have performed over the centuries as icons of nationhood suggests that attempts to alter the perception of woman's place in society would be fraught with fears about the fragmentation of 'national identity' (Edwards 2000). Western feminism, as enunciated in campaigns for 'rights', has become one of those feared attacks on the 'national woman'. But, when framed within the nationalist rubric, the development of women becomes a patriotic act rather than an anti-male one. Nonetheless, even with this careful reconstruction of women's activism, women's rights activists face major challenges, and in some cases, considerable danger.

Because it can be labelled as 'other' or as 'alien', Western feminism that we identify as part of the developmental narrative, has had the effect of reinforcing some traditional patriarchal principles. The case of Singapore described by Jasmine Chan reveals the patriarchal state asserting the specificity of their 'national woman' by way of defining her against the perceived antagonistic, confrontational feminism of the West. Similar to the Asian values debate led by Malaysia's Prime Minister Mahathir, the invocation of the modern Asian woman's difference from the Western feminist woman serves two functions. First, it reaffirms the distinctiveness of a particular national subjectivity from a putative hegemonic Westernising identity. Second, it undermines potentially disruptive claims by less compliant women to government funding and power by linking any such action as un-Asian and likely to be led by traitorous women who have 'sold-out' to the West. In China, prominent women's studies scholars would also eschew assimilation with Western feminism, in the creation of a specific national women's movement that remains distinct from Western hegemony (see Edwards, this volume). In Malaysia the use of the veil has also been seen as an attempt to embrace 'modernity' in non-Western terms (Stivens, this volume and Stivens, forthcoming).

There is a perception by some Asian societies and governments that the developmental narrative is emerging as a hegemonic paradigm that requires a direct challenge. Ruchira Ganguly-Scrase's seminal chapter on India in this volume provides us with a unique insight about the tensions between the developmentalist paradigm and the other emerging gender narratives that object to its superimposition, undiluted, into Indian soil. Ganguly-Scrase shows that the ideals of liberal feminism face critique by religious groups. Religious communalism in India offers other gender narratives and some of these are problematic. As the discourse on women is drawn into the political contest for supremacy between Muslims and Hindus certain invocations of 'woman' may seem to be re-inventions of traditional views on women's roles.

The Peoples' Republic of China (PRC) also offers a unique slant to the study of contesting gender narratives. Louise Edwards argues that since 1949 up until the mid-1980s the official Chinese Communist Party (CCP) rhetoric was that 'Gender equality has been achieved in the PRC'. No dissenting voices were permitted to challenge, dispute or even question this axiom. This slogan of gender equality became the CCP's gender narrative. Since the mid-1980s however, transformations within the PRC stimulated the women's movement including the All China Women's Federation (ACWF), formerly a mouthpiece of CCP directives. As China began to retreat from totalitarian socialism and began to implement economic liberalisation, the ACWF has become more proactive in speaking for Chinese women. Women academics researching on the history of women in China and the emergence of women's studies in China may eventually undermine the totalising CCP narrative that presents the CCP as the liberators of Chinese women. China's feminists now celebrate 'difference' as opposed to 'whatever men can do, women can do' and react against Communist androgyny. Today women themselves critique the gender equality myth arguing that such an equality narrative is only partial and incomplete.

The development narrative and globalisation

The impact of the 'development narrative' on women is monitored
world-wide by such bodies as the United Nations who use international
pressure to introduce legislation to protect women's rights within the
rubric of 'human rights'. The United Nations played an important role in
the establishment of benchmarks and protocols for women's status in
society. In 1946 the UN established its Commission on the Status of
Women, within a year of the formation of the UN itself, and charged the
Commission with monitoring and promoting women's rights. In the
1970s the work of the Commission was made prominent at a global
level with the observation of International Women's Year (1975) and
the International Decade for Women (1976–85). The general goal of the
accompanying programs was to promote equality between men and
women. Mid-way through the decade, on 18 December 1979, the UN's
General Assembly ratified the Convention on the Elimination of All
Forms of Discrimination against Women (CEDAW). This document
was then submitted to national governments for ratification by their
respective legislatures. The process of debating ratification prompted
discussion on women's rights and gave credibility and respectability to
women's groups around the Asian region. Kathryn Robinson's chapter
on Indonesia, Catherine Tang et al.'s on Hong Kong and Sasha
Hampson's on Korea each demonstrate the weight of this UN
benchmark in providing vital impetus to reform—particularly within
those nations keen to promote their emerging civil, judicial and
democratic institutions. Nonetheless, Radhika Coomarasswamy notes
that while the Convention 'enjoys the privilege of having this
exceptionally large membership (121 members in 1996) CEDAW is also
the human rights convention with the largest number of state
reservations'. She argues that these restrictions reveal that 'relative to
other fields, women's rights are more fragile, have weaker
implementation procedures and suffer from inadequate financial support
from the United Nations' (Coomaraswamy 1996, p. 16). Subsequent UN
initiatives have attempted to maintain the importance of women's rights
and the promotion of women's status in the global arena. By 1993 the
Commission on the Status of Women Declaration on Violence against
Women (DEVAW) was established. In 1995 a special rapporteur on
violence against women was appointed and by 1995 rape during times of
war was recognised as a war-crime—giving victims the right to
compensation.
   Within the Asian region the major impetus for measuring national
'performance' came at the Fourth World Conference on Women held in

Beijing in 1995. This venue enabled many Asian Non-Governmental Organisations (NGO) to attend the adjunct conference at Huairou at far less cost than the previous European, African and Central American conferences. China saw this conference as a platform from which to demonstrate its success on women's rights but the NGO forum also unleashed new voices of discontent. China's ongoing problems with female infanticide and the abduction and sale of girls gained international attention as a result of the UN's conference. Regional issues, such as the trafficking in women within Asia, were also widely canvassed because of the large numbers of Asian delegates attending the NGO forum.

The education of national leaders by the UN's statutes has given weight to women's groups within each country and made it useful for governments to address, even at a token level, the relationship between women's status and development. Clearly, documents such as CEDAW and DEVAW can be signed and then ignored by governments—but the very process of signing in itself has served an educational function and provides support for women's rights activists across the region. Moreover, the international pressure to appear 'modern', is a considerable incentive to change. Governments have been prompted to establish committees to create programs directed at women as a result of the UN's support for women's rights. The UN's decade for women prompted changes in numerous government legislative practices.

APEC has also taken initiatives to promote the economic status of women within member countries. In its bid to integrate women into the mainstream of APEC activities, a Ministerial meeting was convened in Manila in 1998. The main concerns of this meeting were to promote equal opportunity for women and men, to encourage the implementation of gender sensitive development projects and to eliminate barriers to women's full contribution to the economic life of member countries. To this end, APEC has produced a *Guide on Gender Analysis* to promote understanding among government officials and development project managers about the best methods for promoting women's engagement with APEC policies.

The UN, CEDAW, DEVAW and APEC are outside forces. Yet through their enactment of legislation which has global implications, when they speak for all women (based on the premise that women's rights are human rights), they introduce a new gender paradigm—that of liberal feminism. This may be in conflict with the gender narrative of a particular Asian country. In most cases the new global legislation for women's rights and women's equality has benefited women in Asia (as the chapters in this book illustrate). However, there is evidence to show that in some Asian countries the older gender narratives (described by some of our contributors as 'traditional attitudes towards women') try to subvert the newly won women's rights. This attempt at subversion or 'resistance' is a strong theme particularly in Confucian based societies such as Japan, Taiwan and Korea. In Korea for example, Sasha Hampson points out that although many Korean women pursue higher education, they do so primarily with the aim of acquiring better husbands. Traditional constructions of women as 'bearers of sons' or as 'wives and mothers' permeate strongly and thus, modern institutions such as higher education for women are perceived in terms of how these new opportunities can be tapped to fulfil basically traditional cultural constructions of women.

Elise Tipton's chapter shows that while international pressures have enforced changes in women's lives, an examination of women's roles in the workplace, politics and popular culture, can unmask the very clear inequalities existing in a society that still places women 'primarily in nurturing, reproductive roles even outside the home'. Despite Japan's affluence women are still assessed on their motherhood roles, particularly their skills in nurturing and educating children. This expectation of womanhood remains strong even if a woman is a participating member of the labour force. Coexisting with the legislation that allows for women to access higher education and the passage of the Equal Employment Opportunity Law (EEOL) in 1985 there are tax incentives which discouraged women from re-entering the labour force for full-time work because husbands could claim their wives as dependants. Superannuation policies discriminated against full-time working wives and the 1972 Working Women's Welfare Law expected women to require help in order to cope with the responsibilities of work and home duties. In the end, although the EEOL should end discrimination against women, the fact that it lacks penalties meant that it could not really increase women's career opportunities. The cultural construction of the Japanese woman as a 'good wife, wise mother' succeeds in subverting the global narrative of equal opportunity and equal rights.

Another potent example of such 'subversion' of 'modern' elements by traditional forces is the introduction of birth control in its many forms, including abortion. Birth control in the West is seen as pro-women— allowing women control over their sexuality as well as limiting their family size and therefore permitting them to fulfil careers as well as motherhood. However, in some of the Confucian influenced societies discussed in this book, birth control has been used merely to reinforce traditional notions of son-preference. New technology made possible the determination of the baby's sex and this new knowledge has been used to terminate pregnancies if the baby was a girl. Instead of modern radical elements 'subverting' traditional narratives, in some Asian countries it is the traditional elements that subvert the more 'modern' definitions of women.

Catherine Tang et al. provide us with a classic case study of a Confucian-influenced territory (Hong Kong) where traditional cultural constructions of women slowly try to erode the progress women have made in the legislative and political arenas. Despite social change and Westernisation 'remnants of traditional Chinese conceptions of womanhood continue to exert an influence on the behaviour and attitudes of Hong Kong people'. And yet, the struggle between gender narratives still persists as emerging counter-narratives led by young, educated women (there are now over 200 local women's groups) have a visible presence and a clear voice in their campaigns to raise women's consciousness.

The case of Taiwan is interesting because here Lan-Hung Nora Chiang argues that it is economic prosperity and economic development that actually raises the status of women rather than feminist activism or government policy. The improvement in women's status was an added 'bonus', an inadvertent benefit that was the fruit of economic progress rather than a result of a feminist agenda. In this sense therefore, Taiwan's success in the global market and the prosperity that accompanied such success elevated women's status. The 'development' mantra has proven beneficial to women in this country case study. A similar point can be made about the Thailand case study comprehensively presented to us by Bhassorn Limanonda. The improvements on the status of Thai women since the 1970s have been phenomenal and most have occurred due to the economic growth of the nation although supported by initiatives from the government, academic institutions and NGOs. The Long-term Women's Development Plan for instance (to cover 1982–2001) emphasised women as an important target group as it integrated gender issues with national economic plans. Government sponsored population control programs and campaigns to expand health services as well as education and employment opportunities, were all harnessed by Thai women in their bid to improve their status.

Structural change in the economies of the region has also played an important role in altering the status of women. Girls who once stayed at home until marriage are now potential earners as they take jobs in the multitude of factories producing clothing and consumer items for export. In Southeast Asia, in particular, farming is becoming less important to the family income as women's labour is drawn into the new industrial sector. The relationships between daughters and parents have altered irrevocably as daughters gain education, experience in the burgeoning urban centres and financial independence. The generation gap in expectations and outlook between the young woman in the 1990s and her mother is profound and this highlights the considerable impact of rapid structural change on women's status. Nonetheless, structural change in the economies of the region has been a gendered process and one that has often served to reinforce male privilege and further embed stereotypes about women's work. As is clear in each of the chapters to follow, both the nature of employment deemed suitable for women within the new industrial sectors and the wages paid to women within these industries reflect the view that women's work is less valuable and less important than men's. The changing economic base of many countries in the region has thus created new opportunities for exploiting old gender narratives in the pursuit of the export dollar. But it has also created multiple opportunities for the emergence of counter-narratives in which the modern Asian woman articulates the expansion of her crucial role within the family and national economies.

'Being women' in Asia 1970–2000

Who is the modern Asian woman? Is it Wan Azizah Wan Ismail and Aung San Suu Kyi who represent the voices of reform, or is it more likely to be Megawati Sukarnoputri, Corazon Aquino, Mrs. Suharto or former Philippine First Lady Mrs. Imelda Marcos? Is it Flor Contemplacíon, the Filipino maid who was hanged in Singapore? Or is it embodied in the Malaysian factory worker, the overseas contract worker (including domestic helpers and 'entertainers'), or the agricultural labourer? One could easily attest that all these women are 'modern'—all embody the many dilemmas, contradictions and complexities that now define what is modern in an Asian woman. Louise Williams' 1998 volume *Wives, Mistresses and Matriarchs: Asian Women Today* provides poignant biographies that belie any attempt to homogenise the modern Asian woman. We would like to resist the temptation of essentialising the modern Asian woman at the end of the twentieth century since all the chapters here have presented the impossibility of locating THE modern Asian woman in one example, in one persona. After all multiple modernities must mean multiple modern women. And yet, if we had to isolate one critical feature it is precisely that the modern Asian woman exudes contradiction and ambivalence as she straddles between tradition and modernity, victimisation and agency, between being a subject and an object.

Using a Philippine case study Mina Roces argues that in negotiating multiple modernities, Filipino women have embraced extreme choices of both modernity and tradition, empowerment and disempowerment, unofficial power and official power, feminisms and traditional cultural constructions of women (see Roces, this volume). In doing so, women can no longer be boxed into categories such as 'victim' or 'agent', subject or object, tradition or modern. The example of Wan Azizah Wan Ismail presented earlier epitomises these complexities. Another prominent example from a non-élite background is Flor Contemplacíon. She is a modern Filipino woman working overseas (in Singapore) as a maid or domestic helper. Working overseas is a post-modern condition as women extend the parameters of working outside the home to its maximum potential—working outside the country and sending remittances back home to their husbands and children. Is she therefore not just a modern woman but a post-modern woman participating in the globalisation of the labour force? The answer is of course affirmative. And yet to read Flor as 'modern' is to over-simply her. She is fulfilling traditional duties associated with women. Though she is no longer caring for her own children, she is still caring for children—someone else's children. The construction of her duties lies still within the ambit of the definition of 'traditional' woman. In the last thirty years Philippine politics saw the emergence of the woman activist—in the martial law years epitomised by the militant nun. Feminist in orientation (and highly influenced by Western liberal feminism) and overtly radical in political orientation, these nuns nonetheless exercised power behind the scenes in the traditional way women exercised power. Being a modern woman in Asia at the end of twentieth century implies unsettling the categories of traditional and modern woman rather than merely replacing one narrative with another.

Maila Stiven's fascinating chapter on 'Becoming Modern in Malaysia' further highlights the point that the 'widespread reshaping of gender of relations' occurs 'within a highly contested process'. Women have been integrated into 'development', they are extensively involved in professional, technical and other white collar work, and have accessed university on par with men. And yet they live their daily lives 'in a context in which "family" is highly politicised'. The discourse on the 'Asian family' inevitably draws in images of the woman and in this case as a warm and supportive helpmate of the father who is head of the family. Women who are workers are also expected to juggle work and home duties and the middle-class solution to this conundrum has been to employ maids (usually women from poorer communities or nations within the region). The Malaysia case study is also important because woman's engagement with all that is 'modern' is also self-consciously reinvented so that Malaysian modernity is packaged as a non-Western type of 'modernity'. As Stivens argues, the classic symbol of this for women is the use of the veil. Asian women, then, are actively creating culturally specific forms of modernity fully cognisant of the diversity in possible models from around the globe.

Focus on the Asian woman: 1970-2000 and beyond

The beginning of the twenty-first century is a good time to look back and reflect on what women have achieved in the previous century, particularly in the last thirty years of rapid change. This book is a starting point for this assessment as it surveys the general changes that have had an impact on Asian women in a number of selected Asian countries from East Asia, South Asia and Southeast Asia. The volume is multi-disciplinary in approach with contributions from anthropologists, historians, political scientists and sociologists. They engage with the debates about 'being women in Asia at the end of the twentieth century', and the 'multiple modernities' this entails. Each contributor has also addressed the tensions between modernity and tradition in women's roles, the impact of globalisation and consumerism on women's status, the conflicts between national feminism and Western feminism, and the impact of greater governmental influence on sexual health, contraception and family size. Taking women themselves as agents of change, as active participants in globalisation, 'modernisation' and 'development', the various scholars examine how Asian women have negotiated these complex processes. For the first time a comprehensive general survey of the status of women which includes up to date statistics on participation in the labour force, education, and politics as well as women's health and demographics is provided for both the undergraduate reader and the area specialist interested in comparative research. Where possible, web-site addresses are provided to enable readers to update the statistical information in future years. The stimulating chapters to follow also discuss the history of the women's movement in each Asian country and the ways in which Asia has engaged with Western feminisms and the 'woman question'. Since contesting gender narratives are an important theme throughout the book, the authors also grapple with the motley of interesting cultural constructions of gender each country or territory produced in the last thirty years. The impact of modern technology, contraception, and even the internet on women's bodies provoke continuing discussion. The list of recommended readings at the end of each chapter becomes a useful guide for further more specialised research. The addresses for relevant sites on the world-wide-web and the homepage associated with this volume provide readers with a constant update to an expanding body of material (http://www.mcauley.acu.edu.au/womenasia/index.html).

Although we are focussing on the changing status of women at the end of the century, we do not abide by the linear model of 'progress'. The history of women in the last thirty years cannot be mapped or measured in the same linear fashion as 'development' is measured with Five Year Plans and national development targets. Two examples from our contributors illustrate the mosaic nature or even zig-zag turns that emerge in an attempt to measure changes in status. Esta Ungar's study suggests that Vietnamese policies have resulted in a major shift from a de-gendering of society (that is, policies were not guided by gender differences and stressed equality) to a re-gendering of society (where women were once again asked to return to more 'feminine' traditional roles). The war years led to a de-feminisation because women broadened their roles to include those normally performed by men. Since 1975 however, the end of the war has seen men return to the workforce and women encouraged to assume home duties.

In Burma, Janell Mills presents us with a unique case where the intense militarisation of the state has led to a 'masculinsation' of the state. Men have long dominated the two most important national institutions—the government and Buddhism. In recent years military rule under the State Law and Order Restoration Council (SLORC) has entrenched 'army/male' authoritarian rule. The emergence of such a masculine state has undermined women's status not only in the political and religious spheres but also in the world of the economy, society and family—areas where women had critical roles in previous eras. Ironically it is a woman, Aung San Suu Kyi, who is the spokesperson for democratic reform in Burma as she heads the National League for Democracy.

The presence of authoritarian regimes in Vietnam and Burma give the state a greater control over the cultural constructions of woman—in the shaping of a totalising, and later hegemonic, gender narrative. Jasmine Chan points out that Singapore is not just an authoritarian state, it is also a patriarchal state. The state's discourse on women became overtly patriarchal in the 1980s stressing the view that men are the heads-of-households and that 'where necessary, women's rights may be subsumed for the "greater good" of society'. Lee Kuan Yew's Great

Marriage Debate in 1986 and the Graduate Mother Scheme policy had the effect of making entry to university easier for men than women. In a country that celebrates patriarchy the women's movement faces incredible obstacles.

Indonesia is another authoritarian regime (until the 1998 'May' revolution which seems to promise some increase in democratic space or a possible repudiation of dictatorship) where the state plays a dominant role in defining woman. In her enlightening chapter exploring Indonesian women from the New Order up until the *reformasi* movement of 1999, Kathryn Robinson reveals how the New Order policies have defined women's citizenship in terms of their difference from men with women assigned the primary roles of wives and mothers. Even women's organisations such as the *Dharma Wanita* originated from the state's policy which enforced women's subordinate status in political power in particular—men were in the state bureaucracy while their wives were required to join the *Dharma Wanita*. At the same time, despite the state's imposition of 'a homogenising vision of women' there is great diversity in the experiences of women in Indonesia. Women have become prominent activists in the union movement (such as Marsinah) and many others have sought employment overseas. Accordingly, in the 1990s there has been government recognition of the importance of women as workers. Political posturing which included the language of gender equity is now creating emergent multiple gender discourses.

The role of women's organisations in the process of reinventing the 'modern' Asian woman at the end of the twentieth century cannot be underestimated. In most of the chapters the many authors examine in some detail the number of women's organisations that have mushroomed in the last thirty years. They outline the achievements women's groups have made by way of empowering women through legislation and by raising women's consciousness along 'feminist' or 'womanist' lines (the Malaysians prefer this because 'feminism' reeks of Western origins, see Stivens, this volume). Although these organisations were inspired by some aspects of Western liberal feminism, many Asian women's organisations have an ambivalent attitude towards Western liberal feminism and other Western discourses on women (Bulbeck 1998). Just as Asians want to experience a non-Western form of modernity, so too, Asian womanists or feminists want to express a non-Western form of women's movements. This does not necessarily imply however, that these women are the most empowered of all. True to the complex and contradictory nature of modernity and women's power, it may be ironical that in certain historically specific contexts (like post-war Philippines), women exercising power through the kinship group have been more influential than the radical women. The latter sought official power and have thus been forced to abide by men's rules (see Roces 1998 and Roces, this volume). But all these complex and contradictory experiences are the precise factors that make the study of women in Asia at the start of the new millennium so very enthralling. The authors of all the individual chapters here have presented a comprehensive review and analysis of these complex changes, discussing the wide gamut of women's experiences in the last thirty years. And since we are all talking about multiple modernities, multiple gender discourses, and multiple gender narratives, each author has given us a unique interpretative argument about being women, being modern, and being Asian at the end of the twentieth century.

References

Bulbeck, Chilla 1998 *Re-Orienting Western Feminisms: Women's Diversity in a Postcolonial World*, Cambridge, Melbourne.

Coomaraswamy, Radhika 1996 'Reinventing international law: women's rights and human rights in the international community,' *Bulletin of Concerned Asian Scholars*, vol. 28, no. 2 (April–June), pp. 16–26.

Edwards, Louise 2000 'Policing the modern woman in Republican China,' *Modern China* (April).

Ong, Aiwha 1990 'Malay families, women's bodies and the body politic,' *American Ethnologist*, vol. 17, no. 2 (May), pp. 28–42.

Roces, Mina 1998 *Women, Power and Kinship Politics: Female Power in Postwar Philippines*, Praeger, Westport.

Stivens, Maila 1998 'Theorising gender, power and modernity' *Gender and Power in Affluent Asia*, ed. Krishna Sen and Maila Stivens, Routledge, London, pp. 1–34.

Stivens, Maila (forthcoming) 'Gender, modernity and the everyday politics of Islamic revival in Malaysia' *Gendered States and Modern Powers: Perspectives from Southeast Asia*, ed. L. Summers and W. Wilder, Macmillan, London.

Williams, Louise 1998 *Wives, Mistresses and Matriarchs: Asian Women Today*, Allen and Unwin, Sydney.

2 Becoming modern in Malaysia: women at the end of the twentieth century

Maila Stivens

Women's Studies
Melbourne University

As the new century unfolds, these are heady times for Malaysia. The country has been riding the waves of *Reformasi*, the reform movement unleashed by Prime Minister Mahathir's sacking of his deputy, Anwar Ibrahim. This has thrown up an unlikely heroine, Anwar's wife, Wan Azizah Wan Ismail. A quietly-spoken medically-trained housewife and mother, she has revealed herself to be a woman possessing the political acumen and presence to form an effective figurehead for the reform movement. While the future of this movement is unclear, it has become a powerful platform for Malaysians to express a series of discontents long submerged under the stunning economic successes delivered by Mahathir's authoritarian ruling coalition.[1] What does Wan Azizah's rise to prominence tell us about the contemporary condition of Malaysian women? One answer might be that she is the very model of a modern Malaysian woman: highly educated, articulate, enjoying a degree of independence but also fiercely loyal to family, religion and a vision of nation within the emerging corporate Islamic modernity envisaged by the new order. Amidst a crisis of governance throughout a region awash with accusations of corruption and a lack of transparency, her perceived 'feminine' qualities of integrity and fidelity and her piety greatly enhance her political credibility. This amply illustrates a key point of this volume—we are not simply looking at how the economic and social transformations of the last three decades have 'affected' Asian women generally and Malaysian women in particular—we are also arguing for understanding these transformations as deeply gendered processes in which women are active players.

Writers and activists dealing with gender issues in Malaysia regard 'development' as producing a very mixed result for women in the country. They acknowledge many of the gains made by the population at large, and the improved employment and educational conditions for women—Wan Azizah is one proof of the new ways of living open to many Malaysian women. But critics also point to disadvantages experienced by women: these include discriminatory laws, poor working conditions in factories, a neglect of rural women, who continue to be virtually invisible in much government planning in spite of some attempts to redress this, continuing problems of family workers, stresses produced by the juggling exercise that contemporary urban life imposes on women, and the continuing emphasis on women's reproductive roles in much representation of women (see World Bank 1999a).

The new Malaysia

Malaysia has seen massive social change since independence in 1957. Before the Asian financial crises of 1997 it had moved from relative poverty and rural backwardness to be propelled within a brave new globalised order towards the goal of Prime Minister Mahathir's Vision 2020—a fully developed Malaysia by the year 2020. With its neighbours, the country had witnessed unprecedented growth rates, and energetic debates about the cultural forms to be either embraced or rejected with modernity. In triumphalist mode the prime minister and neighbouring leaders proclaimed the Pacific Century, with exultant images of the modern: booming economies and consumption, rapidly improving health and life expectancy and expanding education.

Contemporary Malaysian modernity can be seen as a highly specific form of being modern. It has not simply followed the western liberal capitalist path to development but rather one common to many countries in the Asian region, in which the state acts as a 'midwife' to capitalism (Robison and Goodman 1996). There have been a number of core policy initiatives guiding the modernising process: an export-oriented industrialisation policy in the late 1960s; the New Economic Policy (NEP) (1970–90), an affirmative policy aimed at alleviating poverty and redressing some of the perceived imbalances in economic distribution among the different ethnic groups constructed as such within Malayan colonial and post-colonial history (Malays form about 55 per cent of the population, the Chinese 30 per cent, and Indians 10 per cent);[2] an expansion of a highly-developed public sector, with a large growth in public enterprises concentrated in the financial and industrial sectors (Kahn 1996, pp. 10–11); and more recently, a move from heavy involvement in public enterprises towards partnership between the state and the private economic sector (see Jomo 1995). In the last decade, the National Development Policy has seen the government aiming for a Singapore-style Second Industrial Revolution, with a shift from the model of the low-wage factory to the high-tech, highly skilled economy (Kamal Salih and Mei Ling Young 1989; Kahn 1996). These plans, however, have been set back by the Asian financial crises.

The results of the development process have been dramatic by any account, with the country moving into the category of 'upper middle income economy'. Growth rates were spectacular, averaging 6.5 per cent in the 1970s and, after the recession of the mid-1980s, 8.7 per cent per annum from 1991–95. Unemployment was low, falling from around 7 per cent in 1985 to 4 per cent in 1991 (Jomo 1993a, p. 336), and to 2.5 per cent in 1997 (World Bank 1999b). A large shift from agricultural employment to non-agricultural urban employment (see Table 2.1 below) was associated with an exodus of labour from rural areas, including substantial numbers of women (see Jamilah 1992, 1994).

The distribution of the benefits of development and modernity is more problematic. Critics see the NEP as producing new middle classes, and a shift of power to technocrats and bureaucrats, with increasing gaps between rich and poor, rather than poverty alleviation *per se* (Khoo 1992, p. 50). The extensive involvement of the state in economic enterprises has led to accusations of 'crony capitalism' (Gomez 1990; Searle 1999). The exodus from the countryside set the seal on the demise of many small farming economies and communities, which increasingly became highly marginal areas peopled by the old and the very young. Moreover, the Asian economic collapse of 1997 has seen unemployment rates rise back to 5 per cent by the end of 1998. Cutbacks in government spending have affected services and 'hardcore' poverty, reduced from 4 to 2 per cent, is growing again, especially in urban areas (World Bank 1999b). But many critics have shared with supporters of the status quo an expression of their worries about development within elaborated discourses about 'social problems' and so-called 'Asian Values'. Importantly for this chapter, these highlight issues associated with transformations in family structure, women's place in society and women's sexuality. Such changes are seen as important sites for the remaking of 'culture' under attack by the forces of modernity.

Gender and Malaysian development

Discussions of the dramatic effects of 'development' on Malaysian women's lives have appeared in a number of different contexts, including academic writing, Malaysian popular culture, local activism and western representations of the country (see Stivens 1992). We need to be cautious, however, about assuming any simple linear progression in the situation of women in the country (Stivens 1994, 1996, 1998b). Writing about the 'effects' of the development process on women and gender inevitably finds itself drawing on a confused history of theorising the relationship of gender to development, modernity and globalisation (Stivens 1994, 1998a).[3] Modernity has been seen contradictorily both as intensifying gender inequalities through, for example, displacing women from rural production, and as 'freeing' women from oppressive, archaic 'traditions' (Stivens 1994, 1998a). These problems arise in part from the highly androcentric nature of the models available for thinking about these issues. These difficulties are compounded both by the continuing Eurocentrism of much social theory and the problems of voice faced by non-Malaysian scholars (see Stivens 1994, 1998a).

Earlier writings on colonial Malaya tended to concentrate on rural Malay women, stressing the idea of a 'relatively autonomous' Malay woman living in the village or *kampung* (see Firth 1966; Djamour 1965 and discussion in Stivens 1992). Such images were part of a larger set within nationalist imaginings about a core Malay identity both before and after Independence. The essential Malay was either pictured as a (usually) male villager living in an egalitarian rural idyll or as a suffering subaltern united in a brotherhood of suffering and deprivation by the twin forces of colonialism and capitalism.[4] The model has reappeared in some later writings on *adat*, 'customary law', which represent this as an essential 'traditional' sphere offering women a more egalitarian order.[5] The model of the autonomous woman has given way in recent decades to more critical feminist versions, both local and expatriate, in which a previous 'autonomy' is assumed to be lost to versions of a conspiracy between capitalist development and patriarchy (Ong 1987; Ng 1989; see discussion in Stivens 1992, 1994, 1996). Most attention has been paid to the travails of the Malaysian global factory 'girl', who came to stand for the modern for many scholars, journalists, film-makers and activists. Subsequently, her image has been displaced by the late modern figure of the veiled, devout modern Muslim woman, child of the New Economic Policy. Both images speak to the dramatic changes women have experienced in Malaysia in the last three decades. They also speak to the continuing privileging of Malay experience over that of the other ethnic groups in accounts of the nation.

Class, state and gender in the new Malaysia

The British colonial regime left a legacy of large business and plantation interests in ascendancy in the Malaysian economy. These buttressed a hierarchy of local aristocratic-bureaucratic or landed élites (Crouch 1996; Jomo 1986), a mass of the 'peasantry' and other small middle strata. The latter includes what I see as an 'old', rural-based middle class of local officials, school teachers, police and small entrepreneurs who mediated peasant-state relations (Stivens 1996). The contemporary class landscape has altered dramatically with the rise of the new technocratic forces and new middle classes.

Few accounts of class in Malaysia discuss women, apart from young women factory workers.[6] This invisibility contrasts in interesting ways with the attention given to ethnicity: all discussions of economy, class and stratification in Malaya and then Malaysia have been inextricably driven by a powerful ethnicising discourse, with occupational tables and census tabulations zealously dividing the population into ethnic groupings.[7] The discussions of class that do consider women generally subsume the woman's class situation in that of the household/husband's. This subsumption tends to ignore women's paid work, their property relations, their political agency, and the fact that domestic work within the supposed private sphere performed by women (and some men) can be seen as integral to the everyday cultural production and re-production of class situation (see Stivens 1998a; Davidoff and Hall, 1987; PuruShotam 1998).

An examination of rural society reveals the seriousness of this neglect. The role of female members of 'peasant' households as producers and as holders of small landholdings was systematically ignored in much past writing on peasantries, which mostly assumed that the farmer was male (see Stivens 1994).[8] Rural women, however, have formed significant sections of small holder property owners, as I found in my study in 'matrilineal' Negeri Sembilan (1996),[9] and in fact were among the larger landholders there. Women also have had significant property rights in other parts of rural Malaysia (Stivens, Ng and Jomo 1994).

The pragmatic but crude categorisation of occupation gives some indication of class structure,[10] although the census classifications used in Malaysia are not particularly helpful. Table 2.1 shows both the rise of middle-class occupations and the corresponding decline in numbers of both

Table 2.1: Percentages of total number of male and female workers employed in primary, secondary and tertiary industries, 1970–90

Industry	1970		1980		1990	
	M	F	M	F	M	F
Agriculture and forestry	49.6	67.9	37.5	49.3	28.9	28.2
Mining and quarrying	2.3	0.7	1.4	0.3	0.7	0.2
Manufacturing	9.3	8.1	11.8	16.3	15.2	24.3
Electricity, gas, water	1.0	0.1	0.2	0.1	0.9	0.1
Construction	3.1	0.5	6.4	1.0	8.7	0.7
Wholesale, retail trade, hotels and restaurants	11.6	5.8	13.	11.2	16.9	19.7
Transport, storage and communications	5.0	0.5	5.0	0.7	5.9	1.5
Finance, insurance, real estate and business services	—	—	1.9	1.6	4.0	3.9
Community, social and personal services	18.1	16.4	22.7	19.5	18.8	21.4
Total	100	100	100	100	100	100

Source: Malaysia (1991, p. 417).

men and women working in primary industries over the last three decades.

Table 2.2 drawn from Crouch (1996) is an attempt to provide a schematic account of changes in occupational/class structure over the last four decades. These divisions have a complex relationship with ethnic distinctions, but the figures prior to 1970 support to some extent the pictures presented by the ethnicising discourse of Malaysian popular culture. According to this, Malays were largely 'peasants' and civil servants, and non-Malays, especially the Chinese, dominated employment in business and other modern private sectors of the economy (Crouch 1996, p. 183; Jomo 1990). The last three decades have seen a profound shifting of these associations of occupation with ethnicity. For example, many Malays are entering business and other middle-class occupations and similarly other ethnic groupings are moving into areas where they had previously been less represented (see Crouch 1996).

Women's work in the new Malaysia mirrors these developments. Table 2.1 shows the changing patterns of female work, the decline in agricultural work and the rise of tertiary sector occupations. Female participation rates had risen to 46 per cent in 1993 (Malaysia 1993, p. 239). This compares to

Table 2.2:   **Occupational structure**

	1957	1970	1990
Middle class	15.5	20.0	32.6
Upper middle class	(4.0)	(5.9)	(11.3)
Lower middle class	(11.5)	(14.1)	(21.3)
Working class	18.9	27.3	27.6
Agriculture	56.4	44.9	28.3

Source: Crouch (1996, p. 183)

85.8 per cent for men (Malaysia 1995). These rates vary by ethnicity and between rural and urban sectors. In 1991 participation rates for urban Malay women were 43.5 per cent, for urban Chinese women 42 per cent and for urban Indian women 45 per cent. In the rural sector Indian women had the highest participation rate (55.9), followed by Malay and other *bumiputra* (indigenous) women (38.6) and the Chinese (36.9) (Malaysia 1991, Census Table 6.1).

Women today are extensively involved in professional, technical and other white-collar work, although only very small numbers are employed at the highest levels of the occupational structure. The patterns of labour market segregation within these sectors show 'pink-collar' patterns common to more developed countries. About 10 per cent of employed women were engaged in professional, technical, administrative and managerial work in 1986 (having risen from 5.3 per cent in 1970 and 5.6 per cent in 1975, [Jamilah 1992, p. 40; 1994, p. 16]). Only 0.1 per cent of employed women were in the administrative and managerial category in 1970, rising to 0.6 per cent in 1990. (A different set of figures about employment status shows 9 per cent of employers being women in 1980, rising to 11 per cent in 1987, 1988 and 1989, and about 9 per cent in 1990 [Siti Rohani Yahya, cited in Jamilah 1994, p. 16]).

These figures for middle-class occupations appear rather different, however, when the proportions of men and women in each occupational group in the 1991 census are compared. Malay women then come out at 43.5 per cent of the total number of Malays employed in the professional, technical and related category and 17.7 per cent of the total managers. Malay women comprised 28.8 per cent of all Malays employed in the administrative, managerial, technical and professional categories (Malaysia 1991, Census Table 6.3). Women formed 45.65 per cent of the total numbers of those classified as Chinese professional and technical workers and 19 per cent of managers (Malaysia 1991, Census Table 6.3). Corner's comparison of these categories across the region is an interesting exercise, showing broadly comparable figures for neighbouring countries (Corner 1999, p. 8).[11] If one includes clerical workers, a slightly greater proportion of women than men was working in white-collar occupations in the early 1980s (19.9 per cent as compared to 14.6 per cent). By 1990, these figures had risen to 24.1 per cent and 16.2 per cent respectively (Siti Rohani Yahya quoted in Jamilah 1992, p. 16). The figure of 27 per cent of women being own account workers, however, remained constant over the same period (Jamilah 1994, p. 29), most in agriculture and forestry. These are gross classifications, but the proportions of female to male participation in the technical and professional categories across the region is particularly striking evidence of the transformations that have taken place, not only in Malaysia, but across the region.

The work experiences of many rural migrants to urban areas have been very different. Large numbers enter the unskilled and semi-skilled sectors, although there has also been a measure of upward mobility. The young women of my earlier rural study who migrated to the city from rural villages were fairly typical. Their occupations followed the common 'pink-collar' pattern for women, with a predominance of office and 'caring' jobs, such as typists, clerks, factory workers, nannies, and nurses as well as a sizeable number of teachers. An extensive literature has documented the difficulties of such workers, which have included housing problems, sometimes extreme work pressures and harassment and ongoing sexualisation in the popular imagination.[12] There are also growing environmental and occupational health hazards (World Bank 1999a). Aihwa Ong's study of factory women in the early 1980s gives a vivid picture of the daily lives and concerns of factory women—their stresses manifested in mass hysteria and episodes of spirit possession (Ong 1987).

The Malaysian state has undertaken some initiatives with the explicit aim of 'integrating' women into development. (As feminist critics have noted, this implies that women were somehow outside such 'development'.) These initiatives have included the establishment of the National Council on the Integration of Women in Development (NACIWID) in 1976 which provides policy guidelines for the government. Similarly, in 1983 the Secretariat for Women's Affairs (HAWA) was formed to monitor and evaluate projects and services for women and oversee the activities of NACIWID. It has conducted large-scale research, for example, into women workers. The National Policy for Women (NPW) was promulgated in 1989 with the stated aim of ensuring gender equality and the integration of women in all sectors of development in line with their abilities and needs (World Bank 1999b). Critics have suggested, however, that instruments such as the Community Development Division of the Ministry of Rural Development (KEMAS) until very recently have been mostly interested in sustaining ideas of 'traditional' gender roles through cooking and sewing lessons (see Stivens, Ng and Jomo 1994). Federal Land Development Authority Schemes, (FELDA) for example, do not include 'farming background' as a category for women in apportioning points for settler selection.

Education

Education has been a key plank in both the modernising of Malaysia and for promoting 'national unity' in a multicultural society. Core features have included free education since 1956, a national language and common curriculum, widespread provision of scholarships and bursaries at all levels and hostel accommodation to help rural students (Robiah 1996). Girls had been seriously disadvantaged within the colonial system, but efforts were made in the independent era to remedy this. Table 2.3 shows some of the major changes from 1970.

Enrolment rates for both girls and boys at primary school level have been very similar, rising from about 87 per cent in 1980 to 98 per cent in 1989. This suggests that parents have valued education for daughters as much as for sons. The curriculum, however, appears to have reflected parental and social images of femininity with an emphasis on preparation for marriage and motherhood (Robiah 1996). The opportunities for rural children have lagged behind those of their urban peers. According to the 1983 Census Report, while nearly two thirds of urban boys and girls have enrolled in secondary school, fewer than half the rural girls were enrolled. Overall, more girls than boys were attending secondary school by 1993 (61 per cent) (World Bank 1999a), but many students continued to find it difficult to proceed into upper secondary education (about 19 per cent in 1990 figures) because of the limited places available in government schools. Girls also have limited access to vocational and technical education (Robiah 1996, pp. 129–32).

According to 1992 data, female access to university appears to equal that of males. But there are large concentrations of males in engineering (2 per cent women) and in fields like economics, agriculture, medicine and science (20 to 30 per cent women) (Robiah 1996, pp. 132–33). Figures for women decline at higher degree levels, with women comprising only 28 per cent of Ph.Ds in 1990.

Table 2.3:   Female students as percentage of enrolment by level and stream of
              education, 1970–90

	1970	1980	1990
Level of education			
Primary	46.8	48.6	48.6
Secondary	40.6	47.6	50.5
Post Secondary	42.6	45.5	59.3
University	29.1	35.5	44.3
Polytechnics	13.2	21.5	25.2
Teacher Training Institutions	41.9	48.3	56.1
MARA Institute of Technology	32.4	42.9	45.8
Tunku Abdul Rahman College	23.5	33.9	37.2
Stream			
Arts	46.4	61.0	64.8
Science	24.5	36.3	44.7
Vocational	24.5	36.3	44.7
Technical	4.3	27.1	35.9

Source: Malaysia (1991, p. 421).

Family and domesticity

Malaysian women are living their everyday lives in a context in which the 'family' is highly politicised. There is frequent debate in the print media about the new 'working woman' and about the pressures and costs of 'juggling' work and home. In the last few years, for example, there has been a nation-wide moral panic about the role of working parents (for which read 'mothers') in producing 'delinquent' children. This took the form of widespread anxiety about the 'social problems' posed by teenage boys 'loafing' in shopping centres and by teenage girls engaging in 'immoral' behaviour (see Stivens n.d.a). Representations of family in the last decade or so have been embedded within a larger 'Asian Family' discourse strongly supported by the state and by some Muslim elements (see Stivens 1998b; n.d.a). This counterposes the virtues of the 'Asian Family'—filial piety and continuing extended family ties—to the supposed crisis of the western family. A new 'Asian' ethics and morality are to provide a buffer against the undesirable aspects of modernisation, especially the 'toxic' imports of western 'culture', and to provide an alternative 'Asian' path to modernity. The state campaigns about 'happy families' of recent years have invoked versions of this imagined future, often in terms of a crudely patriarchal model of family life, with the father as the clear head and protector of the family and the mother as a warm and supportive helpmeet.

Family, kinship and demographics

Development has brought a swathe of demographic change: rising life expectancy; falling death rates, especially infant mortality;[13] rising ages at marriage; and falling divorce rates, at least among Muslims.[14] The government has also actively campaigned to manipulate birth rates with some success. They first acted to limit birth at the behest of international agencies and later coopted a long-existing pronatalism in the 1984 '70 million Policy', which tried to persuade women to have more children for the nation (Jomo and Tan n.d.; Stivens 1987, 1998c).[15] While secondary marriages among the other groups were outlawed by new marriage laws, polygamy among Muslims appears to be a figure somewhere above 2 per cent, with no evidence of a recent decrease (Jones 1994, p. 275; Reddy 1992). One area where less change is apparent is intermarriage between ethnic groups: there was almost no such intermarriage in 1975 (Hirschman 1975) and low rates continue. In part this is due to religious differences among the various ethnic groups.

Among the more important changes in marriages have been a decline in arranged marriages and a concomitant rise in free-choice romantic marriages. This trend is associated with modernist ideologies of companionate marriage, 'freedom' from arranged marriage and searches for intimacy. Equally important has been an increasing postponement of marriage due in part to women's growing participation in education and paid work (Jones and Tan 1985, p. 276; Jones 1994). (Free-choice marriages accounted for half of all marriages occurring in my 1970s Negeri Sembilan study villages, for example.) Such 'free-choice' marriages are far from proof of declining parental controls over marriage, as is sometimes alleged. Moreover, while it is often claimed that romantic love is relatively new, I suspect that it has a much longer history (see Stivens 1996). It might be better understood as a form of subjectivity refigured within the present conjunctures. The arguments put forward to explain these changes, rising educational levels and prosperity, are also used to explain falling divorce rates among Malays (Jones and Tan 1985; Jones 1994; Stivens, 1996).

Legal and political contests around 'family' have been well-developed. Successive legislation has attempted various reforms in marriage, divorce and maintenance procedures in both the Islamic and non-Islamic communities.[16] Campaigns against domestic violence have been a feature of the last decade, instituted by women's organisations and culminating in the passage of the Domestic Violence Act in 1996. There is a long history of reformist female concern about marriage laws, especially those surrounding polygyny, which continues to wax large in the Malay female imagination. The power of this anxiety among 'independent' middle-class informants in my recent study of the new Malay middle classes was interesting (see Stivens 1998b).[17] Some high profile cases of polygyny among men in hyper-modern occupations, such as pop-stars, have intensified such concern. It finds expression in the alleged widespread use of love magic among Malays to keep a husband's affection. This reconstituted modern magic involves such rites as burning a used sanitary pad and crumbling the residue into food the husband is to consume to keep him faithful.

Juggling work and home

Women's economic contributions to the household are clearly important at all class levels: rural women perform large amounts of 'family' labour, which researchers and government alike have been slow to recognise; the wages of unmarried daughters working in urban areas are often vital to the continuing support of many rural households; and many of the new urban middle-class households could not support their lifestyle without the woman's income. The middle-class women I interviewed in my recent study, for example, mostly enjoyed their work, but felt it came at considerable cost. Such women in particular have found themselves caught in the juggling exercise of the double day so familiar to women the world over. Childcare problems, the demands of the school co-curricular (extra) activities, parental transporting of children and timetabling were dominant concerns for my informants.[18] As one informant summed it up: 'Rush, rush, rush!' There are feminist exhortations for men to do more, but there is little cold evidence about how much domestic work is done by men. Male inputs into domestic work among my middle-class informants, for example, were variable, but generally not great.

A common way to resolve these dilemmas is to employ maids, who are often recruited from neighbouring countries like Indonesia and the Philippines. (About half of the informants in my middle-class study employed a maid.) I have suggested elsewhere that the employment of domestic servants has forestalled some of the negotiation over changing gender relations within the household that might otherwise have been precipitated by the woman's paid employment (1998a). For working-class women, such options are not available, and they have to rely on kin or childminders paid a small fee. Among the less affluent groups, juggling may be forcing greater male participation in domestic work and childcare. Some men in my study, for example, were actively involved in driving children to school and to after school activities such as music and dance tuition or extra tutoring to improve school performance. Such 'co-curricular' activities are clearly important parts of the new middle classes' educational and class re-production projects.[19]

The lives of these maids signal unresolved tensions in the apparent achievements of many middle-class Malaysian women. The labour market for such domestic workers is unregulated, and ethnically-segmented, with Filipino maids earning the highest rates, ostensibly because their superior English talents are thought to be of benefit to their charges. A sizeable number of maids are in fact illegal migrant workers, with zero legal rights (see Heyzer and Wee 1994). The mistreatment of maids receives some public attention, especially from feminist, womanist and other Non-Governmental Organisations (NGOs). More publicity, however, is given to the problems employers feel they have with 'their maids'. A researcher, C. Chin, tells a horrifying story of a maid employed by the household next door to Chin's own parents in Kuala Lumpur. She was chained like a dog in the backyard (1998). The children of the Filipino maids left behind in the Philippines figure very little in the Malaysian consciousness.

The Malaysian state has assumed in its many publications that the emerging dominant family form is a 'nuclear' one, replacing other more extended forms. A declining family size has been associated with urbanisation, but as I have argued elsewhere, while *households* may be smaller, this does not necessarily entail weakening *family* ties. Indeed, the importance of remittances to rural relatives from migrant kin in urban areas may intensify forms of family dependence (Stivens 1996). The identifiable existence of 'kin help' provides evidence to support arguments that wider family ties are of continuing importance for Malaysian women. Many urban dwellers may be living in smaller households, but it can be argued that the pressures of industrialisation have not eliminated such relationships but reshaped them, producing a modified and often female-centred extended family form to support the work and family trajectories of urban life.[20]

Rural women

It will be apparent already that the 1970s and 1980s were periods of profound transformation in Malaysia's rural sectors. Urban and industrial growth saw a mass exodus of most able-bodied young rural dwellers, male and female, to land settlement schemes and the newly-industrialising cities, sealing the fate of many small producer rural economies. Table 2.1 above illustrates some of the scale of these changes. In attempts to raise the flagging small farmer economy, the state became increasingly interventionist, with virtual state management of many village economies (see Stivens 1996; Wong 1987).[21]

The invisibility of rural women in both scholarly models and state agendas continues to be an issue. Elsewhere I have discussed the problems with simply adding 'women' to the classical debates about agrarian transformations, showing the 'effects on women' (Stivens 1992, 1994, 1996). We need instead to show the gendered character of agrarian transformations, particularly the linkages between local level and larger political and economic forces. The experiences of my female informants working in the rural economy in Negeri Sembilan point to the problems in assuming that men, as the supposed heads-of-households, do most of the rural work, that households are places of equitable redistribution of resources and that men are the main property holders (Stivens 1996). Questions of female agency are again important here. Hart, for example, analyses the ways in which the political actions of rural women have been omitted from important analyses of 'peasant' resistance (1992). The categories rural and 'peasant' are also problematic. In Negeri Sembilan, even in the 1970s, nearly three quarters of purportedly rural households had histories of intermittent wage and salaried work, in some cases stretching back into the 1920s and 1930s, illustrating the fluidity of the concepts 'rural' and 'urban'.[22] There have been extensive and ongoing ties between village and city with women carrying out farm work and grandparents undertaking child-minding while the husbands are away on migrant labour.

The twin forces of urbanisation and the green revolution have put rural women under great pressure. Rural production in the last three decades has been marked by: growing commoditisation and mechanisation; the introduction of green revolution technologies like high-yielding varieties of rice; the displacement of village forms of cooperation with more 'rational', market-driven forms of production; the marginalisation by capital-intensive forms of production like large agricultural machinery; labour shortages; and environmental pollution. One response has been an intensification of state management of many rural economies. As a consequence of these changes many women farmers of small land holdings face increased labour demands from new inputs and simultaneously the loss of labour to the cities. In areas of large-scale rice production the loss of seasonal work to harvesting machines has also hit women hard. The sheer hard slog of agricultural work in a blazing tropical sun should never be forgotten. The conditions of Indian women plantation workers have been a site of particular concern for NGOs. As the World Bank's Country Gender Profile on Malaysia notes (World Bank 1999a), most women farmers are disadvantaged in their access to resources and services. In spite of their very significant role in agriculture, women have been largely ignored in government programmes until relatively recently. Current programmes have concentrated on food processing and handicrafts, with the outcomes unclear.[23] Moreover, as I have argued elsewhere (1996) and with Ng and Jomo (1994), development poses a danger to Malay women's reconstituted customary land rights, with both capitalist encroachment of the rural economy and with the Islamisation of recent years. In 'matrilineal' Negeri Sembilan women have had extensive rights to land, possessing almost all ancestral land and in my study area at least half the rubber land. But as almost all rice production ceased in the 1980s and rubber and other crop production has been in crisis due to the absence of younger villagers, such rights have clearly declined to the status of a fallback 'insurance' in a modern world. As well, women's access to credit may be weakened due to the replacement of the informal credit channels or *kutu* by new formal credit arrangements which tend to favour men as farmers (Ng 1989; UNIFEM 1994).[24]

Politics, religion and nation

In recent years, the central government project of nation-building has become inextricably enmeshed with the Islamisation produced by global Islamic forces, local revivalism and the state's promotion of a corporate Islamic modernity (see Othman 1998; Stivens n.d.b.). Some of the strongest supporters of revivalist Islam in Malaysia have been the hard-working, thrifty and devout new middle classes, the children of the New Economic Policy.

The state has faced a complex juggling act in championing what can be seen as a 'moderate', reinvented, neo-traditionalist Islam, while managing revivalist discontents.[25] On occasion, it has been difficult to distinguish state and revivalist postures—unlike many contexts in the Middle East where revivalism and the state have been clearly oppositional. This has meant that neo-traditionalist constructions of 'family' (Stivens 1998b) have been part of both state and revivalist platforms. Such images of 'family', as noted above, have also seen women placed as important bearers of the nation's honour and creators of the Asian families that are to bring the new Malaysia. This underlines the ways in which issues relating to women, gender, family and sexualities have been central to the Malaysian state's political project of producing a non-western modernity—a profound gendering of religious nationalism. As I suggest elsewhere, it can be argued, with some Middle Eastern women writers on Islam, that the active support of revivalist and other versions of Islam by women in contemporary Malaysia is evidence that a version of political agency is opening to women. The adoption by women of Muslim dress in its many variants, especially the veil, speaks to this. Women's dress has not been simply a symbol of religious nationalism or a sign of 'coercion' into such forms of bodily representation—although this has happened, especially on some university campuses. Instead I would argue with Göle that, with the emergence of the veil as a symbol of politicised Islam, women become important religious and political agents (1996). Their everyday practices can be seen as constantly producing and recreating Islamic discourse and practice. Amidst this politicisation of Islam, extreme sensitivity about ethnic religious differences has left non-Muslim women and men (Christian, Buddhists, Hindus, Daoists and Sikhs) highly anxious but often unable to find a voice in which to express those anxieties.

Organising women

There has been a long history of women's organisations active in working for women's interests in pre- and post-independent Malay(si)a (see Manderson 1980). Today a growing number of women's NGOs are affiliated to the National Council of Women's Organisations, which are mostly led by middle-class women. A list of women's organisations can be found on the recently established FemiNet Asia website.[26] They include university gender and women's studies programmes, professional organisations and organisations active against domestic violence. The engagement of various groups with versions of feminisms within the global women's movement has been marked by a predictable ambivalence about imported agendas (see Stivens 1992; Maznah Mohamed and Wong Soak Koon 1994).

A group that has been attracting particular interest is a reformist Muslim women's group, Sisters in Islam. This small group of tertiary-educated women has been part of an internationalist movement working to reclaim a social justice agenda within Islam. It is noteworthy that some members have strategically disclaimed the title 'feminist', opting for 'womanist' instead. The group has been active in publicising its ideas both at home and abroad (see Othman 1994), laying claim to a new space for women to act within the national religious and political projects. There are suggestions that Prime Minister Mahathir has found it useful to coopt their modernist agenda. But their very success in negotiating within the spaces of Malaysian and now global Islamic modernity can also be seen to demonstrate some of the limits imposed by Islamisation on women's voice, notwithstanding the recasting of Malaysian public spaces through the *Reformasi* process. It is also significant that women's organisations have been prominent in the reform movement. Moreover, the emergence of massive new cyberspaces in which Malaysians are able to circumvent some of the controls imposed by an authoritarian government promise important new avenues for political action.

Conclusion

Present-day Malaysia, along with Asia in general, has witnessed a widespread reshaping of gender relations within a highly contested process (Stivens 1998a). I have outlined briefly here some of the parameters of this reshaping and some of the local and wider forces contributing to this process. The changes in the relationships between work and home and of ideas about intimate relationships signal important shifts in the boundaries between public and private with the modernising process and have produced complex and shifting pressures and negotiations for women. Moreover, mass migration to the cities in the wake of state-led industrialisation, the growing middle classes, and rising female education have all produced a critical mass of educated women. These women have articulated both their old and new discontents in modernist language, and are engaging on their own carefully articulated terms with regional and global feminisms. As this is written, Malaysia is amidst political turmoil, in which many former practices and understandings face dramatic challenges. A more democratic future is a distinctly possible outcome, and one in which women will clearly be taking a very active role.

Notes

[1] Mahathir's party, the United Malays National Organisation, is the senior partner in the coalition.
[2] The NEP (1970–90) was promulgated after ethnic tensions erupted in riots in Kuala Lumpur in 1969, with the goal of raising *bumiputra* (Malay or indigenous) ownership of the economy to 30 per cent by 1990. Affirmative action has included scholarships, employment and preferential access to loans and capital.
[3] Elsewhere I have detailed my scepticism about the linear concepts embedded in writing about modernity, including 'tradition', 'development' and 'modernisation', arguing that both feminist and Asianist readings can usefully destabilise the Eurocentric modernity/postmodernity debates (Stivens 1998a).
[4] See Kahn (1992) for a discussion of the famous Malay writer Shahnon Ahmad's *No Harvest but a Thorn*.
[5] For example Karim (1992). I have suggested elsewhere that such 'traditional cultures' were in fact reconstituted in the colonial period in a complex political, economic and cultural process (Stivens 1992; 1996).
[6] Two examples: there is no index heading for women or gender in Crouch (1996). The otherwise very sophisticated account of Malay plantation workers in Zawawi (1998)

barely mentions either the issues of gender involved in the evolution of working class consciousness nor the ways in which both masculinities and femininities are implicated in the construction of class situation.

[7]   This ethnic discourse has a complex history. Writers from a political economy perspective have pointed to what they see as a policy of divide and rule by the British rulers, in which the different ethnic groups were ascribed different economic niches by deliberate policy (Hua Wu Yin 1983).

[8]   Exceptions to this include Peletz (1988), Azizah Kassim (1988) and Fett (1983).

[9]   See my account of this for Negeri Sembilan in Stivens (1996). My original research in Rembau, Negeri Sembilan, was carried out in three adjacent villages in Rembau district, Negeri Sembilan, from 1975 to 1976 funded by a studentship in the Department of Anthropology, London School of Economics, from the then SSRC (UK). Further visits were made in 1982 (funded by the Hayter Fund), 1984, 1985, 1986, and 1987–88 (funded by the Australian Research Grant Scheme). The focus of the original research was on gender and transformation of the agrarian economy. Later research visits have centred more on macro-level change (see note 17).

[10] There are of course multiple problems in using these classifications, including assumptions about the nature of the static classifications staying uniform over the decades, a privileging of occupation as the main indicator of 'class' and an absence of the proprietorial and aristocratic fractions from the classifications. They also of course omit women entirely.

[11] Cf. Australian figures of 25 per cent of professional and technical managers being women, and 43 per cent managers (Corner 1999, p. 8).

[12] See Ong (1987) Grossman (1979), Jamilah (1992; 1994).

[13] Infant mortality fell from 40.8 per thousand live births in 1970 (Jones and Tan 1985, p. 266) to 32.1 in 1975, and 11.9 in 1993 and 1994 (*Malaysia, 1994/5*, p. 212). Under 5 mortality was 15/1000 births, maternal mortality 34 per 100 000 live births, having declined from 140 in 1970. There has been a strong emphasis on primary health care, focussing on maternal and child health (see Manderson 1998). Female life expectancy was 73 in 1993, the second highest in Asia after Sri Lanka (World Bank 1999a).

[14] Divorce rates fell spectacularly among Muslims from the 1940s through to the 1980s. See figures in Djamour (1965), Jones (1994). Malay divorce rates fell from yearly rates of over 90 divorces per 100 marriages a year in some places to rates of about eight or nine divorces per 100 marriages per year by the 1980s. Demographer Jones's clear argument that Muslim divorce rates in Southeast Asia in general and in Malaysia in particular have fallen, in some cases very dramatically, suggests some problems with accounts alleging otherwise (e.g. Ong 1995).

[15] Fertility declines, however, began in the 1960s, especially in urban areas (Jones 1994).

[16] The Islamic Family Act of 1984 set a minimum age of marriage for women of 16 years and for males 18 years. It imposed restrictions on polygamy and divorce and was finally enacted in all states by 1991, although there have been subsequent attempts to undermine it (see Jones 1994; Chung and Ng 1977).

[17] I have recently been engaged in writing up two Australian Research Council funded and related projects on *Work and Family in the New Malay Middle Classes* (1990–93) and *Public and Private: Gender and Southeast Asian Modernities* (1995–96). This extended research project has included a two month period of residence on a Seremban middle class housing estate in 1987–88, and a number of trips gathering materials in Malaysia, Singapore and the UK since. As part of this research, interviews were carried out with 100 households in Seremban, Kuala Lumpur and Penang. I am extremely grateful to

Lucy Healey, Goh Beng Lan, Hah Foong Lian, Zainab Wahidin, Linda Pang, Norani Othman, Clive Kessler, Azizah Kassim, Jomo Sundaram, Ikmal Muhd Said and Joel Kahn for their help during the current project.

[18] See Stivens (1998c; n.d.a) for further discussion of child rearing and child bearing.

[19] See Manderson (1998) and Stivens (1998c) for discussions of mothering.

[20] Elementary family households have been a feature of pre-industrial Malay kinship patterns (Djamour 1965; Stivens 1987).

[21] The increasing commoditisation of small farms where they continue to function means that the category of 'peasant' has grown increasingly inappropriate.

[22] As I argue (1996) these patterns have to be located in the continuing historical experience of extensive male out-migration from Negeri Sembilan in earlier periods, which has been represented by the 'matrilineal '*adat*' system which supposedly provided less opportunity for men (see Stivens 1996).

[23] See Agrolink, Dept. of Agriculture, Malaysia, website. http://agrolink.moa.my/doa/

[24] There have, however, been attempts to introduce credit patterns modeled on the Grameen Bank model from Bangladesh, although the long-term success of that original venture is now debated.

[25] Islam is the official state religion, but Malaysia is not an Islamic state.

[26] FemiNet Asia web-site—http://ideal.upm.edu.my/~gansl/FemiNet/main.html

References and recommended readings

Akbar Ahmed 1992 *Postmodernism and Islam*, Routledge, London.

Amina Wadud Muhsin 1992 *Quran and Woman*, Penerbit Fajar Bakti, Kuala Lumpur.

Azizah Kassim 1988 'Women, land and gender relations in Negeri Sembilan: some preliminary findings,' *Southeast Asian Studies*, vol. 26, no. 2 (September), pp. 132–49.

Chin, C.B.N. 1998 *In Service and Servitude, Foreign Female Domestic Workers and the Malaysian 'Modernity' Project*, Columbia University Press, New York.

Corner, Lorraine 1999 'Women's participation in decision-making and leadership: a global perspective,' Bangkok: UNIFEM. Paper delivered to Conference on Women in Decision-Making in Co-operatives held by the Asian Women in Co-operative Development Forum (ACWF) and the International Co-operative Alliance Regional Office for Asia and the Pacific (ACAROAP) on 7–9 May 1997 at Tagatay City, Philippines. Also published in Report on the proceedings of the Conference *Women in Decision-making Co-operatives: Report of a Regional Conference* 7–9 May, 1997 Tagatay City, Philippines, ACWF and ICAROAP. Also on UNIFEM web-site— http://unifem.undp.org.eseasia/TechPapers/wleaders.html

Chung, B.J. and Ng Shui Meng 1977 *The Status of Women in Law: A Comparison of Four Asian Countries*, Institute of Southeast Asian Studies, Singapore.

Crouch, H. 1996 *Government and Society in Malaysia*, Allen and Unwin, Sydney.

Davidoff, L. and Hall, C. 1987 *Family Fortunes: Men and Women of the English Middle Class 1780–1850*, Hutchinson, London.

Djamour, J. 1965 *Malay Kinship and Marriage in Singapore*, Athlone Press, London.

Enloe, C. 1989 *Bananas, Beaches & Bases: Making Feminist Sense of International Politics*, Pandora Press, London.

Fett, I. 1983 'Women's land in Negeri Sembilan,' *Women's Work and Women's Roles*, ed. L. Manderson, Development Studies Centre, Monograph No. 32, Australian National University, Canberra.

Firth, R. 1966 *Housekeeping Among Malay Peasants*, Athlone, London.

Göle, Nilufer 1996 *The Forbidden Modern: Civilization and Veiling*, University of Michigan Press, Ann Arbor.

Gomez, E.T. 1990 *Politics in Business: Umno's Corporate Investments*, Forum, Kuala Lumpur.

Grossman, R. 1979 'Women's place in the integrated circuit,' *Southeast Asia Chronicle*, vol. 66 (Jan–Feb), pp. 2–17.

Hart, G. 1991 'Engendering everyday resistance: gender, patronage and production politics in rural Malaysia,' *Journal of Peasant Studies*, vol. 19, no. 1, pp. 93–121.

Heyzer, N. and Wee, V. 1994 'Domestic workers in transient overseas employment: who benefits, who profits?,' *The Trade in Domestic Workers: Causes, Mechanisms and Consequences of International Migration*, eds N. Heyzer, G. Lycklama à Nijeholt and N. Weeraloon, Asia Pacific Development Centre, Kuala Lumpur; Zed Press, London and New Jersey.

Hirschman, C. 1975 *Ethnic and Social Stratification in Peninsular Malaysia*, American Sociological Association, Washington.

Hua Wu Yin 1983 *Class and Communalism in Malaysia*, Zed Press, London.

Jamilah Ariffin 1992 *Women and Development in Malaysia*, Pelanduk, Kuala Lumpur.

—— 1994 *Reviewing Malaysian Women's Status: Country Report in Preparation for the Fourth UN World Conference on Women*, Population Studies Unit, University of Malaya, Kuala Lumpur.

Jomo K.S. 1986 *A Question of Class*, Oxford University Press, Kuala Lumpur.

—— 1993 *Industrialising Malaysia*, Routledge, London.

—— 1993a *Growth and Structural Change in the Malaysian Economy*, MacMillan, Houndmills.

—— 1993b *Industrialising Malaysia*, Routledge, London.

—— 1995 *Privatising Malaysia: Rents, Rhetorics, Realities*, Westview, Boulder, CO.

Jomo K.S. and Tan P.L. (n.d.) *Not the Better Half: Malaysian Women and Development Planning*, Integration of Women in Development, Asian and Pacific Development Centre, Kuala Lumpur.

Jones, G.W. 1994 *Marriage and Divorce in Islamic Southeast Asia*, Oxford University Press, Kuala Lumpur.

Jones, G.W. and Tan, P.C. 1985 'Recent and prospective population trends in Malaysia,' *Journal of Southeast Asian Studies*, vol. 16, no. 3, pp. 262–80.

Kahn, J.S. 1992 'Class, ethnicity and diversity: some remarks on Malay culture in Malaysia,' *Fragmented Vision: Culture and Politics in Malaysia*, eds J. S. Kahn and Francis Loh Kok, Allen and Unwin, Sydney.

—— 1996 'Growth, economic transformation, culture and the middle classes in Malaysia,' *The New Rich in Asia: Mobile Phones, McDonalds and Middle Class Revolutions*, eds R. Robison and D. S. G. Goodman, Routledge, London.

Kamal Salih and Mei Ling Young 1989 'Changing conditions of labour in the semiconductor industry in Malaysia,' *Labour and Society*, vol. 14, pp. 59–80.

Karim, Wazir 1992 *Women and Culture: Between Malay Adat and Islam*, Westview, Boulder, CO.

—— ed. 1995 *Male and Female in Developing Southeast Asia*, Berg, London.

Khoo Kay Jin 1992 '"The grand vision": Mahathir and modernisation.' *Fragmented Vision: Culture and Politics in Contemporary Malaysia*, eds J. S. Kahn and Francis Loh Kok Wah, Allen and Unwin, Sydney.

Majid, S. and Majid, A. 1983 'Public sector land settlement in West Malaysia,' *Rural Development and the State*, eds D.A.M. Lee and C. P. Chaudhri, Methuen, London.

Manderson L. 1980 *Women, Politics and Change: The Kaum Ibu UMNO Malaysia, 1945–1972*, Oxford University Press, Kuala Lumpur.

—— 1998 'Shaping reproduction: maternity in early twentieth-century Malaya,' *Maternities and Modernities: Colonial and Postcolonial Experiences of Mothering in Asia and the Pacific*, eds K. Ram and M. Jolly, Cambridge University Press, Cambridge.

Mansor 1991 *Women Managers of Malaysia*, Faculty of Economic and Administration, University of Malaya, Kuala Lumpur.

Malaysia 1991 *Sixth Malaysia Plan, 1991–1995*, National Printing Department, Kuala Lumpur.

—— 1993 *Mid-term Review of the Sixth Malaysia Plan*, Economic Planning Unit, Prime Minister's Department, Kuala Lumpur.

—— 1994/95 *Economic Report 1994/5*, Ministry of Finance, Kuala Lumpur.

—— 1995 *General Report of the Population Census, 1991* (*Laporan Am: Banci Penduduk 1991*), Department of Statistics, (Jabatan Perangkaaan Statistik), Kuala Lumpur.

Maznah Mohamed and Wong Soak Koon eds 1994 *Feminism: Malaysian Critique and Experience, Kajian Malaysia Special Issue*, vol . XII, nos 1 and 2 (December).

Ng, C. 1989 *Women in Development: Malaysia, Country Briefing Paper*, Asian Development Bank, Manila.

Ong, A. 1987 *Spirits of Resistance and Capitalist Discipline: Factory Women in Malaysia*, SUNY University Press, Albany.

—— 1995 'State versus Islam: Malay families, women's bodies and the body politic,' *Bewitching Women, Pious Men: Gender and Body Politics in Southeast Asia*, eds Aihwa Ong and Michael Gates Peletz, University of California Press, Berkeley. (Updated version of 'State Versus Islam: Malay Families, Women's Bodies and the Body Politic,' *American Ethnologist*, vol. 17, no. 2 [May, 1990], pp. 28–42.)

Othman, Norani 1994 'The sociopolitical dimensions of Islamisation in Malaysia: A Cultural Accommodation or Social Change?,' *Shari'a Law and the Modern Nation-State: A Malaysian Symposium*, ed. Norani Othman, Sisters in Islam Forum, Kuala Lumpur.

—— 1998 'Islamization and modernization in Malaysia: competing cultural reassertions and women's identity in a changing society,' *Women, Ethnicity and Nationalism*, eds R. Wolford and Robert L. Miller, Routledge, London.

Peletz, M. 1988 *A Share of the Harvest: Kinship, Property and Social History Among the Malays of Rembau*, University of California Press, Berkeley.

PuruShotam, N. 1998 'Between compliance and resistance: women and the middle-class way of life in Singapore,' *Gender and Power in Affluent Asia*, eds K. Sen and M. Stivens, Routledge, London.

Reddy, R. 1992 *A Handbook of Law for Malaysian Women*, Penerbit Fajar Bakti Sdn Bhd, Petaling Jaya.

Robiah Sidin 1996 'Malaysia,' *Women, Education and Development in Asia; Cross-National Perspectives*, ed. G. C. L. Mak, Garland Publishing, New York.

Robison, R. and Goodman, D. S. G. eds 1996 *The New Rich in Asia: Mobile Phones, McDonalds and Middle Class Revolutions*, Routledge, London.

Searle, P. 1999 *The Riddle of Malaysian Capitalism*, Allen and Unwin, Sydney.

Stivens, M. 1987 'Family and state in Malaysian industrialisation,' *Women, State and Ideology*, ed. H. Afshar, Macmillan, London.

—— 1992 'Perspectives on gender: problems in writing about women in Malaysia,' *Fragmented Vision: Culture and Politics in Contemporary Malaysia*, eds J. Kahn and F. Loh, Allen and Unwin, Sydney.

—— 1994 'Gender and modernity in Malaysia,' *Modernity and Identity: Illustrations From Asia*, ed. A. Gomes, La Trobe University Press, Bundoora.

—— 1996 *Matriliny and Modernity: Sexual Politics and Social Change in Rural Malaysia*, Allen and Unwin, Sydney.

—— 1998a 'Theorising gender, power and modernity in affluent Asia,' *Gender and Power in Affluent Asia*, eds K. Sen and M. Stivens, Routledge, London.

—— 1998b 'Sex, gender and the making of the Malay middle class,' *Gender and Power in Affluent Asia*, eds K. Sen and M. Stivens, Routledge, London.

—— 1998c 'Modernising the Malay mother,' *Modernities and Maternities in the Asia Pacific Region*, eds K. Ram and M. Jolly, Cambridge University Press, Cambridge.

—— (n.d.a) 'The hope of the nation: moral panics and the construction of teenagerhood in contemporary Malaysia,' *The Emerging Adult: Young People, Sexuality and Courtship in South and Southeast Asia*, eds Lenore Manderson and Pranee Liamputtong Rice, Harwood Press, London, in press.

—— (n.d.b.) 'Gender, modernity and the everyday politics of Islamic revival in Malaysia,' *Gendered States and Modern Powers: Perspectives from Southeast Asia*, eds L. Summers and W. Wilder, Macmillan, London, in press.

Stivens, M., C. Ng & K. S. Jomo (with Jahara Bee) 1994 *Malay Peasant Women and the Land*, Zed Press, London.

UNIFEM 1994 *Calling for Change: International Strategies to End Violence Against Women*, Ministry of Foreign Affairs, Netherlands, Hague.

Wong, D. 1987 *Peasants in the Making*, Institute of Southeast Asian Studies, Singapore.

World Bank 1999a *Malaysia—Country Gender Profile*,
         (http://www.worldbank.org/html/prmge/info/malays.htm).

World Bank 1999b *Malaysia Social Sector Support*,
         (http://worldbank.org:80/pics/pid/my.6094.txt).

Zawawi, Wan 1998 *The Malay Labourer at the Window of Capitalism*, Institute of Southeast Asian Studies, Singapore.

See also FemiNet Malaysia (http://ideal.upm.edu.my/~gansl/FemiNet/main.html)

3 The status of women in a patriarchal state: the case of Singapore

Jasmine S. Chan

Department of Sociology
National University of Singapore

In order to understand the changing status of women in Singapore in the past 30 years, we would do well to first understand the social and political context of these changes. Singapore has been described as an authoritarian state (Rodan 1993). Since its independence in 1965 from the Federation of Malaya (see Pang 1971), Singapore has been ruled by one political party, the People's Action Party (PAP).[1] As a result of the domination of that one party in parliament, policies that both directly and indirectly affect women are made and implemented, sometimes with astonishing speed. However, to examine the status of women within the context of Singapore as an authoritarian state is not sufficient. The Singapore state is also an overtly patriarchal state. The authoritarian nature of Singapore therefore enables the swift implementation of national policies that are patriarchal in nature.

The Prime Minister of Singapore, Goh Chok Tong, has openly endorsed the government's position on patriarchy, pointing out that '(in) a largely patriarchal society, minor areas where women are not accorded the same treatment should be expected so long as the welfare of women and of the family is protected. I would not regard them as "pockets of discrimination" or "blemishes" but as traditional areas of differential treatment' (1993, p. 29).

The main concern of the PAP government is to ensure the smooth implementation of policies that are believed to benefit the nation as a whole, and the confirmation of patriarchy in Singapore is seen to be so beneficial. Women's issues and demands are considered within this patriarchal framework. Where necessary, women's rights may be subsumed for the 'greater good' of society. Indeed, the long absence of women from parliament may have contributed to this state of affairs.

Although women were actively involved in the fight for Singapore's independence in the 1950s and 1960s, for a long time after independence women's voices were not represented in parliament. In the 1959 Federation elections eight women candidates were elected to the Legislative Assembly. However, from 1970 to 1984, the Singapore Parliament did not have any women members. Currently there are only six women in parliament—Senior Minister of State, Aline Wong, Members of Parliament (MP) Lily Neo, Lim Hwee Hua and Yu-Foo Yee Shoon, and Nominated Members of Parliament (NMP) Jennifer Lee and Claire Chiang. At present, the PAP's policies are accepted and tolerated because the PAP government has successfully provided for the economic and social needs of the population, and can legitimately claim to have improved the lives of its people, including women.

Changes in women's lives

Since the 1960s, indicators on areas such as education, employment and health show that Singapore women have gained tremendously on these fronts. In terms of health, women's life expectancy rose by ten years from 67.7 in 1957 to 77.6 years in 1990. For women aged 60, the number of years they can expect to live has increased by six years—from 14.9 years to 20.9 years (Shantakumar 1993, p. 211). While there is cause to celebrate these improvements in health and longevity, a number of these women will face economic difficulties. These will result in part because women tend to outlive their married partners on whom they are dependent for economic support and in part due to their low levels of educational qualifications. Only a small proportion of these women is in paid employment. The majority are dependent on their families for financial support. This scenario should improve over time, as cohorts of women who benefited from the universal education policy in the 1960s form the bulk of the elderly population. For example, in 1980, 92.7 per cent of women above the age of 60 had received no or incomplete primary education. By 1990, this percentage had fallen to 77.7 per cent, and the percentages in all other categories showed improvements, with those completing primary/lower secondary education showing the highest increase, rising from 2.4 per cent to 15.2 per cent (Shantakumar 1993, p. 217). Those receiving secondary and upper secondary education rose from 4.7 per cent to 6.7 per cent and those attaining tertiary education increased from 0.2 per cent to 0.4 per cent.

For women aged 15–24, the literacy rate has improved from 84.5 per cent in the 1970s to 96.2 per cent in 1990. Female attendance in schools has increased over the years. The ratio of female to male enrolments at tertiary institutions rose from 34:100 in 1960 to 73:100 in 1991 (Wong and Leong 1993a, p. 7). More women are entering universities than ever before. In 1990, only 4.4 per cent of women aged 20–59 had tertiary education, compared to 9 per cent in 1997. However, they still lag behind men. 12.1 per cent of men aged 20–59 had tertiary education in 1997, up from 6.1 per cent. This also indicates an increase of 6 per cent for men, compared to an increase of 4.6 per cent for women.

Although the enrolment numbers have improved, there are sex-based differences across disciplines at universities, with women being concentrated in areas such as accountancy, and the humanities and social sciences while men are concentrated in disciplines such as engineering and medicine. In 1990 the female to male ratios of enrolment at the National University of Singapore were 0.1 for engineering, 0.4 in medicine and 2.8 in arts and social sciences (Low et al. 1993, p. 94). More recent data shows that this pattern has not changed. 75 per cent of female undergraduates in the National University of Singapore and Nanyang Technological University are enrolled in the faculties of Arts and Social Sciences, Business and Accountancy, and Science, compared to 38 per cent of male students (Singapore Department of Statistics 1998, p. 4). Direct discrimination against women has not helped alter these ratios. In 1979 a quota restricting the number of women entering the medical faculty was set at one third of the enrolment. This was justified on the grounds that the 15–20 per cent attrition rate for women doctors was a loss of investment for the country.

The percentage of economically active women aged 15 and above rose from 29.5 per cent in 1970, to 44.3 per cent in 1980, to 50.3 per cent in 1990. The rise is sharpest amongst married women with 14 per cent being economically active in 1957, 29.8 per cent in 1980 and 43.1 per cent in 1990. Nonetheless, in 1990, 32 per cent of all women, compared to only 0.2 per cent of all men, were identified as fulltime homemakers (Wong and Leong 1993b, p. 24). It is therefore not surprising that the overall labour force participation rate (LFPR) for married women is much lower than that of married men. In 1997, the LFPR for married women was 48 per cent while that of married men was 86 per cent. The demands of marriage and family become evident when we compare the rates to that of single women, at 66 per cent which is almost equal to that of single men, at 67 per cent (Singapore Department of Statistics 1998, p. 6).

At the same time, the percentage of women in various types of occupations also changed. Women's participation in finance and business rose from 3.5 per cent in 1970, to 9.2 per cent in 1980, reaching 12.9 per cent in 1990. Although this is an indication that women are starting to make inroads in other sectors, women are still mainly employed in manufacturing. Statistics show that 39.49 per cent and 25.14 per cent of working women are found in production and clerical work—both low-paid jobs with few chances for advancement. Only 3.9 per cent are found in administrative and managerial jobs (Low et al. 1993, pp. 87–110). The concentration of women in the manufacturing sector makes them prone to retrenchment since jobs in this sector are particularly vulnerable to economic fluctuations. Moreover, when the business cycle improves, these women are re-employed as new workers or, alternatively, new women workers are recruited with lower starting salaries (SAWL 1986, p. 35). Data from 1995 indicate that this pattern has not changed. For workers aged 25 to 39 in occupations such as administrative clerks, assemblers, and secondary and pre-university teachers, more than 70 per cent are women, while men number more than 70 per cent in occupations such as computing, architecture and engineering (Singapore Department of Statistics 1998, p. 9). This concentration of women in low-end routine work is not helped by the perception that women are 'more suited' to these tasks. One of the explanations used by the Singapore Department of Statistics for gender differences in occupations is that 'females are suited for clerical and production jobs that entail repetitive tasks' since they have 'greater manual dexterity and capacity for routine work' (1998, p. 10).

The financial situation of women seems to have improved over time. A survey on women aged 60 and above showed that while only 62.7 per cent were owner-occupiers of their homes in 1980, by 1990 this figure had risen to 87 per cent (Shantakumar 1993, p. 220). With regards to financial remuneration, the median gross monthly wages for female workers rose from 57 cents in 1974 to 73 cents in 1991 for every dollar earned by a male worker. However, this improvement is evident only for women at the two ends of the education spectrum, in part because the wage disparity between males and females in these categories was so great to begin with. Women with primary/lower secondary education and women with tertiary education were earning 54 cents and 57 cents respectively to a male dollar in 1974. By 1991, women in both groups were making 69 cents to a dollar. The earnings of women with secondary/upper secondary education remained practically stagnant from 1974 to 1991, moving only a cent from 74 to 75 cents for every dollar that a man makes (Low et al. 1993, p. 95).

It has been claimed that with time, the income gaps between the sexes will continue to narrow. However, over the five-year period from 1990 to 1995, men's income grew faster than women's income. The average monthly wage for men grew by 13 per cent while that of women rose by only 8.3 per cent. Due to this rapid growth in men's earnings, there seems to be a widening income gap between the sexes. In 1995, women earned 59 per cent of men's incomes, falling from 73 per cent in 1990. Moreover, in 1995, 28.6 per cent of men earned S$3000 per month and above while only 13.7 per cent of women earned as much. Similarly, only 4.4 per cent of men earned below S$500 per month while 16.8 per cent of women did so. The widening of the income gap between men and women is due to faster occupational upgrading among males. There has been a 10 per cent increase in the proportion of men working in professional, administrative and managerial occupations, and only a 3.3 per cent increase among women. Overall, 26 per cent of men and 11 per cent of women work in these highly paid occupations (Yim and Ang 1997). The income gaps for women have narrowed in some occupations and widened in others. I take two examples, comparing percentages from 1990 and 1997 respectively. Women in professional jobs show a narrowing of income gap from 81.1 per cent to 83.4 per cent while those in administrative and managerial jobs show a widening gap from 87.5 per cent down to 85.5 per cent. For women in clerical jobs, their income gap closed from 86.8 per cent to 96.2 per cent while women in production and related jobs saw their income gap widen from 74 per cent to 67.1 per cent (Singapore Department of Statistics 1998, pp. 11–12)

The patriarchal state and women's status

As can be seen in the above discussion, measures utilising hard numbers seem to give us mixed results. On one hand, there is some cause to celebrate some very real improvements in women's lives, even in those areas where women have yet to 'catch up' with men, such as income differentials. While it is important to gauge the relative mobility of the status of women vis-à-vis men and in relation to different cohorts of

44

women over time, the status of women in Singapore is more complex
than such statistics reveal. In order to accurately portray how women are
viewed, I choose to focus on state discourse on 'women' since the
Singapore state makes laws and policies that impact on women's lives on
a daily basis. The experiences of women in Singapore are diverse,
mediated through many varied aspects such as class, age, race and
marital status, to name a few. This renders generalising discussion on
'the Singapore woman' problematic. Yet the state discourse on women
usually hides such diversity. The importance of focusing on this issue
becomes self-evident when we recognise that Singapore as an
authoritarian state is able to establish patriarchy as a guiding principle
for making policies.

The Women's Charter

The status of women in Singapore took a promising turn in the late
1950s and early 1960s during the fight for independence. The Singapore
Council of Women supported the People's Action Party in the 1959
election when the PAP promised to form a society that will not exploit
women. Established in 1952 the Council took as one of its earliest goals
to eliminate polygamy. It currently has about 2000 members (Wee 1987,
p. 6). The PAP's 1959 election manifesto (*The Tasks Ahead* 1959) stated
that 'all people will have equal rights and opportunities irrespective of
sex, race and religion'. The manifesto also outlined a series of steps to be
taken to improve women's status in Singapore (see Wee 1987).

One of the early pledges by the PAP was the promise to enact a
Women's Charter whose main aim was to 'enable women to have their
rights safeguarded by legislation' (*Singapore Legislative Assembly
Debate* 6 April 1960, p. 443). It simultaneously acknowledges women's
influence in politics and the interests of politicians in winning the
'woman's vote'. The then Minister of Labour and Law, K.M. Byrne,
described the Charter as a way to 'consolidate the existing laws relating
to marriage, divorce, the rights and duties of married persons, the
maintenance of wives and children, and the punishment of offences
against women and girls' (Wong and Leong 1993b, p. 81). It is directed
mainly at the non-Muslim population of Singapore, although certain
sections of the Charter are available to those who married under Muslim
law (Leong 1981, p. 104).

Unlike the conciliatory language used by present-day self declared
feminists, language that emphasised women's subordinate and men's
privileged positions in the patriarchal society was used in the Legislative

Assembly debates. PAP Member of Parliament Chan Choy Siong who supported the Bill declared that

> Women in our society are like pieces of meat put on the table for men to slice. The PAP government has made a promise. We cannot allow this inequality in the family to exist in this country. We will liberate women from the hands of the oppressor (Quoted in Wee 1987, p. 7).

Pressure from various organisations and from the desire to win over women voters who were considered to be a political force enabled the Women's Charter to be passed on 24 May 1961. The Charter delineated the rights, responsibilities and duties of women and men in the family. It gave both husband and wife equal ownership rights to property, equal rights to divorce, to be equally responsible for their children, and equal rights to social and economic participation. It gave women the right to act in their own legal capacity. It outlawed polygamy. Over the years, there were numerous amendments to the Charter, amendments that seem to improve the legal position of women over time. One such amendment in 1980 gave women a share of matrimonial property, even if she did not contribute cash to the acquisition of that property.

Given the time and context of its enactment, the Women's Charter has often been regarded as a progressive piece of legislation. Both women and men worked hard towards the enactment of this legislation in the belief that once a woman's legal status is equal to that of her husband, her position will improve (Leong 1981, p. 104). Accordingly, the issues in the Charter deal mainly with family law, although there is a section that is concerned with the protection of women and girls. The Charter is therefore mostly concerned with the roles, responsibilities, duties, and rights of women within the family. It is mainly women's traditional roles as wives and mothers that are protected in the Charter. Perhaps that conventionality enabled the Charter to be passed, even with opposition from some quarters—that 'good women' who perform their roles lovingly as wives and mothers should not be penalised for their service to the family, and they therefore deserve protection from the state.

At the same time, women do not have the right to equal pay for equal work. Singapore did not sign the United Nations' Conventions on (a) equal pay for equal work for both men and women, (b) eliminating discrimination against women, and (c) equal opportunities and treatment for men and women workers. This is despite the fact that the PAP government made a promise in the 1959 election to work towards equal pay for women. However, within the civil service itself, changes were introduced. In response to the request by the PAP Women's Affairs

Bureau for equality of pay, women and men in the civil service were put
on the same pay scale in 1962 (Wong and Leong 1993b, pp. 42–43).
Women civil servants do not, however, receive the same employment
benefits as men—for example, medical benefits (discussed below).
Before the equal pay for equal work policy was instituted, women in the
civil service were receiving 80 per cent of male workers' salaries.
Moreover, when female employees got married, their job status was
reduced to that of temporary staff, and they were denied pension (Wee
1987, p. 7).

While the Women's Charter deals directly with women's position in
the family, many other laws, policies and regulations were put in place
which affected both women's position in the society and their everyday
life decisions. As the PAP government became engrossed in providing
for a basic standard of living in the 1960s and 1970s, and as the party
tightened its rule over Singapore and Singaporeans, the government's
policies have shown progressively that, while women's rights in the
family should be protected by law, it is the men who are and should be
treated as the heads-of-household. From an election manifesto that
promised equal rights irrespective of sex in 1959 to an overt defence of
the patriarchal family in the 1990s, the present government blatantly
prescribes and inscribes patriarchy as a desired and desirable form of
governance.

Man as head-of-household

In 1975, the then Prime Minister Lee Kuan Yew opened a National
Trade Union Congress seminar-cum-exhibition to mark International
Women's Year *(see Proceedings of the International Women's Year
Seminar cum Exhibition* September 1975). In that speech, Lee presages
the government's future concern on the relationship between women as
economic contributors and women's role in the family. In describing the
effects of industrialisation on the roles of women Lee said, 'On the
whole, we have been fortunate in educating our women, opening up jobs
for them, and having them more independent, without too great an upset
in traditional family relationships'. Acknowledging that the position of
women in Singapore had changed with their increased education and
employment, Lee went on to say that, 'what has not yet taken place in
traditional male-dominant Asian societies is the helping of household
work by husbands...This change in social attitudes cannot come by
legislation. Such adjustment should be allowed to develop naturally'.

At the time the speech was given, Singapore was already experiencing
a labour shortage (Wong 1974), and the PAP government was

encouraging women to go to work. In 1971, the government launched a campaign to persuade employers to hire women on the basis that they were under-utilised. At the same time, the government indicated that they would work with *working married women* to help find solutions to pressures induced by their dual roles as mothers with childcare responsibilities and as workers. The government itself defines women's primary role in the family as that of child raising. In the 1980s, instead of helping men 'adjust naturally' to participating in household work, an education policy was introduced that reinforced the traditional division of labour within the family. In 1985, Secondary One and Two female students were not allowed to take Technical Studies. Instead, Home Economics became a compulsory subject for all girls. As the then Minister of State for Education put it, 'girls should be girls' and as such, they must be prepared for their roles as 'wives, mothers and workers' (*The Straits Times* 4 September 1984)—clearly locating women within the home first. Similarly, boys were not permitted to study Home Economics and were enrolled in Technical Studies instead. This policy was rescinded in 1994.

From the 1980s onwards, the government has taken a more overtly patriarchal stance, especially towards policies governing the family. In part, we can locate the change in discourse on women to then Prime Minister Lee Kuan Yew's National Day Rally speech in 1983 when he provoked what was popularly known as the Great Marriage Debate (see section below). Since then, the PAP government has unabashedly described itself as a patriarchal state, where nation and family are pre-eminent concerns, as can be seen in the opening quotation above by Prime Minister Goh Chok Tong. On 2 January 1991, the President presented a White Paper on Shared Values to the Singapore Parliament. Two of the five values detailed in the Paper are 'nation before community and society above self' and 'family as a basic unit of society' (*White Paper* 1991, p. 10). Despite positive changes in meeting the basic daily needs of women, state-endorsed patriarchy meant that certain aspects of women's lives remained unchanged and that the traditional division of labour in the family was given state support. In addition, state-endorsed patriarchy also had the effect of re-locating women back into the home through policies that make her responsible for child-rearing and other household duties, even as the state makes calls for women to contribute to the economy. The PAP government acknowledges the need for women to enter the workforce, and hence the need to educate them. As Lee stated,

> Societies which do not educate and use half their potential because
> they are women, are those which will be the worse off. Those that
> do, and face up to the problems of new social and family
> relationships and new social institutions to *help working wives* bring
> up the next generation, are those most likely to provide better lives
> for their people. We cannot NOT educate and use the energy and
> ability of our women (*Proceedings of the International Women's
> Year Seminar cum Exhibition* 1975). [*emphasis added*]

This quotation is illustrative of the current contradictions in government
policies on women and suggests that such inconsistencies will continue
into the future (For further detail on the effects of policy contradictions
on women see Goldberg 1987).

State-endorsed patriarchy also means that both women and men are
allocated separate duties and responsibilities. Men are to remain as
heads-of-household, and policies are made with this view in mind. PM
Goh in his National Day Rally Speech in 1994 said that 'rights and
benefits targeted at the family would be channelled through the man, and
laws and rules would be framed towards this objective' (*The Straits
Times* 10 September 1994).

One example of how the state supports the patriarchal family is seen in
the on-going debate over medical benefits for public sector employees.
Numerous women's groups, including women members of the PAP
government, have waged a persistent campaign to force changes to the
current medical scheme. Male employees may claim medical benefits for
their families while family members of female employees do not have
access to these benefits. The marital status of women is taken into
account such that widowed or divorced women or women whose
husbands are seriously ill may be eligible for the benefits. The scheme
was first defended in 1986 by Finance Minister Richard Hu (*The Straits
Times* 25 March 1986) on the basis that extending it to women
employees was costly and not in keeping with the government's attempt
to cut back public sector spending during a recession (Kong and Chan
1997). However, in 1993, with the recession over, government officials
took a different stance on the policy. They defended it on the grounds
that it preserves social structures by supporting the principle of husband-
as-head-of-household. Finance Minister Richard Hu declared, 'It is the
husband's responsibility to look after the family's needs, including their
medical needs. This is how our society is structured. It would be unwise
to tamper with this structure' (*The Straits Times* 12 November 1993).

Dependants of women employees will bear their own cost while
dependants of male employees may claim up to 60 percent of their

medical costs. The man as head-of-household is used by the government as a guiding principle for policies, despite the fact that the 1990 Census placed 110 568 out of 661 730 households as headed by women *(Forum Page, The Straits Times* 17 November 1993). Moreover, it ignored the fact that the contribution of working married women to the family income has increased over time, from 36 per cent in 1980 to 41 per cent in 1990. In addition, the Country Report prepared for the UN's Fourth Conference on Women, acknowledged that the women's financial contribution to the family is even more important in lower income families. Among couples earning less than S$2000, 43 per cent had wives contributing at least half of the combined income *(Women in Singapore: A Country Report* 1995, pp. 15–16). This guiding principle seemed to have contravened two other acts. First, the government's own 1962 position on equal pay for equal work in the civil service, and second, that of the Women's Charter which places equal rights and responsibilities on both men and women in running the home and caring for the children.

While women may protest that the patriarchal stand contradicts the PAP's 1959 election manifesto, and may also point to the Women's Charter as legislation that protects women's rights within the family, yet the Singapore Constitution itself does not guarantee against sex discrimination. Article 12 of the Singapore Constitution states only that '(t)here shall be no discrimination against citizens of Singapore on the grounds only of religion, race, descent or place of birth in any law...'. Both men and women are not protected against discrimination on the basis of sex/gender, which enabled the enactment of policies and rules favouring one sex over the other at different points in time, including those found in the Women's Charter. Therefore when male privileges and benefits are extended to women, they are done as a *privilege* to women, not as a right. In part, this means that women have to constantly keep an eye out for policy changes that may have a detrimental effect on hard-won rights and/or benefits.

The principle of man-as-head-of-household has also meant that it is men who are made financially responsible for the family. A husband may be made to maintain his wife and children under the Women's Charter, and this is enforceable by court order. Moreover, Singapore citizenship is given to children of Singaporean males even if such children were born abroad whereas the children of Singaporean women married to foreign citizens do not have such a right unless they are born in Singapore (NTUC 1994, p. 10). In 1990, then Prime Minister Lee Kuan Yew said the government should think about revising this law since it meant the loss of a group of people who tend to be highly-educated (*The Straits Times* 4 June 1990). Moreover, special provisions in the Constitution also made it easier for foreign wives of Singaporean men to get citizenship while the case is not so for foreign husbands of Singaporean women (SAWL 1986, p. 20). Recently, the government has made it easier for foreign husbands of Singaporean women to receive Permanent Resident (PR) status. Singaporean women may now sponsor their foreign husbands whereas previously foreign husbands had to qualify for PR status on their own ground.

The government therefore views the relationship between men and women, especially within the context of the family, as having a 'natural' division of duties and responsibilities. Occasionally the family will need an injection of support from the state in the form of pro-family policies and/or incentives—with 'family' defined in distinctly traditional terms. The government continually warns of social decline if the family unit with the man as head-of-household is not supported. During the debate on extending the medical benefits scheme to women civil servants, a Ministry of Finance spokesman wrote,

> Many Western countries have, through unwise social and welfare policies, unintentionally but irreversibly undermined the basic unit of husband, wife and children. Their experience warns us of the dangers of even the most well-intentioned government intervention to alter the natural balance and division of responsibility between the sexes, which has evolved over many generations (Tan Eng Beng, *The Straits Times* 19 November 1993).

As can be seen from the above example, women are both penalised and at the same time protected under state patriarchy. The government has enacted a few structures that protect women and has provided some benefits for women. However, both protection and benefits are related mostly to her traditional role as wife and mother. For example, women are given eight weeks' paid maternity leave, and it is illegal for the employer to dismiss a woman worker during such leave. Women civil servants can claim up to four years' unpaid childcare leave after the birth of her child without a loss in the job status. Married women with children have five days' unrecorded paid leave to care for sick children if the children are six years old or under but it is subject to the women having a maximum of three children. Flexible work schemes for female employees with children under the age of six have been initiated. While these have somewhat eased women's burden in juggling their dual role as worker and mother (Goldberg 1987), at the same time, these benefits have reinforced the view that it is essentially women's responsibility to care for home and hearth.

Equal opportunities, yes, but we shouldn't get our women into jobs where they cannot, at the same time, be mothers...You just can't be doing a full-time job heavy job like a doctor or engineer and run a home and bring up children' (Lee Kuan Yew, *The Straits Times* 15 August 1983).

'Bearing' responsibility: home and nation.

As stated above, the discourse on 'women' became overtly patriarchal in the 1980s. This may be traced to the Great Marriage Debate which began in 1983, and eventually culminated years later in high level government officials publicly expressing regret over the 'equal' status of women and men in Singapore.

The Great Marriage Debate began in 1983 when then Prime Minister Lee Kuan Yew observed that graduate women were more likely to remain single or to have fewer children. He deduced from this observation that that Singapore's competitiveness could be at stake, based on his belief that intelligence is primarily genetically determined. Educated women in Singapore tend to marry later, postpone parenthood, and have fewer children. Mr Lee said that the government needed to encourage better-educated women to have more children.

Our most valuable asset is the ability of our people. Yet we are frittering away this asset through the unintended consequences of changes in our education policy and equal career opportunities for women. This has affected their traditional role as mothers. It is too late for us to reverse our policies and have our women go back to their primary role as mothers, the creators and protectors of the next generation. Our women will not stand for it. And, anyway, they have already become too important a factor in the economy (1983, p. 44).

Based on this concern, he created a policy popularly known as the Graduate Mother Scheme in 1984. The scheme gave children of women with tertiary education priority in school registration while less educated mothers were given a S$10 000 incentive to sterilise themselves after having two children. This applied to those families with a monthly income of S$1500 or below and those with less than O-level educational qualifications if the mother undergoes sterilisation after the first or second child when she is below 30 years of age. Due to the overwhelming negative response from the public, the scheme was stopped a year later, although other forms of incentives such as enhanced child relief and unpaid childcare leave took its place. Other efforts to

encourage graduate women to marry resulted in the setting up of the
Social Development Unit which acted as matchmaker between graduate
women and men. Population policies formulated as a national issue were
targeted solely at women and impacted on women's lives (see Saw
1990).

Having stirred up controversy, Mr Lee added fuel to the fire, by
remarking in 1986 that polygamy might be a solution to the problems of
procreation in Singapore. He said 'You must have the physically and
mentally vibrant and vital reproduce. We are doing the opposite. We
introduced monogamy. It seems so manifestly correct...It was wrong, it
was stupid'. In spite of the criticisms his remarks received then, he
reiterated his views in 1994 that the 'government has been "young,
ignorant and idealistic" when it gave women equal rights' (see *The
Straits Times* 26 April 1994 and 30 July 1994).

The Great Marriage Debate had far-reaching consequences for women,
going beyond the procreation issue. Education policies were changed.
For example, in 1983, the National University of Singapore modified
entry requirements making it easier for male applicants to enter the
university. This included changes in second-language requirements in
which men seem to do badly compared to women. These changes were
to address the 'lopsided situation', as exemplified by the 1982 university
enrolment numbers where female students entering the National
University of Singapore outnumbered the males 5563 to 5530.[2] The
Vice-Chancellor supported the change by stating that the gender
imbalance in the university would worsen the problem of unmarried
graduate women. Lee Kuan Yew first highlighted the 'problem' of
unmarried graduate women since Singaporean men tend to marry their
educational equals or inferiors, leaving a pool of unmarried graduate
women whose intelligent genes will therefore not be passed on to the
next generation (Lee 1983).[3]

The women's movement in Singapore

In many ways, the Great Marriage Debate, the speeches of high ranking
government officials and some policy changes galvanised women into
action, to protect and defend rights which they have so far taken-for-
granted. Singaporean women realise that, given the domination of the
PAP in parliament, policies that are detrimental to women's status could
be easily passed. As a result, the Association of Women for Action and
Research (AWARE) was formed with the intent to ensure equal
opportunities for women, attain full equality, and increase women's

awareness and participation in all areas of life (Wee 1987, p. 11). AWARE was registered as a society in December 1985. Although there were other women's groups in existence at that time, such as the Singapore Council of Women's Organisations established in 1980, AWARE was the first to describe itself as a feminist organisation (see PuruShotam 1998).

AWARE claims to represent a constituency concerned with women's issues. Its approach to change is essentially non-confrontational—its members preferring negotiation and dialogue with governmental bodies. A book celebrating the women's movement in Singapore stated, 'Because of the country's traditional Asian roots, feminism in Singapore has taken a quiet, behind-the-scenes form based on sound, logical reasoning' (Lin 1993, p. 35). Another declared, '...in an Asian context, where closed door negotiation worked better than loud public lobbying, militants ran the risk of losing their credibility' (Chew and Tan 1993, p. 88).

Some of the methods used by AWARE to voice their concerns and express criticisms are public talks, open forums, seminars, and letters to local newspapers. It has, on occasion, provided information and given feedback to the government (Rodan 1993, pp. 92–96). Open discussion on women's issues did heighten women's awareness of their experiences within the patriarchal structures of everyday life. AWARE became seen as *the* women's organisation, and when the Nominated Member of Parliament Scheme was adopted, an AWARE president, Dr Kanwaljit Soin, became the first woman NMP to sit in parliament. She made it her mandate to speak on and for women (*Business Times* 9–10 January 1993).[4]

Although Dr Kanwaljit Soin raised many issues pertaining to women during parliamentary debates, one of the more significant events was her tabling of the Family Violence Bill, an issue that generated considerable public discourse. Parliamentary debates surrounding the tabling of the Bill reiterated the government's position on women and family, and women's subordinate position in the patriarchal family (see Chan 1996). The Bill was eventually defeated in parliament in 1995. However, it had by then generated much public discussion on the problem of family violence. Accordingly, the Women's Charter was amended in May 1997 to deal with the issue of family violence.

Women's voices were increasingly heard in the public arena, and women's perspectives were sought by the state. However, after serving two terms as NMP, Dr Soin stepped down from parliament in 1996, and with that, a feminist voice was lost in parliament. Even though the form of feminist discourse, and hence the representation of women's issues, is limited by both the ideology of the 'normal family' (PuruShotam 1998) and by the authoritarian politics of the Singapore state, the parliament was one forum in which women, as represented by Dr Soin, and women's concerns could legitimately be raised and opened for public discourse.

Conclusion

The political context in Singapore has made the fight against patriarchy an uphill battle. Feminist literature has long identified the state as patriarchal (see MacKinnon 1989). However, feminist movements within democratic patriarchal states have access to arenas in which their voices may be heard, even as they work against the constraints of state patriarchy. Authoritarian states like Singapore, on the other hand, play a significant role in defining the boundaries of any discursive activities. Since political spaces for feminist voices are controlled by the state, feminists in Singapore have to work within these boundaries, using strategies deemed appropriate by the state. In order to 'get things done' for women, the effect of this is the tendency for feminists to self-police their own discursive strategies (see Chan 1996). As a result, feminists in authoritarian patriarchal states face overwhelming resistance to feminist work, both structurally and discursively.

However, this does not mean the outlook for the position of women in Singapore is totally pessimistic, even with the authoritarian state's support of patriarchy. We should not judge the state of feminism in Singapore solely via the activities of women's organisations or the speeches of public servants. Feminist knowledges and discourses are disseminated through institutions, sometimes overtly and sometimes unobtrusively (see Katzenstein 1990). While anecdotal, it is useful to note that, at the National University of Singapore, we see courses being offered on gender, and other courses may now include a gendered analysis, feminist theorising or women's perspectives. Research and publications on women's issues are proliferating, not least because there are more women faculty in the university than ever before, but also because researchers, scholars and students are exposed to a variety of feminist knowledges and discourses.

Singaporean women, whether identifying themselves as feminist or not, are grappling with the changing social conditions that economic development brings. As their everyday life experiences expose the contradictions of 'being' women, opportunities are raised for re-thinking what 'woman' entails. I end this article with a powerful quote and a plea from PuruShotam,

> Singaporean women require a blueprint that will involve working with and forging bonds with ourselves: we need to recognise the gossamer threads we may desire are only a web of someone else's construction, a trap. We must start with the basics: ourselves, and an understanding of our real power as fully equal citizens of the nation we belong to and care about...the contemporary Singaporean woman has the potential to ensure growth and development of the truly civil society to which both...men and women in Singapore aspire (1998, p. 162).

Notes

[1] In 1958, self-government for Singapore by 1959 was legally approved. During the 1959 general election, the PAP contested all fifty-one seats, and won forty-three. Lee Kuan Yew, the secretary-general of the PAP became Singapore's first Prime Minister. However, independence for Singapore was sought within the context of a Federation of Malaya. This took place in 1963 when Singapore officially became part of the Federation. Due to the political and social differences that arose after the merger, the alliance dissolved on 9 August 1965 making Singapore an independent state.

[2] The term 'lopsided' is itself gender-biased because it is used to describe situations in which women outnumber men at the tertiary institution and not the reverse.

[3] Delivering a speech at the 1983 National Day Rally, Lee stated that 'A person's performance depends on nature and nurture. There is increasing evidence that nature, or what is inherited, is the greater determinant of a person's performance than nurture (or education and environment)'. He cited a study that had concluded 80 per cent of performance is affected by inherited factors and 20 per cent by environmental factors.

[4] In the late 1980s and early 1990s, the government made several changes to the parliamentary system in response to the call for better representation of different constituencies. The Nominated Member of Parliament Bill was introduced in 1989 and allows for up to six nominated members of parliament. NMPs are individuals nominated by the public to serve a two-year term, and eventually appointed after approval is given by a selected committee of elected MPs.

References and recommended readings

After–5 Collective 1984 *Labour Pains: Coming to Grips with Sexual Inequality*, Asiapac Publishers, Singapore.

Anuar, Hedwig and Lim Kek Hwa 1987 'Recent writings on or by women in Singapore, 1980–' *Commentary*, vol. 7, no. 2–3, pp. 79–93, 129.

AWARE 1988 *The Singapore Woman*, AWARE (Association of Women in Action and Research), Singapore.

——— 1996 *The Ties That Bind: In Search of the Modern Singapore Family*, AWARE, Singapore.

Bungar, Joan Baptista 1991 *Sexuality, Fertility and the Individual in Singapore*, Unpublished Masters' Thesis, Department of Sociology, National University of Singapore.

Chan, Jasmine 1996 'Legislating feminism in a paternalistic state.' Paper presented at the Joint International Conference of the Law and Society Association and Research Committee on Sociology of Law (ISA), July 10–13 in Glasgow, Scotland.

Chew, Phyllis and Tan Ee Sze 1993 'Singapore women—looking back (1950–89)' *Voices and Choices: The Women's Movement in Singapore*, ed. Jenny Lam Lin, Singapore Council of Women's Organizations, Singapore.

Commentary: Journal of the National University of Singapore Society, 1987 Special Issue on Women, vol. 7, no. 2–3.

Goh, Chok Tong 1993 'Guarding the sacred institutions of marriage and family,' *Speeches: A Bi-Monthly Selection of Ministerial Speeches*, vol. 17, no. 3, pp. 28–33.

Goldberg, S. 1987 'Mixed messages: public policy and women in Singapore,' *Commentary*, vol. 7, no. 2–3, pp. 25–37.

Heng, Geraldine and Janadas Devan 1992 'State fatherhood: the politics of nationalism, sexuality, and race in Singapore,' *Nationalisms and Sexualities,* eds A. Parker, M. Russo, D. Sommer, and P. Yaeger, Routledge, New York.

Heyzer, Noeleen 1986 *Working Women in Southeast Asia: Development, Subordination and Emancipation*, Open University Press, Philadelphia.

Huang, Shirlena and Yeoh, Brenda S.A. 1994 'Women, childcare and the state in Singapore,' *Asian Studies Review*, vol. 17, no. 3, pp. 50–62.

Katzenstein, Mary Fainsod 1990 'Feminism within American institutions: unobtrusive mobilization in the 1980s,' *Signs*, vol. 16, no. 1, pp. 27–54.

Kong, Lily L.L. and Chan, Jasmine S. 1997 *Women and the State in Singapore: Continuity and Change*. Paper Presented at the ASEAN Inter-University Seminar on Social Development, 16–19 June in Pekanbaru, Riau, Indonesia.

Lee Kuan Yew 1983 'Talent for the future.' Prepared text delivered at the National Day Rally (14 August 1983). In Saw Swee Hock (1990), 'Changes in the Fertility Policy of Singapore,' *IPS Occasional Paper*, Appendix A, no. 2. Institute of Policy Studies, Singapore.

Leong, Wai Kum 1981 'A brief survey of the Women's Charter,' *Commentary*, vol. 5, no. 1, pp. 104–10.

Lin, Jenny Lam ed. 1993 *Voices and Choices: The Women's Movement in Singapore*, Singapore Council of Women's Organizations, Singapore.

Low, Linda, Toh Mun Heng, Euston Quah and David Lee 1993 'Economic participation,' *Singapore Women: Three Decades of Change*, eds Aline Wong and Leong Wai Kum, Times Academic Press, Singapore.

MacKinnon, Catharine A. 1989 *Towards a Feminist Theory of the State*, Havard University Press, Cambridge.

Murugason, Sudha 1987 'Women, marriage and divorce: changes in the legal and social situation,' *Commentary*, vol. 7, no. 2–3, pp. 38–50.

NTUC (National Trade Union Congress) 1994 *Legal Rights and Support Services for Women Workers*, Singapore National Printers, Singapore.

Pang Cheng Lian 1971 *Singapore's People's Action Party: Its History, Organization and Leadership*, Oxford University Press, Singapore.

PuruShotam, Nirmala 1992 'Women and knowledge/power: notes on the singaporean dilemma,' *Imagining Singapore*, eds Ban Kah Choon, Anne Pakir and Tong Chee Kiong, Times Academic Press, Singapore.

——— 1998 'Between compliance and resistance. gender and the middle class way of life in Singapore,' *Gender and Power in Affluent Asia*, eds Krishna Sen and Maila Stivens, Routledge, London.

Rodan, Garry 1993 'Preserving the one-party state in contemporary Singapore,' *Southeast Asia in the 1990s*, eds Kevin Hewison, Richard Robison and Garry Rodan, Allen and Unwin, Sydney.

Saw Swee Hock 1990 'Changes in the fertility policy of Singapore,' *IPS Occasional Paper*, No. 2. Institute of Policy Studies, Singapore.

SAWL (Singapore Association of Women Lawyers) 1986 *Legal Status of Singapore Women*, Asiapac Books and Educational Aids, Singapore.

Shantakumar, G. 1993 'Demographic and socio-economic characteristics of older women: issues and policy implications,' *A Woman's Place: The Story of Singapore Women*, eds Aline Wong and Leong Wai Kum, PAP Women's Wing, Singapore.

Singam, Constance 1993 'Feminism is civic consciousness,' *Commentary*, vol. 11, no. 1, pp. 70–74.

Singapore Association of Women Lawyers 1986 *Legal Status of Singapore Women*, Asiapac Books and Educational Aids, Singapore.

Singapore Department of Statistics 1998 'Social progress of Singapore women: a statistical assessment,' *Occasional Paper on Social Statistics*, November 1998.

Soin, Kanwaljit 1996 'National policies: their impact on women and the family,' *The Ties That Bind: in Search of the Modern Singapore Family*, eds AWARE, Singapore.

Thio Li-Ann 1997 'The impact of internationalisation on domestic governance: gender egalitarianism & the transformative potential of CEDAW,' *Singapore Journal of International and Comparative Law*, vol. 1, pp. 278–350.

Wee, Vivienne 1987 'The ups and downs of women's status in Singapore: A chronology of some landmark events, 1950–87,' *Commentary*, vol. 7, no. 2–3, pp. 5–12.

White Paper on Shared Values 1991 Presented to the Singapore Parliament by Command of the President of the Republic of Singapore.

Women in Singapore Country Report 1995 Fourth UN World Conference on Women, Beijing, 4–15 September 1995, Ministry of Community Development, Singapore.

Wong, Aline 1974 'Women as a minority group in Singapore,' *Working Paper No. 29*, Department of Sociology, University of Singapore.

Wong, Aline and Leong Wai Kum 1993a *Singapore Women: Three Decades of Change*, Times Academic Press, Singapore.

—— 1993b *A Woman's Place: The Story of Singapore Women*, PAP Women's Wing, Singapore.

Yim Seow Hua and Ang Seow Long 1997 'Income trends: the gender income gap,' *Statistics Singapore Newsletter*, vol. 10, no. 3, pp. 2–6.

4 Women in the People's Republic of China: new challenges to the grand gender narrative

Louise Edwards

School of Arts and Sciences
Australian Catholic University

At the beginning of the 1970s, young women in the People's Republic of China (PRC) were presented with a simple picture of their status in relation to their grandmothers'. 'Before 1949 women were oppressed by Confucianism and lived in misery. After 1949, under the leadership of the Chinese Communist Party (CCP), women have been liberated from the shackles of tradition.' In this grand narrative the CCP had saved Chinese women from centuries of oppression and misery. In the grim Cultural Revolution days of the early 1970s, individuals expounding views that deviated from the official perspective faced persecution and imprisonment. As a result, people were compelled to mouth official slogans ignoring the schism between their daily reality and the propaganda. By the start of the decade-long Cultural Revolution (1966), a generation of citizens interpreted the history of Chinese women in a linear fashion with the CCP bestowing the ultimate dream of equal status. Women uniformly spoke about their happy, liberated status to gullible foreign authors (see Kristeva 1977) while sexual abuse and discrimination remained unacknowledged.

In the 1950s, 1960s and early 1970s non-CCP voices were few and far between and the emancipation rhetoric was unremitting—'Gender equality had been achieved in the PRC.' At the end of the twentieth century this official monotone has been joined by a plurality of differing voices that relate vastly contradictory and diverse narratives about women's lives and experiences in China. CCP control of the rhetorical space in the nation has diminished over the past thirty years. Since the implementation of the Open Door Policy in the mid-1980s a wider variety of narratives about women's lives are competing with and undercutting the 'gender equality' myth. Commercial influences creating women as objects of desire and sexuality intermingle with popular magazine images of women as domestic experts (Hooper 1998). Opposing voices now expose the equality narrative as partial and incomplete—victims of domestic violence or rape can now ring emergency hotlines (Evans 1997), women's studies centres have been established to explore problems of unemployment, unfair dismissal, sexual discrimination and female infanticide.

In thirty years the CCP's monotone that gender equality has been achieved in Communist China has been replaced by a multiplicity of voices about the diversity of the modernities Chinese women experience. This chapter explores these transformations in a survey of the political, economic and social indicators of women's status in the PRC. It argues that there have been real improvements for women between 1970 and 2000 but these are a result of general improvements for all China's citizens and do not relate to specific policy initiatives directed at raising the status of women. In fact, as will be clear below, there has been a dismantling of structures that protected women since 1970. The re-invention of Asia's largest socialist, totalitarian state, as it gradually integrates into the global capitalist economic and political system, has had dramatic impacts on the status of women. As the most populous nation in the world—representing one quarter of the world's population—any transformation in the status of women in the PRC is significant for the global status of women.

Building China's socialist modernity

In 1949, at the culmination of a bloody civil war, the CCP defeated the ruling Nationalist Party. Supporters of the Nationalist Party fled to the island of Taiwan where they established a separate government (see chapter on Taiwan). From 1949 the national government politics of 'mainland' China, as the PRC came to be known, were informed by Marxist principles and the government's claim to legitimacy stemmed from the notion that the CCP had liberated the masses from an oppressive ruling minority. The espousal of gender equality was central to this emancipation rhetoric. This progressive line has been tempered by the adherence to the overarching Marxist maxim that the liberation of women follows as a natural consequence of the liberation of all classes. Thus, national interests have always overridden gender interests in the PRC. Nonetheless the new government took great pains to promote and implement its progressive policies on women's liberation and made repeated attacks on the strong patriarchal heritage of Confucianism (see Croll 1978).

Women's equality with men was pronounced in the constitution of 1950 and has been reiterated in every subsequent revision. In 1950 the government also implemented the Marriage Law which included the right of women to initiate divorce proceedings on the basis of incompatibility decades before many Western nations. It was so successful it became nicknamed the 'divorce law'. The Electoral Law of 1953 stipulated that women enjoyed the same electoral rights as men. The Land Reform campaigns included women as 'land-owners' eligible for land allocation. Provisions for maternity leave and childcare were made within state owned enterprises and women were exhorted to work outside the home to rebuild a strong, prosperous China.

These policies encouraged women to participate in economic and political reconstruction alongside men on the basis of gender equality but two radical campaigns undercut the project of nation building and retarded the economic growth that would have truly alleviated much of the hardship women suffered. The Great Leap Forward (GLF) of 1958– 60 created large commune farms where labour and rewards were shared across the villages. This collectivisation policy resulted in a massive decline in productivity and, in combination with the natural disasters that swept across China in the early 1960s, between twenty and thirty million Chinese citizens had died of starvation and related diseases. Less than six years later the blunder of the GLF was followed by the infamous Great Proletarian Cultural Revolution of 1966–76. This movement plunged the country into further political and economic chaos directing savage attacks on intellectuals, teachers, researchers and CCP cadres. During both the GLF and the Cultural Revolution women's rights were highlighted and women were exhorted to participate in politics and labour for the national benefit. In reality, China's economy was stagnating and one quarter of the world's population remained internationally isolated. 'Building socialism by self-reliance' was the motto used to justify China's distance from the rest of the world from the mid-1950s to 1970.

In September 1976, Mao Zedong, Chairman of the CCP and the main proponent of both the GLF and the Cultural Revolution, died. China's new leaders embraced a policy of economic liberalisation and further engagement with the West that had been slowly beginning during the last years of Mao's life. The PRC replaced Taiwan, formally called the Republic of China, in the UN in 1971. The years since are typified by the gradual opening of China's economy and society to Western influences under a CCP inspired 'Open Door Policy'.

China has become more democratic since 1979—most of its citizens do not live in fear of political criticism. Open elections have been held at the local level since the mid 1980s but nationally the CCP leadership remains defiantly unrepresentative and ultimately holds all political power and controls large sections of the economy. Events like the 1989 Tiananmen Square massacre demonstrate the CCP's commitment to continuing its one-party rule and ruthlessly enforcing government directives. One justification for continued CCP control is the need for political stability during the period of rapid economic reforms required to modernise the nation. Indeed, the economic reforms presided over by the CCP during the years since 1978 have been far-reaching, carefully monitored and largely successful to date. A centrally controlled command economy has been dismantled to permit individual ownership of land and factories, the establishment of stockmarkets, private banks, and public markets where individual producers sell their goods without government mediation.

Economic indicators reflect the positive nature of the political and economic reforms. The per capita GDP of China's citizens has risen dramatically: From around US$280 in 1971 to US$2800 in 1999 (FEER 1999a, p. 56). The post-reform years averaged double digit growth in GDP. The period from 1984–88 posted 11.6 per cent average GDP growth (FEER 1990) and the period from 1990–96 averaged 12.3 per cent (FEER 1999). Nonetheless, China is still a very poor country by Western standards. Overwhelmingly a rural nation, 70 per cent of its population live outside of urban areas (down from 80 per cent in 1970). Moreover, the rewards of the rapid economic growth of the past 25 years have been unevenly distributed with the urban and coastal regions receiving most benefit and the remote, rural areas remaining much poorer. The rising numbers of disgruntled unemployed are a potential source of political instability and corruption and nepotism also threaten the impressive economic growth.

Dismantling socialism and consequences for women

China has not been alone in its retreat from totalitarian socialism. Maxine Molyneaux noted that the collapse of socialism in Eastern Europe and the Soviet Union would bring both benefits and losses to women (Molyneaux 1990). The state's retreat from its paternalistic role as the liberator and protector of women is only partially balanced by the benefits arising from the emergence of a civil society. A civil society implies the existence of legally enforceable rules and punishments and a political openness that permits the emergence of women's organisations to meet the needs of women. China is currently somewhere between the two points—paternalistic socialist and civil democratic—consequently the independent social and political networks designed to protect and advance women's rights are still numerically insignificant and politically impotent.

Economic liberalisation has not altered the fundamental government espousal of the need to protect women's rights, but it has altered the nature of the relationships between rhetoric and reality on women's status. Since the 1980s the experiences of women and girls have been increasingly publicly discussed and the official rhetoric shows recognition that more work is needed to improve the status of women. The solution to 'women's problems' presented by the CCP is modernisation through economic growth. The logic being; as China becomes wealthier the status of women will improve. The government makes little effort to examine the effects of its reform policies on the status of women. After all, gender concerns have consistently been secondary to, rather than implicit in the CCP's economic policies since 1949.

In 1994 the Information Office of the State Council of the PRC published a document titled 'The Situation of Chinese Women' as part of its preparation for the 1995 Fourth World Conference on Women. Beijing hosted this conference for the UN and was keen to demonstrate to the international community the remarkable progress made in Chinese women's rights since 1949. The report declares:

> New China proclaimed that Chinese women enjoy equal rights with men in all aspects of political, economic, cultural, social and family life and that they have become, like all Chinese citizens, masters of the state and society. Chinese laws guarantee that women and men enjoy the same rights and status and have equal personal dignity. The Chinese government employs legal, administrative and educational means to eliminate all kinds of discrimination against

women and protect their special rights and interests (Information Office 1994, p. 9).

In later paragraphs, the report acknowledges that problems remain in the realisation of gender equality.

China is a developing country. Owing to the constraints of social development and the influence of old concepts, the condition of Chinese women is still not wholly satisfactory. There exist various difficulties and resistance which have prevented the full realisation of equal rights to women.... Instances of...discrimination against women and even infringement of their rights still occur from time to time (Information Office 1994, p. 9).

The current official explanation for the continued existence of problems for women draws on 'development' rhetoric which places China on a teleology stretching from underdeveloped nation through developing nation to developed nation. In this problematic view the woman problem will be solved once 'developed' status has been achieved. Gender equality is conceived as a luxury of wealthy and 'modern' nations that have discarded tradition (see Stivens 1998). However, even this CCP-authorised refinement of the grand narrative is being undercut by an increasing diversity of stories on women's lives in China.

Representatives of women: the Women's Federation

The most significant remnant of the CCP's paternalism as the emancipator of women is the All China Women's Federation of (ACWF). The ACWF was responsible for the promotion of the CCP's aphorism that 'Gender equality had been achieved' up to the late 1970s. Established by the CCP in 1949, the ACWF was dedicated specifically to communicating the government's policies to women and, less commonly, women's concerns to the government. As such the ACWF was never conceived as a 'feminist' organisation. Rather, it is first and foremost a CCP organisation. Its cadres are appointed and paid by the Party-government and all women who are members of the CCP are automatically members of the ACWF. A typical CCP's perspective on the ACWF-CCP relationship is:

The Party is a representative and guardian of women's interests...the Chinese Communist Party has always been the leader of the Chinese women's movement...women's organisations are highly unified. Although there are women's national, regional and

industrial organisations...they are mostly affiliates of the All-China
Women's Federation... The Chinese Communist Party and the
people's government exercise leadership over the women's
movement via ACWF which acts as the spokesperson for all women
in China. No other women's organisation in the country can
substitute for the ACWF (Min 1995, pp. 533–34).

The presence of the ACWF, even in the mid-1990s appears to obviate
the need for 'independent' women's organisations. However, the CCP's
enthusiasm for ensuring that this monopoly is protected has waned and
the ACWF has shown itself to be more responsive to women and not
merely a mouth-piece for CCP directives. Consequently a healthy
tension in the ACWF's function has emerged over the past two decades
as the totality of the CCP influence has fragmented and the ACFW has
now become part of the plurality of voices that undercuts the CCP's
totalising narrative of the success of gender equality in China. The
ACWF increasingly feels twin responsibilities—to the CCP and to the
women of China (Howell 1996). It has reinvented itself in important
ways that suggests it will continue to be the dominant advocate of
women's rights into the future even as the state draws back from its
controlling role and the private sector expands.

    Like most of the CCP's mass organisations the ACWF ceased
operation during the turbulent years of the Cultural Revolution. By 1967
it had stopped functioning and when it recommenced its activities in
1977–78 the CCP had vastly different plans for China and Chinese
women. The ACWF, as an official organ of the CCP, tailored its actions
accordingly but soon found that the increasing complexity of China's
liberalising economy and society rendered this reactive mode ineffective.
The ACWF entered the 1980s in drastic need of rejuvenation—a task
made more difficult by the fact that CCP membership is no longer the
sole path to power, career advancement and privilege in the new post-
reform China. Nonetheless, the ACWF has gone some way to achieving
this shift towards a more proactive role with a fresh new leadership.

    Croll notes that in the ACWF's regular National Women's Congresses
there has been a distinct increase in emphasis on women's rights and a
corresponding diminution of focus on eliciting support for CCP policies
among women since 1978 (1995, pp. 137–39). When it became apparent
that the One Child Family Policy was increasing the incidence of female
infanticide and the abuse of women who gave birth to daughters, the
ACWF was at the forefront of the prevention strategies. Croll argues that
the ACWF's 1983 decision to take strong action against the reappearance
of these 'feudal' practices was the turning point in the ACWF's history

(1995, p. 140). They conducted research into the extent of the problem and initiated forceful campaigns to promote the value of girls and the role of male sperm in sex determination. From this point the ACWF undertook to protect women from abuse and advance women's interests with more certainty and clarity than it had at any other time since 1949.

Jude Howell describes other examples of the ACWF's proactive role. In some counties the ACWF has been active in promoting skills among women entrepreneurs. Others have served as employment agencies helping rural women find domestic jobs in urban areas and providing retraining for unemployed women in computing, secretarial skills, and foreign languages (Howell 1996). It encouraged the development of research into women by establishing first the National Institute for Women's Studies in 1983 and later, numerous provincial branches. The 1992 Women's Law was another important national initiative to emerge from the ACWF's new purposeful role as defender of women.

Women's Law

As China became more involved with the international agreements through the UN, the ACWF was able to win legal reforms for women. Demonstrating a commitment to women's rights was an important signifier of respectability in the UN and China was keen to publicise its success. This gave the ACWF greater influence in government. In 1980 China was among the first to endorse the 1979 UN Convention on the 'Elimination of All Forms of Discrimination against Women.' During 1985, at the close of the International Decade for Women, the ACWF raised the issue of writing a new Chinese law on the rights and interests of women (Keith 1997, p. 31). This resulted in the promulgation in 1992 of the 'Law on Protecting Women's Rights and Interests.' The document (reprinted in Croll 1995, pp. 184–92) drew together all existing laws and constitutional provisions relating to women's rights and initiated new articles for areas omitted in earlier documents. The document is divided into nine sections including Political Rights, and Rights and Interests Relating to Culture and Education, Work, Marriage and the Family. In each aspect equality of the genders is emphasised. Special provisions that reflect the vulnerability of women in poorer regions are included— for example, prohibition on trafficking in women, female infanticide, maltreatment of women who give birth to girl babies are listed explicitly in 'Rights Relating to the Person.'

Problems with this document have become apparent in the years since its promulgation. Primarily these relate to the absence of clear legal responsibilities for those who violate the law. The Law stipulates in

Article 48: 'When a woman's lawful rights and interest are infringed upon, she has the right to request the competent department concerned for a disposition or bring a lawsuit in a people's court according to law.' Only 75 per cent of the 54 articles in the Women's Law delineate consequences and legal responsibilities for infringement and with the current underdeveloped state of China's civil law courts the effectiveness of the Women's Law is diminished. Article 3 anticipates the problem: 'The State shall take effective measures to provide the necessary conditions for women to exercise their rights.' Moreover, as the private and foreign owned component of China's economy has expanded relative to the state owned sector the ability of the government to monitor the treatment of women has diminished. The real benefits of the Law will emerge when its punitive and educational functions are given full bureaucratic support as a civil society develops complete with enforceable legal codes. It is too early to dismiss the Law as mere window-dressing.

Four Self's: the collective retreats and the individual returns

The ACWF has maintained an active propaganda role in promoting the importance of women's participation and gender equality through the last three decades. The dominant slogan since the 1988 Sixth National Women's Congress has been the 'Four Selfs'—self respect, self-confidence, self-reliance and self-strengthening. The focus on the responsibility of women themselves to develop the desired character attributes is indicative of the CCP's retreat from paternalism. It posits Chinese women as potential creators of their own individuality—the focus on 'self' development was inconceivable even in the early 1970s when the collective, the nation, or the work unit were emphasised. During the Cultural Revolution, concern for individual personality attributes was harshly criticised as bourgeois sentimentalism. The current Four Self's movement places greater responsibility on women for their psychological and economic independence and in a rhetorical shift it absolves the Chinese government's responsibility for meeting these needs or solving these problems. At no stage prior to this campaign had there been any recognition of the psychological aspects to women's subordination in the PRC's gender equity rhetoric.

In 1993 the ACWF embarked upon a campaign to address the commercialised objectification of women. In particular they focussed on the rising popularity of beauty contests. Their slogan, the 'Four Don'ts—don't endorse them, don't promote them, don't organise them and don't participate in them'—was a rather feeble attempt to counteract an increasingly popular urban phenomenon. 'Talent' contests even extend to the internet. During 1999 a Miss Net competition was held with selection criteria weighted 30 per cent on beauty/personality and 70 per cent on internet expertise (Lawrence 1999, pp. 54–55). Attempting to provide an alternative model, the ACWF's journals promoted the 'strong woman' who was able to compete with men on multiple fronts. However, this campaign merely indicated to younger women that the ACWF was still tied to its 1960s puritanical, CCP inspired promotion of a drab, grey Mao-suit androgyny. Women in 1990s China, particularly younger women, are more inclined to be influenced by television, advertising, employment and their peers than they are by a campaign on self-confidence from the ACWF. The increasing diversity of the discourses competing for women's attention threatens to marginalise the ACWF as the dreary official voice of the past.

Politics in the communist state

Politics in the PRC is entirely dominated by the CCP. Involvement in politics implies involvement with the CCP. The highest ruling body in the party structure is that of the Standing Committee of the Politburo, and while three women have been full members of the Politburo, none have joined the Standing Committee since the formation of the party in 1921. The three that have reached the Politburo were wives of extremely powerful men—Jiang Qing (wife to Mao Zedong), Ye Qun (wife to Lin Biao) and Deng Yingchao (wife to Zhou Enlai). A handful of women have become alternate members of the Politburo and the most significant of these for the reform period is Chen Muhua. She has held numerous important posts in the CCP and the government and is currently the president of the ACWF. During the Cultural Revolution and the years immediately following the percentage of women in politics was at its highest since 1949. In 1969 10.5 per cent of the Politburo were women compared with 4 per cent in 1982 and 0 per cent in 1977, 1987 and 1992. A similar pattern emerges with the percentage of female members in the Central Committee of the CCP. In 1973 10.3 per cent of the 195 members were women; in 1982 this had slipped to 5.2 per cent and in 1992 it had risen slightly to 6.4 per cent (Rosen 1995, pp. 318–19). The period of economic and political liberalisation has thus been a period of decline in numbers of women reaching the top level of power in the CCP. Those that have attained positions of authority usually have some close connection with the ACWF indicating that within the CCP there is a certain expectation that women perform 'women's political work' and do not venture into the broader political realm.

If we examine the National People's Congress (NPC) (ostensibly a non-CCP organ but effectively a 'rubber stamp' for Politburo decisions), a similar pattern emerges. In 1975 women formed 22.6 per cent of the delegates to the 4th NPC and 25.1 per cent of all Standing Committee members. By 1993 at the 8th NPC women still comprised about 21.03 per cent of all delegates but their share of the Standing Committee members had halved to a 12.68 per cent. Rosen has noted that women in the NPC are often expected to represent other 'minorities' (e.g. small democratic parties, ethnic minorities) (1995, p. 324). This custom amplifies their 'exceptional' status and reaffirms them as non-threatening tokens rather than women with the raw political career ambition accepted in men. Those who do manage to win higher positions find themselves allocated to the soft issues of education, health, and culture—but overwhelmingly all have had some contact with women's affairs.

At the local level the situation is even more bleak. In the early 1970s a quota system guaranteed a certain number of positions to women in both party and local councils. With the market reforms and democratisation women have not be able to compete successfully against men in open elections. Women with previous experience in politics find that their areas of expertise (education, health and welfare) are not regarded as evidence of 'real experience'. These soft portfolios are 'extras' rather than 'earners' for the economy. Male candidates often have the experience in the prestigious portfolios of industry or agriculture that ostensibly demonstrate economic and financial management skills.

The greatest shift during the last three decades has been the removal of the quotas guaranteeing women access to positions of political authority that existed from the 1950s. The liberalisation of the political realm has opened women to direct competition without the protective quotas of the state. Even if the development of a legal system allows the Women's Law to protect women's rights, it is doubtful that it can ensure women equal political representation. The increasing political freedoms that have accompanied the Open Door Policy have not been beneficial for women with political aspirations. The official line now rather vaguely declares, the number of women deputies to the NPC and local people's congresses should include 'appropriate numbers of women and the proportion should be increased step by step' (Information Office 1994, p. 12). Rosen summarises the situation of the years since the mid 1980s as

a decision to rely solely on the market, without a concomitant reduction of state intervention, seems likely to lead to less, rather than more participation in social life by Chinese women, at least in the short term. At the same time, it has contributed to the resurgence of traditional cultural prejudices which have prevented women from taking an active part in public life (Rosen 1995, p. 339).

As will be clear from women's participation rates in various employment sectors, government and party positions are second only to construction in their low rates for women.

Problems for paid employment

Since the establishment of the PRC the government has encouraged all citizens to participate in the building of the New China—primarily this has meant by joining the paid workforce. The CCP upheld the Engelsian notion that paid employment was an important step towards improving women's status. Women in the 1950s joined the rural workforce in large numbers and an estimated three-quarters of rural women were working outside the home by the end of the GLF (see Andors 1983). It was politically astute to work in the new peasant/worker dictatorship of the PRC. However, it soon became clear that women were in reality regarded as an auxiliary workforce to be encouraged in times of perceived labour shortage and discouraged in times of less need. Thus, in the 1950s women were encouraged to leave the home, in the early 1960s they were exhorted to rediscover the delights of unpaid domestic labour, and in the late 1960s and early 1970s they were welcomed back into the workforce (Wolf 1985; Andors 1983). Currently, one proposal to solve China's growing unemployment problem involves pushing women out of the paid workforce. Despite the fluctuation in political rhetoric women still make up almost 40 per cent of the total workforce (Croll 1995, p. 117) Only in urban areas are husbands inclined to help with the domestic chores when wives worked outside the home. Women in China, for the most part, are still carrying the double burden undertaking between 2–3 hours more housework each day than men (ACWF 1991, p. 590).

In the last three decades the nature of work in China has changed dramatically. Unemployment has emerged as a major problem for China's citizens with the dismantling of socialist job-protection. In the early 1970s there was almost no private ownership of land or industry—the government or the collective owned all property, means of economic production and controlled all retail outlets. Everything you ate, bought, wore and read was created in a government controlled or collectively-owned industry. It was difficult to access housing, rice ration tickets or clothing ration tickets without a link to a 'work-unit', as all communes, collectives, institutions and factories were called. Since the early 1980s the private sector has been allowed to return to China's economy. The collective farmland has been allocated to individual farmers, all items of machinery allocated to individuals or small groups, permission for private entrepreneurs to raise chickens or pigs for private sale has returned (Jacka 1997). Foreign companies have been welcomed to establish factories that produce toys, textiles and increasingly, electronic equipment for a Western market. The shift away from loss-making state owned enterprises to the private or foreign has resulted in massive redundancies. Women, as 'auxiliary workers' are particularly vulnerable to sackings and currently account for 70 per cent of the urban jobless (Keith 1997, p. 47).

The conditions for those in employment have also been jeopardised. The protection and rights afforded women by the paternalistic state are not necessarily available in the private sector. For example, maternity leave was guaranteed in state or collective industries but may not be in the private sector. The Constitution of the PRC and the 1992 Women's Law established an admirable legal framework for protecting women in the workforce. However, the general retreat of the state and the undeveloped legal system means that many of these rights are ignored by new foreign and local employers (see Woo 1994). The government position is:

> Women enjoy equal working rights with men...the right to work and be employed, equal pay for equal work...The law stipulates that any unit...is not allowed to refuse to employ women or raise the recruitment standards for women under any pretext. It cannot fire women... on the pretext of marriage, pregnancy, maternity leave or baby nursing. It is not allowed to discriminate against women in terms of promotion, award of academic and technical titles, allotment of housing and enjoyment of welfare benefits, nor to assign women to tasks that are not suitable for them. Women enjoy special protection during menstruation, pregnancy, childbirth and baby nursing period (Information Office 1994, p. 12)

Nonetheless, Honig and Hershatter cite a case in 1984 where the Post Office and Telegraph Bureau in Shanghai favoured men in recruitment by 20:1 (1988, p. 245). This instance was not unique. Croll points to a survey conducted by the ACWF which reports that 75 per cent of employers preferred to hire men and sometimes required the women candidates to pass employment exams with 12 per cent higher grades than male counterparts (1997, p. 120). Employers argued variously: women were weaker than men; once women marry they no longer devote themselves fully to their employment; women require expensive maternity leave and kindergartens.

The difficulty for women in finding and keeping jobs makes them vulnerable to exploitation. There is strong evidence to suggest that women in China earn far less that men and that the wage-differentials have worsened during the last decade. A 1999 study showed that Chinese women earned 0.501 of the male wage in 1991, and 0.418 in 1994. This is in comparison with 1994 figures for Sri Lanka, Hong Kong and Germany where women earned 0.749, 0.635 and 0.742 of the male wage respectively (Maurer-Fazio et al. 1999, p. 67). This differential results from the concentration of women in lower paid jobs—they do not face discrimination within industries but find more difficulty gaining employment in higher-waged industries. Croll notes that 'Women have constituted a high proportion of the new causal labour force, much of it migrant, contracted to produce electronics, textiles, clothing and automobile components...for the export market (1995, p. 123). Women are concentrated in those industries favouring piece-work with low rates of pay. Croll estimates that 80 per cent of workers in the new foreign factories are young women who migrate from the countryside to work. Conditions in many of these factories are appalling and with the weak state of China's labour movement there are no advocates for these exploited workers. For women remaining in agricultural work new challenges are also emerging in the age of liberalisation. Labour intensive and low-paid agricultural work is gradually becoming feminised and regarded as a 'domestic' chore as the men head to the cities to higher paid labouring jobs (Kelkar and Wang 1997, p. 73).

In 1996 women comprised 20 per cent of construction workers, 23 per cent of CCP and government workers, 37 per cent of agricultural workers, 44 per cent of manufacturing workers, 45 per cent of retail and wholesale workers, 57 per cent of catering workers, 56 per cent of health and welfare workers and 41 per cent of education workers (SSB 1997, pp. 106–107). The greatest rates of increase in the years since 1982 have been in the commercial sector—primarily because this sector was almost non-existent prior to the economic reforms (Croll 1995, p. 118). From these figures it is clear that despite the government's rhetoric about gender equality the party and government sector of the workforce remains one of the most difficult for women to enter. Women concentrate in those areas with the least job security or those linked to 'feminine' skills such as health and welfare. Ultimately, women workers in China remain highly vulnerable and undervalued workers. Until the labour movement is able to lobby freely in the PRC, the grand narrative about worker's rights will continue to dominate, and the problems faced by China's modern women workers will remain obscured.

Women and population control

The most controversial social policy initiative of the last three decades is the One Child Family Policy. Women have been the main targets for this policy as the main receivers of contraception and sterilisation. Many girls and girl-babies face grave threats to their survival as a consequence of this draconian policy. Fertility control is regarded as a key national development responsibility and women carry the burden for ensuring that this national development goal is reached while girls and girl-babies have become its unwitting victims. Communist China was not always preoccupied with population reduction. In the 1950s and 1960s China's vast population was regarded as a precious resource to be harnessed in the building of national wealth (White 1994). However, by the early 1970s advocates of serious population control were on the ascendancy and the Chinese government embraced the global development paradigms which promoted the notion that rapid population growth inhibits improvements in living standards. The campaign to restrict the numbers of children being born began in earnest.

Over 83 per cent of couples use contraception—this is one of the world's highest rates. The main methods used during 1994 demonstrate that contraception is regarded as a woman's concern and a national rather than individual matter. 40.30 per cent of couples relied on female sterilisation, 39.99 per cent relied on inter-uterine devices and only 11.44 per cent relied on male sterilisation. Only 3.6 per cent of women used the contraceptive pill and only 3.6 per cent of men used condoms (Lu Chunheng et al. 1994, p. 481). Both sterilisation and IUDs empower the medical practitioners above the woman. An IUD cannot be removed without professional medical attention whereas barrier or oral contraceptive pills permit human error and demand individual compliance to function. The urban-rural divide is clear with sterilisation more common among rural couples than metropolitan couples. In Shanghai and Beijing only 7.2 per cent and 10 per cent of women respectively were sterilised, while 72 per cent and 63 per cent had IUDs inserted. The incidence of HIV/AIDS remains low in China relative to Europe, America and Southeast Asia so condom use has not been encouraged on health grounds.

The targets for population control explain the reason for such high use of contraception. In its Fourth Five Year Plan (1971–75) the government aimed to reduce the urban growth rate to 1 per cent and the rural growth rate to 1.5 per cent by 1975. In its Fifth Five Year Plan (1976–80) the goal was 1 per cent for both urban and rural areas by 1980, 0.5 per cent by 1985 and zero growth by 2000. Initially, these targets were encouraged through a policy of 'later, longer, fewer'—delayed marriage (ideally 24 to 26 years for women and 26 to 29 years for men), longer space between births and fewer children over all. Accompanying slogans included 'One is good, two is all right, three is too many' (see Kane 1987). Throughout the 1970s contraception was free, work units were instructed to give paid leave for women who had undergone sterilisation, IUD insertions or abortion procedures. The success of these campaigns is clear. The annual growth rate reduced from 2.6 per cent in 1970 to 1.17 per cent in 1979 (SSB 1997, p. 69). In 1996 this had risen slightly to 1.3% (FEER 1999, p. 14). A concerted government effort to reduce the rate of maternal deaths in childbirth has accompanying the family planning measures. The results are impressive for a country of limited financial capacity. China has only 95 maternal deaths per 100 000 live births compared to Indonesia's 650 and India's 570 (Neft and Levine 1997, pp. 506-507).

Where are the girl babies?

The population control policy began by encouraging rather than coercing couples. This changed over the course of the 1980s when it became apparent that China's population was expanding beyond the capabilities of the government to provide the promised improvements in living standards even with the reduced growth rates. The post-liberation baby boom of the 1950s and the post-famine baby boom of the mid 1960s brought millions of couples into child-bearing age over the late 1970s and 1980s. To prevent the children of these couples from creating a super-baby boom in the following generation a One Child Family Policy was regarded as the only solution. Initially, this policy was implemented with incentives for couples choosing to have one child—extra work-points, provision of child health-care fees, priority housing and job allocation for urban residents, private land and housing lots in rural areas. By the mid 1980s more coercive measures were implemented and reports of forced abortions, late abortions (even into the third trimester), forced sterilisation and compulsory IUD insertions were appearing.

Although the government could enforce the One Child Family Policy with some degree of success they could not easily change the cultural preference for boys. Consequently, female infanticide, abuse by husbands and parents-in-law of women who give birth to girls, and an under-reporting of births of daughters increased (Honig and Hershatter 1988). Such unregistered daughters are non-persons within the highly bureaucratised Chinese state. To counteract the abuse of mothers of daughters, the government posted bills to explain that the father determines a baby's sex not the mother. Posters of 'ideal families' routinely featured girls rather than boys in an effort to establish girls as 'real' children. In the past, particularly in poorer families, daughters had not been valued. Inheritance was passed through the male line, sons performed religious rituals (such as ancestor worship), and it was sons not daughters, who were responsible for care of elderly parents. Daughters were the first sold or dumped in times of starvation and hardship. Residues of these old practices remained well into the 1990s. While much has improved in the status of women in China the continued practice of female infanticide demonstrates that women are valued less than men.

Official PRC statistics for 1997 illustrate the effects of son-preference on the national sex ratio at birth. The naturally occurring sex ratio is 100 girls to 106 boys but the national ratio for the PRC in 1996 was 100:111—demonstrating a considerable and unnatural weighting towards boys. The figures vary according to region. Wealthy urban areas like Beijing and Shanghai have slightly higher weighting towards girls than the naturally occurring ratio, with a rate of 100:105. Poorer rural regions reveal the locus of the skewed national ratio: Guangxi 100:115, Jiangxi 100:116 and Anhui 100:115 (SSB 1997, p. 84). The One Child Family Policy is clearly the reason for these appalling figures because changes in the sex ratios over a series of years follow changes in the degree of rigidity used to enforce the regulation. In Fujian province the stable rate of 100:108 for the four years from 1974–1978 jumped to 100:112 in 1979 and reached a peak of 100:120 in 1986 (Fujian sheng 1989, p. 127). Each sharp rise correlates directly to periods of increased emphasis on population control with the strict enforcement of the One Child Family Policy in 1985 causing a dramatic drop in the number of girls born or reported born in 1986. Further evidence for the linking of the One Child Family Policy to the skewed birth ratios is clear from the fact that both Tibet and Xinjiang, despite being poor and rural, have ratios within the normal range. In neither of these areas has the One Child Family Policy been implemented for the majority of the population (who are ethnic minority peoples rather than majority Han). The ACWF has taken seriously its responsibility to prevent the murder or under-reporting of baby girls. Some success is evident with the Fujian rate for 1997 dropping back to 100:115. Nonetheless, this is still well above the

Fujian average of 100:108 common prior to the implementation of this policy.

The extent of son-preference is amplified by the sex ratios for second and third children. Some families are prepared to ignore both official coercion and encouragement to have one child only and in these families the sex ratios show dramatic son-preference in the second and third births. In 1993 the sex ratio at birth for second births is 100:130 and for third births it is 100:126. A snap-shot of selected non-metropolitan regions (where the policy is more likely to be ignored) demonstrates an even greater disparity. In Henan the sex ratio for the second child is 100:149; in Fujian it is 100:175. Sex ratios for the third child demonstrate that families in metropolitan areas, where the social, economic and housing pressures to have only one child are greatest, go to great lengths to ensure that their third child is a boy. Beijing figures show a ratio of 100:600 in favour of boys for third births (Lu Chunheng et al. 1994, p. 61). Such a figure could only be possible with the assistance of ultrasound sex-determination technologies. Abortions on the basis of sex have been illegal in China since the mid 1990s but for those very few citizens prepared to risk the social and economic penalties for having a third child such legal technicalities are irrelevant.

One consequence of the decline in the number of girls relative to boys will be the increasing scarcity of marriageable women. The children born after the One Child Family Policy was implemented in the early 1980s are only now reaching marriageable ages. The reports of abductions and forced marriage of women are increasing. 'According to statistics for 1991 and 1992, Chinese public security departments solved [more] than 50 000 cases of abduction of women and children' (Min 1995, p. 535). The number of unsolved cases would probably exceed this amount. Most gangs that traffic in women target the transport hubs of towns and cities to trap the unsuspecting rural girls who have left home in search of work. Once abducted they are sold to men as 'brides'. The abducted women are kept as prisoners in their new 'homes' with the complicity of the parents, relatives and neighbours of the 'husband'. Once the bride has a child she is generally resigned to her fate but the period prior to this can be peppered with desperate escape attempts. The market economy has made the traditional bride-price, paid by the prospective husband to the bride's parents, beyond the reach of the poorer peasants. The problem will worsen as the number of men born since the implementation of the One Child Family Policy entering marriageable age increases relative to women. The ACWF has been instrumental in educating rural women about the new dangers of abduction and forced-marriage.

Educating the modern Chinese woman

In the 1950s and 1960s the CCP embarked upon major campaigns to eradicate illiteracy as part of its commitment to emancipating the masses from oppression and ignorance. Women were a major focus of these early campaigns. Min Jiayin describes the transformation:

> In Old China nine out of every ten women were illiterate. Three nation-wide illiteracy drives were launched within a few years beginning in 1952 and as many as 1.6 million illiterate women learned to read and write. The illiteracy rate among Chinese women today has dropped to 32 per cent. The education of women has received particular attention and made rapid growth. School attendance of school age girls has reached 96.2 per cent and women students accounted for 43.1 per cent and 33.7 per cent of the student body at secondary schools and colleges respectively in 1992 (1995, p. 532).

By any measure this is a dramatic improvement—nevertheless, the problems of female illiteracy remain endemic (Billard 1999). There is evidence that girls face greater difficulties gaining access to schooling than boys. Over 71 per cent of China's 164 million illiterates are women (SSB 1997, p. 77) and 80 per cent of the nearly 3 million unschooled primary-age children are girls (Rai 1993, p. 3). In 1997 25.54 per cent of the female population over the age of fifteen was designated as illiterate or semi-literate. Vast differences exist between urban areas and the distant poor rural areas—only 11 per cent of Beijing women but 69 per cent of Tibetan women and 45 per cent of Guizhou women fall into this category. Nonetheless, even *within* regions women fare considerably worse than men. Only 3 per cent of men in Beijing are illiterate or semi-literate, while 52 per cent of Tibetan men and 16 per cent of Guizhou men are in this category (SSB 1997, p. 77).

In the last three decades the education system has undergone a major overhaul. Schools were closed at the peak of the Cultural Revolution as urban youngsters were instructed to go to the countryside to learn from the peasants rather than fall under the influence of the then reviled intellectual class of which their teachers were a major component. When schools and universities reopened in the 1970s, the heavy political content in the curriculum was reduced. By 1977 a national university entrance examination was implemented, fees were introduced, universities were encouraged to gain support from the emerging private sector and by 1985 university students were allowed to apply for jobs rather than be allocated employment by the state.

Shirin M. Rai notes,

> As the eighties rolled on, the impact of these reforms on education, employment and the social position of women in China began to cause concern...First, the increasing drop-out rates among school girls, especially in rural areas. Second, the difficulty faced by women college graduates in finding employment under the partially opened job market (Rai 1993, pp. 2–3).

As is clear from the experience of women politicians discussed above, once market forces take the lead women are unable to compete successfully with men for scarce resources. In 1988, women comprised 80 per cent of the People's University graduates who were rejected by employers still in the state allocation employment system (Rai 1993, p. 10). Unemployment rates are higher among people with only primary education and women are more likely to be in this category than men (Women Workers' Dept 1998, p. 104). Prejudice against women has re-emerged within the gender blindness of the economic policies aimed to produce the modernisation of China.

The percentages of women and girls enrolled as students show a slight increase in the past three decades. In 1973 women made up 30.8 per cent of the students enrolled in higher education, in 1989 they comprised 33.7 per cent. In 1997 they comprised 36.4 per cent of tertiary students. The figures for secondary and primary schools show a marginally greater increase. In 1973 girls comprised 33 per cent of secondary students whereas in 1989 they comprised 41.4 per cent. By 1997 the upward trend had slowed with girls comprising 42.1 per cent of secondary students (SSB 1997, p. 79). At the crucial level of primary schooling girls comprised 40.7 per cent in 1973, 45.9 per cent in 1989 (Rai 1993, p. 3) and close to 50 per cent in 1997 (SSB 1997, p.79).

There is an important distinction to be made between China's urban residents and the majority who live in rural areas. Discrimination against schooling daughters is lower in the cities and with the success of the One Child Family Policy amongst this section of the population, schooling for girls has actually improved. If you only have one child you make sure 's/he' gets the best education possible. In the countryside, economic liberalisation and reduced family sizes has concentrated the labour performed by children on a few—increasingly these are daughters. Girls now work in handicraft industries, till the family's private plot, tend the family's private herd or carry out the household chores while their mothers work in local factories. Compounding this problem is the considerable rise in school fees and incidental costs of schooling during the period of reform. As rural families made hard choices about household expenditure, girls' education was easy to cut. The generation of private wealth is no longer a politically dangerous act, as it had been from the mid-1960s until about 1980, so the financial incentives to keep girls back from school are compelling. In the bustling and wealthy metropolis of Shanghai 51 per cent of primary school children are girls whereas in poor provinces like Yunnan and Qinghai only 45.2 per cent and 40 per cent respectively are girls (SSB 1997, pp. 78–79).

Intellectualising feminism and academic work

Those women privileged with access to higher education have participated in a dramatic shift in academic work during the years 1970–2000. From 1949 until 1978 almost all academic work was assessed for its political leanings. Unless the research followed Marxist principles and could demonstrate its commitment to the working masses and the CCP, it would rarely be conducted. From the late 1970s the political restraint on academic research lifted and women's history was among the new areas opened. The ACWF led the movement, sponsoring a large research project on the history of the women's movement from 1919 to 1949. Gilmartin described this project as 'a breakthrough' (1984, p. 57). The CCP had maintained tight control over the historical narrative—there had been no women's movement worth speaking of prior to the CCP and it was the CCP who showed the women of China the path to liberation (Wang Zheng 1999). By encouraging the excavation of a history of a women's movement prior to the existence of the CCP, and independent of the CCP, the ACWF opened this narrative to question. The result of the ACWF initiative was a string of publications and the establishment, in 1983, of the Institute of Women's Studies. From this point women's studies departments or groups emerged in tertiary institutions around the country (Wang Zheng 1997). The first non-governmental women's studies unit was established by Li Xiaojiang in Zhengzhou University, Henan Province. It remains a foremost centre of activity for women's studies in China.

For the most part, the women's studies that developed has not adopted an antagonistic role in relation to the state (see Li Xiaojiang 1997, Li Xiaojiang et al. 1997 and Sha Jicai 1995). As Li Xiaojiang and Zhang Xiaodan wrote,

> Unlike the development of women's studies in the West, the rise of women's studies in China was not the result of a distinct feminist movement; on the contrary, women's studies grew out of an attempt by a few liberal women leaders in governmental women's

organisations as well as some intellectuals, both male and female, to reobserve, rethink, and redefine the liberation of Chinese women. In other words, rather than theoretically claiming or appealing for equality between men and women, the discipline of women's studies in contemporary China was initially designed to mediate upon the equality that Chinese women had supposedly achieved according to law established by the socialist revolution in 1949 (1994, p. 140).

After an initial period of tension there has been increasing co-operation between women in the academies and the researchers in the ACWF. The academics are attempting to stretch the theoretical boundaries beyond the strictures of Marxist methodology and CCP hagiography favoured by the ACWF (see Li Xiaojiang 1994). Literature, sociology and history are the three most active fields with the social-sciences experiencing a boom in the liberal 1990s.

The emergence of women's studies will eventually undermine the totalising CCP narrative that the women of China were liberated by the CCP. Currently, however prominent women's studies academics continue to assert that 'Chinese women's equality was guaranteed for the first time by the Constitution of 1950' after the 'Communist Party's rise to power' (Li and Zhang 1994, p. 138). In fact, Chinese women struggled for and won the right to equality and suffrage through the first three decades of the century and were awarded equal rights with men in the 1936 draft constitution promulgated in 1946 (Edwards 1999). So far, women's studies academics have not challenged the narrative that posits the CCP as the patriarchal saviour of women. Moreover, there is evidence that even the independent women's studies units remain heavily influenced by the 'unofficial-official line' that relegates women to the auxiliary workforce. As China's unemployment problems increase, women's studies scholars are examining the importance for women to stay at home and occupy themselves with domestic duties. Some argue that the link between work and independence is oversimplified and simply locks women into the double-burden of paid-work and housework (see discussion in Li and Zhang 1994, p. 147). ACWF officials actively opposed this line maintaining that economic independence was fundamental to women's liberation.

One unique aspect of women's studies in China is the rejection of 'equality-based' feminism exemplified by the Western feminist movement. The Cultural Revolution promoted slogans like 'Whatever men can do, women can do'. To scholars like Li Xiaojiang equality-feminism merely concealed the fact that men were yardsticks for female difference. Feminism in 1990s China asserts and celebrates feminine difference. During the early 1970s women were dressed in shapeless, drab Mao-suits and wore no cosmetics—any deviation from communist androgyny was politically dangerous and morally reprehensible. The assertion of the right to be feminine has become central to women's studies in the PRC. The celebration of supposedly specific female attributes by women's studies activists is a rejection of the Maoist-state's promotion of a masculine ideal for women. This move is not, however, contrary to the current leadership's notions of the roles of the sexes since women, constructed as naturally and essentially concerned with beauty, make superb consumers. The opposition to communist androgyny is a reaction against a historical hegemony that many university-age women have seen only in newsreels or photos in their mothers' albums.

Moreover, most women's studies scholars, women authors and ACWF officials would object to being labelled 'feminist' (Edwards 1998). From the ACWF perspective, feminism is a bourgeois ideology that has the potential to distract from the central force driving historical change—class struggle. This classic Marxist line always subordinates gender to class. The independent women's studies scholars reject the label 'feminist' arguing it is loaded with Western ideological baggage and therefore is inappropriate for the exploration of the experiences of Chinese women. Others distance themselves from the term simply because it has negative social and political connotations.

Conclusion

During the past thirty years the totalising narrative of the CCP's liberation of Chinese women has gradually been dismantled. At the start of the twenty-first century, women in China are more likely to see their diverse views, aspirations and needs expressed in public discourse than at any point since 1949. This expression of plural female modernities in China does not necessarily equate to an improvement in women's status in the country. Indeed, the increasing diversity in economic and political power characteristic of the period has clearly widened the gap between men and women's opportunities and expectations across a number of spheres. One of the voices that has, as yet, remained muted in this period of tentative and controlled liberalisation, is that of an independent feminist movement. The overarching nationalistic development rhetoric of the government still holds such gender specific campaigning as treasonous, bourgeois selfishness. However, such a speaking position, may soon be possible as the CCP's grand narrative crumbles further and

82WOMEN IN ASIA

the gap between the opportunities presented to men and women increases.

References and recommended readings

All China Women's Federation (ACWF) eds 1991 *Zhongguo funü tongji ziliao 1949-1989* (Statistics on Chinese Women), Zhongguo tongji chubanshe, Beijing.
Andors, P. 1983 *The Unfinished Liberation of Chinese Women 1949–1980*, Indiana University Press, Bloomington.
Billard, E. 1999 'The female face of illiteracy in China,' *China Information*, vol. xiii, no. 4 (Spring), pp. 27–65.
Croll, E. 1978 *Feminism and Socialism in China*, Routledge and Kegan Paul, London.
—— 1995 *Changing Identities of Chinese Women: Rhetoric, Experience and Self-Perception in Twentieth Century China*, Zed, London.
Croll, E., Davin, D. and Kane, P. eds 1985 *China's One Child Family Policy*, Macmillan, London.
Edwards, L. 1998 'Consolidating a socialist patriarchy: the women writers' industry and "feminist" literary criticism,' *Dress, sex and text in Chinese Culture*, eds Antonia Finanne and Anne McLaren, Monash Asia Institute, Clayton.
—— 1999 'From gender equality to gender difference: feminist campaigns for quotas for women in politics 1936–1947,' *Twentieth Century China*, vol. xxiv, no. 2 (April), pp. 69–105.
Evans, H. 1997 *Women and Sexuality in China*, Continuum, New York.
FEER 1990 *Asia Yearbook 1990*, Far Eastern Economic Review, Hong Kong.
—— 1999 *Asia Yearbook 1999*, Far Eastern Economic Review, Hong Kong.
—— 1999a 'Economic indicators,' *Far Eastern Economic Review* (February 4), p. 56.
Fujian sheng tongjiju 1989 *Fujian sheng renkou tongji ziliao huibian* (Materials on the population statistics of Fujian province), Fujian tongji chubanshe, Fuzhou.
Gilmartin, C. 1984 'Recent developments in research about women in the PRC,' *Republican China*, vol. 10. no. 1 B (November), pp. 57–66.
Hershatter, G., Honig, E., Mann, S. and Rofel, L. eds 1998 *A Selected Guide to Women's Studies in China*, Center for Chinese Studies, Berkeley.
Honig, E. and Hershatter, G. 1988 *Personal Voices*, Stanford University Press, Stanford.
Howell, J. 1996 'The struggle for survival: prospects for the women's federation in post-Mao China,' *World Development*, vol. 24, no. 1, pp. 129–43.
Hooper, B. 1998 ' "Flower vase and housewife": women and consumerism in post-Mao China,' *Gender and Power in Affluent Asia*, eds Krishna Sen and Maila Stivens, Routledge, London.
Information Office of the State Council of the People's Republic of China 1994 'The situation of Chinese women,' *Beijing Review* (6-12 June), pp. 9–23.
Jacka, T. 1997 *Women's Work in Rural China*, Cambridge University Press, Cambridge.

Johnson, K. A. 1983 *Women, the Family and Peasant Revolution in China*, Chicago University Press, Chicago.

Judd, E. 1994 *Gender and Power in Rural North China*, Stanford University Press, Stanford.

Kane, P. 1987 *The Second Billion: Population and Family Planning in China*, Penguin, Harmondsworth.

Keith, R. C. 1997 'Legislating women's and children's "rights and interests" in the PRC,' *The China Quarterly*, no. 149 (March), pp. 29–55.

Kelkar Govind and Wang Yunxian 1997 'Farmers, women and economic reform in China,' *Bulletin of Concerned Asian Scholars*, vol. 29, no. 4 (October–December), pp. 69–77.

Kristeva, J. 1977 *About Chinese Women*, Urizen, New York.

Lawrence, Susan V. 1999 'Widening web,' *Far Eastern Economic Review*, 18 November, pp. 54–55.

Li Xiaojiang 1994 'Economic reform and the awakening of Chinese women's collective conscious,' trans. by S. Katherine Campbell, *Engendering China: Women, Culture and the State*, eds Christina K. Gilmartin et al., Harvard University Press, Cambridge, Mass..

—— 1997 *Guanyu nüren de dawen* (Questions and answers on women), Jiangsu remin chubanshe, Nanjing.

Li Xiaojiang and Zhang Xiaodan 1994 'Creating a space for women: women's studies in China in the 1980s,' *Signs*, vol. 20, no. 1, pp. 137–51.

Li Xiaojiang et al. 1997 *Pingdeng yu fazhen* (Equality and development), Sanlian shudian, Beijing.

Lu Chunheng et al. 1994 *Zhongguo renkou tongji nianjian* (Annual statistics on China's population), Zhongguo tongji chubanshe, Beijing.

Maurer-Fazio, M., Rawksi, T. and Zhang, W. 1999 'Inequality in rewards for holding up half the sky: gender wage gaps in China's urban labour market, 1988–1994,' *The China Journal*, Issue 41 (January), pp. 55–88.

McLaren, A. 1998 'Chinese cultural revivalism: changing gender constructions in the Yangtze river delta,' *Gender and Power in Affluent Asia*, eds Krishna Sen and Maila Stivens, Routledge, London.

Min Jiayin 1995 *The Chalice and the Blade in Chinese Culture: Gender Relations and Social Models*, China Social Sciences Publishing House, Beijing.

Molyneaux, M. 1990 'The "women question" in the age of perestroika,' *New Left Review*, no. 183 (September/October), pp. 23–49.

Neft, N. and Levine, A. 1997 *Where Women Stand: An International Report on the Status of Women in 140 Countries*, Random House, New York.

Ono Kazuko 1989 *Chinese Women in a Century of Revolution 1850–1950*, Stanford University Press, Stanford.

Rai, Shirin M. 1993 'Gender, education and employment in post-Mao China: issues in modernisation,' *China Reports*, vol. 29, no. 1, pp. 1–14.

Rosen, S. 1994 'Chinese women in the 1990s: images and roles in contention,' *China Review 1994*, eds Maurice Brosseau and Lo Chi Kin, Chinese University Press, Hong Kong.

—— 1995 'Women and political participation in China,' *Pacific Affairs*, vol. 68, no. 3 (Fall), pp. 315–41.

Sha Jicai ed. 1995 *Dangdai Zhongguo funü jiating diwei yanjiu* (Women's domestic status in contemporary China), Tianjin renmin chubanshe, Tianjin.

Stacey, J. 1983 *Patriarchy and Socialist Revolution in China*, University of California Press, Berkeley.

SSB—State Statistical Bureau 1997 *China Statistical Yearbook 1997*, Zhongguo tongji chubanshe, Beijing.

Stivens, M. 1998 'Theorising gender, power and modernity in affluent Asia,' *Gender and Power in Affluent Asia*, eds Krishna Sen and Maila Stivens, Routledge, London.

Wang Zheng 1997 'Maoism, feminism and the UN conference on women: women's studies research in contemporary China,' *Journal of Women's History*, vol. 8, no. 4, pp. 126–52.

—— 1999 *Women in the Chinese Enlightenment: Oral and Textual Histories*, University of California Press, Berkeley.

White, T. 1994 'The origins of China's birth planning policy,' *Engendering China: Women, Culture and the State*, eds Christina K. Gilmartin et al., Harvard University Press, Cambridge, Mass.

Wolf, M. 1985 *Revolution Postponed: Women in Contemporary China*, Stanford University Press, Stanford.

Women Workers Department of All-China Federation of Trade Unions 1998 'Guanyu xiagang nü zhigong zai jiu ye nandian wenti de diaocha baogao' (Survey on the difficulties and problems for laid-off women workers to be re-employed), *Shiji zhi jiao de Zhongguo funü yu fazhen* (Chinese women and development at the turn of the century), ed. Jin Yihong, Nanjing daxue chubanshe, Nanjing.

Woo, Margaret Y.K. 1994 'Chinese women workers: the delicate balance between protection and equality,' *Engendering China: Women, Culture and the State*, eds Christina K. Gilmartin et al., Harvard University Press, Cambridge, Mass.

Zhang Naihua 1996 'The All-China Women's Federation, Chinese women, and the women's movement: 1949–1993,' PhD diss., Michigan State University.

Zhang Shaoling 1998 *Funü yu renquan* (Women and human rights), Xinhu chubanshe, Beijing.

5 Diversity and the status of women: the Indian experience

Ruchira Ganguly-Scrase

School of Humanities and Social Sciences
Charles Sturt University

'The secondary status of woman is a pan-cultural fact'
…So argued Sherry Ortner in 1970 in her now famous essay, 'Is female to male as nature is to culture?' At the end of the twentieth century it is impossible to universalise the subordination of the world's women in such a fashion, let alone homogenise the mass of Indian women. Grappling with diversity and difference is central to understanding the position of women in India. Since the heydays of the women's liberation movement in the 1970s, when there was a sense of women's solidarity and sisterhood, feminist theorists have shifted their attention to the study of difference among women. Scholarly analysis used to focus on women's shared oppression and male domination, but more recent research has shown that male domination and female subordination is far from uniform. On the contrary, women's experiences are distinguished by their specific locations within particular ethnic, class and religious groupings.

Thus, no unitary categorisation of Indian women is possible. For example, in India over the past two decades the achievements of urban

middle-class women in salaried and professional jobs have been as
spectacular as the relentless exploitation and acute deprivation of female
agricultural labourers (Bardhan 1993). There are many powerful and
influential Indian women in the professions, business, bureaucracy and
government who enjoy the privileges and benefits of their class position.
Such women have also gained from the anti-colonial struggles of the
Indian nationalist movement, which gave them a voice in the political
arena. After independence from British colonial rule in 1947 these
women had relatively easy access to the expanding civil service as well
as representation in parliament. However, the vast majority of women in
India do not belong to this affluent middle class. Their lives are
constrained by problems typical of a post-colonial developing economy.

At a discursive level there are also contradictions. On the one hand
there are belief systems in India which relegate women to an inferior
position in society. On the other, competing views construct women as
powerful, life-giving and forceful. Similarly, Indian women face a huge
gulf between the constitutional guarantees of formal equality and the
every-day reality of inequalities generated by divisions of caste and
class. Despite the formulation of specific government policies designed
to improve the position of women over the past several decades, the
majority of women have seen little real progress. For example, in 1976
the Equal Remuneration Act was introduced, which prohibited gender
discrimination in recruitment and required employers to pay equal wages
for equal work. However, this legislation only covered those in
government employment. As most women do not work within this arena,
only a fraction of women workers have benefited from this act. This
chapter shows that the efforts of the women's movement to improve the
status of women over the past several decades have been undercut by
conflicting sources of community authority flourishing in the diversity
that is Indian society.

The general indices on the status of women, such as literacy, life
expectancy, male/female sex ratio, and labour force participation,
indicate the precarious position of Indian women at the end of the
twentieth century.

Male/female sex ratio

One of the startling aspects of gender relations in India is the
male/female sex ratio. Despite the biological advantage of the female
foetus and globally higher female life expectancy, the situation is
reversed in India. Infant mortality rates for girls are higher than boys.
The sex ratio has been declining steadily since 1901. The 1991 census

shows the number of females per males to be 92.9 to every 100 males. In most countries around the world, regardless of relative wealth and prosperity, the sex ratio is weighted in favour of women (e.g. Colombia 102 females:100 males; France 105:100; Thailand 102:100) (Neft and Levine 1997, pp. 482–84). Though there was a slight rise in the female numbers in India's sex ratio from 93 to 93.4 during the decade 1971–81, scholars attribute this to better data collection methods rather than an improvement in the status of women (Desai and Patel 1985, p. 17).[1]

Literacy

Between 1971 and 1991 female literacy leapt from 18.7 per cent to 32.6 per cent. Although this indicates an absolute increase in female literacy, there remain wide disparities between male and females rates and between rural and urban areas. Only 20 per cent of rural women are literate compared to 50 per cent of men. Among the urban population 45 per cent of females are illiterate compared to only 20 per cent of men. Primary school enrolment for boys is 99 per cent compared to only 66 per cent for girls. This is because girls from poorer backgrounds have the heavy burden of domestic chores and child-minding and face a general apathy towards the education of girls. It is assumed that boys require a better education since they will be future earners. In higher education there is a relatively favourable attitude towards education of girls, particularly in the cities among the upper and middle classes (Desai and Patel 1985, p. 28). However, university educated women only constitute 3 per cent of the female population.

Labour force participation

Officially, the labour force participation of women is low. In 1971 only 12.06 per cent of the labour force was female compared to 22.3 in 1991. Moreover, only 6 per cent of the female workforce is employed in the relatively well paid, secure, 'formal' organised sector jobs while 94 per cent are found working in the casual and informal sector of the labour market. Here they face adverse conditions of low pay, lack of protection from unscrupulous employers and job uncertainty. The low rate of participation partly reflects the narrow official definition of 'economic activity'. Large areas of women's work are excluded from official statistics. For example, women in rural households collect edible roots, greens and fruits. In urban areas women prepare fuel from dung cakes and collect half-burnt coals; among artisan communities, they actively participate in the production within the family. Yet, these activities are excluded from official statistics (Bannerjee 1985). Another reason for the low participation rate is the real lack of employment opportunities for women—especially in areas where women are displaced in large numbers from their traditional occupations as a result of mechanisation and commercialisation. As will be discussed below, there is also a strong cultural expectation that women will not be employed outside the home on marriage. Cultural practices and expectations relating to status and hierarchy remain strong influences on women's status in India.

Cultural constructions of gender and sexuality

Dominant brahmanical versus subaltern folk traditions

One of the major distinguishing aspects of the Indian traditions is the tension between the dominant brahmanical traditions drawn from élite Hinduism and the subaltern heritages drawn from daily life of the ordinary people. Variously described as the 'great' tradition versus the 'little' tradition (cf Marriot 1955) or the orthodox versus the popular, the brahmanical is derived from textual and scriptural sources, while the subaltern is based on fluid localised oral traditions at the village level. These oppositions provide an important conceptual framework that underpins female power and feminine principles in India's cultural traditions. Although the notion of *Shakti* (female power embodied in a mother goddess) is present in both traditions, the brahmanical cosmology embodies the passive aspects of femininity while the latter often reflects the assertive (Babb 1970).

These traditions are expressed with enormous regional variations. Northern India is characterised by patrilineal kinship systems and patriarchal values which rigidly circumscribe the lives of women. The existence of the Dravidian kinship system in southern India and the influences of the matrilineal traditions in northeastern India afford a more positive view of females. These competing cultural constructions are reflected in the demographic outcomes of women's lives (Miller 1981; Dreze et. al 1996; Dreze and Sen 1995). For example, in the southern state of Kerala female life expectancy is 72 years and the female to male sex-ratio is 104 women per hundred men compared to the northern Indian state of Utter Pradesh, where it is 87.9 females per hundred—one of the lowest in the world. Generally speaking, women in the south live longer, are more valued and are regarded as more critical to their natal kin than are women in north India (Wadley 1980, p. 161).

Caste is an important principle of social organisation in Indian society, which significantly shapes gender relations. It is a system of hereditary social ranking associated with Hinduism, which governs social relations and the distribution of power in Indian society. It is both a cultural and economic system of stratification. Divided into hierarchically ordered castes, *Brahmins* (priests) occupy the highest rank, followed by *Khshatriyas* (warriors/noblemen) *Vaishyas* (traders/merchants) and *Sudras* (artisans/labourers). There are numerous sub-castes and outside the caste system are 'untouchables', the lowest strata of society. In India today, as part of a process of self-affirmation and political mobilisation, the formerly untouchable and other subordinate castes have come to refer to themselves as '*dalits*' or 'the oppressed'—a term that I use later in the chapter. Classifying society into different groups is not unique to India, but what is characteristic of the Hindu social order is the notion of ritual purity and impurity, which is sanctioned by religious principles. Caste remains a pan-Indian phenomenon (Dumont 1972, p. 257) despite its religious association with Hinduism. In other words, although ritual purity does not have the same religious connotation in other non-Hindu communities in the Indian subcontinent, caste distinctions based on descent and birth are also found among Muslims (Ahmad 1973) and other minority groups. Consequently, low-caste Christians are likely to experience the same level of cultural humiliation as non-Christian untouchables as well as suffer economic hardships.

In contemporary India caste intersects with class inequalities and low caste is frequently synonymous with low socio-economic status and poverty. The relationship between caste and the position of women is particularly evident in the beliefs surrounding female sexuality. Female sexuality is seen to pose a danger to caste purity due to the perceived threat of lower caste men gaining sexual access to upper caste women (Liddle and Joshi 1986, p. 60). Therefore, within higher castes, religious ideologies prescribe a greater control over women to ensure caste purity. Historically *brahmin* women have been subjected to greater control over their mobility than have lower caste women. Rules of marriage and inheritance have circumscribed the freedom of upper caste women. We will consider the instances of dowry and *sati* later in this chapter. In modern India, the phenomenon known as 'sanskritisation' (Srinivas 1966), whereby lower castes emulate the practices of upper castes to gain higher status, have meant that men within such communities have invariably imposed greater restrictions over women's mobility.

Traditionally *Brahmin* men have exerted control over lower caste women's sexuality as a means to demean and humiliate lower caste men. Today many of these upper caste practices continue to have serious consequences for women. As I noted at the beginning of the chapter, among urban upper middle-class, high caste families, the position of women is quite high due to the legacy of the nationalist movement. The women's movement in 1970s was able to draw upon the positive gains of the anti-colonial struggles. However, more recently feminists have focused on the centrality of gender in reproducing caste inequalities. This is particularly significant when we look at the caste/class nexus and violence against women. As Rege argues

> Violence against women reveal definite variations by caste; while upper castes are subjected to control and violence within the family, it is the absence of such controls that makes lower caste women vulnerable to rape, sexual harassment and the threat of public violence (1995, p. 19).

Activities of the women's movement

Despite the relatively dismal statistics on women's status in India and the strictures posed by the caste/class system, it would be inaccurate to characterise women in India as passive victims of their circumstances. On the contrary, the Indian women's movement has provided a powerful challenge to continued subordination of women. Legal reforms as well as struggles to maintain a livelihood and guarantee safety from violence have all been part of the Indian women's movement. Clearly, legal improvements in women's status do not necessarily equate to real qualitative improvements in the lives of individuals, especially when broader economic and social contexts remain unaltered. Nevertheless, it is important to recognise that the emergence of the women's movement in India enabled hundreds of thousands of women to participate in activities significantly empowering them both individually and collectively to enforce changes. For a village woman in a highly stratified community, unaccustomed to interacting with males outside the confines of family and kin, a bus-ride to town without a chaperone and attendance at a rally may be phenomenal achievements.

The activities of the women's movement highlight a number of seemingly contradictory and complex factors governing women's lives. The deep class and caste divisions in Indian society have inhibited the emergence of a unified feminist movement. Nonetheless, the campaigns to address specific women's problems have occasionally brought middle-class and poor women together. For the most part, working-class and peasant women confront exploitation through their own specific organisations, but middle-class women with feminist ideals have become involved in these struggles performing roles as lawyers and lobbyists for the working-class and peasant groups. By examining a selection of the campaigns waged by the Indian women's movement I will explore the critical issues concerning the changing nature of women's position in the last two decades.

The experience of colonialism had an important influence on women's activism. During the 19th century women supported the fight against colonial rule and in turn were supported by nationalists in their quest for formal equality as citizens. Yet the nationalist discourse ignored the realm of women's rights within the family. It was within the domain of the home that the colonised subject could remain sovereign (Chatterjee, 1995). During this period women's innate qualities were utilised as mothers of the nation. After independence, women were guaranteed constitutional equality. However, by the 1970s such legal claims ceased to have any meaning and feminists began to challenge the patriarchal nature of Indian society. Focussing on legal reform feminists utilised state mechanisms to bring about changes, but they were well aware that the state itself was a patriarchal institution.

An important departure for the women's movement was the emergence of 'autonomous' women's groups in the 1970s. Previously women's organisations were affiliated to political parties such as the women's wing of the Communist Party of India. Many of the new women's groups were left oriented but they remained independent by eschewing political party affiliation. There was also a proliferation of scholarly work on women's status, the establishment of research organisations on women's studies such as the Centre for Women's Development Studies in New Delhi and the Research Centre for Women's Studies, SNDT Women's University in Bombay. In 1975 the appearance of a number of publications gave a boost to the women's movement and highlighted the stark inequalities experienced by women. These included *Towards Equality*, the report of the National Committee on the Status of Women, and several journals in various Indian languages and especially the bilingual (Hindi and English) magazine *Manushi: A Journal of Women and Society*.

In the 1970s the world-wide recession and the expansion of capitalist relations of production had a serious impact on Indian society. It is not surprising that many of the issues taken up by women during this period related to working-class, peasant and tribal women (Omvedt 1980). These included the right to better working conditions, campaigns against inflationary prices, land rights and so on. Emphasis was placed on issues of basic survival and the articulation of economic transformation with pre-existing patriarchal ideologies and their mutually reinforcing influences, which continued or heightened gender inequalities. Let us now turn to an exploration of some of these struggles.

Chipko movement

The vast majority of Indian women live in rural areas. Landlessness is a major problem for the rural poor. The ways in which women have been particularly affected is their diminishing opportunities for subsistence activities and loss of control over land (Agarwal 1994). Felling of forests and clearing land for large development projects such as dams, and large scale capitalist farming posed greater threats to survival needs of the rural poor. During the period 1961–71, many poor peasants were dispossessed of their agricultural land and became dependent on wage work for survival. However, during this period, male agricultural work increased by more than double the rate of female wage work. Women were further marginalised into casual and unskilled labour (Sharma 1985). Traditional access to forest produce particularly among communities that relied on gathering became increasingly scarce. For women there was also the growing burden of travelling far to collect water and fuel for cooking. For many their working day extended to 14–15 hours per day.

Against this background the Chipko or tree hugging movement became emblematic of women's struggle for basic survival needs and a safe environment. In the early 1970s in the foothills of the Himalayas spontaneous protests erupted against plans to fell trees by timber contractors. The form of protest was to protect trees by embracing them in order to prevent logging. By 1975 women in surrounding villages had formed *Mahila Mangal Dals* (women's welfare organisations) to extend their struggle to general issues on protecting fields and forests (Sharma et al. 1985). One of their actions included targeting the male dominated *panchayat* (village council). Women were critical of men within their communities who usually moved their grazing cattle through the fields, where women grew their crops. Women's protest resulted in the head of the council filing a case against them. However, the district magistrate dismissed the case when faced with combined protest from the women (Kumar 1993, p. 184). Interestingly, Chipko was not regarded as part of the women's movement in the 1970s but gained importance in the 1980s as a manifestation of eco-feminist principles (Mies and Shiva 1993) and as a symbol of 'woman centred' feminism.

Self-Employed Women's Association (SEWA)

In 1972 in the western Indian state of Gujerat, women employed in the 'informal' sector of the labour force (street vendors or home-workers engaged in piecework) united to form the Self-Employed Women's Association (SEWA). It was effectively a trade union of self-employed women. This form of organising among women was unique since the vast majority of women in India do not work in large factories or enterprises where they can be protected by labour regulations, government legislation or become unionised. The organisation evolved from India's oldest union the Textile Labour Association (TLA), and was also inspired by Mahatma Gandhi's campaign against the mill owners (Bhatt 1998). Initially the Department of Labour refused to register the union on the grounds that there was no recognised employer. Finally SEWA was granted recognition as the activists argued that its members had the right to 'freedom from exploitation, assurance of regular wages and access to opportunities for advancement' (quoted in Kumar 1993, p. 102).

According to SEWA's secretary Renana Jhabvala (1994, p. 115), 'the United Nations decade for women gave a boost to the growth of SEWA, placing it within the women's movement'. She further adds that SEWA's adoption of a unique structure combining the strategies of a trade union and co-operatives enabled it to struggle against the everyday oppression of women (Jhabvala 1994, p. 118). SEWA now claims that it is turning from an organisation into a movement, with a membership of 46 000 across five states. The organisation played an important role in securing credit for low-income women. A further significant outcome for the movement came when its general secretary became a member of the National Planning Commission giving SEWA influence at the national policy level. Moreover, SEWA was instrumental in the formation of the National Commission on Self-Employed Women.

Anti-dowry campaign

In the 1980s the campaigns against dowry and dowry harassment became major foci of feminist protest across India. The protests fundamentally challenged the nature of patriarchy within the private domain of family and kinship. More significantly, they echoed an important feminist critique about the effectiveness of legal reform concerning women's property rights. Women's property in India is intimately linked with the custom of dowry. The changes in dowry practices and the pressure of ever increasing demands on the amount paid by the bride's parents to the bride's parents-in-law raise a number of questions about the status of women in India. Upon marriage daughters are given gifts of household goods such as furniture, crockery, electrical appliances (in recent years refrigerators, televisions etc.) as well as personal items of clothing, jewellery and cash. Additionally gifts are made to the groom and his family. However, dowry is more than a simple economic transaction; it is deeply embedded in the cultural practices of patrilineal kinship systems, the cultural valuation of a 'woman's worth' as well as brahmanical religious principles.

Within the dominant brahmanical culture the giving away of a bride is a ceremonial 'gifting' of a virgin daughter. In the transfer of this gift the 'wife-givers' accrue merit. Further, the ceremony surrounding the exchange expresses symbolically the responsibility of the bride's father to furnish the household of the newly married couple. Hence the dowry frequently consists of an elaborate array of household goods as well as cash. The assumption here, of course, is that a wife is not expected to be gainfully employed, and therefore she is an economic liability in her husband's household. As a result, she has to be compensated for in marriage. The gift of the daughter is considered to be the best form of marriage in brahmanical ideology because of the accumulation of merit and the gain of rank and prestige (Fruzetti 1982). The opposite is the practice of accepting a bride price that is categorised as a morally inferior form of marriage. In most agricultural land-holding upper caste groups the seclusion of women is closely associated with giving elaborate dowries. In contrast, the practice of bride price generally occurs within communities where women actively participate in agricultural production.

In 1956 the Hindu Succession Act enabled daughters to inherit land. In a predominantly agrarian society, where land is an important asset, it was hailed as radical legislation since it reversed the traditional practice where women were only eligible to inherit movable property. However, since the implementation of this reform, women have rarely exercised this right. They generally waive their claims in favour of their brothers or are intimidated into relinquishing their rights (Agarwal 1988). While this applied largely to upper caste land-owning families, a new phenomenon was now emerging in communities which previously had no custom of dowry. They were turning away from customary bride price and were adopting the giving of 'dowry'. For some scholars this change signified 'sanskritisation' while others attributed the rise in demand for dowry partly to the monetisation and commercialisation of the economy (Srinivas 1984; Ram 1991, pp. 185–99; Randeria and Visaria 1984).

Dowry, far from being a marker of a 'backward' traditional mentality, has emerged as a very modern phenomenon, with educated men demanding more in accordance with their professional status (Caplan 1984). A number of women's groups brought to public attention increasing cases of women who were being abused emotionally or physically for the amount of dowry they brought into marriage. In a growing number of cases women were murdered. In the late 1970s a number of feminist organisations in Delhi carried out a sustained campaign of demonstrations, street theatre and exhibitions to highlight the dowry-related crimes which were previously ignored by the media and the general public. Dowry deaths that had been hidden in police reports as suicides were now exposed as murders. In May 1979 a young woman, Tarvinder Kaur, was killed because of her parents' inability to fulfil the demands of her in-laws. It seems that like many women throughout India she was under constant pressure to procure more money from her parents to finance her husband's business (Das 1984). The protests that followed her death drew wide media coverage. 'Within weeks, feminists reversed the indifference of decades, linking death-by fire with dowry harassment, showing that many official suicides were in fact murders (Kumar 1993, p. 119).'

The campaigns against dowry harassment have continued in the form of protests, often involving demonstrations in the husband's neighbourhood or workplace. In response to these actions the state has been prompted to adopt legal measures. These include, compulsory investigation and post-mortems of married women who have died within seven years of marriage; changes to criminal laws which encourage prosecution of dowry murders; and the establishment of anti-dowry harassment cells within the police force where women report dowry harassment. Amendments to the Indian penal code made cruelty to a woman by her husband or any relatives a crime punishable by imprisonment. In a significant departure from earlier laws, the definition of cruelty was extended to include mental cruelty (Calman 1992, pp. 132–33). Whether these actions have resulted in any marked improvement in the status of women remains open to question. Paradoxically, demands by the women's movement to protect women against violence may have the unintended effect of relegating women to the familial sphere (Mukhopadhyay 1998). Nevertheless, one of the major gains of the period is the public way violence against women was linked to the cultural dimensions of gender relations in India.

Anti-rape campaigns

The print media in India has sympathetically reported the issues of violence against women. In the late 1970s the acquittal of two policemen accused of raping a young woman at a police station provoked national outrage. The anger galvanised a major campaign for the women's movement and subsequently laid the foundation for the emergence of a number of feminist organisations. These include the Bombay based Forum Against Rape (which later changed its name to Forum Against Oppression of Women, to indicate its wider objective), *Stri Sangarsh* in Delhi, and the *Stri Mukti Andolan Sampark Samiti*.

The 'Mathura rape case', as it came to be known, sharpened the focus of public discussion about the endemic violation of women's rights in India.

> Mathura a sixteen year old tribal girl, who had lost both her parents in childhood and who worked as a maid servant, was raped by two policemen within a police compound in Desai Ganj, a small village in Chadrapur District of Maharashtra. She was brought to the police station around 9 pm on 26 March 1972, on a complaint filed by her own brother that she had eloped with her lover. When she along with her relatives, were about to leave the police station around 10.30 pm, she was detained by two constables, Tukaram and Ganpat. She was taken to the rear side and was raped by Ganpat, while Tukaram looked on. He too would have raped her, but was too drunk to do so. So he had to content himself by merely molesting her (Agnes 1993, p. 104).

In 1974, the Sessions Court found the two constables 'not guilty' on the grounds that Mathura must have consented since she was an unmarried girl 'habituated to sexual intercourse'. It was also noted that she did not display any visible signs of physical injury. On appeal, the High Court reversed this decision and concluded that passive submission under threat did not imply consent. The accused men, who had been dismissed from the police force, appealed to the Supreme Court, which in turn reversed the High Court's ruling. In 1978 the Supreme Court justices found, 'no reason to doubt that a *nice* girl—impoverished, powerless and frightened though she might be—would have resisted the orders of two armed police officers' [original emphasis] (Calman 1992, p. 66).

The Supreme Court's judgement was widely condemned. In particular four eminent law professors (two of who were women) wrote an open letter to the Chief Justice of India. The letter was also circulated widely, revealing the antiquated rape laws, the biased and conservative views of the judiciary and above all the utter failure of the legal system to extend human rights to the protection of women, especially the poor, illiterate and the powerless. Following the circulation of the letter, agitation around rape issues gained momentum, involving not only feminist organisations, but also civil liberties groups, lawyers and political parties. It generated massive public debate and exposed the systematic sexual assault of women by those in positions of authority such as the police, the armed forces, prison wardens, hospital management and so on. The significance of mass rape in Indian society as a retaliation and assertion of power against groups who are in the process of challenging their subordinate status and the rape of individual women in marginalised communities became the focal points of these debates.

As a result of the mounting pressure the government established the 84th Law Commission and submissions were heard from women's groups throughout India. Consequently, in 1983 the Criminal Law (Amendment) Bill focused almost exclusively on custodial rape. The burden of proof rested on the accused only in cases of custodial rape and there was to be a minimum sentence of 10 years. Although the Law Commission's recommendations included the major demands of the women's organisations—such as the onus of proof being placed on the accused; the women's right to privacy regarding her past sexual history; immediate medical examination of both the accused and victim—in practice these were ignored. Several women's organisations had argued that custodial rape should not only apply to state officials but should also be extended to include employers, money-lenders, contractors and land lords who routinely terrorise economically vulnerable women into submission either by the threat or actual committal of rape. In other words, a specific category—'economic rape' or 'power rape'—should be included. The emphasis on custodial rape also left unchallenged familial rape, particularly rape within marriage.

Women's groups had demanded that there be *in camera* trials. Instead the government imposed a ban on press reporting of rape cases on the pretext of protecting the identity of the victim. This was an ironic outcome since it was largely due to the positive role of the media that the campaigns became widely known. The legal changes were a minor victory for women's rights. The most important aspect of the agitation, once again, was the increasing public awareness of violence against women and the breaking of the taboo surrounding rape (Agnes 1993). Social attitudes towards rape have remained ambiguous; violation of honour and the stigma attached to the victim have not disappeared. Yet it seems more women now have the courage to report it (Agnes 1990, cited in Kumar 1993).

Communalisation of gender identity

As we have seen through the 1970s and 1980s, violence against women was a rallying point for the women's movement. During this period there was broad ideological unity about the key issues affecting women's status. However, this situation changed in the mid-1980s for two reasons —the emergence and growth of identity politics and the rise in fundamentalist and religious revivalist ideologies. A combination of social forces underpinned these developments including, rapid economic transformation; general feelings of the loss of identity; and reactions against the assertion of new confidence by those inspired by feminist and other egalitarian ideologies. Of particular concern was the confidence of the rising 'backward' castes—the hitherto marginalised groups who were gaining a political voice. On the whole, political actions of the 1980s were characterised by the struggle to control meaning and symbols rather than material resources.

Since independence the government of India has made some attempts to provide affirmative action for historically disadvantaged groups. There are quotas reserved for 'scheduled' castes and tribes in government employment and education. In the Indian Constitution disadvantaged groups are classified under a schedule for taking affirmative action in their favour. This is largely based on the census classification of communities developed during the colonial period. In 1990 the government implemented the recommendations of the Mandal Commission that the quotas should be extended to 'other backward castes' (OBCs). This resulted in a backlash from the dominant castes in many parts of India. If the recommendations are followed this would offer greater opportunities for women from *dalit* communities (oppressed castes).

The centrality of women in the construction of community identity gained significance during this decade. Previously within the movement issues about the woman's body representing the community had been widely debated in the analysis of rape as assertion of male power— particularly its use as a form of reprisal against women of 'other' communities. This practice entails notions of the violation of male honour, i.e. loss of control over 'their' women. Feminists during the 1970s and early 1980s had spoken out on issues of violence in terms of domestic violence, individual, familial and mass rape. By the end of the 1980s a different threat of violence came from fundamentalism, which, in this case, was largely Hindu.

The rise of fundamentalism is a global phenomenon. It is difficult to identify the exact reasons for its emergence at this particular juncture. It has been argued that resurgence in crises of cultural identity are more pronounced in areas of uneven capitalist development where the advantages of economic development have not benefited people equally. The resulting frustration over the inability to control resources has led some groups to seek self-affirmation through a return to 'traditional' community. Here, women's roles are used as markers of community (Mogadham 1994). We also find that during colonial periods, the status of women was used as a measure of civilisation. The identity of people centred on women (Chatterjee 1995). Currently, as post-colonial states are engaged in a similar process of constructing their identity in a rapidly changing world, women's roles are used to symbolise the cultural essence of communities or even the nation. Whatever the reasons, in the current Indian context it becomes increasingly evident that the state has adopted a communalist posture (Chhachhi 1989). When disenchantment grew with the failure of the Indian state to deliver the fruits of development, it cynically utilised the 'communal card' to win electoral support. The impact of communalism seriously jeopardised the questions of gender justice. The following two cases—the Shah Bano controversy and the death of Roop Kanwar—exemplify how demands of communalist forces were utilised to side-step the issue of gender justice.

In India there are no uniform civil laws with regards to the rights of women in matters of family, marriage, child custody and inheritance. This was part of the British legacy, and although it aimed to allow for the maintenance of customary laws of different communities, in practice it had the effect of rigidly codifying practices that were previously fluid and localised. However, uniform criminal laws were developed under colonial rule. After independence, the government was unwilling to confront the question of implementing a uniform civil code due to the devastating communal riots and disunity that followed partition.

The lawmakers, with their emphasis on a secular India—which guaranteed the freedom of all religious communities—were reluctant to interfere in matters of personal law. After all, it was envisaged that personal laws would enable the communities to maintain their distinct identity. By contrast, women's organisations had pressed for a uniform civil code since 1936. Their aim was to formulate common laws that would provide gender justice since the rights of women were secondary within *all* religious communities. Here we see the contradictory aspects of the Constitution relating to women's rights. On the one hand, it promises equality for women as individual citizens. On the other, women's individual rights conflict with their membership of collective communities.

The following discussion of the Shah Bano case highlights the complex relationship between gender and community identity. A 73-year-old Muslim woman, Shah Bano, petitioned the courts to obtain maintenance from her husband who had divorced her after forty-three years of marriage. She applied under the Criminal Procedure Code Section 125, which entitles destitute, deserted and divorced women to maintenance from their former husbands. The courts ruled in her favour, but her husband Mohammad Ahmed Khan, himself an advocate, appealed to the Supreme Court. He argued that laws relating to marriage and divorce were outside of the court's jurisdiction, adding that as a Muslim he had abided by Muslim Personal Law which required him to pay maintenance during the initial three months of separation—a period known as *iddat*. However, he was not obliged to pay maintenance from three months after the divorce. In order to arrive at a judgement the Supreme Court consulted the *Quran* since Shah Bano's counsel had cited verses from the *Quran* to lend support to the idea that the righteous had a duty to provide a reasonable maintenance (Kumar 1994, p. 227). The Supreme Court's ruling in 1985 can be described in the following terms:

> First it upheld Shah Bano's right to maintenance and both under Section 125 and under Muslim personal law. Second, it asserted that Section 125 'cut across the barriers of religion', that is, it transcended the personal laws of the religious communities which a given married pair might belong to. Third, it was critical of the way women 'have been traditionally subject to unjust treatment' and urged the government to frame a common civil code (Kumar 1994, p. 227).

Although, most of the liberal Muslim intelligentsia along with women's groups and democratic organisations supported the court's decision (whilst remaining critical of the judiciary's attempt to link religious matters to the civil code), this ruling enraged a section of the Muslim community. Fundamentalist Muslims mobilised populist support against the uniform civil code, arguing that such interference with Personal Laws meant an end to a distinct Muslim identity and began a campaign of 'Islam in Danger'. Feminists campaigning for a uniform civil code were joined by the most unlikely of supporters—Hindu communalists. However, Hindu chauvinists did not support the demand for a uniform civil code because they were interested in the rights of Muslim women. Rather they wanted Muslims to conform to the 'national mainstream'. Inflammatory remarks about 'barbaric Muslims' were made frequently and communal violence was incited across northern India.

Meanwhile a Muslim League MP drafted the Muslim Women's (Protection of Rights on Divorce) Bill that would exclude divorced Muslim women from section 125. The ruling Congress Party government opportunistically supported the bill, which stated that husbands were not obliged to maintain their wives three months after the divorce. It would be the responsibility of the woman's natal family to support her and those who could not afford to do so could appeal to their local *Waqf* board (private Islamic charitable organisations). Women's organisations, the progressive Muslim intelligentsia and major political parties opposed the Bill. The government had previously suffered an electoral backlash as Muslims turned away from the Congress Party, so, in a bid to capture the 'Muslim vote' the government appeased Muslim conservatives and finally passed the Muslim Women's Bill in February 1986. The Shah Bano was case was a blow to the demand for a uniform civil code.

In 1987 Roop Kanwar, an educated 18-year-old woman committed *sati* (widow self-immolation), on the funeral pyre of her husband in the northwestern province of Rajasthan. After it had been announced that Roop Kanwar would undergo *sati-daha* (the act of committing *sati*), the Rajasthan government, under pressure from several groups, prohibited the ceremony. However, thousands gathered at the ceremony in defiance of a court order. Later the location was accorded the status of a pilgrimage site.

In their opposition to this incident feminists were portrayed as a Westernised urban élite with little sympathy or understanding of the deeply held beliefs of 'real' people. For example, Prabhash Joshi wrote in the newspaper *Jansatta* on 18 September 1987,

> This incident is one of the innumerable contradictions of our country where millions of people think in a way that is radically different from that of a handful of those who man the courts and the government, and who live among English educated people...*sati* is not an ordinary occurrence. One out of a million widows takes a vow to commit *sati* and it is but natural that her [Roop Kanwar's] supreme sacrifice becomes the centre of people's worship and reverence. Therefore, this cannot be seen either as an issue of women's civil rights or of discrimination between men and women. It is simply a question of a society's social and religious beliefs.

An issue of fundamental women's rights was suddenly framed in terms of a simplistic tradition/modernity dichotomy—a struggle of the religious majority against an irreligious minority. Presented in this way, feminists were ridiculed as agents of evil Western ways. Yet, as a

102   WOMEN IN ASIA

number of observers indicate, this was the re-invention of tradition
(Kumar 1994; Sangari 1995; Thapar, 1987). Far from being a place of
worship, the *sati-sthal* resembled a political rally. Thousands of young
men in their 20s and 30s gathered to chant slogans (Thapar 1987). The
sentiments expressed among the supporters of *sati* were remarkably
similar to the Shah Bano case. As Prof Zoya Hasan (1987, p. 1948), has
explained,

> The issue is not one of conflict between tradition and modernity, but
> the organised revival of tradition made worse by the Indian State's
> compromise with the forces of tradition for the sake of political
> survival...*sati* or dowry deaths or the denial of the rights of Muslim
> women have become contemporary phenomena. *'Sati'* as indeed the
> reactions against the Shah Bano judgement, were not spontaneous
> responses of people who were steeped in tradition, and therefore
> determined to protest their religious identity. As a matter of fact,
> both issues were set off by an organised campaign that involved
> evoking religious sanction to assert a distinct political identity.

Sati had become a symbol of identity in response to the declining
legitimacy of the land owning *Rajput* community. The *Rajput* (warrior)
and *Marwari* (money-lending) castes had lost their traditional power as a
consequence of the land reforms that took place in Rajasthan in the
1950s. The revival of *sati-daha* was a reassertion of their identity.

In the wake of communal violence the complex nature of identity and
difference among women became apparent. What were the implications
for those seeking change under a common umbrella of women's
interests? First, it was evident that women did not speak with one voice
in their efforts to construct identities. Nor did their interests cut across
classes and communities. Second, it was incorrect to assume a
convergence of their political orientations. For example, in the 1970s and
early 1980s women's groups were guided by a broadly left orientation.
By the end of the 1980s the presence of women within the religious right
had gained prominence (Butalia and Sarkar 1995). Third, it seemed that
at times women's rights could be at odds with rights of minorities
(Ganguly-Scrase and Julian 1998). In the case of Roop Kanwar
thousands of women supported *sati-daha*, while the Shah Bano
judgement, an apparently just cause for women's rights had turned into a
ploy to harass a religious minority. As a consequence, women's rights
were sacrificed. In the decade that has passed since the Shah Bano
controversy erupted communal tensions have intensified and the prospect
of a uniform code seems remote.

Communalism and feminist scholarship

The aggressive communalism of Hindu chauvinists has sparked scholarly efforts to trace the roots of the current communal tensions to the emergence of nationalism in the nineteenth century (see Pandey 1990). Studies investigating stereotypes that were created by colonisers as well as the oppositional identities that were constructed by Indian nationalists were examined. Focusing on a majority Hindu identity, this research was devoted to the study of the colonial period and understanding the formation of colonial subjectivities through 'colonial discourses'. These studies emphasise colonial domination and its response to the creation of a nationalist identity and as such overlook much of the pre-colonial origins of caste hierarchies and domination. In the context of feminist scholarship this uncovered the notion that nationalist discourse categorised the 'Indian woman' as Hindu, urban, *brahmin* (upper caste) and middle-class (Sangari and Vaid 1989). Over a period of time these specific markers were not mentioned and the interventions of non-*brahmin* women were rendered invisible (Rege 1997).

In post-independence India, particularly in the 1970s and 1980s feminists pursuing women's rights invoked the language of citizenship that implicitly denied caste and community. However, as far as women's rights in the uniform civil code is concerned, some observers in India contend that it is no longer possible to produce feminists concerns in terms of unproblematic 'human rights' or 'citizen's' rights (Menon 1998). Given the evolution of current communal politics women's groups are now completely rethinking issues of gender. There is an urgency within the women's movement to 'evolve a new form of politics that will among other things seriously engage with issues of caste and religious community' (Anveshi Law Committee 1997). In order to mobilise women, the feminist movement in India tried to appropriate symbols from the Indian tradition, such as the use of the goddess imagery, as source for empowerment. This was particularly necessary because they had consciously tried to develop a mode of feminism that was distinct from Western feminism. Madhu Kishwar, the editor of *Manushi* once argued the need to draw from Indian cultural traditions which people hold dear (see Kishwar and Vanita 1984). It was important to have an understanding of the images that have a powerful force in the hearts and minds of women 'to identify their points of strength and use them creatively'. She claimed this at a time when religious fundamentalism was on the increase. It was especially important that 'anti-women' forces did not seize a monopoly on religious and cultural symbols. However, the search for this kind of gender symbolism today is fraught with problems. At the time the goddess image was an effective and powerful source for the women's movement, but in recent years it has been shown to be alienating for minority women (Agnes 1995) since it derives from the majority Hindu tradition.

Towards the future?

Redressing the disparity between formal political equality and the meaningful exercise of political power was one of the major platforms of the women's movement. Bridging the gap between rhetoric and reality is seen as a precondition to the empowerment of women. Two issues that I want to take up now are the conditions surrounding women's economic and political participation. The changes that have taken place in recent years will radically impact on women's lives in the new century. These changes concern the Indian government's efforts to liberalise the economy and the constitutional amendments to statutory reserve quotas for women in local self-government.

Panchayati Raj and the 73rd Constitutional Amendment

An important political innovation since Indian independence has been the creation of *Panchayati Raj*—elected self-governing bodies at the village level. Its architects believed that efforts had to be made to democratise local institutions, without which development would be ineffective (Government of India 1957). As we have seen, the growth of informal political activity through the women's movement has been widespread. Yet, women's participation in the formal political structure has not improved greatly. During the period 1971–77 women constituted 3.8 per cent of the representatives in the *Lok Sabha* (the lower house of Parliament). This had only increased to 7.2 per cent by the end of 1992 (Santha in Mohanty 1995, p. 3346). To expand women's participation in grass roots political institutions—the *Panchayati Raj*—legislation was introduced to reserve 30 per cent of the total seats for women. Within this quota one third of seats are reserved for women from scheduled castes and tribes.

As early as 1959, recommendations were made to secure representation of minorities and especially women in the *Panchayati Raj*. The underlying reasoning was the recognition of the crucial role of women as active participants in the development process rather than passive recipients of its benefits (Manikyamba 1989, p. 14). However, it was not until 1993 that the 73rd Constitutional Amendment Bill was enacted to reserve one third of the seats for women. Effective implementation of the 73rd Amendment would mean that about a million women would be able to enter national politics. However evidence to date on participation in decision making in decentralised governance shows that in most cases, women's roles have been actually performed by male members of the family (Pal 1998). A recent study by Bhaskar. (1997) on the social backgrounds of women candidates has also revealed a conventional social pattern of gendered public activity. That is, the overwhelming majority of women members are married (95.2 per cent). They are generally older (aged 35–45), the ideal age when they can combine family and political roles (mostly after completing their reproductive tasks) and only 3 per cent are in full-time paid employment. Their occupational status shows that 55 per cent are non-earning members, dependant on either their spouses or fathers.

Economic liberalisation and global integration

In the late 1980s India reversed earlier policies of protecting domestic industry and began to pursue economic liberalisation. In 1991 this direction was consolidated in the New Economic Policy. In keeping with the requirements of international lending institutions such as the IMF and World Bank, structural adjustment policies have been formulated with the aim of increasing global competitiveness via trade liberalisation and export-led growth. The Indian government's structural adjustment policies have proposed reductions in public sector employment, limitations on agricultural subsidies, de-nationalisation of banks and insurance companies and reductions in public expenditure.

Some social scientists have considered the implications of economic liberalisation and forecast that the dramatic shift in economic policy, and especially the rapid opening up to the world market will polarise Indian society as never before (Singh 1993; Vanaik 1993; Acharya 1995). In particular, it has been argued that economic liberalisation and marketisation will reinforce asymmetrical gender relations (Sen 1995; Ghosh 1996). While it is clear that marginalised groups will be adversely affected, it is the expansion of the middle class that has influenced the direction of economic policy. Its growth has already attracted considerable world attention in terms of the size and number of consumers in the global market (Kulkarni 1993; Lakha 1999). To foreign investors and government officials it offers a very attractive market for transnational corporations. Forty million Indians have annual incomes with the purchasing power of US$600 000 per annum and a further 190 million have incomes of US$20 000.

The effects of structural adjustment policies on women elsewhere suggest that with growing inequalities the burden will be shifted to women (Beneria and Feldman 1992; Vickers 1991). Feminists in India are concerned that gender issues will be seriously compromised as liberalisation proceeds. The evidence suggests that 'privatisation of public sector enterprises, reduction in investment in public sector units and lower government expenditure on poverty eradication programs will hurt the interests of women' (Panini 1995, p. 57). Moreover, the proportion of women workers will fall because it is the public sector rather than the private sector that has favoured the recruitment of women.

Reduced employment opportunities resulting from the new economic policy have affected women directly and indirectly (Kalpagam 1994, pp. 39–50). The trade liberalisation policies have attempted to integrate women into the global economy, particularly through export processing industries and the expansion of export processing zones. However, their job securities are threatened by the prohibition on unionisation and decentralisation though subcontracting (Dalal 1995). A recent study examining the impact of the New Economic Policy on 610 women workers in five industries shows that 'the status of women's employment has moved toward being irregular and casual and the few who had some measure of protection are now facing the threat of losing their jobs' (Shah, cited in Bhandari 1997). On the one hand, it is anticipated that the unorganised sector will grow since the absence of labour legislation makes it attractive for employers to recruit women. On the other, in areas like the agro-processing industry where women work in large numbers, the import of modern technology in industries which are to be taken over by corporations such as Kellog, Pepsi, Nestlé and General Foods will reduce employment in low-skilled jobs (Mathew 1995). At the same time, because the provision of education is now premised on 'user-pays' principles, the prospects for the retraining of women in technical skills seems limited—particularly for poor women.

However, let us be clear that prior to liberalisation women did not fare substantially better, as I have shown at the beginning of this chapter. Although the state created jobs for women as rural functionaries and reservation policies allowed *dalit* women to gain education and employment, the development model did not benefit women. Lip-service was paid to 'socialism', but in reality it did not seriously challenge class interests. For example, the 'green revolution' created a capitalist class in the countryside, while rural landlessness increased. Nevertheless, market reforms are unlikely to offer better solutions to women in changing the sexual division of labour in Indian society. Earlier studies of women producing for the world market show this to be the case. In the 1970s a major study of lace makers in India showed that caste ideology of female seclusion was compatible with the piecework system of lace production. The lace industry rapidly expanded during the 1970s due to international demand. However, the exporters made no efforts to improve conditions and women continued to work on a piece-rate basis from home since the prevailing ideology saw the work of the 'housewife' as supplementary (Mies 1982).

Conclusion

At the beginning of the new millennium the major challenges for women in India present a conundrum—the need to forge alliances to fight against the adverse socio-economic conditions of women comes into direct conflict with the reality of differences among women. It is clear that interests of Indian women are not identical. Yet, whether these differences become divisive and a hindrance to gender justice remains to be seen. Women are now caught in a bind. If they speak of common roots, they will not only end up idealising tradition but also risk drawing from symbols that are unacceptable to a cross-section of women. The alternative may be to invoke a secular cosmopolitanism—but neither is this view shared by all women. In this scenario the existence of a syncretic tradition, removed from both uppercaste brahminism and ascetic Islam, seems to be forgotten. Until some form of new syncreticism emerges the scope for alliance will be hampered.

Thus, at the end of the twentieth century the differences among Indian women are more than an empirical fact of diversity. A complex picture emerges of the ways in which gender, caste and class influence one another. More significantly, despite the need to recognise diversity and difference there are certain homogenising forces at work, namely the normalising process of the nation-state and the increasingly powerful forces of the global economy.

Notes

[1]   Editors' note: Sex ratio figures in India are normally expressed in terms of 1000 rather than 100. However, because elsewhere in Asia the 100 ratio is more common we have translated India's figures to this base. In this way it is hoped that readers will be able to drawn cross-national comparisons more readily.

References and recommended readings

Acharaya, S.K. 1995 'Spatial implications of New Economic Policy—reflections on
    some issues for Northeast India with special reference to women,' *Man &
    Development*, vol. 17, no. 1 (March), pp. 56–64

Agarwal, B. 1988 'Who sows? who reaps?: women and land rights in India,' *Journal of
    Peasant Studies*, vol. 15, no. 4, pp. 531–81.

—— 1994 *A Field of One's Own: Gender and Land Rights in South Asia*, Cambridge
    University Press, Cambridge.

Agnes, F. 1993 'The anti-rape campaign: the struggle and the setback,' *The Struggle
    Against Violence*, ed. C. Datar, Stree, Calcutta.

—— 1995 'Redefining the agenda of the women's movement within a secular
    framework,' *Women and the Hindu Right: A Collection of Essays*, eds U. Butalia
    and T. Sarkar, Kali For Women, New Delhi.

Ahmad, I. ed. 1973 *Caste and Social Stratification among Muslims in India*, Manohar,
    New Delhi.

Anveshi Law Committee 1997 'Is gender justice only a legal issue? political stakes in
    UCC debate,' *Economic and Political Weekly*, March 1–8, pp. 453–58.

Babb, L. 1970 'Marriage and malevolence: the uses of sexual opposition in a Hindu
    pantheon,' *Ethnology*, vol. 9, pp. 137–49.

Bannerjee, N. 1985 *Women Workers in the Unorganised Sector*, Sangam Books,
    Hyderabad.

Bardhan, K. 1993 'Social classes and gender in India: the structure of differences in the
    condition of women,' *Gender and Political Economy: Explorations of South
    Asian Systems*, ed. A. Clark, Oxford University Press, New Delhi.

Beneria, L. and Feldman, S. eds 1992 *Unequal Burden: Economic Crisis, Persistent
    Poverty and Women's Work*, Westview Press, Boulder CO.

Bhandari, N. 1997 'Women labour for less under free market.' Paper presented for the
    forum on 'Policies and Strategies for Working Women in the Context of
    Industrial Restructuring,' Institute of Social Studies, The Hague.

Bhaskar, M. 1997 'Women Panchayat members in Kerala: a profile,' *Economic and
    Political Weekly*, Special Issue: Review of Women's Studies, April 26, pp. W13–
    20.

Bhatt, E. R. 1998 'Doosri Azadi: SEWA's perspective on early years of independence,'
    Economic and Political Weekly, Special Issue: Review of Women's Studies,
    April 25, pp. W25–27.

Butalia, U. and Sarkar, T. eds 1995 *Women and the Hindu Right: A Collection of Essays*,
    Kali For Women, New Delhi.

Calman, L. 1992 *Toward Empowerment: Women and Movement Politics in India*,
    Westview Press, Boulder CO.

Caplan, L. 1984 'Bridegroom price in urban India: class, caste and 'dowry evil' among
    Christians in Madras,' *Man (N.S)*, vol. 19, no. 2, pp. 216–33.

Chatterjee, P. 1995 'The nation and its women,' *The Nation and Its Fragments*, Oxford University Press, Oxford.

Chhachhi, A. 1989 'The state, religious fundamentalism and women: trends in South Asia,' *Economic and Political Weekly*, vol. 24, no. 11, pp. 567–77.

Dalal, M. 1995 'Rural women of India in the global economy,' *Development*, vol. 3, September, pp. 40–42.

Das, M. 1984 'Women against dowry,' *In Search of Answers: Indian Women's Voices from Manushi*, eds. M. Kishwar and R. Vanita, Zed, London.

Desai, N. and Patel, V. 1985 eds *Indian Women: Change and Challenge in the International Decade 1975–85*, Popolar, Prakashan.

Dreze J. et. al 1996 'Demographic outcomes, economic development and women's agency,' *Economic and Political Weekly*, July 6, pp. 1739–45.

Dreze, J. and Sen, A. eds 1995 *India Economic Development and Social Opportunity*, Oxford University Press, New Delhi and Oxford.

Dumont, L. 1972 *Homo Hierachicus: The Caste System and Its Implications*, Paladin, London.

Fruzetti, L. 1982 *The Gift of a Virgin: Women, Marriage and Ritual in Bengal*, Rutgers University Press, New Brunswick.

Ganguly-Scrase, R. and Julian, R. 1998 'Minority women and the experiences of migration,' *Women's Studies International Forum*, vol. 21, no. 6, pp. 633–48.

Ghosh, R. 1996 'Economic liberalisation and its impact on women and women's education,' *Alberta Journal of Education*, vol. 42, no. 2, pp. 115–20.

Government of India 1957 *Report of the Team for the Study of Community Projects and National Extension Service*, Committee on Planning Projects.

—— 1975 *Towards Equality*, Report of the Committee on the Status of Women in India, Ministry of Education and Social Welfare,

Hasan, Z. and Qadeer, I. 1987 'Deadly politics of the state and its apologists,' *Economic and Political Weekly*, Nov. 14, pp. 1946–49.

Jhabvala, R. 1994 'Self-Employed Women's Association: organising women by struggle and development,' *Dignity and Daily Bread: New Forms of Economic Organising Among Women in the Third World and The First*, eds. S. Mitter and S. Rowbotham, Routledge, London.

Kalpagam, U. 1994 *Labour and Gender: Survival in Urban India*, Sage, New Delhi.

Kishwar, M. and Vanita, R. eds 1984 *In Search of Answers: Indian Women's Voices from Manushi*, Zed Books, London.

Kulkarni, V.G. 1993 'The middle class bulge,' *Far Eastern Economic Review*, March 11.

Kumar, R. 1993 *The History of Doing: An Illustrated Account of Women's Rights and Feminism in India*, Verso, London.

—— 1994 'Identity politics and the contemporary Indian feminist movement,' *Identity Politics and Women: Cultural Reassertions and Feminisms in International Perspective*, Westview Press, Boulder CO.

Lakha, S. 1999 'The state, globalization, and the Indian middle class identity,' *Culture and Privilege in Capitalist Asia*, ed. M. Pinches, Routledge, London.

Liddle, J. and Joshi, R. eds 1986 *Daughters of Independence*, Zed Press, London.

Manikyamba, P. 1989 *Women in Panchayati Raj Structures*, Gyan Publishing House, New Delhi.

Marriot, M. 1955 *Village India: studies in the little community*, University of Chicago Press, Chicago.

Mathew, G. 1995 'New Economic Policy, social development and sociology,' *Sociological Bulletin*, vol. 44, no. 1.

Menon, N. 1998 'State/gender community: citizenship in contemporary India,' *Economic and Political Weekly*, January 31, Special Issue: Review of Political Economy, pp. PE3–15.

Mies, M. 1982 *The Lace Makers of Narsapur: Indian Housewives Produce for the World Market*, Zed, London.

Mies, M. and Shiva, V. eds 1993 *Ecofeminism*, Fernwood Publications; Zed, London.

Miller, B. 1981 *The Endangered Sex: Neglect of Female Children in Rural North India*, Cornell University Press, Ithaca.

Mogadham, V. ed. 1994 *Identity Politics and Women: Cultural Reassertions and Feminisms in International Perspective*, Westview Press, Boulder CO.

Mohanty, B. 1995 'Panchayati Raj, 73rd Constitutional Amendment and women' *Economic and Political Weekly*, December 30, pp. 3346–49.

Mukhopadhyay, M. 1998 *Legally Dispossessed: Gender, Identity, and the Process of Law*, Stree, Calcutta.

Neft, Naomi and Levine, Anne D. 1997 *Where Women Stand: An International Report on the Status of Women in 140 Countries*, Random House, New York.

Omvedt, G. 1980 *We will smash this prison! Indian women in struggle*, Zed, London.

Ortner, S. 1970 'Is female to male as nature is to culture?' *Women, Culture and Society*, eds M. Rosaldo and L. Lamphere, Stanford University Press, Stanford.

Pal, M. 1998 'Women in Panchayat: experiences of a training camp,' *Economic and Political Weekly*, Jan. 24, pp. 150–52.

Pandey, G. 1990 *The Construction of Communalism in Colonial North India*, Oxford University Press, New Delhi.

Panini, M 1995 'Social logic of economic liberalisation,' *Sociological Bulletin*, vol. 44, no. 1, pp. 31–62.

Ram, K. 1991 *Mukkuvar Women: Gender Hegemony and Capitalist Transformation in a South Indian Fishing Community*, Allen and Unwin, Sydney.

Randeria, S. and Visaria, L. 1984 'Sociology of bride-price and dowry,' *Economic and Political Weekly*, vol. 19, no. 15, pp. 648–52.

Rege, S. 1995 'Caste and gender: the violence against women in India,' *Dalit Women in India: Issues and Perspectives*, Gyan Publishing House, New Delhi.

——— 1998 'Dalit Women talk differently: a critique of 'difference and towards a dalit feminist standpoint position,' *Economic and Political Weekly*, Special Issue: Review of Women's Studies, October 31, pp. W39–45.

Sangari, K. 1995 'Politics of diversity: religious communities and multiple patriarchies,' *Economic and Political Weekly*, December 23, pp. 3287-310 and December 30, pp. 3381-389.

Sangari, K. and Vaid, S. 1989 *Recasting Women: Essays in Colonial History: 600 BC to the Present*, Feminist Press, New York.

Sen, G. 1995 'Gender, markets and states: a selective review and research agenda,' *World Development*, vol. 24, no. 5, pp. 821–29.

Sharma, M. 1985 'Caste, class and gender: production and reproduction in North India,' *Journal of Peasant Studies*, vol. 12. no. 4, pp. 57–88.

Sharma, K. et al. 1985 'The Chipko movement in the Uttarkhand region, Uttar Pradesh, India: women's role and participation,' *Rural Development and Women: Lessons from the Field*, ed. S. Muntemba, ILO, Geneva.

Sharma, U. 1984 'Dowry in India: its consequences for women,' *Women and Property, Women as Property*, ed. R. Hirschon, Croom Helm, London.

Singh, A. K. 1993 'Social consequences of New Economic Policies,' *Economic and Political Weekly*, vol. 28, no. 7, pp. 279–85.

Srinivas, M. N. 1966 *Social Change in Modern India*, University of California Press, Berkeley.

——— 1984 *Some Reflections on Dowry*, Oxford University Press, New Delhi.

Thapar, R. 1987 'Traditions versus,' *Manushi*, no. 42–43.

Wadley, S. ed. 1980 *The Powers of Tamil Women*, Maxwell School of Citizenship and Public Affairs, Syracuse University, Syracuse, N.Y.

Vanaik, A. 1993 'Imperialism, Soviet collapse and implications for the post colonial world,' *Economic and Political Weekly*, vol. 38, no. 5, pp. 37–46.

Vickers, J. 1991 *Women and the World Economic Crisis*, Zed Press, London.

Vyas, Anju and Singh, Sunita 1993 *Women's Studies in India: Information sources, services and programmes*, Sage Publications, Newbury Park.

6 Negotiating modernities: Filipino women 1970–2000

Mina Roces

School of History
University of New South Wales

Pulling the trajectory of women's history in multiple, often contradictory directions, the twin impacts of globalisation and the various feminisms have, since 1970, been largely responsible for altering the status of women in the Philippines. The history of Filipino women in the later half of the twentieth century cannot be mapped using a linear, progressive, modernist or developmentalist paradigm where it is assumed that women's status is ever improving. Instead, the phenomenal changes that were introduced have blurred the lines between woman as victim and woman as agent, woman as mother and woman as worker, woman as object and woman as subject. In the three decades between 1970–2000, the Philippine political government itself experienced an extreme swing from an authoritarian regime (1972–86) to a democratic one (1986–99). How have women negotiated the choices thrust on them by the forces of modernity and post-modernity between 1970–2000?

This chapter suggests some answers to this question through a survey of women's engagement with the plethora of changes that altered their lives in the last three decades of the twentieth century. I argue that in negotiating modernities, Filipino women expressed ambivalence—simultaneously embracing extreme choices between modernity and tradition, empowerment and disempowerment, unofficial power and official power, feminisms and traditional cultural constructions of women. In the experience of negotiating multiple modernities, Filipino women have blurred the distinguishing boundaries between these polar opposites, revealing the complexities that women's changing status has compelled them to face. For instance, women's power is a site where the contradiction between traditional kinship politics (defined as utilising political power for the kinship group) and modern values (such as nationalism where the loyalty to the state is raised above that of the kinship group) is played out. In the gendering of power and politics women are ascribed unofficial power and as the support system of the kinship group given the space to exercise power behind the scenes.

In granting women unofficial power, kinship politics makes them vulnerable to modern criticisms that women are manipulating or scheming (interview: Patricia Licuanan 1993), wielding power that is illegal, undemocratic and unaccountable. The attacks against the blatant use of power by First Lady Imelda Marcos, particularly in the zenith of the martial law years, and more recently the 'scandal' involving the very visible influence of President Fidel Ramos's alleged former mistress Rosemarie 'Baby' Arenas, are outstanding case studies. At the other end of the equation, the female politician's frequent involvement in the exposés and crusades against graft and corruption is doubly legitimised through both the 'modern' discursive prioritising of the nation-state and women's traditional gendered roles as moral guardians. Thus, Senator Miriam Defensor Santiago, who launched her political career as the most avid and vocal female campaigner against graft and corruption, can be seen simultaneously as a modern 'nationalist', 'gun-wielding' feminist, and as a woman performing the roles ascribed to her gender.

The militant nuns who dominated the image of political activism in the martial law period represented another classic example of the conflict between kinship politics and modernity contested and negotiated through women's power. The nuns were not only strident political activists but also feminists. But their *moral* power was exercised unofficially. Refusing to claim official power, the nuns preferred to act as a pressure group, lobbying politicians to initiate political and social change. Perhaps that is the reason they were so effective—though they demanded modern ideas of full equality and empowerment for women, their exercise of power remained within traditionally accepted modes.

In the area of globalisation and women's labour, the gendered nature of the Filipino diaspora reifies the complexities and ambivalences associated with the modern economy. Two important diasporic movements are clearly associated with women: the overseas contract worker who is a domestic and the migrant-for-marriage phenomenon often referred in pejorative terms as the 'mail-order bride'. If globalisation means the destruction of the family as we know it, how does one explain the pattern of Filipina marriages to Australian men which are initiated by women for the purpose of preserving the family institution? Although economic reasons are important, Filipinas who marry Australian men are largely motivated by the desire to become wives and mothers. While the woman's decision to leave the country as a migrant is 'modern', her motivation for participating in the diaspora is the perpetuation of the traditional gendered dynamics of symbolic capital—the fulfilment of Filipino womanhood in the roles of wife and mother (Roces 1998b). These women were *solteras* (bachelor women) in the Philippines—most were either past marriageable age or were single mothers (Cooke 1986).

Even the labels 'victim' or 'agent' become problematic when discussing specific women's experiences in this period. Is the mail-order bride or overseas contract worker a victim or an agent? The sensationalised literature presents them as victims but a close examination of oral histories reveals them to be challenging not just the stereotype but the exclusive nature of the categories themselves. Take the story of Ruthie Paredes (pseudonym), a prostitute from Manila who marries her Australian customer for financial security. Six months pregnant she is hospitalised for severe bruises inflicted by her husband. With the help of government subsidies and the Housing Commission, she succeeds in beginning a new life on her own. Contacting me months after the interview she informs me that her husband wants to get back together with her. When I asked her what she will do, she replies with '*Kakapit nalang ako sa patalim*' (I will hold on to the blade). Her choice to grasp the blade is an act of courage and agency, but the fact that the blade cuts her shows that her agency brings her victimisation. Her motives are to gain a husband and fulfil Filipino womanhood, a poignant example of the gendered valence of symbolic capital (Roces 1998b).

I will examine the impact of new changes and women's responses to them in four general areas: women and power and women and politics; women and labour including the diaspora; legislation affecting the status of women; and cultural constructions of the feminine. More detailed analysis of specific responses by women to particular issues are analysed by specialist readings recommended at the end of this chapter.

Women and power/ women and politics

Philippine politics is not male-dominated but gendered. In the gendering of power and politics, men exercise official power as senators, congressmen, mayors, and councillors. Women are ascribed unofficial power and traditionally expected to occupy the space behind the scenes wielding power as part of the support system of the kinship group. Filipino concepts of power (*malakas* /strong or powerful) see power held not just by the individual in office but by the entire kinship alliance group. Women therefore exercise power through their kinship and marriage connections with powerful politicians (Roces 1998a).

Women have also exercised official power since 1937 when Carmen Planas became the first woman councillor. Although, the number of women in office has increased in the post-war years up until the elections of 1998, they still represent only a small percentage (11 per cent in 1992, small increase in 1998) of politicians in electoral office (NCRFW 1995, p. 9). Women politicians are a minority in a culture where official power is considered a male domain. Clearly they are disadvantaged in an environment where the men still make the rules and have stronger links with established political party machines and patronage networks. That women in official power are still marginalised is obvious from the fact that the congresswomen had to form POWER (Philippine Organisation of Women Elected Representatives) in 1992 to lobby for the passage of women-centred legislation. Women politicians are also disadvantaged because there is as yet no 'women's vote' (NCRFW 1995, p. 17; Domingo-Tapales 1991–92). This remains the case despite the influence of feminist groups, the increasing number of women politicians, and the birth (and now comatose state) of an all-female political party (KAIBA or *Kababaihan Para sa Inang Bayan*, Women for the Mother Country). Perhaps the absence of a 'women's vote' and the failure of KAIBA affirm the dominant perceptions of the gendering of power where women are traditionally assigned the space behind the scenes.

The period 1970–99 was a watershed for women's power as it produced both the most powerful woman to exercise unofficial power and the first woman president. Between 1972–86 First Lady Imelda Romualdez Marcos wielded so much unofficial power that the martial law period was sometimes referred to as the 'conjugal dictatorship of Ferdinand and Imelda Marcos'. The career of Mrs. Marcos as First Lady marked the zenith of women's unofficial power. It maps the extent to which *de facto* power can be deployed from patronage of the arts and civic work, to building bridges, hospitals and hotels, to exercising kinship politics and acting as the unofficial diplomat for the head of state. (The Romualdez family built a larger business empire than the Marcos family).

After 1972 Mrs. Marcos became known for her 'edifice' complex, because she was obsessed with construction projects of enormous proportions. At her insistence the CDCP (Construction and Development Corporation of the Philippines) constructed the longest bridge in the Philippines in 1974 (the San Juanico Bridge), which linked the two relatively undeveloped islands of Leyte and Samar. At her instigation pavilions were built for the delegates of the May 1979 UNCTAD conference in Manila (Manapat 1991, p. 278). She built the Folk Arts Theatre, several tourist hotels, the Manila Film Centre, the Coconut Palace, and the Palace in the Sky in Tagaytay. Where before she merely raised funds for hospitals, she now built hospitals: the Philippine Heart Centre, the Lung Centre, the Kidney Centre, and the Children's City or *Lungsod ng Kabataan*. She also organised the Nutrition Centre of the Philippines and developed the Research Institute for Tropical Medicine (RITM) in Alabang Muntinlupa (Manapat 1991, pp. 14–15). Invading the field of education, she built and inaugurated her very own University of Life.

Though not an official diplomat, she eventually earned the epithet 'Marcos's Secret Weapon in Diplomacy'. She was sent on official diplomatic missions to see US Presidents Nixon, Carter, and Reagan, to visit Mao Zedong in China, to negotiate with Libya's President Ghaddaffi over his support of the southern Moro National Liberation Front in the Philippines, to the Soviet Union to meet with Premier Aleksei Kosygin, and to Cuba to meet with Fidel Castro. She signed a loan agreement worth US$88 million with the World Bank and addressed the United Nations! (Bonner 1987, pp. 81, 83, 139, 156, 160, 201, 247, 250, 300).

In displaying the maximum potential of women's unofficial power, Mrs. Marcos literally set the parameters for all wives and women kin of politicians. Her legacy has been to inspire the more visible and aggressive use of unofficial power in the subsequent post-Marcos era (1986–99). Since the Marcos regime, more and more wives of politicians and female kin of politicians have shown a more aggressive participation in political civic work. Simultaneously, they are growing more vocal, assertive, and ambitious despite their official pronouncements that they exist only to support their husbands. This behaviour is doubtless inspired by the new feminisms and globalised notions of the empowerment of women, or perhaps it is simply because they had seen the potential of women's unofficial power. At the same time, the government itself has recognised or maybe even endorsed women's exercise of unofficial power. Congressional wives or spouses pledge an oath of office to the President of the Philippines and the Congressional Spouses Foundation Inc. (CSFI) holds office, complete with its own staff of secretaries, in the Batasan or the Congress building. The establishment of a ritual oath of allegiance and the allocation of physical space in the congressional building to these wives represent not only overt recognition of unofficial power but an institutionalisation of the wife or spouse as a partner in politics as well. Moreover, it provides recognition that she, as wife, is *malakas* (powerful). CSFI since 1992 (particularly under the leadership of Mrs. Gina de Venecia, wife of then Speaker of the House Jose de Venecia 1992–98) has been the most active group of wives in twentieth century history. The case of Mrs. Rosemarie 'Baby' Arenas, President Ramos' alleged former mistress, provides a current indicator that women exercising power in kinship politics have become more assertive, vocal, public, visible and ambitious. She exerted massive power and influence in politics during the Ramos administration (1992–98). It is not the first time a perceived mistress exercised power—there have been several cases (at least two mayors in Metro-Manila had mistresses who were seen to be exercising unofficial power), but the other women have hardly projected as prominent a profile as Mrs. Arenas, nor have they exercised as great an influence as she has reportedly done. Her case is evidence of the increasing visibility, assertiveness, and aggressiveness of women since the 1970s.

The other continuing trend is the increasing number of politicians' wives who become politicians themselves. The statistics show a creeping but steady increase in the number of female politicians. It is expected that more women will enter politics not only because of the direct influence of globalised ideas of feminisms or of equal opportunity for women but also because of the perpetual adjustment of kinship politics to a 1986 constitutional rule. This limits the term of senators to two terms of six years each and congressmen and local government officials to three consecutive terms of three years each. If politicians (generally male) are restricted to only two or three consecutive terms, then to prolong the kinship group's hold on political office or to keep the kinship alliance group *malakas*, the wife will be pressured to run for office in her husband's place once his two or three terms are over (personal communication, Narciso Pineda). It is still the dynamics of kinship politics that affects the gendering of power. In this new era, wives of politicians will more often be given access to the symbols of power to keep the dynamics of kinship politics alive. Thus, without disregarding the possibilities of globalised ideas of women's empowerment and First and Third World feminisms inspiring the assertiveness of women, ironically, it is to serve the ends of kinship politics that women will increasingly be given the symbols of office. In the clash between kinship politics and new constitutional attempts to curb its influence kinship politics is fighting back by giving women official power at last. In the future, many active wives of politicians will be transformed into politicians themselves, all with the aim of perpetuating the dynamics of kinship politics.

The first woman president Corazon Cojuangco Aquino (1986–92) was first a wife of a politician before she became president. Cory, as she became known, was the wife of Senator Benigno Aquino who in the martial law years became the star political prisoner of the Marcos regime. When Aquino was assassinated in 1983, allegedly by the Marcos administration, Cory became the rallying symbol for all victims of martial law. A snap election called by Marcos made her a presidential candidate. But before Marcos proclaimed himself the winner in the midst of allegations of massive cheating, a *coup d'état* launched by Defense Minister Juan Ponce Enrile, the RAM (Reform Armed Forces Movement), and General Fidel Ramos was discovered by Marcos and the rebels were forced to retreat to Camp Crame. But 2 million people came out to protect the rebels and the generals sent to disperse the crowd refused to order their troops to fire. Faced with a rapidly disintegrating army, and pressured by the US, Marcos left the country to spend his last days in exile in Honolulu, Hawaii.

Though she gained power as the alter-ego of her husband, Corazon Aquino as president in a revolutionary atmosphere, was heir to an enormous amount of official power. But even granting that her position was precarious and that there were seven coups instigated against her in the six years she was in office, her popularity was so high that she could directly access people power to strengthen her hold as a legitimate president. As the first female president of the Philippines how did she wield her power? The most common adjective used to describe her government was 'weak'. In fact, the cabinet and some of her officials deliberately refrained from discussing critical economic policies or complex international negotiations with her because they believed that she was intellectually incapable of understanding them. Isolated from critical negotiations, excluded from government international 'schemes', and denied access to important information, Aquino swiftly defaulted official power. Instead, power was exercised behind the scenes by her *cordon sanitaire*, made up of close kin and a menagerie of advisers.

Mrs. Aquino's personal political panache contrasted sharply with Mrs. Marcos's who meddled in all affairs of state. This contrast introduces a woman's personality as a factor in analysing women's exercise of power, be that official or unofficial power. It also raises the question of whether official power is the best or only option for women in the Philippines. The complexities in the road toward women's full empowerment is highlighted by Imelda and Cory and the parameters established by *both* official (as a woman marginalised in a male dominated arena) and unofficial power. To maximise empowerment for Filipino women the Filipina feminist challenge lies precisely in exploring the vast potential of unofficial power, and in reworking traditional codes, practices and even the dynamics of kinship politics. For women to gain official power in a male-dominated structure with male-centred rules would prove Pyrrhic *if* it is at the sacrifice of the existing unofficial power women already wield.

Nonetheless a statistical analysis of women politicians shows a consistent though creeping increase in numbers from 1970 to 1998, the last national election prior to the close of the millennium. From 1970–86, an authoritarian regime made election results dubious. Participation was limited primarily to Marcos supporters and only a few opposition members, like Justice Cecilia Muñoz Palma, who ran for office in the Marcos created legislative assembly or *Batasan Pambansa* (both Congress and the Senate had been abolished). There were ten women in the 1978–84 assembly and another ten in the 1984–89 assembly (abolished in 1986 however by Corazon Aquino) (Aguilar 1992a, p. 25) comprising around 5.52 per cent in 1984 (Tancangco 1996, p. 182). In the 1989 elections women composed 9.79 per cent of politicians in elective posts (Tancangco 1996, p. 183) and by the 1992 elections, the average was raised to 11 per cent (NCRFW 1995, p. 3). In 1998 women Senators were 17.39 per cent, District Representatives 12.14 per cent, Governors 17.33 per cent, Vice Governors 12 per cent, Board Members 13.74 per cent, Mayors 15 per cent, Vice Mayors 11.36 per cent and Councillors 16.84 per cent. There were 2 women in the Senate in 1987, 4 in 1992 (Aguilar 1992b, p. 17; NCRFW 1995, p. 3), peaking to 5 in the 1995 elections and returning to 4 in 1998. In 1995 and 1998, the Senators who topped the election results, were both women (Gloria Macapagal in 1995 and Loren Legarda in 1998) revealing that despite the disadvantages women face in election campaigns and their lack of patronage networks, they can outdistance their male rivals. The numbers of congresswomen have altered little since 1986 with 21 in 1987 and 25 in 1999. In 1967 there were 29 women mayors compared to 39 in 1971. By 1980, 80 women mayors were elected, 88 in 1988 (Aguilar 1992b, p. 18), 119 in 1992 (NCFRW 1995, p. 3) and by 1998, 15 per cent of the Mayors were women. In 1988 there were 1588 women Councillors (Aguilar 1992b, p. 18), in 1992 there were 1644 (NCFRW 1995, p. 3) but by 1998 they reached 2141 or 16.84 per cent of all Councillors. Despite these small victories, there is evidence to suggest the existence of a 'glass ceiling' for women politicians. The first woman Vice-President was only elected in 1998 (Gloria Macapagal), the first woman Senate President pro-tempore appeared only in 1994 (Leticia Shahani), and as of this writing (1999) there has never been a female Speaker of the House or Senate President. Official power is still very much the domain of men.

Women activists

Feminists from the early 1970s up to 1999 have concentrated so far on the pursuit of official power and equal opportunity for women. Subscribing by and large (with the exception of the militant nuns) to Western feminist paradigms, women's groups have shunned the path of unofficial power and competed with men for the right to equal positions and power on male terms. The first feminist organisation MAKIBAKA (*Malayang Kilusan ng Bagong Kababaihan*, or Free Movement of New Women) began as an offshoot of the *Kabataan Makabayan* (Nationalist Youth). It was organised initially to mobilise women as part of the student activism of the late 1960s and early 1970s. This group protested social injustices, the Vietnam War, US influence on domestic affairs, oil prices, inflation, the Marcos government's fascist tendencies, and the wide disparity between the rich and poor. On the other hand, MAKIBAKA also reflected its connections with Western radical feminism by launching its organisation with a protest outside the Miss Philippines beauty contest. Locked into the frameworks of Western feminism and Marxist feminism, it had not yet gone beyond grafting imported feminist theories onto the Philippine situation. Perhaps because this proto-feminist group was born at the height of student activism and in the midst of 'national liberation' struggles, tensions between feminism and nationalism prevented any sophisticated theorising of feminism and its adaptation to the Philippine cultural matrix. In fact, the tension was resolved in favour of nationalism, where women were pressured to keep feminist concerns or women's issues secondary in importance to the aims of national liberation—a prioritisation that characterised women's activist groups all the way into the 1980s. In effect, national liberation was seen as a prerequisite to women's liberation (Angeles 1989). The first feminist group members refused to be labelled feminists, and even today women political activists evade the word (except the militant nuns). MAKIBAKA was dominated by young students, although it also incorporated the mothers of these students (who were initially drawn in and politicised as chaperones for their daughters) (interview: Ceres Alabado 1995), as well as women workers, housewives, and professionals (Angeles 1989, p. 149). But MAKIBAKA never self-consciously thought to enlarge its membership, for example, by mobilising the mothers further or extending its membership beyond the students (Ronquillo 1984, p. 52). In any case, its potential as a burgeoning feminist movement was never realised as martial law forced it to go underground, aborting prematurely its mutation into a feminist movement with a nationalist orientation or, alternatively, a nationalist movement with a feminist orientation.

During the martial law years, women in radical politics joined organisations not exclusively comprised of women. These included: the Communist Party of the Philippines (CPP); KASAPI (social democrats); April 6th Liberation Movement; human rights activists; KAPATID (*Kapisanan Para sa Pagpapalaya at Amnestiya ng mga Detenido sa Pilipinas*, or Organisation for Freedom and Amnesty for the Detainees in the Philippines); Movement for a Free Philippines (this in the US); and the Task Force Detainees or TFD, an organisation set up to speak for the political detainees. Although women fought in the CPP's New People's Army as *amasonas*, they were still relegated mainly auxiliary roles as cooks, childcarers and housekeepers; as support staff appended to military organisations; and as journalists and teachers (interview: Carolina 'Bobbie' Malay 1994; Hilsdon 1995, p. 75, p. 82). They were marginalised in the top leadership positions even if they had become martyred, imprisoned and tortured. In the entire history of the CPP, women theoreticians were conspicuously absent. The TFD on the other hand, led by the militant nuns, eventually metamorphosed into a female dominated organisation.

The militant nuns (though small in number, around 200 out of a total of 9000 nuns) were the most vocal of women activists in the 1972–86 period. They joined illegal labour strikes and risked their lives for the rights of workers and tribal minorities fighting to retain ancestral lands. They wrote newsletters reporting on current events (*IBON Facts and Figures*) and rallied against prostitution in American bases (TW-MAE-W, Third World Movement Against the Exploitation of Women). From 1972 until the people power revolution, they symbolised political activism in the Philippines, so much so that the main character in Mike de Leon's Tagalog film *Sister Stella L.* is a nun who delivers the activist

slogan: *'Kung hindi tayo kikilos, sino pa, kung hindi ngayon, kailan pa*
[If we do not act, who will, if not now, when else]? The choice of nun
over a priest or a Communist Party member, whether male or female,
attested to the nuns' visibility in radical politics as well as the strong,
consistent identification of nuns with protest politics. In the martial law
era, the ideal activist was symbolised by a militant nun. That they held
one form of unofficial power—*moral power*—was evidenced by the fact
that even Mrs. Marcos would invite a nun, Sister Christine Tan,
(interview: Sr Christine Tan 1995) for a discussion in Malacañang. Nuns
also took the forefront at rallies because it was believed that the military
would hesitate to harm them. The force of moral power was tested in the
people-power revolution where nuns armed with rosaries triumphed over
armoured personnel carriers sent to shoot and dispel the crowds.

When Senator Benigno Aquino was assassinated in 1983, women's
groups mushroomed. Between 1945–72, and even during martial law,
women were pivotal in charity and civic work organisations—although
many were founded and run by wives and female kin of politicians with
the goal of boosting their husband's civic profile. Extending the
traditional definition of 'politics' and 'political activity' to include these
organisations, it would appear that women have been organising
themselves politically and for political ends for most of the twentieth
century but particularly in the post-war era. Between 1945 and 1980
women's groups were formed for the purpose of charity or civic work or
as campaign-support groups for male politicians. After 1983, the tenor
changed and women began to organise themselves for reasons other than
supporting their male kin. Though initially they organised themselves to
fight the Marcos dictatorship (with the exception of PILIPINA and
KALAYAAN which were consciously feminist in orientation),
eventually they began to include women's issues as an important part of
their agenda. Their aims were primarily to mobilise women as a
gendered force and to politicise them against the Marcos regime. Onto
the scene burst Women for the Ouster of Marcos (WOMB), the Alliance
of Women for Action Toward Reconciliation (AWARE), and Women
Writers in Media Now (WOMEN), composed of middle-class women.
Samahan ng Makabayang Kababaihan (SAMAKA), composed of
women students and youth, Concerned Artists of the Philippines
Women's Desk, and *Kilusan ng Manggagawang Kababaihan* (KMK)
were others with a broader range of class membership.

Some peasant groups who were still active were the KaPaPa
(*Katipunan ng Bagong Pilipina*) and *Amihan* (Tancangco 1992, p. 70).
KaPaPa members were mostly peasant women, urban poor workers, and
housewives. Its basic focus was education of grassroots women

(Angeles 1989, p. 172). The CWP (Concerned Women of the Philippines, a group of élite women who agitated for better conditions for political detainees), and the TFD were still active. Another active group was the aforementioned Third World Movement against the Exploitation of Women. It formed in response to Japanese sex tours and prostitution around military bases. It later expanded to include the phenomenon of mail-order brides (the 'export' overseas of Filipina brides, who proved to be victims of domestic violence, murder, and other forms of victimisation), and Filipino prostitutes abroad, particularly the *Japayukis* in Japan. Finally, in March 1984, these loose groups of women's organisations coalesced to form GABRIELA (General Assembly Binding Women for Reforms, Integrity, Equality, Leadership and Action). GABRIELA brought together about 50 organisations in Manila and 38 in Mindanao (Tancangco 1992, p. 70). By 1992 it had links with 120 organisations though it is believed that more than 200 women's organisations now exist (*Laya* 1992, p. 32). As members began to see themselves as women they developed a gendered outlook and a realisation that they could attain power as a women's group. While not criticising directly the gendering of politics, the women of GABRIELA began to see the potential of women's power and attempted to unite women's groups of all flavours under its umbrella. After Marcos was deposed in 1986, GABRIELA became increasingly more feminist in orientation, viewing issues from a more gendered perspective. Interest focused on the problems of: mail-order brides; prostitution; rape; domestic violence and battered women; the comfort women of the Japanese Occupation years; domestic helpers and maids in Singapore, Hong Kong, and the Middle East; pornography; and sex tourism.

The history of women's activism reveals an evolutionary feminine politics. It is women's involvement in activist politics that awakens them to the possibilities of women's empowerment as a group. But the history of women's power from the 1970s onwards questions established scholarship that sees only women activists or women's movements as representing politically active or empowered women. While scholars writing on women and politics in the Philippines (and elsewhere in Southeast Asia) tend to focus only on women activists, interpreting them as *the* sublime example of empowered women or political agents, the experience of women activists in the Philippines disproves this viewpoint. These women activists, who shunned kinship politics and women's exercise of unofficial power within their group, were eventually marginalised from official power by the male leadership of the radical organisations they joined. Deprived of official power and refusing to exercise unofficial power, women activists were practically impotent. Compared to their sisters who practised kinship politics, women activists were severely limited in functioning as political agents, their leadership roles hardly commensurate with their contributions to the movement.

On the other hand, the militant nuns appear to have negotiated the conflict and contradictions between feminism, modernity, traditional kinship politics, and the gendering of power to their advantage. As feminists, they spoke up for women's issues and women's rights. Ironically, while rejecting official power (not a feminist stance), they became effective practitioners of moral power behind the scenes. These nuns represent the classic contradictions and ambivalences women encounter while negotiating modernities.

Women and labour

Since the martial law years the Philippines has lagged behind the tiger economies of the region. Both men and women workers shared the burden of economic problems and, in an attempt to cope with increasing poverty, participated in both the export processing zones at home and the globalisation of the labour market which sent them overseas on temporary job contracts. This labour participation at home and abroad was highly gendered. Though women's participation in both local and global labour has been very significant, their contributions have not been rewarded in monetary terms. In their own country they were prominent in the service sectors, hospitality industries, teaching and nursing, and in factory chores associated with 'feminine or delicate skills'. Overseas they have been identified with the image of domestic helpers, prostitutes or entertainers (*Japayukis* for example), or mail-order brides.

The woman as worker at the end of the twentieth century reveals the complex challenges facing the modern woman who, in the Philippine context, has to survive in an economy experiencing very slow growth. Those élite women in plum family corporations may have to sublimate their power and achievements behind the facade of male company presidents. For the majority of women, the choices involve more poignant sacrifices. If factory work offers little pay and no future prospects, a job in the tourist/hospitality sector might prove more lucrative although the woman becomes a 'sex object', open to victimisation and abuse by male customers (both local and foreign). If the woman opts for an even more 'modern' scenario of working overseas as a domestic helper or entertainer, her earnings increase significantly but she pays the high price of victimisation from her employers and estrangement from her family. This modern 'woman as worker' has completely redefined 'woman as mother', for as a domestic helper in Singapore in the process of bringing up other people's children, she forfeits the chance to fulfil her own motherhood.

Filipino women have high education status with more women than men in the college level and in graduate school (Licuanan 1991, p. 16; Eviota 1992, p. 94). But women's strong educational qualifications do not translate to parity in employment. Women's participation in the labour force is lower than that of men, and women have higher rates of unemployment and underemployment (Eviota 1992, p. 91, 94). Women comprised 40 per cent of the labour force in 1988 (Samonte 1990, p. 13), and 37 per cent in 1990 (29 per cent of the rural labour force and 39 per cent of those employed in urban areas) (Chant and McIlwaine 1995, p. 23). Statistics are not always consistent with one 1998 study placing women's labour participation rate at 50 per cent (Roffey 1998, p. 49).

There is also a gendering of occupations. Women's labour concentrates in specific industries: the service sectors; handicrafts; electronics (in 1981 90 per cent were women); hawking and vending (in the 1970s 2 out of 3 hawkers in Manila were women); domestic service; and prostitution or sex tourism (employing 350 000 women in the late 1970s) (Eviota 1992, pp. 17, 120, 130, 137). In agriculture women continue to be relegated the label of 'farm workers' rather than 'farmers' (Eviota 1992, p. 110) leaving farming largely a male dominated sphere. In one export processing zone, female labour statistics echo the general trend of women's labour participation representing 38.9 per cent of the workers in the Mactan Export Processing Zone in 1990. In a booming city like Cebu, women's labour participation is higher; up to 45.4 per cent in 1992. Women's participation in the labour force is higher than average in a tourist spot like Boracay island, where it reached 45 per cent in 1993 (Chant and McIlwaine 1995, pp. 77, 79, 81). Hospitality work and sex tourism provide ample scope for women's employment (whether one should rejoice at such figures is problematic since such occupations are associated with the commodification of women). In Nabas, a coastal municipality in the province of Aklan, the weaving of hats and mats was perceived as women's craft. For example, Buenavista had 148 female weavers but only 5 male weavers. Though the income generated from this occupation is very low, it is crucial to the financial security of the household, particularly for women who are keepers of the household finances (Rutten 1990, pp. 76–77, 89).

Wages show a clear-cut discrimination against women. Equal work most definitely does not receive equal pay and women's wages trail far behind those of men. There are some slight differences in statistics presented but figures still show women's wages are lower than men's in most occupations except sales. In one 1986 study women received 37 centavos for every peso a male earned (Licuanan 1991, p. 19), and where women's earnings were averaged from 1978 to 1986 the figures showed women earning 0.54 cents for every peso a man earned (Eviota 1992, p. 89). In the 1990s women still receive only between 50 per cent and 80 per cent of male wages for the same job (Hoffarth 1989 quoted in Roffey 1998, p. 22). There are also a number of occupations where women perform unpaid labour. These include the 70 per cent of women trading in *sari-sari* stores, markets and in manufacturing sectors, 54 per cent of women service workers, and 50 per cent of agricultural workers (Roffey 1998, p. 50).

There are encouraging signs however, in the statistics on women business managers and entrepreneurs, particularly when compared to other Southeast Asian countries. The 1994 figures show 28 per cent of Filipino women in administrative and manager levels and 63 per cent in professional and technical positions. Thailand scored only 22 per cent in administrative and manager levels and 53 per cent in professional and technical positions; Singapore offered 16 per cent and 40 per cent; Malaysia 8 per cent and 38 per cent; and Indonesia 7 per cent and 41 per cent in these same two categories (Roffey 1998, pp. 51–52). The high rate of women in professional and technical occupations reflects the large proportion of women teachers and nurses. In 1975 about 60 per cent of professionals were teachers and 74 per cent of all teachers were women (Eviota 1992, p. 88). Ranking 130 countries using a Gender Empowerment Measure (which measures women's share of earned income, proportion holding legislative positions, and the percentage of women managers, administrators, and professional and technical workers) the Philippines performed well, ranking 28th, with Singapore, Malaysia, and Indonesia, designated as 35th, 29th and 56th respectively (Roffey 1998, p. 51). There is also a healthy pattern of increasing female participation in administrative and managerial positions. In 1986 women comprised a mere 22.7 per cent of administrators and managers but by 1995, their numbers had increased to 32.8 per cent (Roffey 1998, p. 53). These figures reflect the high numbers of women with tertiary qualifications (and beyond) in business, accounting and finance.

Abandoning statistics as the sole method in which to assess women's leadership roles in the professional business sectors, and exploring other qualitative perspectives, one may discover a similar gendering of business power as was found in the political arena. Elite women who run business corporations or educational institutions would often place their husband or male kin as the official public director. A woman will give her husband or brother the title of company president while she actually runs the business and makes all the decisions. Although the male holds the institutional symbols of office and the cultural capital associated with the title of president or chairman of the board, the woman is the real power holder. Furthermore, the perception that she is the one in charge is well-known publicly despite the fact that formally the male enjoys all the prestigious titles. This arrangement has proved effective for many large businesses (the Rustan's Commmercial Corporation and Philippine Women's University readily come to mind), precisely because the role of women as a supporter operating behind the scenes is more socially accepted than a visibly aggressive woman who publicly outshines her husband (Roces 1998a). These women have chosen to wield actual power in business without holding the symbols of power. Like the militant nuns these women have blurred the lines between traditional and modern behaviour—running a business corporation but through the traditional gendering of power.

Globalisation has had a major impact on the gendering of labour ironically reinforcing gender stereotypes in a wide gamut of occupations. The employment of women in the electronics industry, particularly in export processing zones is a clear example of women being given 'modern' tasks in locations intimately linked to the tentacles of globalisation. But the reasons they are assigned these tasks derives from the categorisation of women as best suited to perform duties that are considered painstaking or requiring dexterity and/or infinite patience. Furthermore, it is particularly *young, single* women who are in much demand (Eviota 1992, p. 120). For example, in the Bataan Export Processing Zone (BEPZ), the 1975 figures show that 9 out of 10 workers employed were female (in garments and electronics) and out of these, more then 8 out of 10 were single women in the 15–24 age group (Eviota 1992, p. 121). The post-colonial plantations run by multinational companies of the globalised economy make similar assumptions about women's work. For example, women who comprise 30 per cent of the labour in the banana industry are employed in packing and weighing bananas—a chore seen as requiring delicacy and an assignment that is usually part-time and piece-rate (Eviota 1992, p. 108).

International tourism, another sector of the globalised economy, finds women highly visible in the hospitality and sex industries. Particularly since tourism became the forerunner of the Philippine economy in the 1970s, the Filipino woman became commodified—often marketed as one of the country's main tourist attractions. The reputation of Manila as an 'international sex city' or as the 'sex capital of Asia' is evidence of the gendered aspects of tourism particularly during the martial law period. Though international tourism dropped to fourth place in foreign exchange earnings in the 1990s (Chant and McIlwaine 1995, p. 63) and attempts have been made to deflect the conflation of 'Filipina' with 'sex object', the legacy of the 1970s remains. In the 1990s, there was still a continuing male bias in foreign tourist composition in the 83 per cent of visitors travelling for pleasure (Chant and McIlwaine 1995, p. 65). This is evident despite the Department of Tourism's formal stand against sex tours and the agitation of women's organisations. Even though the American military base at Subic was closed in 1992, the image of the country as a supplier of prostitutes is carried over by the *Japayukis* or the Filipina prostitute overseas (in Japan).

The Filipino diaspora epitomised by the overseas contract worker (OCW) can be cited as the classic example of the Philippine engagement with globalisation. The OCW has become a major symbol of the modern Filipino since the 1970s. Filipinos had been emigrating throughout the twentieth century. But the economic problems of the martial law period, which gave the Philippines the title of 'sick man of Asia,' compelled an unprecedented number of citizens to seek employment (both temporary and permanent) overseas in such places as the Middle East, Hong Kong, Singapore, Malaysia, and Europe. The difference between previous migrations and those of the 1970s and beyond is the temporary, often contractual nature of the move and the involvement of the Philippine government in recruitment and deployment. Remittances from these overseas Filipinos have been in the billions (in 1993 US$2.2 billion) (NCRFW nd, overleaf), prompting the government to baptise them as the country's *'bagong bayani'* or 'new heroes' because these remittances have been crucial to the recovery of the Philippine economy.

The statistics provided by the National Commission on the Role of Filipino Women reveal that in 1991, 40.6 per cent of the Filipino OCWs (a total of 752 700) were women (almost commensurate to the Filipino women's labour participation rates at home). Most male OCWs were sea-based while most women OCWs were entertainers and domestic helpers, nurses, choreographers and dancers. If only land-based figures are utilised, a marked feminisation of labour migration is exposed. The Philippine Overseas Employment Administration (POEA) recorded 382 299 land-based OCWs, of which 47.2 per cent were women. By 1991, 50.6 per cent of the estimated 742 700 Filipinos overseas were women. In 1994 the proportion increased to 55 per cent (Beltran, Samonte and Walker 1996, p. 16). In Hong Kong 10 out of 12 OCWs are women and in Singapore there is a corresponding pattern of 6 women out of every 8 OCWs. The ratio of women to men in European countries was: Italy 2:1,

Greece 8:1, Germany 5:1, Spain 7:1, and Belgium 2:1 (1992 statistics NCRFW nd, p. 3).

A significant number of the women working on contracts abroad are domestic helpers so much so that the term 'Filipino' has become synonymous with 'domestic helper'. This is particularly the case in Singapore and Hong Kong where Filipino women have a visible presence particularly on Sundays (their day off) at Lucky Plaza in Singapore, and Liberty Plaza in Hong Kong. Many of these women have college degrees and are seeking employment overseas either because they were unable to find jobs (in 1990 there were 9.78 million unemployed women graduates and 7.28 million unemployed male graduates in the Philippines, NCRFWb, p. 6), or wages were too low at home. The Filipina as domestic helper or as *atsay ng mundo* ('maid of the world'), has heightened globalised images of the modern Filipina as a victim or as a 'slave' particularly in countries like the Middle East where Filipina maids have very few human rights, if any at all. The case of Sarah Balabagan who murdered her employer because he had raped her (Torrevillas 1996, pp. 59–66) essentialised the plight of the young Filipina OCW domestic who was not only marginalised and exploited but also harassed and abused physically and sexually. In Singapore, the hanging of Flor Contemplacíon for the murder of another Filipino domestic and her employer's son (Torevillas 1996, pp. 46–59) also politicised the issue of the Filipina as domestic helper. In 1995 relations between Singapore and the Philippines were strained by this incident as Filipinos expressed their anger and frustration not only at the Singapore government, but also at the Philippine government. The latter was perceived to be encouraging labour migration by arranging it through the POEA but failing to come to the aid of these temporary migrants. The Contemplacíon case certainly had an impact on the 1995 local elections when the entire rationale for the existence of the OCW was raised—if the Philippine government were to solve the problems of employment and wages, then these Filipinos would not be forced to seek low status employment overseas.

Next to the image of the OCW Filipina as a domestic helper or maid is the image of the Filipina temporary migrant as an entertainer, choreographer, dancer or sex worker. The Filipina OCW as entertainer is epitomised by the *Japayukis* or *Japayuki-san* whose jobs as entertainers and hostesses often involve prostitution. Like the Filipino domestic helper the term *Japayuki* is pejorative and the occupation holds the lowest status as the 'bottomline of Japan's economic structure' (Javate de Dios 1992, p. 45). Again the numbers of *Japayukis* reflect the feminisation of temporary overseas land-based labour migration. Based on the data generated from those given 'entertainers visas', accurate statistics can be released for Filipino entertainers going to Japan from 1981 onwards. These numbers increased from 9125 in 1982 to 57 038 in 1991. These numbers are large even in comparison to the other foreign entertainers working in Japan. Filipino women were a majority, representing 65.28 per cent of all foreign entertainers in Japan in 1992 (Javate de Dios 1992, p. 44). The gendering of Filipino workers in Japan is quite glaring with 24.3 per cent males and 75.7 females in 1989, 23.0 per cent males and 77.0 females in 1990 and 20.4 per cent males and 79.6 females in 1991 (Osteria 1994, p. 11).

By and large the prevailing image of these women is that of exploited sex object and victim. The *Japayuki* has her Flor Contemplacíon and Sara Balabagan equivalent in Maricris Sioson, a 21-year-old entertainer who left for Japan and came home in a coffin. Although the Japanese doctors declared that she had died of a natural cause (fulminant hepatitis), a Philippines Senate Committee Report of 1991 argued that medico-legal experts saw signs of apparent torture and physical injuries (Javate de Dios 1992, p. 39). There were also those who became mentally deranged due to enforced prostitution, rape, or beatings. A report from the Labour Office of the Philippine embassy in 1991 revealed that there were 11 mentally ill females most of whom were entertainers. One woman committed suicide. The death of 18 females in Japan in 1991 (6 were entertainers) (Ballescas 1992, pp. 90–91) highlights women's victimisation as entertainers cum prostitutes.

Despite the horror stories sensationalised in the press involving the torture, rape and violence inflicted on Filipino entertainers in Japan, interviews with entertainers themselves reveal that they are reluctant to support a government ban against overseas deployment of female entertainers. In fact several thousand of them demonstrated against the ban in 1991 (Ballescas 1992, pp. 101–107). Though holding low status in Japan, they acquire some new status as returnees because they come back with the material trappings of success: televisions, video recorders, walkmans, jewellery, CD recorders, electrical appliances, money and other 'gifts' (Ballescas 1992, pp. 87–89). How their new status or income was earned becomes subliminal upon arrival. They no longer want to work in the Philippines because the pay is low and the work '*hindi sosyal*' (not socially accepted as high status or classy) now that they had experienced working in Japan (Ballescas 1992, p. 105). (The seemingly contradictory point that their job in Japan is low status is sublimated.)

The woman as *Japayuki* is another site where women's negotiation with modernity or postmodernity (if the globalisation of labour is seen as a post-modern phenomenon) explodes in contradiction and ambivalence. Her decision to leave the Philippines though fuelled by economic considerations is 'modern' as she extends the territorial parameters of women's work outside the home to its maximum potential by accepting employment overseas. But her occupation conforms to the traditional commodification of women as 'sex objects', exploited for their bodies. Is she a victim or an agent? She is definitely experiencing victimisation not only from customers but also from recruiters, the *mama-san*, and others. Yet in one study (Ballescas 1992), where these women speak for themselves, they express a desire to return to Japan and would like their daughters to be *Japayukis*—a clear sign of agency. Like the mail-order bride who used the image of '*kapit sa patalim*' (hold on to the blade), the *Japayuki-san* is an agent whose decision may turn her into a victim.

And what of the role of the POEA or the Philippine government as promoter and protector of these women? By sending women overseas to become prostitutes, the government is reduced to acting as an 'official pimp' (Javate de Dios 1992, pp. 52–56). If one takes into consideration the government's benefits in terms of remittances, the label 'official pimp' assumes appalling accuracy.

Another type of Filipino migrant behaviour that is also visibly gendered is the migrant-for-marriage phenomenon more commonly referred to in the press as the mail-order bride.[1] Since the 1970s increasing numbers of Filipino women have left the country to become wives for Australians, Swiss, Americans, Japanese and Germans. Economic reasons are cited as the explanation for why women seek pen-pals or place themselves in marriage agencies (Cooke 1986). Oral histories also show that these women also seek husbands to become wives and mothers—thus fulfilling Filipino cultural constructions of womanhood (Roces 1996 and 1998b).

In Australia in particular, the plight of these women has been much sensationalised in the print media. The murders and disappearance of some of these Filipino 'brides' in Australia, called attention to their vulnerable state as new immigrants solely dependent on their husbands and without the support of a much needed kinship-alliance group. Research for the Institute of Criminology confirmed that 'Filipino women are over-represented as victims of homicide' (Cunneen and Stubbs 1997, p. 31). Furthermore, the emergence of the serial sponsor (the Australian man who sponsors a series of Filipino 'brides' who he then abuses or divorces), highlighted the dehumanisation of the Filipina as bride, stressing once more the image of the Filipina as 'sex object' to be bought and dispensed with at the whim of a male.

It is difficult to 'locate' the Filipina migrant-for-marriage—she is not strictly an OCW but she is a migrant; she is neither exclusively a victim nor is she an agent; and she is neither modern nor traditional. In this sense, she represents all that is contradictory about the Filipino 'modern' woman. She is modern because she leaves her country even if it is to reinforce traditional constructions of the Filipina as a wife and mother who is expected to fulfil traditional wifely duties (such as cooking, cleaning and child-minding). She may be a victim of domestic violence and/or someone who contributes to multicultural Australia by volunteering in civic work and local cultural festivals (Roces 1996). Though not an OCW she remits whatever she can to the Philippines even without her husband's knowledge. And, despite her attempts to embrace citizenship she remains liminal; marginalised in the dominant white Australian culture and community, often in isolated, remote areas like Mount Isa (a small mining town in north Queensland).

Legislation and women's status

The 1987 Constitution espoused gender equality officially recognising the role of women in nation-building (Feliciano 1993–94, p. 13). In the 1970s Imelda Marcos created the National Commission on the Role of Filipino Women (NCRFW) and in 1989 the Senate passed Resolution No. 77 requesting it to assist the Committee of Women and Family in working towards recommending appropriate legislation to ensure women's equality with men (Feliciano 1993–94, p. 14). Women's political and civic rights are on par with men's although in practice men dominate high official positions in government. Women have the right to vote, to run for and hold public office, and have freedom of speech, press, association, peaceful assembly and the right to petition for the redress of grievances (Samonte 1990, p. 19). Between 1991–92 a new law granted women equal opportunities for 'appointment, admission, training, graduation, and commissioning in all military or similar schools of the Armed Forces of the Philippines and the Philippine National Police' (Feliciano 1993–94, p. 19). The Family Code has been improved now granting women 'joint administration by husband and wife of the absolute community of property and the conjugal partnership of gains, the joint parental authority of father and mother, the joint management of the affairs of the household, the right of the wife to exercise her profession or engage in business without the consent of the husband, and the joint right of the husband and wife to fix the family's domicile' (Samonte 1990, p. 19).

The Comprehensive Agrarian Reform Law (Republic Act No. 6657) passed in 1988 promised women members of the agricultural labour force equal rights to the ownership of land and shares in the farm's produce as well as representation in decision-making organisations. Unfortunately in practice titles to land which are part of conjugal property are still being registered under the husband's name (Samonte 1990, p. 15). In 1990 Republic Act No. 6955 specifically addressed the issue of sexual exploitation of women (trafficking in women) when it outlawed the practice of matching Filipino women for marriage to foreign nationals through the mail-order system or any introductions involving payment (Samonte 1990, p. 17). In the same year considerations of the complex responsibilities of women as mother/worker were made explicit through Republic Act No. 6972. This law made it compulsory for every *barangay* (smallest political unit) to have a day care centre (though in practice only a few were actually established) (Samonte 1990, p. 18).

The Sexual Harassment Act (Republic Act 7877) was passed in 1995 to protect women from sexual harassment in the workplace. Republic Act No. 7322 (1992) amended the Social Security Law to increase the maternity benefits for women in the private sector. Unfortunately, despite the laws on equal opportunity in the workplace, wages testify to the continuing inequity in practice. In 1997 RA 8353 expanded the definition of the crime of rape and in 1998 RA 8505 created a Rape Crisis Centre for each province and city.

The Philippines has not yet passed a divorce law (although one can file for legal separation). Though the legislators addressed the issues of male adultery, they stopped short of addressing divorce. In a society where a man's infidelities are tolerated, where the role of the mistress is accepted, one could argue quite convincingly that the absence of a divorce law is oppressive to women. The society's privileging of a 'macho culture' means that women have to endure men's infidelities. On the other hand, it encourages complacency among men, who know for certain that despite their transgressions (women's infidelities are frowned upon), the wife has no choice but to put up with them.

Cultural constructions of women

Definitions of Filipino femininity have altered little despite the major breakthroughs made by women throughout the entire twentieth century. Marriage is still viewed as the destiny of women regardless of educational attainments. According to scholar Elena Samonte: 'The best

things that could happen to a woman are: to study and to get married.'
(Samonte 1990, p. 30). The definition of woman is still interchangeable
with her role as wife and mother, and her major concern is still the
management of the household affairs, the family's needs and the
organisation of the family's economic, spiritual and physical life. The
woman must do the washing, ironing, cooking, cleaning, caring for the
children as well as budgeting and marketing (Samonte 1990, p. 29;
Licuanan 1991). While some might argue that women have economic
power because they are in charge of the purse strings, it has been
observed that for women in the lower economic scale (and this would
comprise almost half the population since 37.5 per cent in 1997 or 27.25
million lived below the poverty line), the control over the budget is not
as empowering as it seems. The money they are given to handle is so
little compared to the funds required to make ends meet, thus women
experience the added pressure of trying to make the tight budget fit the
family's needs or else search for alternative forms of income (Licuanan
1991).

The definition of woman as wife or mother (which feminist scholar
Elizabeth Eviota analyses as women being attached to men, as they are
defined primarily in terms of their relationships with men) means that
'women who are not attached to men in one way or another are either
suspect (e.g. witches) or incomplete (e.g. 'old maids') because they have
failed to achieve the main purpose of their existence' (Eviota 1994, p.
61). The pressure to get married, a value linked to cultural constructions
of the feminine, is felt across all classes. Women migrants-for-marriage
for example, marry foreigners and leave the country not only solely for
economic advancement and material well-being, but as noted earlier,
also to fulfil traditional constructions of Filipino womanhood (Roces
1998b).

Conclusion

Filipino women have taken up the many challenges posed by
globalisation, modernity and post-modernities. Their responses to the
complex problems posed by new frontiers have encouraged them to
explore different, sometimes contradictory, strategies in the attempt to
maximise women's empowerment. To access political power, they have
explored unofficial power in a political field where men dominated
official positions and commanded patronage politics. At the same time,
women have also opted for official power, joined women's movements,
and participated in radical politics. As activists they fought as *amasonas*

or like the militant nuns risked their lives for issues of social justice. As wives of politicians they dominated civic organisations, claiming a prominently visible space in the public sphere for their contributions in this area. They have attempted to alter the definitions of woman as wife and mother to include woman as worker.

Filipino women's responses to economic and social change have largely been informed not by a 'feminist project' but a 'modernising project' as women became proactive in improving their lives alongside that of their kinship group. Women politicians and women wives of politicians exercise power to practice kinship politics, women overseas contract workers including domestic helpers and *Japayukis* send money home to help the family's finances and improve the family's status in society. There are some exceptional women who are informed by ideological principles apart from the dynamics of kinship—women activists like the militant nuns, women in the Communist Party, and women who join women's organisations. In this sense women's engagement with the 'women question' has still been largely framed in the context of 'family' of 'kinship' and the new emerging cultural construction of the Filipino modern woman in an ideal modern Filipino kinship group. Negotiating modernity also implied negotiating the family and the kinship group. Women's status and women's power at the end of the twentieth century remains inextricably linked to the discourse of kinship politics and the dynamics of the kinship group.

Notes

[1] 'Mail-order brides' is not an appropriate term to use here since the women themselves object vociferously to this label because it has derogatory overtones. Also, few are technically mail-order brides. Many women married to Australian men met their husbands through Filipina friends or relatives married to an Australian or met their husbands when they were vacationing in the Philippines.

References and recommended readings

Aguilar, Carmencita 1992a 'Filipino women in electoral politics,' *Filipino Women and Public Policy*, ed. Proserpina Domingo Tapales, Kalikasan Press, Manila.

——— 1992b 'Women's political involvement in historical perspective,' *Lila Asia Pacific Women's Studies Journal*, no. 2, pp. 14–23.

Aguilar, Delia 1988 *The Feminist Challenge: Initial Working Principles Toward Reconceptualizing the Feminist Movement in the Philippines*, Asian Social Institute, World Association for Christian Communication, Manila.

Alabado, Ceres 1995 Interview. Quezon City, Metro-Manila, January 25.

Angeles, Leonora Calderon 1989 'Feminism and nationalism: the discourse on the woman question and politics of the women's movement in the Philippines,' MA Thesis, University of the Philippines.

Azarcon-de la Cruz, P. 1988 *From Virgin to Vamp: Images of Women in Philippine Media*, Asian Social Institute, Metro-Manila.

Ballescas, Ma. Rosario P. 1992 *Filipino Entertainers in Japan: An Introduction*, Foundation for Nationalist Studies, Quezon City.

Beltran, Ruby P., Samonte, Elena L. and Walker, Sr. Lita 1996 'Filipino women migrant workers: effects on family life and challenges for intervention,' *Filipino Migrant Workers: At the Crossroads and Beyond Beijing*, eds Ruby Beltran and Gloria Rodriguez, Giraffe Books, Quezon City.

Beltran, Ruby Palma and Javate De Dios, Aurora 1992 *Filipino Women Overseas Contract Workers: At What Cost?*, Women in Development Foundation, Manila.

Bonner, Raymund 1987 *Waltzing with a Dictator: The Marcoses and the Making of American Foreign Policy*, Times Books, New York.

Cahill, Desmond 1990 *Intermarriages in International Contexts*, Scalabrini Migration Center, Quezon City.

Chant, Sylvia and McIlwaine, Cathy 1995 *Women of a Lesser Cost: Female Labour, Foreign Exchange and Philippine Development*, Ateneo de Manila University Press, Quezon City.

Cooke, Fadzilah M. 1986 *Australian-Filipino Marriages in the 1980s—The Myths and the Reality*, Griffith University, Brisbane, Queensland.

Cunneen, Chris and Stubbs, Julie 1997 *Gender, 'Race' and International Relations: Violence Against Filipino Women in Australia*, Institute of Criminology Monograph Series, no. 9, Sydney.

Domingo, Lita, Gastardo-Conaco, J., Ma, Cecilia, Yordan, Eileen S., Baltazar, Marie Joy D. 1995 'Women in political affairs: a study of women councillors in 1990,' in 'Gender Issues in Philippine Society', *Philippine Sociological Review*, vol. 52, nos. 1–4, pp. 15–41.

Domingo-Tapales, Proserpina 1991–1992 'Is there a women's vote?' *Review of Women's Studies*, vol. II, no. 2, pp. 9–18.

Eviota, Elizabeth U. 1992 *The Political Economy of Gender: Women and the Sexual Division of Labour in the Philippines*, Zed Books and Institute of Women's Studies St. Scholastica's College, London and Manila.

—— 1994 'The social construction of sexuality,' *Sex and Gender in Philippine Society*, ed. Elizabeth U. Eviota, National Commission on the Role of Filipino Women, Manila.

Feliciano, Myrna 1993–94 'Legal and political issues affecting the status of women, 1985–1993,' *Review of Women's Studies*, vol. IV, no.1, pp. 13–31.

Francia, Beatriz Romualdez 1988 *Imelda and the Clans: A Story of the Philippines*, Solar Publishing Corporation, Metro-Manila.

Gonzalez-Yap, Miguela 1987 *The Making of Cory*, New Day, Quezon City.

Guerrero, Sylvia H. 1995 'Overseas migration of women: realities and consequences,' *Filipinas in Dialogue: Muslim-Christian Women's Response to Contemporary Challenges*, ed. Erlinda H. Bragado, De la Salle University Press, Manila.

Hilsdon, Anne-Marie 1995 *Madonnas and Martyrs: Militarism and Violence in the Philippines*, Ateneo de Manila University Press and Allen and Unwin, Quezon City and Sydney.

Hoffarth, V.B. 1990 *Women Managers in Southeast Asia*, Women for Women Foundation Asia, Manila.

Javate de Dios, Aurora 1992 'Japayuki-san: Filipinas at Risk,' *Filipino Women Overseas Contract Workers...At What Cost?*, eds. Ruby Palma Beltran and Aurora Javate de Dios, Women and Development Foundation. and Goodwill Trading, Manila.

Javate de Dios, Aurora 1996 'Participation of women's groups in the anti-dictatorship struggle: genesis of a movement,' *Women's Role in Philippine History: Selected Essays*, University Center for Women's Studies, University of the Philippines, Quezon City.

Komisar, Lucy 1987 *Corazon Aquino: The Story of a Revolution*, George Braziller, New York.

Laya. 1992 vol. 1, no. 2 *Feminist Quarterly*, Second Quarter.

Licuanan, Dr. Patricia 1991 'A situation analysis of women in the Philippines,' *Gender Analysis and Planning: The 1990 IPC-CIDA Workshops*, ed. Jeanne Frances I. Illo, Institute of Philippine Culture Ateneo de Manila University, Quezon City.

—— 1993 Interview. Quezon City, Metro Manila, January 19.

Malay, Carolina 'Bobbie' 1994 Wife of Satur Ocampo, Leader of the Communist Party of the Philippines. Interview. Quezon City, Metro-Manila, February 1.

Mananan, Sr. Mary John, Azcuna, Ma, Asuncion, Mangahas, Fe. eds. 1989 *Sarilaya: Women in Arts and Media*, Institute of Women's Studies, St. Scholastica's College, Manila.

Mananzan, Sr. Mary John 1991 *Essays on Women*, Institute of Women's Studies, St. Scholastica's College, Manila.

Manapat, Ricardo 1991 *Some Are Smarter Than Others. The History of Marcos's Crony Capitalism*, Aletheia Publications, New York.

NCRFW—National Commission on the Role of Filipino Women 1995 *Women and Politics*, NCRFW, San Miguel, Manila.

—— nd *Women Overseas Workers*, NCRFW, San Miguel, Manila.

Osteria, Trinidad 1994 *Filipino Female Labor Migration to Japan: Economic Causes and Consequences*, De La Salle University Press, Manila.

Pedrosa, Carmen Navarro 1987 *The Rise and Fall of Imelda Marcos*, Manila.

Roces, Mina 1996 'Filipino brides in Central Queensland: gender, migration and support services,' *Futures for Central Queensland*, eds Denis Cryle, Grahame Griffin and Dani Stehlik, Rural Social and Economic Research Centre, Central Queensland University, Rockhampton.

——— 1998a *Women, Power and Kinship Politics: Female Power in Post-War Philippines*, Praeger, Westport and London.

——— 1998b '*Kapit sa Patalim* Hold on to the Blade: victim and agency in the oral narratives of Filipina women married to Australian men in Central Queensland,' *Lila Asia Pacific Women's Studies Journal*, no. 7, December.

——— 1998c 'The gendering of Philippine post-war politics,' *Gender and Power in Affluent Asia*, eds Maila Stivens and Krishna Sen, Routledge, London.

Roffey, Bet 1998 'Women and business leadership in the Philippines: a study of Filipina managers and entrepreneurs,' Phd Dissertation, Flinders University.

Ronquillo, Salome 1984 'MAKIBAKA remembered,' *Diliman Review*, vol. 42, no. 3–4, May–August, pp. 31–53.

Rutten, Rosanne 1990 *Artisans and Entrepreneurs in the Rural Philippines*, VU University Press, Amsterdam.

Samonte, Elena L. 1990 *Status of Women in the Philippines*, Psychological Association of the Philippines Module No. 4, Manila.

Santos-Maranan, Aida F. 1991 'Do women really hold up half the sky?,' *Essays on Women*, ed. Sr. Mary John Mananzan, Institute of Women's Studies, St. Scholastica's College, Manila.

Sister Stella L. 1984 Film.

Tan, Sister Christine 1995 Interview Leverisa, Malate, Metro-Manila, February 7.

Tancangco, Luzviminda 1992 'Voters, candidates, and organizers: women and politics in contemporary Philippines,' *Filipino Women and Public Policy*, ed. Proserpina Domingo Tapales, Kalikasan Press, Manila.

——— 1996 'Women and politics in contemporary Philippines,' *Women's Role in Philippine History: Selected Essays*, University Centre for Women's Studies, University of the Philippines, Quezon City.

Tapales, Proserpina Doming 1992 'Filipino women in politics and public affairs: activism in the patriarchal system,' *Filipino Women and Public Policy* ed. Proserpina Domingo Tapales, Kalikasan Press, Manila.

Torres, Amaryllis T. ed. 1995 *The Filipino Woman in Focus: A Book of Readings*, University of the Philippines, Quezon City.

Torrevillas, Domini M. 1996 'Violence against Filipina OCWs: the Flor Contemplacíon and Sarah Balabagan cases,' *Filipino Women Migrant Workers: At the Crossroads and Beyond Beijing*, eds. Ruby Beltran and Gloria F. Rodriguez, Giraffe Books, Quezon City.

7 Indonesian women: from *Orde Baru* to *Reformasi*

Kathryn Robinson

Anthropology RSPAS
Australian National University

May 21 1998, the day that President Suharto announced an end to his 32-year Presidency, has achieved an almost mystical potency. On that day Indonesia entered an era of reform—*reformasi*—which promises a dismantling of the apparatus of authoritarian rule that had characterised the New Order (the self-descriptor of the Suharto regime). Student demonstrations at the national parliament were the immediate catalyst for change. These actions elevated the symbolic importance of the legislature as a seat of people's power (in contrast to its role as a captive of executive authority under the New Order) (see Forrester and May 1999 for a discussion of these events). Students—or more generally youth—have had a role as political actors in Indonesia from the days of the struggle for independence. Furthermore, the mobilising of a particular 'interest group' was in accord with the ideology of the New Order, which required political participation by individuals as members of 'functional groups' that were formally organised by the state as people's organisations (for women, farmers, workers and youth). The social role of women (as wives and mothers) had been valorised as a basis of the authoritarian power of the New Order (Robinson 1994).

139

Women were active in the demonstrations at the parliament. Prior to these events, women's groups had already been involved in protests about the damaging effects of the 1997 monetary crisis (which precipitated the political crisis) for the mass of the people. For example, the group *Suara Ibu Peduli* (Voice of Concerned Mothers) had organised the distribution of milk and other basic commodities to the worst affected, and had held several well publicised demonstrations protesting at the rising prices for basic commodities. They invoked the valorisation of women as mothers (used by the New Order for repressive ends), stressing the important role of women as providers of basic livelihood for their families. During the occupation of the Parliament, women supplied logistic support, especially by providing the demonstrators with food. Echoing the role played by women in the struggle for independence, other women drove ambulances to collect the wounded during the days of rioting and protest in mid-May. Activist women at the parliament organised themselves into a new political coalition, the *Koalisi Perempuan Indonesia untuk Keadilan dan Demokrasi* (Coalition of Indonesian Women for Justice and Democracy), to address the issue of women's rights in the hoped-for democratic political reform. Publicly announced on 20 May 1998, this group brought together individual women, and activist groups, which had been involved in an increasing volume of activism around issues of women's rights in the last decade of Suharto's rule (see Robinson 1998a).

Women's activism was galvanised by the revelations of the rapes of Chinese women as part of the political terror of the May riots. Throughout Indonesia, women condemned the violence. For example, some Muslim women's organisations refused to endorse the suggestion that the attacks on Chinese women were part of a *jihad* (holy war) understanding it as an attack by men on women. The analysis which has wide circulation among women's organisations is that women are used as instruments of terror in war, and the parallels of the rapes associated with 'ethnic cleansing' in the former Yugoslavia have not been lost on them.

Public discussion of the rapes (the reality of which were contested at the time by members of the government, including the Minister for Women's Affairs, Tutty Alawiyah) has created a new space for discussions about the situation of women in Indonesia. Public discussion of the issue of violence against women had been muted as it ran counter to the prevailing gender ideology of the New Order, and the ideology of social harmony which that supported (see below). The reform of gender relations is very much on the agenda for women in post-Suharto Indonesia—but the implications of the reform of gender ideology and gender relations go far beyond the specific realm of relations between men and women. They reach right to the heart of the authoritarian character of the state.

This chapter will review the consequences of New Order policies for Indonesian women. The homogenising imperatives of state policy contrast with the diversity of women's lives throughout the archipelago. Women have been largely absent from the accounts of the New Order and its policies (Blackburn 1991), including recent research on the growth of the middle class, which looked for the possible catalysts for change under conditions of capitalist development in the 'Asian Tigers' (see Robinson 1997). This chapter will map out some of the directions of change for women in the current climate of *reformasi*. The recent events in Indonesia have underscored the importance of giving credence to women as political actors, as both subjects and agents of change.

The gender order of the New Order

New Order policies for women have been characterised by the promotion of gender difference, with officially sanctioned images of femininity locating Indonesian women as subordinate to men within the family and the State. Formally, women's citizenship is defined in terms of their difference from men, within the notion of *kodrat* (biologically determined difference) and their primary civic duties are performed in their roles as wives and mothers (see Robinson 1994). A gendered model of political authority with its origins in an imagined tradition of a patriarchal family is a cornerstone of the repressive ideology that has underpinned the New Order. Consequent repressive and restrictive representations of women and circumscribed roles in social life have been part and parcel of the dominant forms of the Indonesian political system (Robinson 1994). The polity was theorised as resting on the family foundation (*azas kekeluargaan*) which put collective above individual good, and required 'democracy with leadership' (McDonald 1980, p. 95), leadership understood implicitly as the 'natural authority' of the father. Thus, the patriarchal family has been invoked as the basis of authority relations within society, and the family at the core of the state has been institutionalised. President Suharto was known as *Bapak Pembangunan* (the father of development) and civil servants also use the familial form of address (Father-*Bapak*) to their (usually male) superiors (see Suryakusuma 1996; Sunindyo 1998).

Women are enjoined, as citizens, to carry out their wifely and motherly duties. These values have been 'socialised' through their incorporation into

official women's organisations. Indonesia has a long history of women's
organisations (see Vreede de Stuers 1960; Wieringa 1988). The major
factions of the nationalist movement, which were the basis of parties in the
post-independence period, had women's sections, and they had been
meeting together in National Congress of Women since 1928. (The
anniversary of this date is celebrated as Mother's Day.)

In its attempt to impose a repressive order on the nation, the new
regime banned mass organisations in the villages. Village women's
organisations were incorporated within the new state organised women's
groups (the Family Welfare Movement or PKK) (see Sullivan 1983).
Underpinning state power, they were politically controlled by the
Ministry of Home Affairs, and organised to propagate the state ideology
of natural patriarchal authority in the family that entrenched women's
subordinate status. Civil servants' wives nation-wide are required to join
a hierarchical organisation called *Dharma Wanita*, their position in its
structure reflecting the position of their husband in the state bureaucracy.
In the official women's organisations (in the manner identified by Yuval-
Davis 1994) women's relations in the private domain determine their
status in the public domain.

New Order gender ideology, in rendering the family as a cornerstone
of the nation, and a particular model of gender relations as a microcosm
for the power relations in the state, imposed a homogenising vision of
women on the peoples of the archipelago. There is, however, a wide
diversity in women's social participation, in family systems and juridical
rights, and in the cultural construction of gender difference in the
cultures of the archipelago. The following section will outline some
parameters of these differences.

Gender diversity in Indonesia

In spite of the oft repeated claims concerning the high status of women in
island Southeast Asia, there are still limited studies which rigorously
investigate the 'position of women' in the various societies of the
archipelago (Errington 1990, p. 3). Dube's (1997) review of gender and
kinship reminds us of the significance of systems of reckoning descent,
residence customs, marriage practices and inheritance for the relative social
positions of men and women, and their capacity to make choices
concerning their own lives and those of others.

While a variety of principles of social organisation are found throughout
the archipelago, Dube focuses on the 'ego-centred bilateral kinship with
variations in its inclination towards matrilineality and matrilocality

[characteristic of much of Indonesia] that does not seem to have the compulsive character that the patrilineal, patri-virilocal pattern [which she finds dominant in South Asia] has' (1997, p. 7). The Javanese are the most numerous cultural group in Indonesia and they have a bilateral kinship system (as do most of the peoples of South Sulawesi where I have conducted research). In such social orders, the male and female lines are of equal import, in terms of reckoning relatedness, but also usually in terms of inheritance.

In bilateral societies, there does not tend to be a marked preference for male over female children, the ideal family including at least one of each. There is none of the sense one gets in patrilineal societies that girls are 'thrown away'. Whereas male children leave their natal homes to make their mark on the world, it is assumed that female children will stay near to their parents and support them in their old age. A tendency to uxorilocal residence in some of these bilateral societies reinforces this. For example, I found that in the South Sulawesi village of Soroako, it was assumed that the youngest daughter and her husband would live with her parents and take responsibility for them, and eventually inherit the house.

Principles of social organisation are not immutable, and coexist with other ideological systems that attempt to regulate personal and social life. Islam has been taking root in Indonesia since the fifteenth century, and Islamic principles of inheritance, favouring men, are in conflict with more gender-equal customs in many places. There can be a difference of interest between men and women in this regard, with women championing traditional principles, and the men Islamic principles. (This has been noted in South Sulawesi, for example). For the matrilineal Minangkabau of West Sumatra, men and women inherit through the female line (for example, from mother's brother to sister's son). However, there is evidence that some men try to subvert matrilineal principles by passing land to their sons, and this is made possible by the complexity introduced to the system by the commodification of land (van der Meer 1997).

Uxorilocal residence after marriage, where the new husband takes up residence in the wife's parent's home, until the couple established an independent dwelling house, is a common feature of some bilateral societies as well as the matrilineal Minangkabau. Contrast this with the situation of the new bride in patrilineal Bali, who most usually goes to live in the house compound of her husband and his kin, where she joins other in-marrying women (who can all be strangers). Balinese women prefer to marry a close affine as it promises a smoother transition. However, many cannot exercise this option, and go to live among strangers. If the marriage fails, the children belong to the husband's group, and the wife may have to relinquish them. Such differences are not just formal. They have profound significance for the power relations of everyday life, and in the practice of everyday affairs. The uxorilocally dwelling husband is likely to establish economic partnerships with his wife's kin, for example, by working his parents-in-law's land. After the wedding, it is the new husband who is the stranger, who creeps around self-consciously, while the wife lives almost as before in the home she grew up in. In the case of marriage break up, in bilateral societies, the children generally stay with the mother. For ordinary people in bilateral societies, there is not a strong notion of father-right.

The kin terminological systems in these societies tend to stress differences of generation, while gender is not always terminologically distinguished. That is, people are referred to by terms meaning sibling, cousin, grandparent, grandchild, which are often not gender specific. For example, in Soroako, South Sulawesi there is only a single term for spouse. Teknonymy (the practice whereby an adult is referred to as the mother/father or grandparent of the first-born child) reinforces this stress on generation. In terms of gender ideology, teknonymy also valorises parenthood as the basis of adult social identity or personhood. It does so in a way that transcends an assumption of the association of women with reproduction as being some kind of natural basis of gender difference (see also Errington 1990, p. 17 for a discussion of bodies and personhood).

These bilateral systems of social organisation contrast with what Errington characterises as the 'Exchange Archipelago' in eastern Indonesia and parts of Sumatra:

> The social organisation of these societies is very complex, but the gist of it is that the entire system of marital exchanges they practice is predicated on the distinction between male and female, and the fact that women must leave their natal Houses (social groupings) in order to marry men who are not their 'brothers' (Errington 1990, p. 39).

These societies are also characterised by cultural systems

> ...in which dualisms of every sort pervade ritual and everyday life' ...[and] a rhetoric of gender could be used to characterise 'male and 'female' cosmic energies, roles, activities, functions in a particular society, but without a presumption that they either reflect or are anchored in physical differences between men and women, or that the sexed bodies of individual men and women are required to fulfil or enact those roles. The ties between physical sex and gendered energies may be much looser than we usually imagine them to be (Errington 1990, p. 18).

Errington wants to go beyond questions of social organisation and relate the differential power related to gender differences to ideas of power in a broader sense. Western commentators have seized on women's economic participation, and their apparent relative economic autonomy in the region as one of the indices of their social power. Errington, however, is critical of the limited notion of power in western thought, which takes it for granted as a 'secular relation between people' (1990, p. 41). The idea of spiritual potency and its connection with power is widespread throughout the archipelago, and she links this to the question of gender differences:

> ...[W]omen in many of these societies are assumed to be more calculating, instrumental, and direct than men, and their very control of practical matters and money, their economic 'power' may be the opposite of the kind of 'power' or spiritual potency that brings the greatest prestige; it may assure them of lower rather than higher prestige...to pull out of context their economic and instrumental power and to designate it as the most important factor in high prestige is to create an optical illusion based on the importation of Eurocentric ideas about the relations of power and prestige (Errington 1990, p. 7).

Thus, women's place in the prestige system has to be understood in terms of their access to and ability (or lack of) to control sources of spiritual potency. In a related argument, Millar (1983) (who like Errington worked with Bugis people in South Sulawesi) sees prestige and power arising on the basis of presumed divine descent which outweighs the power arising on the basis of gender.

Sullivan makes an argument similar to Errington's when she refutes the claim that women's control of household finances is a source of power— money is low prestige (*kasar*) (Sullivan 1994). Hatley (1990) and Keeler (1990) similarly stress the ideological devaluing of women and the feminine in Java. Women are regarded as having lower prestige because they are held to be less able to control their 'animal' passions and to succeed in the ascetic practices associated with the control of spiritual power. Hence they are associated with material actions, such as maintaining household finances. (A similar argument was presented by Djajadiningrat-Nieuwenhuis' 1987 model for the bases of women's power in modernising Indonesia). But, ideological systems are complex and not always seamless. Brenner complicates the understanding of the bases of gendered power in pointing out that, in the case of the Javanese there is a countervailing ideology, one which is encountered just as frequently. This suggests that women of necessity control the household purse because men are less able to control their baser passions, and are likely to spend money irresponsibly, on gambling, drinking or other women (1995, p. 80).

While Errington focuses on gender as 'a cultural system of practices and symbols implicating both women and men' (1990, p. 3), Ong and Peletz (1995, p. 2) focus on the 'need to continuously negotiate and invent' forms of identity in postcolonial Southeast Asia:

[I]ndigenous notions bearing on masculinity and femininity, on gender equality and complementarity, and on various criteria of prestige and stigma are being reworked in the dynamic postcolonial contexts of outmigration, nation building, cultural nationalism and international business (1995, p. 2).

The homogenising imperative of the New Order definitions of appropriate gender roles mask profound differences in the patterns of gender relations and in gender ideologies found throughout the archipelago. They also mask the manner in which gender intersects with other bases of power, such as spiritual potency, but also with other principles of social differentiation such as generation or class. This intersection of gender and class was exposed in Stoler's classic paper (1977) which argued that women's social power in Java derives from their family's control of resources rather than simply their gender. The homogenising of gender definitions also masks the 'renegotiations and inventions' occurring as a consequence of New Order economic strategies, which have sought integration with the global economy. The positioning in the global economic order has been accomplished through an authoritarian political system and has been accompanied by global cultural flows, which all have had consequences for constructions of femininity.

Marriage law

Within the modernising regime of the New Order, the 'private' aspects of women's lives have been brought very firmly into the state arena. The state is now challenging the claims of other dominant ideologies—in particular Islam, but also local cultural traditions—to have pre-eminent rights in the regulation of personal and family relations. This was evident in the conflict over the introduction of a secular marriage law in the early days of the New Order. In the face of stringent opposition from religious groups, particularly Islam that challenged the right of the state to intervene in matters of personal life, the New Order government pushed though a new secular marriage law in 1974. This law established a minimum age for marriage, promised women protection from marriage against their will, and gave women the same rights to initiate divorce as their husbands (Soewando 1977). However, in the case of citizens professing Islamic faith, divorce was still to be handled by religious courts. In another move to strengthen the rights of women vis-à-vis men, men were forbidden to take second wives without the permission of the first wife. This law was, on the surface, the act of a secular, modernising regime, continuing the agenda of nationalist groups that aimed to weed out feudalism from the realm of personal relations as well as from society at large. Indeed, the introduction of a secular marriage law was one of the principle demands of the first congress of Indonesian women's organisations, held in 1928 (see Vreede de Stuers 1960).

In many ways, the law exemplifies the contradictions of the New Order. While apparently giving voice to the liberal sentiments of the nationalist movement, it was in fact supporting the population control agenda of the New Order through the family planning program. This initiative, as much as any other, symbolised the shift from the radical nationalism of the Sukarno regime (the Old Order). The marriage law enshrines the notion of the husband as the head of the family and the wife as the keeper of the household. Official data collection is based on the presumption of a male household head. This is regardless of local practices, in which, for example older women have social power. During fieldwork in Soroako, I knew old women, especially widows who were significant, or even principal decision-makers in issues such as the disposition of land, or the family response to a proposal of marriage for one of their grand-daughters. Such women appeared in official documents as living in households headed by their sons, even when the latter were young unmarried men with no authority. Men are always the representatives of the household in dealing with the state (except in the context of official women's organisations). For example, in the case of a water supply project in Lombok (which I reviewed for the foreign donor in 1989), despite the fact that the principle users of water were women, the official members of Water User Groups, who were deemed responsible for the maintenance of facilities on a daily basis, were all male—the household heads. In practice, the maintenance of the facilities was organised informally by the women, side-stepping the inappropriate organisational initiatives of the local government.

What have been the consequences of the new law? In the past thirty years, there has been a rise in the age at marriage for men and women so dramatic as to be termed a 'revolution' by one commentator (Jones 1994, p. 61), but this cannot be attributed to legislative change. There are many relevant factors, including the expansion of primary school education and the opening of new employment opportunities for women (see Jones 1994). While differential power exists between men and women, and between generations, it is difficult for young women living at home to refuse their parents' request for them to marry a particular young man. Similarly it is difficult for a woman to refuse her husband's request for her agreement to his taking a second wife. However, the new law is in circulation as part of public discourse, providing a powerful sanction for young people who wish to exercise their choice of a marriage partner. Also, economic changes which put resources in the hands of young people rather than the old provide a material basis for the exercise of free choice (Robinson 1986). (This is not to say that arranged marriage is always negative for women— see the discussion of the sexualisation of culture below)

A curious sequela of the new Marriage Law has been an attempt to limit the rights of civil servants to polygamous marriages even further. Probably as a consequence of women in *Dharma Wanita* lobbying the President's wife in 1983, the President ordered that civil servants required the permission of their superior before taking a second wife (Suryakusuma 1996). Logsdon noted that this instruction, intended to strengthen the vulnerable position of these women as dependent spouses in fact made them more vulnerable to their husbands in that it provided an incentive for men to engage in clandestine relationships with other women (1985, p. 87). Also, if the civil servant's wife requests divorce, for reasons other than that he has taken a second wife, she forfeits any claim on his wage (Logsdon 1985, p. 86). Logsdon commented that this would force women to stay in unhappy unions.

Her comments have been born out in subsequent years. There are frequent reports of high ranking men having illicit second wives, including news reports of cases in which an abandoned second 'wife' makes public demands to have the man (who has often fathered several children) continue to support them. The state ideology encourages civil servants' official wives to be 'career wives', supporting their husbands in their careers. Their time is absorbed in the activities of the official women's organisation, thus increasing their economic vulnerability should the marriage fail.

New Order social policy

The Indonesian constitution of 1945, still the legal and frequently invoked symbolic basis of the political system, guarantees all citizens equal rights regardless of sex. Women and men benefited equally from some of the material improvements in the term of the New Order until the onset of the monetary crisis at the end of 1997. Increases in average per capita income (from US$70 in 1969 to US$835 in 1994 [UNICEF 1995, p. 3]) are reflected in an increase in average life expectancy, from 59.8 in 1986 to 63.48 in 1995 (Republik Indonesia 1996, p. 67). The average life expectancy for women rose from 54 in 1976 to 65.31 in 1993 (Republik Indonesia 1996, p. 7 and p. 66). The Suharto regime used the windfall profits from the oil price rise in the mid-1970s to fund an expansion of social infrastructure, in particular the building of primary schools and health centres. Under Presidential instruction, the schools were built in even remote villages, and more teachers were trained to staff them. A minimum of six years compulsory schooling was introduced in 1973. This resulted in a dramatic increase in school participation rates; by 1995, 94 per cent of boys and girls aged 7–12 were in primary school, up from 83 per cent in 1980 (Republik Indonesia 1996, p. 10). Women's organisations at village level (The Family Welfare Movement or PKK) have been mobilised to establish integrated health posts (POSYANDU) in villages, which further extend the reach of health centres, especially in the delivery of maternal and child health services. Health centre staff travel out on a regular basis to these village posts. Where this works well, it has had dramatic effects on infant mortality rates which have almost halved in the period 1976 to 1995, from 109 per 1000 births to 55 per 1000 births (Republik Indonesia 1996, p. 65). The decline has been uneven nationally, however: in the poor eastern province of Nusa Tenggara Timur, for example, the rates were 70 per 1000 live births for girls and 85 per 1000 live births for boys in 1994. Maternal mortality remains high. At 425 per 100 000 births (Republik Indonesia 1996, p. 66), it is amongst the highest in the ASEAN region. The government set a target of 225 deaths per 100 000 births by 1998 (UNICEF 1995, p.7), but the economic crisis has now made it unlikely that this will be achieved. In the current political climate, which has seen women challenging many of the old assumptions about their social participation, the high maternal mortality rate is regarded by some women as an indication of deep underlying gender inequity or injustice, or even an underlying systemic violence against women.

Family Planning is another New Order social program that has won international accolades due to its achievement of high rates of contraceptive use. While the radical nationalist regime of Sukarno (immediately following independence) regarded Indonesia's growing population as a basis of strength, the rationalising economic doctrine of the New Order saw the checking of population growth as a precursor of economic growth. Hence a state sponsored program for the distribution of modern contraceptives was introduced in 1970. The program promotes the idea that women express responsible citizenship by controlling their fertility and having only two well-spaced children.

While notionally the 'targets' of the program are fertile married couples (*pasangan usia subur*, or PUS) in practice it is mainly female methods which are promoted, and the acronym PUS is generally used by family planning workers as a shorthand label for their female clients. Prevalence of contraceptive use (both traditional and modern) has grown from 47.7 per cent in 1987 to 57.4 per cent in 1997 (Haryanto 1998, pp. 1–2). Modern contraception has been enthusiastically embraced in the densely populated regions of Java and Bali, although it has been less successful in the poorer and less populated outer regions. In 1994, only 32 per cent of fertile married women in Nusa Tenggara Timur were using contraception, for example.

There is anxiety that many of the improvements in quality of life will be rapidly eroded by the monetary crisis. The government introduced nine years compulsory schooling in 1994, a goal which will be more difficult to achieve for girls than boys as high school attendance will often involve travel further from home than for primary school. The government has for the moment (1998–99) withdrawn the low compulsory school fees for primary school, but there is evidence that large numbers of children in the regions hardest-hit by the crisis are not attending school. There is anxiety about plummeting nutritional levels, as families struggle with rising food prices and shortages of basic commodities. There are fears that infant mortality rates will rise, and that it will be even more difficult to achieve improvements in maternal mortality. Health centres have been short of basic drugs, as the country lacks the foreign exchange to import pharmaceutical raw materials. The family planning program has been adversely affected by the lack of availability of the modern technical methods which people have come to depend on (Darmadi 1998; Wilopo et al. 1998).

Economic policies

The economic policies pursued by the New Order have transformed the social and economic participation of men and women in ways that contradict the prevailing state ideology that emphasised domestic roles for women. In the last three decades, Indonesia has successfully pursued an industrialisation strategy, focused particularly on light manufacturing. Agriculture as a share of GDP declined from 53.9 per cent in 1960 to 19.55 per cent in 1991, while manufacturing as a share of GDP climbed from 8.4 per cent to 21.3 per cent in the same period (Robison 1996, p. 79). The opening of new world market factories, producing clothing, textiles, footwear and electronics have been accompanied by rapid growth in the employment of women. According to the Central Statistics Bureau (*Biro Pusat Statitik* or BPS) figures, there has been an overall feminisation of Indonesia's industrial workforce in the period 1971–94. Out of 24 sectors for which longitudinal data is available, 19 evidence 'feminisation' (for example, in the clothing, textiles and footwear, lime and cement sectors). Only a few sectors have experienced 'masculinisation'. These include paper and paper products, chemicals and the declining rubber industry (Biro Pusat Statistik 1997). This largely feminised industrial work force has been a new element in the Indonesian economy. The world market factories have been the site of much industrial disputation, the most common cause being the failure of employers to pay legislated minimum wages and to recognise legislated workers rights (such as menstruation, maternity leave and breastfeeding breaks). The minimum wage is in practice the maximum wage, and women often work for wages below subsistence levels (The INGI Labour Working Group 1991, p. 5).

Activist women in Indonesia have been able to utilise UN declarations in their quest for changes in the policy treatment of women, in particular the Convention on Elimination of Discrimination Against Women (CEDAW), which Indonesia ratified in 1984 (although it still has no enabling legislation). It is also a signatory to the ILO (International Labour Organisation) convention on equal pay for equal work. However, one of the chief causes of industrial disputes in Indonesia is the failure of employers to pay legislated minimum wages. Activists have also been able to point to the Constitution that also guarantees women's equality. By tying their critique to CEDAW and the Indonesian government's reporting responsibility, they have been able to publicise the poor working conditions in factories (Robinson 1998a).

The problems in the industrial sector of the economy became symbolised in the person of Marsinah, a young woman factory worker and labour activist from Surabaya. In 1993, during an industrial dispute in her factory, Marsinah was found raped, tortured and murdered. Her killers have never been arrested (Waters 1993). Her bravery in struggling for workers' rights and the violent nature of her passing—generally regarded as an act of political intimidation by the military—have made her an important symbol of the repressive character of the New Order (see Sarumpaet 1998). Ratna Sarumpaet has written a play entitled 'Marsinah: a Song from the Underworld' which deals with the life and death of Marsinah. Sarumpaet has commented 'the way Marsinah was treated, her raped and mutilated body simply discarded in a forest, symbolised the deep, trivialising contempt which men, especially powerful men, feel towards women who dare to speak out' (Hatley 1998, p. 8).

Several studies have been published on the conditions and lives of young female industrial workers, and it has been argued that their entry into the workforce has had contradictory effects. On the one hand, they work under exploitative conditions, on the other hand, as wage earners they have a greater degree of independence in their families (Wolfe 1996; Mather 1983). In the context of the monetary crisis of the late 1990s, many of the factories that utilised this new feminised labour force have closed down, further limiting the employment possibilities for women. The work creation projects funded by overseas donors tend to be only for male workers (Darmadi 1998). In the situation of economic crisis, there is a real concern that women will be forced into even more exploitative forms of employment, such as in the sex industry.

Since the early 1980s rapidly increasing numbers of Indonesian workers, the majority of them women, have been seeking work overseas (see Hugo 1997, Robinson forthcoming). This is a consequence of the general greater opening of the Indonesian economy to the world economy. Women have been going to the Middle East, mainly to work as housemaids, and in more recent years, increasing numbers have been going to Hong Kong and Malaysia (see Hugo 1997, Robinson forthcoming). This issue first came to national prominence in 1984 as a consequence of public criticism of both the treatment of women workers in Saudi Arabia and the Indonesian government's handling of overseas labour recruitment. There were allegations of corruption and extortion by the labour recruiting agencies, and of mistreatment including long working hours, violence and sexual predation in Saudi Arabia. Under the Suharto regime, there was a refusal to acknowledge the problems being faced by the women, in spite of the activism of groups like *Solidaritas Perempuan* (Women's Solidarity for Human Rights) in promoting their case. The monetary crisis in Indonesia has led to an increase in workers seeking to go abroad, and in the new political climate of *reformasi*, there has been a new willingness to acknowledge the problems of Indonesians working overseas. The government has been trying (since late 1998) to implement a new agreement with the Saudi Arabian government, which would establish better protective mechanisms for Indonesian migrant workers, but the initiative is being resisted by the Saudi government.

Much has been written about the effects of New Order polices in agriculture, and consequences for women's labour in that sector. It has been argued that the New Order commitment to 'Green Revolution' technology in agriculture—high yielding hybrid varieties of rice seed which need massive fertiliser inputs and the protection of chemical pesticides—have had the consequence of displacing women's labour in agriculture. This result is clear in Java where most of the studies have been conducted. The new varieties have been accompanied by changes in harvesting technology, the replacement of the finger knife (*ani ani*) with the sickle, which has been accompanied by a change to the use of migrating bands of contract workers, usually male. Local labour, which included women, has thus been displaced. Similarly, the new rice lends itself to the use of mechanical rice hullers, which have replaced hand pounding of rice, formerly a source of employment for rural women. So even in agriculture, the preserve of family labour and personalised connections, there has been an increase in the use of waged labour that has been associated with marginalisation of women. Chris Manning has reviewed the evidence on women's labour and he concludes that while 'labour-augmenting technology generally favoured males' (1998, p. 247, n. 17) the overall trend in Java in the period 1971–90 is a 'slight tendency for females to increase their share of agricultural jobs. Returns to labour for women remained much lower for women than men, however (1998, pp. 245–46).

Manning further comments that although there has been a lot of attention to the opening up of manufacturing employment for women in Indonesia and East Asia generally, the 'increase in female share of service and trade sector employment' has been far more significant (1998, p. 245). Alexander (1987) and Jellinek (1976; 1978) discuss women traders, trading being an established area of women's economic participation. Women traders suffered from the tighter regulation of the informal sector, and regulations favouring the formal sector, under the New Order. Some of the expansion of women's involvement in the service sector is a consequence of the entry of educated women into the professions, including the expansion of employment in the civil service (see below). For less educated women, prostitution and domestic service are the most significant service sector occupations (Manning 1998, pp. 247–48).

In the early 1990s, women held approximately a third of Indonesian civil service positions. Although few women are in the highest levels of the public service, they are well represented in the middle ranks, particularly in the departments of education and health. Reflecting a pattern of sex segmentation of the work force found in industrialised societies, just over half of all primary school teachers and nearly a fourth of government doctors are women. Their prominence in public education and public health, which are managed and staffed by the central government helps explain why women are more strongly represented in national than in regional administration.

Many commentators have linked the economic growth engendered by the New Order to the growth of the middle class. The wealth generated by industrial expansion has led to an increase in consumer spending— the phenomena most studied in discussions of the New Middle Class (Robison 1996, Tanter and Young 1990). The growth of a culturally defined group united by consumption and lifestyle has been accompanied by a pressure on middle-class women to conform with an emerging middle-class ideology (see also Jayawardena 1986, p. 9) while capitalist development is also leading to the proletarianisation of women from lower strata. Hence, the period of the New Order has seen further fracturing of the presumed unity of women's roles. Some of the activism by women's groups that was a feature of the last few years of the Suharto regime, and the changes in official women's policy (see below), reflect the concerns of a middle class. These include a growing consciousness of issues of equity and political democracy, and encompass feminist concerns.

Political representation

Middle-class women have been at the forefront of demands for increased female representation in positions of political power. Since the 1995 Fourth World Conference on Women in Beijing, the issue of women's participation in the institutions of government has been more vocally addressed in the campaigns and publications of women's groups. For example, many of the contributions to the recent book edited by Oey-Gardiner et al. (1996), including the introduction to the volume emphasises women's role in decision making. This concern is also reflected in the recent government publication *Profil Kedudukan dan Peranan Wanita* (Profile of the Status and Role of Women) (Republik Indonesia 1996).

Women's representation in the institutions of the modern state remains low. In the early 1990s only 1.4 percent of village heads were female. There has been a slight increase in the number of female representatives in the national legislative bodies: the People's Consultative Assembly (DPR) and the People's Representative Council (MPR). In the MPR, the proportion of women representatives has risen from 5.5 per cent of the total in 1971, to 10.1 per cent in 1992. Can this be seen as empowerment of women? The Indonesian legislatures are circumscribed in their power—nonetheless, Indonesian women legislators (and activists) see increasing representation of women in the national and provincial legislatures as an important goal. It is regarded as valuable for its symbolic significance and also because they feel it gives them an opportunity to influence the manner in which government policies impact on women. There is no doubt of the passionate commitment of many Indonesian women to place the issue of gender equity on the political agenda, and it is common to hear them express quietly their sense of injustice at the manner in which they are treated by many men in public life. I have often heard middle-class women in public life express the view that a woman has to be twice as good as a man to succeed.

The 1997 election was the first in which women's issues became campaign issues (Sadli 1997). Representatives of all three parties contesting the elections (Fatimah Achmad of PDI—the Democratic party; Siti Hardianti Rukman of Golkar—the government party; and Aisyah Amini of PPP—the Islamic Party), all discussed the necessity of increasing women's participation in development programs in order to realise the officially sanctioned goal of gender equity (*kemitrasejajaran*, see below). They all pointed to the obstacles women faced in achieving equity in public and family life, including discrimination, cultural practices, and access to health and education. Fatimah Achmad presented the most sustained critique of the barriers facing women in their quest for greater social participation, focusing on their lack of power in both family and public life. She argued that legislation should be put in place to ensure women's enjoyment of the equal rights guaranteed by the 1945 constitution. She was also critical of the existing women's organisations for their failure to promote increased political participation by women. As I write, Indonesia is coping with the aftermath of the first elections since the fall of Suharto, held in June 1999. In the free flowing atmosphere of the 1999 elections, with 48 parties contesting seats, women's issues do not seem to be emerging on the party's platforms. The 'gladiatorial' aspect of the 1997 elections was the implicit struggle between the deposed leader of the PDI (Democratic Party), Megawati Sukarnoputri, and then President Suharto's daughter, Siti Hardianti Rukmana (known as Tutut) of Golkar. At one point in time, Tutut was being touted as a possible successor to her father, but her political star has waned with his decline. Megawati is regarded as a serious possibility for assuming the Presidency after the 1999 elections. She would appear to have been the indirect target of a campaign by some Islamic groups, in late 1998, who instigated a public debate concerning whether or not a female President was allowed according to Koranic prescriptions. The *Majelis Ulama,* or Council of Religious Scholars is preparing to deliver a *Fatwah* on the issue. The motive seems to be as much to curb the possibility of Megawati—a populist leader seen by many as the symbol of democratic reform—becoming president, as it is a concern for Islamic political values. Opinion has been divided amongst prominent Islamic figures, but in the 1999 campaign the two major Islamic leaders, Amien Rais and Abdurachman Wahid, announced an alliance with Megawati.

Sexuality and personal freedom

The dramatic social changes in Indonesian society resulting from the development strategy of the New Order government and the related opening of the archipelago to the global economy and culture have affected not only the manner of women's economic participation, but also the modes of expression of femininity. Women have become more able to make choices for themselves, as a consequence of both new economic roles and exposure to mass media images of differing norms of female behaviour. At the same time, however, the commercially driven circulation of sexual images and norms of sexual attractiveness and the growth in prostitution have created new opportunities for exploitation of women. Hence, the effects of these changes are contradictory.

The family planning program exemplifies the contradictory effects of policies that directly impact on constructions of masculinity and femininity. The program has had the consequence of separating sexuality from reproduction. On the one hand, increasing numbers of women are using contraception, enabling them to have intercourse without having to worry about pregnancy. The mainly female-focused birth control technologies—pills, IUDs, implants, injections—has made it easier for them to make reproductive decisions without consulting male partners, but at the same time has substituted the controls on personal life arising from kinship-based forms of power for those originating from the state. The program has made fertility control a woman's concern, with modern methods replacing traditional methods, which imposed disciplines and responsibilities on both women and men. But several decades of contraceptive use have also changed how women experience their own sexuality. One study, for example, found Balinese women increasingly likely to view their sexuality not within the context of family and motherhood but as an expression of their own personal freedom (Parker forthcoming). This consciousness was attributed in part to decades of widespread contraceptive use: Bali has had the highest contraceptive prevalence rate—71.9 percent in 1991—of any province in the country (Biro Pusat Statistik 1991, p. 109).

The growing importance of prostitution as a source of income for Indonesian women reflects not only economic changes but also the sexualisation of Indonesian culture that has accompanied modernity. The mining town of Soroako in South Sulawesi illustrates this tandem influence well. Mining work-forces are predominantly male. Like many mining companies in remote locations, the company in Soroako recruits sectors of the labour force on 'single status'—the company takes no responsibility for housing their families. The high proportion of single males in the community creates a market for bars and brothels. Employment opportunities for women are limited in mining towns, hence there are strong economic imperatives for women to become sex workers. Women are also drawn into commercial sexual arrangements as 'contract wives', who live with men for the duration of their man's contract. Murray (1991) describes similar arrangements between Indonesian women and expatriate men in Jakarta. In her study of sex workers, Murray disputes the official view that prostitution is the consequence of moral depravity. In Indonesia, prostitution is not criminalised and is dealt with by the social welfare system, not the criminal justice system. Sex workers are officially termed *wanita tuna susila*, women without morals. Murray argues that just as a woman may choose factory work as a means of escaping the economic and social constraints of village life, so might a woman choose sex work because she prefers it to working in a factory. Or there may be no alternative—the likelihood of this has risen as opportunities for employment in the informal sector have declined under government pressure to modernise petty commerce.

But the implications of sex work for Indonesian women are not unambiguously beneficial. Elite, high-income prostitutes are a small minority of all the women involved in the sex industry. The majority of sex workers face substantial risk to their health, from STDs including the rising risk of HIV/AIDS, as well as from alcohol and drug abuse. Women also face the threat of violence and intimidation from both clients and 'protectors'. I have heard accounts that suggest that sex workers' requests for clients to use condoms to protect sexual health is a common cause of violence against sex workers. It has been recently revealed that entrepreneurs frequently trick young women into sex work by pretending to be offering them jobs in restaurants. In some cases, the women have been kept against their will and denied access to money to prevent them from returning home. Many are young and inexperienced, and unable to negotiate the journey home (often over a long distance).

There is evidence that the number of sex workers has increased as a consequence of the economic crisis of the late 1990s. The informal sector, traditionally a site of 'family labour' has undergone a renaissance since the monetary crisis, as the formal sector shrinks. This development will also affect the kinds of opportunities available to Indonesian women. The growth in prostitution illustrates the impact of rising commercialisation and sexualisation, trends that in turn reflect the penetration of Indonesian society by global cultural flows, as well as capital flows. The impacts of new cultural forms have been contradictory and often in tension with official images and norms of femininity. These contradictory effects are well exemplified by the issue of free choice marriage. In the mining town of Soroako, a new kind of sexualised culture has manifested in the desire of the young for romantic love. In a community where marriage was once a family affair, the arrangement of a marriage by two families taking account of the need to establish a harmonious and economically viable household, the young are now in the grip of a desire for free choice marriage based on romantic love. The arranged marriages of their parents were based on a presumption that sexual passion followed the conclusion of the arranged marriage, rather than passion serving as the 'spark'. The young are able to exercise their choice because (due to economic changes) the old no longer control the resources necessary to conclude a marriage. This may be read as signalling some advance in personal autonomy in that it frees the sexuality of young men and women from kinship-based forms of power and control. But the shift to marriage choice based on romantic love can also be read as a form of self-subjugation, based on an enslavement to the values of the consumer market place, founded on a new model of sexualised femininity, which is promoted in magazines, on television and in film. The consequences of free choice marriage were all too clear to older women in Soroako, who may have entertained the idea of a love match, but settled for the partner of their parents' choice. They explained to me, if you followed your parents' will and the man turned out to be a bad husband, for example not supporting you and your children, the two sets of parents, as instigators of the match, had a responsibility to look after you. If you married according to your own will, you also had to live by the consequences of that decision. Ironically, in the contemporary situation where women had lost independent access to the means of production (land) the issues at stake were of even greater consequence than in the pre-capitalist economy (see Robinson 1998b). Under conditions of modernity, women may be increasingly freed from ties to the family and its reproduction, but they have simultaneously been introduced to new forms of subordination and exploitation.

New definitions of gender difference

Indonesia has actively participated in the series of international fora beginning with the 1975 Nairobi Conference in the International Decade for Women. During the 'Decade', the Indonesian government was responsive to the UN policy agenda, most notably in establishing the Ministry for Women's Affairs (*Menteri Peranan Wanita*) in 1978. Initially established as a Junior Ministry, it became a full State Ministry in 1983. Other policy initiatives have emerged out of this involvement in international organisations, for example the ratification of CEDAW referred to above. Another consequence of the 'Decade' was the inclusion of a chapter on women in the Broad Outlines of State Policy (*Garis Besar Haluan Negara* or GBHN). The 1978 version, the first to include a chapter on the Role of Women in Nation Building, identifies women's citizenship in terms of their status as wives and mothers. Changes to this document, produced every five years, have reflected the concerns articulated in the international arena.

During the period of the last five year plan (*Repelita* VI, 1995–99) there appears to have been a significant shift, to what Krishna Sen (1998) has termed 'the discovery of the woman worker'. This is particularly evidenced in a change in the wording of the section on women in the GBHN. The 1993 guidelines have a more comprehensive focus on women's economic roles (as opposed to their domestic roles and responsibilities) stressing the need to 'upgrade women's human resources', in particular increasing their capabilities in the areas of science and technology. This GBHN also introduced the new policy expressed in terms of the goal of men and women as equal partners (*mitra sejajar*) and a stress on the importance of women's role in decision making. In these changes policy makers refer to the clauses in the 1945 constitution, which acknowledges the equality of rights, duties and responsibilities of men and women as citizens. The language of gender equity is a new element (or perhaps more accurately a recovered element from earlier nationalist rhetoric) in official policy for women.

These initiatives have been accompanied by the development of new language for discussing relations between men and women. In particular the concept of *kemitrasejajaran* (officially translated as 'harmonious gender partnership', but assumed by women policy makers and activists as a rendering of the concept of gender equity), and the concept of gender (*jender*). *Pendekatan jender* (gender approach) have to an extent displaced the official language of *peranan wanita* (women's roles) in the discussion of relations between men and women in government documents. Ideally, officials in the Ministry of Women's Affairs hope that gender analysis, and the introduction of a mechanism for the more effective integration of women's programs in the regions (see below) will bring about 'mainstreaming' of gender polices and approaches in the current Five Year Plan. In terms of the importance of language noted by many commentators on New Order ideology, it is interesting that the term *mitra sejaajar* (derived from Sanskrit) is used as a gloss for 'equal relations'. Equally interesting, while the officially sanctioned women's organisations use the polite term *wanita* for women, the new organisations and publications are more likely to use the more down-to-earth *perempuan*.

The new language is particularly directed at government officials who are involved in the development and application of policy. The task of 'socialising' officials into this task is not an easy one. Recent research on the institutionalisation of these concepts (Raharjo and Robinson 1997) found little understanding of the concepts by people outside of the circles of government. This is not surprising as they tend to been used in discussions about policy, and only occasionally appear in this context in newspapers. The understanding was not much better among the officials charged with policy implementation, although many of them had at least heard the term *jender*. The information campaign by the Women's Ministry to develop public awareness of concepts like *kemitrasejajaran* do not seem to have had wide effects. There is outright hostility from many of the men charged with implementing the new policy direction. For example, Wijaya (1996) reports a hostility and trivialising of the issues of women's equality in the workplace by high level officials. A commonly expressed anxiety equated a movement for women's equality with 'men being ordered to wash the dishes'. On one level this is a somewhat paranoid and trivialising reaction, but at another level it is recognition of what is at stake in terms of the radical social change involved in a commitment to equality between the sexes.

Political violence and women

The latter decade of the Suharto regime saw the paradoxical flowering of NGOs including many organisations championing women's rights. Hence, as the movement for reform grew in the context of the monetary crisis, women's organisations were one of the community groups poised to take advantage of the new political climate. Women were involved in the demonstrations of May 1998 and the occupation of the Parliament building. The coalition of women's organisations that formed during the occupation (*Koalisi Perempuan Indonesia Untul Keadilan dan*

Demokrasi—(Coalition of Indonesian Women for Justice and Democracy) issued a proclamation calling, amongst other things, for Suharto to resign, and that he and his cronies be investigated and tried for corruption. They take credit for being first to demand that Suharto be tried for his crimes in office, a demand to which the government was eventually forced to respond. The women's group protested at the exclusion of women (and non-Muslims) from the political negotiations with the President, and they were critical of the male leaders of the reform movement, who they saw as too willing to compromise with the Suharto regime.

Women's groups galvanised around the issue of the rapes of Chinese women during the riots and looting which shook Jakarta on May 13 and 14 1998. Established NGOs, such as the women's organisation *Kalyanamitra* and the humanitarian organisation *Tim Relawan* (Volunteers for Humanity), became caught up in supporting the victims of the brutal and politically-motivated rapes of Chinese women. The victims were tortured and mutilated and many were killed—or died as a result of their injuries. The government initially denied the reports of rape, and the individuals and groups working to support the victims and document their cases were threatened. Many victims have been too frightened or ashamed to publicly declare their experience and seek justice. The new President, Habibie, was persuaded by a delegation of women activists and intellectuals to support a fact finding team. The occurrence of the rapes was undeniably documented by a team appointed to investigate the riots, although estimates of numbers vary, because of the reluctance of many victims to speak publicly about their ideal. Many have been supported to travel overseas for treatment after their experiences of indescribable violence and terrorisation.

Public discussion of the rapes (including the government's controversial initial denial) has had the effect of putting violence against women on the political agenda. The discussion of the May events were quickly followed by revelations of the use of rape in systematic violence by military personnel against civilians in the provinces of Aceh and Timor Timur, both of which have had long campaigns of armed resistance against the Indonesian state. While stories of these atrocities had been circulating for some time, they had never been the subject of public discussion in Indonesia and overseas. Women's organisations (in particular *Solidaritas Perempuan*—Women's Solidarity for Human Rights) had been trying for several years to have the government take action on the issue of the violence (rape and even murder) inflicted upon Indonesian housemaids employed in the Middle East, usually by their employers (see Robinson forthcoming). Following the emergence of violence as a key issue for women in the current crisis, the issue of the need to protect the rights of overseas migrant workers is also now receiving public (and government) attention. During October 1998, a television news bulletin reported the action of a group of former housemaids who had become pregnant as a consequence of being raped by their former Saudi employers. They demonstrated outside a labour supply organisation, demanding they fulfil a promise to give financial support for raising the children. On International Women's Day 1999, a group of former housemaids marched on the Ministry of Women's Affairs, demanding that the Indonesian government offer them more protection while they work abroad.

Women's groups are making the issue of violence a focal point of their activities. For example, on Human Rights Day (December 10) in 1998, there were large demonstrations by women in Jakarta, and other urban centres. They demanded action on the issue of violence, including not just the acts of war in the context of military repression, but also violence routinely experienced by women, for example at the hands of their husbands (*Jakarta Post* 26 November 1998). Women also demonstrated on the Anti Violence Against Women Day, on 25 November. For some women, the continuing high maternal mortality rates, and the evidence of duress in the Family Planning program, are included in their characterisation of systematic and institutionalised violence against women. Interestingly, *Dharma Wanita* (the official organisation for civil servants wives) and *Kowani* (the official national women's congress) joined with activists, women academics and NGO representatives to form the People Opposed to Violence Against Women (*Masyarakat Anti-Kekerasan terhadap wanita*). This alliance successfully lobbied the President on the issue of violence, in July 1998. President Habibie responded to their submissions by establishing a Commission to investigate violence against women, including the violence of May 1998, and has appointed leading women activists and scholars to this body. However, lack of funding has hampered its effectiveness.

Mothers Day (*Hari Ibu*) is celebrated as a national holiday in Indonesia. It is the day commemorating the anniversary of the first Indonesian Women's Congress, held by the women's sections of the nationalist organisations in 1928. Under the Suharto regime, the celebrations provided an opportunity to reinforce the duties of the 'citizen mother', rather than truly memorialising the agendas of those nationalist women (who argued for women's right to education, for their rights in marriage and so on) (see Robinson 1994, Suryakusuma 1996). The 1998 celebrations, the first in the period of reform, saw some radical departures from the New Order model. Many women's groups took the opportunity to raise the issue of institutionalised violence against women. Others took the opportunity to criticise the circumscribed models of femininity that had characterised the New Order, and to demand changes, including calls for the disbanding of *Dharma Wanita*. Also in December 1998, the Indonesian Women's Coalition (formed during the May occupation of Parliament) held a Congress in Jogjakarta. In 1999, Indonesian women for the first time celebrated International Women's Day (8 March), an international date that had not been acknowledged by the Suharto regime. Street marches highlighted the issue of violence against women and this was also the date chosen by the former migrant workers for their march on the Ministry of Women's Affairs, mentioned above.

Conclusion

In recent years, political scientists and political commentators have focussed primarily on the issues of the future direction for Indonesia, in particular analysing the significance of the development of a 'middle class' as a consequence of the erstwhile spectacular economic growth. There is considerable debate as to whether the growth of a middle class will necessarily be associated with the growth of civil society and demands on the state for greater political freedom and influence. The term 'middle class' is itself

> much used and little defined often referring only to consumption patterns. It is used by commentators in relation to distinct social categories which can be differentiated in class terms, including an emergent bourgeoisie (McVey 1994, p. 12, n. 6).

Analyses of the middle class have not specifically addressed gender relations as a dynamic factor in Indonesian society and the Indonesian polity.

The state bureaucrats are an important group within the emergent middle class in Indonesia (see Crouch 1994): 'They have emerged in a social vacuum as a discrete political stratum and, in many cases, are the appropriators of the state apparatus' (Robison 1995, p. 80). The development of official policy in relation to women, in particular the official commitment to gender equity can be seen to arise on the basis of feminist initiatives which are closely tied to the growing demands of the Indonesian middle class. In particular the demand for the kinds of freedoms associated with the development of civil society—for the protection and promotion of individual rights. These are the women who participate in the international meetings and in international women's networks. Middle-class women are involved in the growing number of NGOs with gender interests. They have raised issues such as the situation of women workers, and have put issues such as violence against women and harassment in the work place on the public agenda. As well as including a number of class groups (such as the emerging bourgeoisie, and bureaucrats) the middle classes are comprised of many ethnic and religious groups. These differences are reflected in the positions that sections of the middle class take on women's issues. For example, Islamic women's groups and some of the secular feminist NGOs would take different positions on the cultural construction of gender (one embracing the veil, the other jeans and t-shirts). Nonetheless, they are united in a commitment to a political championing of women's rights (see Istiadah 1994, esp. pp. 9–11).

The current public debates about women's roles reflect changes in the social participation of women that in part are a consequence of the economic program of the New Order. Some of these changes are unintended consequences of economic policies such as industrialisation and the broad pursuit of economic growth. There is some suggestion, for example, that the urban middle classes are becoming (as in countries like Australia) two income families of necessity, due to rising real estate prices and increasing consumer expectations. (This is a group that has been hard hit by the economic crisis—it is not unusual for both jobs to disappear.) But the changes are also the result of conscious interventions by bureaucrats and NGOs. In Indonesia we see the effects of the international discourse on rights in spreading new constructions of human rights. While international fora (like the International Women's Conferences, or the ILO), are agents for disseminating the discourse of human rights, these ideas are not altogether new in Indonesia, and have historic roots in the struggle for independence. Nationalist organisations formed a vision of what a free society might be, a vision which was in some measure reflected in the policies of the period of liberal democracy (to 1957).

Indonesia is currently undergoing dramatic changes as reformers attempt to seize the moment and create an Indonesia in an image of democracy. The forces of the old New Order have been vanquished in the short term, but still exert massive economic and political power. The entrenchment of a particular model of family relations and gender order was fundamental to the exercise of political power in Suharto's Indonesia. The reform of gender relations is very much on the agenda in contemporary Indonesia. It is an issue that is not just important for women, but is crucial to the shape of the Indonesia of the future.

Sections of this paper are based on previously published work, especially Robinson 1994 and 1998 (in the journal *Communal/Plural*) and Robinson 1997 (in *RIMA*).

References and recommended readings

Alexander, J. 1987 *Traders and Trading in Rural Java*, Oxford University Press, Singapore.

Biro Pusat Statistik 1991 *Indikator Sosial Wanita Indonesia*, Jakarta.

—— 1997 'Profil statistik buruh dan trend gender dalam industri pengolahan yang sedang dan besar menurut sektor dan gender,' *Jurnal Perempuan*, Edition 3 May/June, p. 86.

Blackburn, S. 1991 'How gender is neglected in Southeast Asian politics,' *Why Gender Matters in Southeast Asian Politics*, ed. M. Stivens, Monash Papers on Southeast Asia 23, Centre of Southeast Asian Studies Monash University, Clayton.

—— 1994 'Gender interests and Indonesian democracy,' *Democracy in Indonesia: 1950's and 1990's*, eds D. Bourchier and J. Legge, Centre of Southeast Asian Studies, Monash University, Clayton, Victoria.

Blackwood, E. 1995 'Senior women, model mothers, and dutiful wives: managing gender contradictions in a Minangkabau village,' *Bewitching Women, Pious Men: Gender and Body Politics in Southeast Asia*, eds A. Ong and M. G. Peletz, University of California Press, Berkeley

Brenner, S. A. 1995 'Why women rule the roost: rethinking Javanese ideologies of gender and self-control,' *Bewitching Women, Pious Men: Gender and Body Politics in Southeast Asia*, eds A. Ong and M. G. Peletz, University of California Press, Berkeley.

Crouch, H. 1994 'Democratic prospects for Indonesia,' *Democracy in Indonesia: 1950's and 1990's*, eds D. Bourchier and J. Legge, Centre of Southeast Asian Studies, Monash University, Clayton, Victoria.

Darmadi, C. 1998 'Women do it tough,' *Inside Indonesia*, October–December, pp. 26–27.

de Vreede, S. 1960 *The Indonesian Woman: Struggles and Achievements*, Mouton, The Hague.

Djajadiningrat-Nieuwenhuis, M. 1987 'Ibuism and priyayization: path to power?' *Indonesian Women in Focus: Past and Present Notions*, eds E. Locher-Scholten and A. Niehof, Foris Publications, Dordrecht-Holland/Providence-USA.

Dube, L. 1997 *Women and Kinship: Perspectives on Gender in South and South-East Asia*, United Nations University Press, Tokyo.

Errington, S. 1990 'Recasting sex, gender, and power: a theoretical and regional overview,' *Power and Difference: Gender in Island Southeast Asia*, eds J. M. Atkinson and S. Errington, Stanford University Press, Stanford.

Forrester, Geoff and May, R.J. 1999. *The Fall of Soeharto*, Select Books, Singapore.

Haryanto, R. 1998 'Arah kebijaksanaan dan prioritas penelitian untuk pelembagaan norma keluarga kecil bahagia sejahtera.' Paper to the conference Pembangunan manusia berkelanjutan di masa krisis, on October 20–21, LIPI (Indonesian Institute of Sciences) Jakarta.

Hatley, B. 1990 'Theatrical imagery and gender ideology in Java,' *Power and Difference: Gender in Island Southeast Asia*, eds J. M. Atkinson and S. Errington, Stanford University Press, Stanford.

—— 1998 'Ratna accused, and defiant,' *Inside Indonesia*, July–September, pp. 7–8.

Hugo, G. 1997 'Changing patterns and processes of population mobility in Indonesia,' *Indonesia Update: Population and Human Resources*, eds G. W. Jones and T. H. Hull, Australian National University and Institute of Southeast Asian Studies, Canberra and Singapore.

Istiadah 1994 'Muslim women in contemporary Indonesia: investigating paths to resist the patriarchal system,' Working Paper no. 91, Monash University, Melbourne.

Jayawardena, K. 1986 *Feminism and Nationalism in the Third World*, Zed Books, London.

Jellinek, L. 1976 *The Life of a Jakarta Street Trader*, Monash University Papers on Southeast Asia, no. 9, Melbourne.

—— 1978 *The Life of a Jakarta Street Trader: Two Years Later*, Monash University Papers on Southeast Asia, no. 13, Melbourne.

Jones, G. W. 1994 *Marriage and Divorce in Islamic South-East Asia*, Oxford University Press, Kuala Lumpur.

Keeler, W. 1990 'Speaking of gender in Java,' *Power and Difference: Gender in Island Southeast Asia*, eds J. M. Atkinson and S. Errington, Stanford University Press, Stanford.

Krier, J. 1995 'Narrating herself: power and gender in a Minangkabau woman's tale of conflict,' *Bewitching Women, Pious Men: Gender and Body Politics in Southeast Asia*, eds A. Ong and M. G. Peletz, University of California Press.

Logsdon, M. G. 1985 'Women civil servants in Indonesia: some preliminary observations,' *Prisma*, no. 37, pp. 77–87.

Manning, C. 1998 'More women in the workforce: regress or progress?' *Indonesian Labour in Transition: An East Asian Success Story?* Cambridge University Press, Cambridge.

Margold, J. A. 1995 'Narratives of masculinity and transnational migration: Filipino workers in the Middle East,' *Bewitching Women, Pious Men: Gender and Body Politics in Southeast Asia*, eds A. Ong and M. G. Peletz, University of California Press, Berkeley.

Mather, C. E. 1983 'Industrialization in the Tangerang Regency of West Java: women workers and the Islamic patriarchy,' *Bulletin of Concerned Asian Scholars*, vol. 13, no. 2, April–June, pp. 2–17.

McDonald, H. 1980 *Suharto's Indonesia*, Fontana/Collins, London.

McVey, Ruth 1994 'The case of the disappearing decade,' *Democracy in Indonesia: 1950's and 1990's*, eds D. Bourchier and J. Legge, Centre of Southeast Asian Studies, Monash University, Clayton, Victoria.

Millar, S. B. 1983 'On interpreting gender in Bugis society,' *American Ethnologist*, vol. 10, no. 3, pp. 477–493.

Murray, A. J. 1991 *No Money, No Honey: A Study of Street Traders and Prostitutes in Jakarta*, Oxford University Press, Singapore.

Oey-Gardiner, M., Wagemann, M.L.E. et al., eds 1996 *Perempuan Indonesia: Dulu dan Kini*, Penerbit PT Gramedia Pustaka Utama, Jakarta.

Ong, A. and Peletz, M. G. 1995 'Introduction,' *Bewitching Women, Pious Men: Gender and Body Politics in Southeast Asia*, eds A. Ong and M. G. Peletz, University of California Press, Berkeley.

Parker, L. (forthcoming) 'Fecundity and fertility decline in Bali,' *Borders of Being*, eds M. Jólly and K. Ram, Michigan University Press, Ann Arbor MI.

Peletz, M. G. 1995 'Neither reasonable nor responsible: contrasting representations of masculinity in a Malay society,' *Bewitching Women, Pious Men: Gender and Body Politics in Southeast Asia*, eds A. Ong and M. G. Peletz, University of California Press, Berkeley.

Raharjo, Y. and Robinson, K. 1997 'Wanita Dalam Pembangunan: Dua Kasus Dari Kawasan Timur Indonesia,' *Eastern Indonesia Population and Development Research Project Newsletter*, Jakarta, pp. 8–11.

Republik Indonesia 1996 *Profil Kedudukan dan Peranan Wanita Indonesia Tahun 1995*, Kantor Menteri Negara Urusan Peranan Wanita/Biro Pusat Statistik, Jakarta.

Robinson, K. 1986 *Stepchildren of Progress: The Political Economy of Development in an Indonesian Mining Town*, State University of New York Press, Albany.

—— 1987 'What price equality? Kartini's vision of the position of women in Indonesia,' *Mankind*, vol. 17, no. 2, pp. 104–14.

—— 1989 'Choosing contraception: cultural change and the Indonesian family planning program,' *Creating Indonesian Cultures*, ed. P. Alexander, Oceania Publications, Sydney.

—— 1994 'Indonesian national identity and the citizen mother,' *Communal/Plural*, vol. 3, pp. 65–82.

—— 1997 'Indonesian women: a survey of recent developments,' *Review of Indonesian and Malay Affairs*, pp. 141–62.

—— 1998a 'Indonesian women's rights, international feminism and democratic change,' *Communal/Plural*, vol. 6, no. 2, pp. 205–23.

—— 1998b 'Love and sex in an Indonesian mining town,' *Gender and Power in Affluent Asia*, eds K. Sen and M. Stivens, Routledge, London.

—— (forthcoming) 'Gender, Islam and nationality: Indonesian domestic servants in the Middle East,' *Home and Hegemony*, eds K. Adams and S. Dickey, Michigan University Press, Ann Arbor MI.

Robison, R. 1995 *The Emergence of the Middle Class in Southeast Asia*, Asia Research Centre on Social, Political and Economic Change, Murdoch University, WA.
—— 1996 'The middle class and the bourgeoisie in Indonesia,' *The New Rich in Asia: Mobile Phones, McDonalds and Middle Class Revolution*, eds R. Robison and D. Goodman, Routledge, London.
Sadli, S. 1997 'Politisi Wanita Berbicara tentang Wanita,' *Kompas*, 17 Juni, pp. 4–5.
Sarumpaet, R. 1998 'Marsinah accuses,' *Inside Indonesia*, July–September, p. 9.
Sen, K. 1998 'Indonesian women at work: reframing the subject,' *Gender and Power in Affluent Asia*, eds K. Sen and M. Stivens, Routledge, London.
Soewando, N. 1977 'The Indonesian Marriage Law and its implementation regulation,' *Archipel*, vol. 13.
Stoler, A. L. 1977 'Class structure and female autonomy in rural Java,' *Signs*, vol. 3, no. 1, pp. 74–89.
Sullivan, N. 1983 'Indonesian women in development: state theory and urban kampung practice,' *Women's Work and Women's Roles: Economics and Everyday Life in Indonesia, Malaysia and Singapore*, ed. L. Manderson, Development Studies Centre, Australian National University, Canberra.
—— 1994 *Masters and Mangers: A Study of Gender Relations in Urban Java*, Allen and Unwin, Sydney.
Sumardi, S. 1998 'Rape is rape,' *Inside Indonesia*, October–December 1998, pp. 19–20.
Sunindyo, S. 1998. 'When the earth is female and the nation is mother: gender, the armed forces and nationalism in Indonesia,' *Feminist Review*, no. 58, pp. 1–21.
Suryakusuma, J. I. 1996 'The state and sexuality in new order Indonesia,' *Fantasizing the Feminine in Indonesia*, ed. L. J. Sears, Duke University Press, Durham.
Tanter, R. and Young, K. eds 1990 *The Politics of Middle Class Indonesia*, Centre of Southeast Asian Studies, Monash University, Melbourne.
The INGI Labour Working Group 1991 'Button up, button down: women workers and overtime in Indonesia's garment and textile industry,' *Inside Indonesia*, June, pp. 5–6.
UNICEF 1995 *The Situation of Children and Women in Indonesia: A Summary*, Government of Indonesia? United Nations Children's Fund, Jakarta.
Vreede de Stuers, Cora 1960 *The Indonesian Woman: Struggles and Achievements*, Mouton, The Hague.
van der Meer, A. 1997 'Cultivating connections: kinship, land and labour strategies in a Minangkabau village,' PhD thesis, Department of Sociology and Anthropology, University of Newcastle.
Waters, B. 1993 'The tragedy of Marsinah: industrialisation and worker's rights,' *Inside Indonesia*, September, pp. 12–13.
Wieringa, S. 1988 'Aborted feminism in Indonesia: a history of Indonesian socialist feminism,' *Women's Struggles and Strategies*, ed. S. Wieringa, Gowers, Aldershot.

Wijaya, H. 1996 'Pelecahan dan tindak kekerasan terhadap perempuan di tempat kerja,' *Seminar Nasional: Perlindungan Perempuan dari Pelecahan dan Kekerasan Seksual*, Universitas Gajah Mada-Ford Foundation, Jogjakarta.

Wilopo, Siswanto and Sri Moertiningsih Adioetomo 1998 'Impact on population and reproductive health in Indonesia,' *Southeast Asian Populations in Crisis: Challenges to the Implementation of the ICPD Programme of Action*, United Nations Population Fund and Australian National University, New York, UN Population Fund.

Wolfe, D. L. 1996 'Javanese factory daughters,' *Fantasizing the Feminine in Indonesia*, ed. L. J. Sears, Duke University Press, Durham.

Yuval-Davis, N. 1994 'Women, ethnicity and empowerment,' *Feminism and Psychology*, vol. 4, no. 1, pp. 179-97.

Yuval-Davis, N. and Anthias, F. eds 1989 *Women-Nation-State*, St. Martin's Press, New York.

Zain'ddin, A. G. T. 1986 'What should a girl become? Further reflections on the letters of R. A. Kartini,' *Nineteenth and Twentieth Century Indonesia: Essays in Honour of Professor J.D. Legge*, eds D. P. Chandler and M. Ricklefs, Centre of Southeast Asian Studies, Monash University, Melbourne.

8 Rhetoric or reality? Contesting definitions of women in Korea

Sasha Hampson

National Korean Studies Centre
Swinburne University of Technology

The status of South Korean women has improved dramatically over the last thirty years and yet gender inequality is still a distinguishing feature of modern South Korean society (hereafter Korea and Korean). The rapid development of a capitalist economy and a democratic political system during these years has given Korea entry into the developed nations club. In emulation of other developed nations, and also in response to the active lobbying by Korean women's groups in the 1980s, the Korean government enacted several pieces of legislation that would apparently enhance gender equity in the nation. Undoubtedly these legislative changes, such as the Equal Employment Act, have improved the lives of Korean women by setting benchmarks for behaviour and providing avenues for redressing discriminatory practices. However, the full and effective implementation of this progressive legislation has been hindered by the resilience of traditional social and cultural norms restricting women's behaviour and participation in society. Korea's rapid social, political and economic transition has changed the family structure, weakened the traditional value system and broadened employment practices and each of these shifts has provided women with new opportunities. Yet Korean women's choices are still constrained by the key axioms of Confucian thought: filial piety, family loyalty, conformity to group norms and chastity. This chapter demonstrates that there is a dramatic difference between the rhetoric and the reality of gender equality in Korea. The diversification of the South Korean economy, from agriculture to industry and commerce, has not been matched by an equal diversification in social and cultural norms and the removal of this disparity is the most pressing challenge for Korean women in the twenty-first century.

The continuing strength of the traditional definition of Korean women as 'wives and mothers' or 'bearers of sons' undermines attempts to redefine women as workers, leaders or educated individuals. In a society that is extremely status conscious, the high prestige given to the traditional Confucian definition of women and the corresponding low status affiliated with other contesting definitions of women means that the new regulations and changes can be subverted or co-opted by the traditional paradigm. Thus, although women are increasingly receiving tertiary education, such education is perceived as a mechanism for attracting a higher status husband. Moreover, women engaged in paid employment have lower status than house-wives because their need for money is perceived to indicate their lower class. This chapter explores this and other contradictions presented by the evolution of the modern Korean woman. The traditional definitions of femininity are challenged by changes in the political and economic basis of Korea as a nation. In this dynamic interaction new definitions of womanhood are created that are at once modern but also distinctly Korean in nature.

Changing Korean families: the resilience of Confucianism

The rapid growth of the Korean economy in the last three decades has altered the Korean family structure in significant ways, nonetheless, adherence to Confucian family values remains strong. As the economy shifted away from its reliance on agricultural production the population has become more urbanised—almost 75 per cent of Koreans currently live in urban areas, up from only 28 per cent in 1960 (KWDI 1994, p. 12). Urbanisation has reduced the size of the Korean household and in the 1990s two-generation households are more common than the traditional three or four generation extended family model. In 1990 two-generation households accounted for 66.3 per cent of households while three-generation households accounted for only 12.2 per cent (KWDI

1994, p. 12). The number of single parent families has increased from
642 000 in 1975 to **888 823** in 1994 (KWDI 1994, p.13) but unlike the
two-generation household, this is still not a socially acceptable family
structure. As a result of a rigorous government family planning program
over the last thirty years the fertility rate in Korea has declined from 6.0
births per woman in 1960 to 1.6 births in 1990 (KWDI 1994, p. 15). For
women these demographic changes have meant fewer years are devoted
to the care of children or elderly relatives. This factor is important
because on marriage, women take full responsibility for domestic matters
even if they work outside their home. The reduction of family size has
reduced the amount of time Korean women spend on domestic duties.
However industrialisation has reinforced, rather than challenged, the
sexual division of labour in Korean families.

Marriage remains a major concern for the parents of the young women
and men involved—it represents an opportunity to improve the status of
the family and is far more than simply a manifestation of a young
couple's mutual affection. Traditionally, Korean parents arranged
marriages with the young couple having minimal control over the choice
of partner. Today, Korean marriages include the following possible
formats; 'fully arranged' as was traditionally the case, 'half arranged/
half love', and 'fully a love match'. Most marriages in the 1990s fall into
the second category—parents, relatives or parents' friends provide a
'suitable' introduction and the couple are left to decide whether they find
each other compatible or not. Both the men and women in this form of
introduction would have equal rights to accept or reject a future partner.

Of paramount concern to all parties involved in the arrangement of a
marriage is the implication of the marriage to the status of the families
being joined. Although the traditional hereditary status system was
abolished in 1894, and thereby no longer has any legal standing, social
relations of Koreans continue to revolve extensively around status. In
modern Korea social and class status are derived from wealth,
educational level, and employment. Even in 'love matches', those where
the young people involved choose their partners without external
involvement, the individuals will consider the impact of their
relationship on the status of their family. The preservation or preferably
elevation of one's family status is often given as much weight in a
decision about 'love' as is the depth of mutual affection. To ensure that
the status of the respective families is not being jeopardised,
matchmakers may be involved in the arrangement of introductions.
Informally, a matchmaker may simply be a friend or relative providing
an introduction. Professional yet unlicensed matchmakers known as
Madame Ttu also exist and are paid for each introduction and a bonus for

a successful introduction. The higher the socio-economic status of the family the greater the chance of involvement by a matchmaker (Lett 1997, p. 44). For middle-class families the presence of a matchmaker is often used to demonstrate improving family prestige.

Typically of Confucian cultures, marriage is a strong expectation in Korea and an unmarried woman older than 30 is a cause for concern amongst her friends and relatives. Currently the average age of marriage for women is 25.3 years and 28.4 years for men (Roh 1991, p. 5). As educational opportunities for women have expanded the average age of marriage has increased. Women's average age at first marriage has increased from 21.6 years in 1960 to 25.3 years in 1991 while men's average age has increased from 25.4 years in 1960 to 28.4 years in 1991 (Roh 1991, p. 5). The importance of marriage for women before the age of 30 relates directly to the Confucian family custom whereby the production of sons who can continue the family name remains of paramount concern. The continued preoccupation with marriage for women is indicative of the primacy given to domestic duties for women. It is overwhelmingly the domestic sphere that defines womanhood in Korea.

The Confucian concern for the production of heirs has come into direct conflict with the population control policies embraced as part of the development drive of the central government. Traditions encourage the production of sons where development policy encourages a reduced birth-rate. As will be clear below the conflict between the two ideologies has had a dramatic impact on women's reproductive behaviour. The government's enthusiasm for a reduced population growth rate has been rewarded with strong results. In 1993 the population growth rate was 0.9 per cent and a zero population growth rate is expected by 2021 (KWDI 1994, p. 61).

One reason for this low figure is the high percentage of married Korean couples using some form of contraception and this has increased rapidly over the past four decades as a wider range of contraceptive technologies has become available. In 1964 only 9.0 per cent of couples used contraception but by 1991 this figure had increased to 79.4 per cent (Cho 1997, p. 110). Female oriented methods such as intra-uterine devices (IUD) and tubal ligations are far more common than male-oriented methods such as vasectomies and condoms. Female sterilisation is the major method employed. There is reluctance amongst Korean women to use contraceptives such as the birth control pill. In 1994 only 1.8 per cent of couples practising contraception used the pill (Cho 1997, p. 112). Korean women's reluctance to use oral contraceptives can be explained in two ways. First, the contraceptives sold in Korea during the

1960s contained high levels of hormones and the pill has continued to be associated with extensive side effects even today. Many Korean women believe the pill to be dangerous, and they are worried that they may give birth to children with defects or become sterile after taking the pill. Second, the reluctance to take the pill can be attributed to the conservative Confucian values that still permeate Korean society. Women are not encouraged to have control over their bodies or their sexuality and many unmarried women are still ignorant about sex and contraception. If a woman takes the pill she would be denying her sexual innocence and ignorance (i.e. virtue) and admitting to sexual knowledge and activity (i.e. profanity). This cultural preoccupation with female chastity also helps explain the preference for medical intervention in the contraception used—IUDs and sterilisation—both take the control and responsibility away from the women by providing an authoritative and medico-technocratic intermediary.

One consequence of the low use of the contraceptive pill is the high incidence of abortion in Korea. Abortion has been a key factor in decreasing fertility in Korea. Official surveys show that 49 per cent of Korean women of child-bearing age have had at least one abortion (ROK 1998, p. 94) and the ratio of abortions to every 100 normal births was 76:100 in 1991 (Cho 1997, p. 113). This figure may be much higher given that abortion is technically illegal except in a specified set of circumstances. Although it was commonplace a decade earlier, abortion was legalised in 1973 if the pregnancy is deemed harmful to the mother or the foetus. Amendments to the law in 1986 eased restrictions by legalising abortion to prevent illegitimate births. Despite these restrictions abortions are widely performed and the termination of pregnancies has become a form of contraception. Abortions are readily available for around US$125 and in some clinics no appointment is necessary and abortion procedures comprise the bulk of the Korean gynaecologist's income. In most cases there is no counselling or support available for women terminating their pregnancies.

Korean feminists, in contrast to their western counterparts, are among the most vocal critics of Korea's high abortion rate. For women in the West the abortion debate is framed around issue of choice and the right of a woman to have control over her own fertility. However, in Korea abortion poses an entirely different set of problems for women because of the overarching Confucian culture of son-preference. Currently, with the advent of ultra-sound technology and a general increase in disposable income among the broad population, gender-selective abortions are occurring at such a rate that there is an identifiable decrease in the female population at birth. If continued into the future such a decline could further reduce women's power in an already staunchly patriarchal society by simply reducing the number of women's voices able to speak on their own behalf. In 1994 the male to female ratio at birth reached 115 to 100 (ROK 1998, p. 96). For the first child in a family the rate is 100 boys to 102 girls however for the fourth child it is 199 boys to 100 girls. Generally speaking families will only have more than two children if they do not have a male child. In large families of six or seven children the youngest is often male. The Korean government addressed the problem in 1995 when it introduced legislation prohibiting gender-specific abortions and regulating the use of technology to determine the sex of a foetus. The legislation has been largely ineffective since enforcement of the rulings has been intermittent and fraught with difficulties. The projected ratio for 2010 is 123:100 (ROK 1998, p. 96). This imbalance will become a serious social issue once today's children reach marriageable ages. Such disparities in the Korean sex ratio challenges the view often espoused in the People's Republic of China that as the wealth of a nation increases the strength of son-preference will decline. The Korean case suggests that wealth and son-preference comfortably co-exist in Confucian cultures.

The privileged status of boys over girls within the family has been challenged only recently with the passage of the revised Family Law Act on December 19 1989. After more than 30 years of persistent lobbying women in Korea have won considerable advances in their status in the family. Traditionally women were discriminated against in the inheritance of property. Since December 1989, in the absence of a will all property is divided equally between all children regardless of sex. A childless widow is now entitled to receive half of her husband's property with the remaining half going to his parents. In the event of divorce both husband and wife have equal rights to properties gained after marriage and custody of children is no longer automatically granted to the father. Custody is now decided by mutual agreement or by family court intervention.

Another important 1989 legal gain for women in relation to their domestic roles was the Mother–Child Welfare Act. This Act is designed to safeguard the security and welfare of fatherless families by guaranteeing single mothers welfare allowances to cover the cost of raising their children (including education and vocational training fees). Although the Mother–Child Welfare Act represents significant protection there are a number of problems remaining. It does not provide protection for motherless families, an income threshold excludes all but those on very low incomes, and the provisions are not legally binding. The Act represents a first step towards the improvement of welfare for single mothers but there is still a desperate need for further welfare facilities for fatherless families.

Women creating the 'economic miracle'

Korea's economy has grown dramatically in the last 30 years and, until the collapse of the stock market and the currency in 1998, Korea was regarded as an 'economic miracle' and given the tag of 'a tiger economy'. Industrialisation and export driven manufacturing has seen South Korea's Gross National Product increase from US$80 in the early 1960s to US$10 000 in 1996 (DFAT 1999, p. 1). This success has been in large part the result of the labour of women working in low status and low wage jobs within the manufacturing industries. The labour force participation rate of women increased from 26.8 per cent in 1960 to 47.6 per cent in 1995 (KWDI 1996) as women left the rural areas and moved to the cities for work in the new factories and businesses.

During the period from 1960 to the late 1980s women were employed in the labour-intensive sectors such as textiles, clothing, rubber products, food processing, electronics and computer component industries. These industries are typified by their low wages, poor conditions and limited scope for promotion. It is these very sectors that have provided the export goods that created Korea's economic growth and yet the contribution of women to the development of Korea remains undervalued. In the 1990s the service sector has expanded and in 1996 33.1 per cent of women were employed in this sector (ROK 1998, p. 80). Women undertake the worst jobs regardless of the industry. In the manufacturing sector women work on the production lines and are monitored by male supervisors. In the clerical sector 94.7 per cent of typists and 62 per cent of bookkeepers are women, but only 1.4 per cent of clerical supervisors are women (Chang 1998, p. 6). In the 1980s gender wage differences in Korea were among the highest in the world (Amsden 1989). The situation has improved with the introduction of the 1989 Equal Employment Act but in 1995 women still earned only 61.5 per cent of the average monthly male wage (ROK 1998, p. 86). This figure is an encouraging 8.1 per cent increase from 1990.

Koreans have continued to regard women's participation in the paid labour force as a temporary condition that will cease once they assume the roles of wives and mothers on marriage. Few Korean men and women (single and married) regard women workers as 'real workers'. There is a great deal of prestige afforded the full-time housewife—it implies that the family is well-off (the second income is not needed) and it invokes the filial respect for the wise mother common in Confucian cultures. Accordingly, the vast majority of female workers are in the 20–24 year age bracket. Moreover, as is found in Japan, the labour participation rate for women forms an M curve when mapped on a distribution graph. Women's participation drops with marriage, pregnancy and child-rearing in the 25–35 age bracket, picks up when these responsibilities fade in the late thirties and drops again with retirement.

The exhortations of the government to encourage women to join the industrial workforce and strive to build a strong Korean nation gave rise to the term 'industrial soldiers' (*sanop chonsa*) (Kim 1997, p. 9). The 'industrial soldiers' were praised for their loyalty, diligence, obedience and selflessness in a direct echo of the traditional Confucian prescriptions for women. In later years the labour movement invoked the female factory worker as a victim of both the capitalist economic systems and South Korea's repressive political system. In rhetoric loaded with nationalist overtones, Korea's factory women were referred to as 'daughters of the Korean peninsula' (*hanbando ui ttaldul*) (Kim 1997).

Conflicting with this ostensibly positive invocation of the female factory worker in both national development rhetoric and labour movement rhetoric is the denigration and disdain of women factory workers. This tendency is best demonstrated by the emergence of the term *kongsuni*—the joining of the word for factory (*kongjang*) and a common female name (*Suni*)—and its overwhelming derogatory connotations. The term could be translated as Factory Sally or Factory Susie and is imbued with notions of factory women as 'poor, coarse, unintelligent and predisposed to sexual immorality' (Kim 1997, p. 10). Although there is an equivalent male term, *kongdori*, it does not carry the same degree of negative connotations since *kongsuni* emphasises the 'contrast between the proper behaviour and status of young women and their lives as factory workers' (Kim 1997, p. 10).

Throughout the 1960s and 1970s factory work was predominantly undertaken by young unmarried women and was regarded as a transitional stage between school and marriage—after which they assume the respectable roles of wife and mother. Marriage was the path to remedy the taint of one's past as a *kongsuni*. Factory workers have attached considerable significance to the 'temporary' nature of their employment in order to reduce the stigma and negative stereotyping of their status as *kongsuni* (Kim 1997). However, in the 1980s and 1990s, married women have increasingly returned to work in the factories to supplement the family income. The cost of living in Korea has risen as have the expectations of the population. The desire to provide better education opportunities for children has encouraged women back to the factory jobs they left as young brides. The participation rate of married women in the manufacturing sector grew from 13 per cent in 1983 to almost 20 per cent in 1989 (Kim 1997, p. 51). Although the participation of these married factory workers is more acceptable now than in earlier times, the women involved tend to view their jobs as temporary—just helping the family out during a brief period of increased expenditure. Young women tend to look down on these married women workers. A young factory worker in Masan comments 'I feel sorry for the married women (*ajumma*). They have to work just like us and then they have to go home and work for their families again. I guess they really need the money, but I would never come back to work at the sewing machine again' (Kim 1997, p. 22). Traditionally, *ajumma* referred to older women or female relatives but the economic and social changes that have drawn older and married women into the workforce have given new meaning to the term. It now refers to the hard-working older working woman who typically neglects herself and stands in contrast to the respectable mother and wife—a Korean Sadie, perhaps. It now connotes specific positions of little power and low class rather than age and marital status.

Despite the growth in numbers of married women in factory work, the overwhelming number of married women who work are concentrated in the informal sectors of the economy—those businesses with fewer than six employees. Both wholesale and retail businesses (peddlers, small street stands, shops and restaurants) as well as domestic and personal services (cleaning) are large employers of married women. This sector is characterised by unstable employment, unregulated working conditions and low wages. Unpaid work conducted by women for the family business is included in this informal sector and accounts for a declining 36.7 per cent of all female workers. It is estimated that more than 60 per cent of women workers are active in the informal sector (Cho 1986; ROK 1998). Many married women choose to work in the informal sector because of the flexibility provided by the smaller workplace. Nonetheless, employment is tenuous and wages are low.

The tenuous nature of women's place in the Korean workforce has been amply demonstrated by the impact of the IMF Agreement implemented throughout 1998 after the economic collapse of 1997. The IMF bailout of the Korean economy has resulted in substantial economic restructuring and massive lay-offs. Women have borne the brunt of this economic upheaval. Irrespective of their qualifications, experience or length of service, women are dismissed before men. Again this is a reflection of the perception that women's employment is temporary. The two groups most affected are young women and women with little education (KLI 1998). Once unemployed, women are discouraged from seeking work again so that any figures on female unemployment are skewed. The Korean Development Institute estimates that once the figures include those unemployed women who are not actively seeking work the female unemployment figure would jump almost three times above the 5.8 per cent currently touted. The government has issued ordinances providing serious penalties for employers who dismiss women before men without due cause. In companies where a proportionally large number of female employees are dismissed, the company will be placed under special review to determine any violations of the Equal Employment Act. In addition a special section within the Ministry of Labour has been set up to receive reports on gender-discriminatory dismissals.

The effectiveness of such measures is yet to be seen given that even before the IMF agreement the Labour Standard Law, that prohibits sexual discrimination against employees by employers, was ineffective. Women activists sought to improve on the Labour Standard Law and in 1987 the Equal Employment Act (EEA) was passed promising to guarantee equality between men and women in employment. It was revised in 1989 to include provisions on equal pay for equal work regardless of the worker's sex. The Act makes punishable discrimination against women in recruitment, employment, placement, promotion, and retirement. It also provides for maternity leave and childcare facilities. However, even though the EEA provides many practical and concrete measures to protect the rights of working women, in reality the Act has not been particularly effective in its implementation. The Act does not provide concrete standards for distinguishing sexual discrimination or an adequate definition of equal work.

Education for social mobility

Education has not proved to be the doorway to greater employment status or career opportunities in Korea as it has in other parts of Asia because of the continued privileging of domestic roles for women. The Korean education system has expanded dramatically since the Korean War (1950–1953) and the educational level for both men and women has risen dramatically over the past three decades. In 1960 the average number of years of education was 4.78 years for men and 2.92 years for women, but by 1998 the figures had increased to 11.18 years for men and 9.37 years for women (ROK 1998, p. 58). The persistence of a gap between the genders reflects the overall domination of men in the

burgeoning higher education sector. At the primary school level, because
education is compulsory and government funded, the male–female ratio
is almost identical. Similarly, there is no significant difference in
participation rates at the middle school level where free compulsory
education is partially in force. As the costs to families increase the
participation rate of women and girls decreases. In 1998 the female
enrolment rate for high-schools was only slightly lower than males but
the situation in tertiary education differs considerably. Despite rapid rises
in the participation of women in the tertiary sector during the 1990s
women are still vastly under-represented. In 1990 24 per cent of women
of student age (18–21) were enrolled in tertiary education and by 1997
this had risen to 50.9 per cent. This dramatic rise, taking place in less
than a decade, reflects an expansion in the tertiary education sector rather
than an improvement for women relative to men. Over the same period,
the percentage of men of student age enrolled has risen from 50 per cent
in 1990 to 85.7 per cent in 1997 (ROK 1998, p. 59). At a tertiary level
women concentrate in education and the humanities while men dominate
the science and technology programs.

For those women who graduate with tertiary qualifications there are
considerable barriers inhibiting full participation in the workforce. The
labour market has been slow in accommodating women with tertiary
qualifications. In 1997 only 52.5 per cent of female college graduates
found employment (ROK 1998, p. 66). This represents a lower
participation rate than for all women of the same age-group of 20–24
year-olds. While only 3.9 per cent of female workers have the
educational level of college graduate or above, 65.2 per cent of female
workers have an educational level of middle school or below (Roh 1991,
p. 40). As a result Korea faces the peculiar situation where the more
educated a woman is the less likely she is to work (Lee 1998, p. 105).
This phenomenon is a result of the division of labour between the
genders which has confined women to lower skilled, lower status and
lower paid jobs within all industries. Women with tertiary qualifications
are unlikely to engage in these forms of employment. Moreover,
employers are reluctant to employ women in positions of responsibility
within the professions because of the intense family and peer pressure
for women to resign from employment upon marriage. A professional
women's working life is expected to be very brief—less than a decade
given the pressure to marry before 30—and this makes an educated
woman an expensive employee.

The predominance of the view that women's roles are primarily
domestic has resulted in the fact that the pursuit of higher education for
Korean women has become an opportunity to elevate one's social status

in the hope of attracting a higher status husband (Lett 1997; Lee 1998). Commitment to careers or academic inquiry remain of low priority and middle-class parents will aim to educate as many of their daughters to as high a level as possible in the hope of 'marrying up'. Upward social mobility for women is thus determined by level of education. Not because educated women gain access to better paying employment, but rather because education will provide them with a higher-paid husband.

Women's participation in politics and government

After the UN's International Year of Women in 1975, the Korean government established numerous committees charged with developing policies addressing women's concerns. Under President Kim Dae Jung women's rights have gained increased prominence as part of the broad emphasis of his government on human rights. The Presidential Commission on Women's Affairs (PCWA) was established in 1998 to replace the Ministry of Political Affairs II (MOPA II). Unlike MOPA II, which operated under the auspices of the Office of the Prime Minister, the PCWA is overseen directly by the President. The PCWA functions primarily as an advisory body but it also formulates women's policies aimed at increasing women's leadership, participation and equal representation and also carries out research on gender-discrimination.

The Korean Women's Development Institute (KWDI), established by the government in 1983, performs a similar function to the research wing of the PCWA. It provides materials on the status of women for public and government debate as well as opportunities for education and training of women and remains a strong advocate of women's social participation and welfare interests. Recent evidence of the government's commitment to equal representation has been the appointment of two women to ministerial positions in the new cabinet—Shin Nakyun as the Minister for Culture and Tourism and Kim Mo-im as the Minister for Health and Welfare. Korea's first female ambassador, Lee In-ho, was also appointed as ambassador to Russia.

These high-level appointments come after decades of low levels of participation of women in Korean politics (see Park 1999). Since independence in 1953 there have been 66 women legislators—a mere 2 per cent of the total 3 233 (KWDI 1994, p. 42). In the judicial branch women account for a mere 1.2 per cent of the total 3 958 judges, prosecutors, and lawyers (Roh 1991, p. 58). Currently women make up less than 30 per cent of civil servants with 90 per cent concentrated in the low levels of Seventh Class or below. In 1995 the government established a female public employee target system which aims to redress this imbalance by facilitating the recruitment of a set number of women into the public sector each year. Target ratios are expected to rise to 20 per cent by the year 2000 from the 10 per cent base in 1996.

While women's representation may be low at political decision-making levels, women have actively exercised their right to vote. In the December 1997 presidential election women voters constituted 50.8 per cent of total eligible voters (ROK 1998, p. 45). Female members constitute between 30 and 40 per cent of political party membership, but few are represented at the higher decision-making levels (Roh 1991, p. 61). The greatest influence women have on the political decision-making process derives from the activities of pressure groups that have effectively mobilised public opinion on women's issues.

The Korean women's movement

Western feminism has many limitations as a tool for understanding women's situation in non-Western societies. Korean women's issues need to be understood within the framework of the Korean historical and social context. Most importantly it needs to be understood that the aims and activities of the Korean women's movement have been heavily influenced by the development of the nationalist movement. Historically, gender issues in Korea have been overshadowed by the nationalist and anti-imperialist struggle. In past decades this was understandable to an extent but today progressive women's groups are challenging the nationalist–feminist relationship.

Highlighted by harsh political oppression, widespread corruption and rapid industrial growth, the 1970s and 1980s was a period of massive political and social turmoil in South Korea. Accordingly, in response to the oppressive totalitarian rule, Korea experienced a growth in the number and strength of social movements struggling for change, the women's movement being no exception. In this period of harsh political oppression however, it was difficult for any social movement to achieve real change. Without democracy all Koreans would be oppressed and hence many social movements placed the political struggle for democracy and national independence ahead of their own concerns. Thus out of necessity the Korean women's movement was forced to give priority to the national political struggle before that of women's emancipation. This has continued until today where, any gender-related issue in Korea has been largely determined by its strategic value to the nationalist movement. This manipulation of gender issues by the nationalist movement has been exemplified by the support for the so-called 'comfort women'. Issues of rape and violence against women have never attracted much attention from women's groups in Korea, let alone a nationalist movement largely dominated by men. Yet the campaign for apologies and reparation for the comfort women (women forced into prostitution for the Japanese military during World War Two) has been well supported across all sectors of Korean society. One explanation is that the issue has been perceived as one of imperialist violence rather than sexual violence (see Kim and Choi 1998). It is a case of violence by Japanese men against Korean women rather than an issue of violence against women committed by men. The nationalist movement claims to represent a shared past and future and yet like all other facets of Korean society the nationalist movement is characterised by patriarchal and paternalistic beliefs.

The 1970s and 1980s saw a close alliance between the nationalist and women's movement but in the 1990s the strengthening of democracy in Korea has allowed the women's movement to focus on its own agenda. Although it can be argued that gender issues in Korea continue to be manipulated and distorted by nationalist sentiment it seems that today with a more open and liberal political environment, the women's movement has begun to deal with matters beyond those of importance to national survival. In the 1990s the women's movement is now challenging problems of gender politics, sexuality and patriarchy that have previously been ignored.

In 1980 the first public discussion (academic or otherwise) on sexuality emerged and twenty years later the first signs of change in perceptions of sexuality is emerging. Nonetheless, chastity for women and sexual freedom for men outside of marriage remain the dominant ideologies. Gradually, through increasing sexual education programs and a more open and liberal lifestyle, the core issues of sexuality and the politics of sexual relations are being addressed. The changes indicate that sex is now regarded as more than procreation—sex is increasingly discussed as pleasure (Shim 1998, p. 36). Accordingly, in contrast to the contraceptive advertising of the 1960s and 1970s, which emphasised the importance of fewer children to the creation of a happy family, contraceptive advertising today appears in magazines for young singles with slogans that acknowledge sex is possible outside of marriage. This new concept of sex for pleasure is not only for young singles but is also for married couples. This has introduced a new dynamic into Korean married couples' lives. As romantic love becomes a more common form of marriage, mutual sexual pleasure is becoming a new dimension of married life. Traditionally sexual pleasure has been men's domain but increasingly through film, literature and advertising the concept of Korean women's sexual pleasure is being publicly explored.

Korean women's groups were once geared largely towards recreation and friendship especially amongst the middle class. In contrast, today they are much more socially and politically focussed on the advancement of women in Korean society. Many have transformed themselves in their aims and activities. The 1970s women's movement focussed primarily on the plight of female factory workers, but as working conditions and the standard of living in general has improved, the women's movement has broadened its focus to encompass a far broader range of issues. The 1980s and 1990s has also seen a growth of organisations with a specific agenda. These specialised or single-issue organisations are not fragmented—in 1987 they formed a coalition of women's organisations known as the Korean Women's Associations United (KWAU). The KWAU is a progressive union of 27 women's groups that work for women's rights and democracy. Their target audience includes rural women, women workers, low-income earners and sex workers. In the past decade the KWAU has played a key coordinating and leadership role on a number of important campaigns. For example, in 1992 seventy-four groups gathered to successfully lobby for legislation against sexual violence.

Sexual and domestic violence

According to a 1989 study conducted by the Korea Criminal Policy Institute, Korea held the third highest rate of reported sexual assault in the world, topped only by the U.S. and Sweden (Louie 1992). Despite the high incidence Korean women are reluctant to report sexual assault crimes. The high moral value placed on female virginity and chastity in Korea means that in the situation of rape the victim will often feel, or be considered to be, responsible for what has happened to them. For female rape victims in Korea the prevailing culture is one of shame. Currently only 2 per cent of rapes are reported (Shim 1998, p. 40). In response to these distressing statistics and the reporting of a number of shocking incidents of sexual violence the 1990s a collective of Korean women's groups has actively campaigned for the introduction of legislation addressing sexual and domestic violence against women. The Women's Sexual Violence Relief Centre (SVRC) and the Women's Hotline were established in the 1980s to specifically deal with these issues. The SVRC has directed attention to the issue of sexual violence through well-publicised reports and counselling services. The Women's Hotline provides counselling and a safe house for abused women. In December 1993, as a result of the active campaigning of these groups, the Act Relating to Punishment of Sexual Violence and Protection of Victims was promulgated and came into effect in April 1994. In its original form this law was far from satisfactory and further campaigning has resulted in amendments that came into effect in January 1998.

Prior to the passage of this law rape had been defined as a crime against chastity; that is, the male's violation of the female's precious purity. The degree to which the victim resisted and her sexual history were the basis of court decisions. The law did not allow people to file suit against their parents or relatives, leaving incest victims with no avenue for redress. The new law emphasises the protection of and assistance to the victims. It defines rape as an act against the free will of the person being attacked. The new law covers previously neglected areas such as rape by relatives, rape of handicapped persons, and rape of minors. In cases of rape by a relative or rape of a handicapped person it is now possible for a third party to report the crime to authorities. This is not yet possible in all rape cases. Marital and date rape are not specifically covered in any legislation. Since domestic violence was not covered in the special law on sexual violence (it was initially included but had to be dropped) the Korean Women's Hotline continued to campaign for legislation against domestic violence. According to various surveys between forty and sixty per cent of women have experienced physical abuse by their husbands.

The Korean Women's Hotline also felt it was important to include the public in the campaign against domestic violence. To this end it has conducted many surveys, held public education workshops and distributed information pamphlets widely. In November 1997 as a result of this hard work the Special Law Regarding Domestic Violence and the Punishment of Offenders and the Law on Sexual Assault Crimes and Assault was passed in the National Assembly. According to this new legislation domestic violence is a social issue, not just a private problem. The law allows anyone to report the crime to police, not just offenders. Police are now obliged to act to stop the violence. Offenders can no longer claim that their actions are nobody else's business. Under the law victims will have access to counselling centres and temporary shelters (although the number of these is relatively limited). Offenders will be ordered to receive counselling through a special correctional program. Although the passing of this legislation has been a great success for the Korean Women's Hotline the next challenge lies in changing social and cultural attitudes which see domestic violence as a private and commonplace family matter.

Conclusion

Industrialisation has occurred in Korea at a rapid pace and has dramatically affected the social and economic status of Korean women as well as realising significant changes to the Korean family structure. The industrialisation of the 1960s and 1970s saw a large scale increase in female waged labour. This was followed by a period of politicisation in the 1980s where the growth of the economy and improved standard of living allowed for a stronger focus on social issues. Various women's organisations were established and significant legislative changes improved women's legal status. In the 1990s we are now seeing women's increased political power as women become more actively involved at decision-making levels. The Korean women's movement is dealing for the first time with issues of sexuality and sexual relations— moving beyond an agenda of economic and political concerns as prescribed by nationalist aims. Entrenched patriarchal and paternalistic values continue to run deep as do traditional notions of gender roles but the past thirty years have seen a definite elevation of women's status and the future looks brighter.

References and recommended readings

Amsden, Alice 1989 *Asia's Next Giant*, Oxford University Press, Oxford.

Byun, Wha Soon 1991 'Women and population policy,' *Women's Studies Quarterly*, vol. 3, pp. 110–14.

Chang, Pilwha 1998 'The gender division of labour at work,' *Korean Women and Work*, Asian Center for Women's Studies, Seoul.

Cho, Hyoung and Chang, Pilwha eds 1994 *Gender Division of Labour in Korea*, Ewha Women's University Press, Seoul.

Cho, Hyoung 1986 'Labour force participation of women in Korea,' *Challenges for Women*, ed. Chung Sei-wha, Ewha Women's University Press, Seoul.

—— 1997 'Fertility control, reproductive rights and women's empowerment in Korea,' *Asian Journal of Women's Studies*, vol. 3, no. 1, pp. 103–32.

Chung Sei-wha ed. 1986 *Challenges for Women*, Ewha Women's University Press, Seoul.

DFAT—Department of Foreign Affairs and Trade eds 1999 *Korea Rebuilds: From Crisis to Opportunity*, DFAT, Canberra.

Gelb, J. and Palley, M. eds 1994 *Women of Japan and Korea, Continuity and Change*, Temple University Press, Philadelphia.

Hicks, George 1995 *The Comfort Women*, Allen and Unwin, Sydney.

Howard, K. ed. 1995 *True Stories of the Korean Comfort Women*, Cassell, London.

Kendall, L. 1996 *Getting Married in Korea: Of Gender, Morality, and Modernity*, University of California Press, Berkeley.

Kim, Elaine and Choi, Chungmoo eds 1998 *Dangerous Women*, Routledge, New York.

Kim, Seung-kyung 1997 'Productivity, militancy and femininity: gendered images of South Korean women factory workers,' *Asian Journal of Women's Studies*, vol. 3, no. 3, pp. 8–44.

—— 1997a *Class Struggle or Family Struggle: The Lives of Women Factory Workers in South Korea*, Cambridge University Press, Cambridge.

Kim, Yung-Chung 1976 *Women of Korea—A History from Ancient Times to 1945*, Ewha Women's University Press, Seoul.

Korean Labour Institute (KLI) 1998 *Factor Analysis for Unemployed Women and Policy Recommendations*, Korean Labour Institute, Seoul.

Korean Women's Development Institute (KWDI) 1994 *Korean Women Now*, KWDI, Seoul.

—— 1996 *Yearly Report on Women's Statistics*, KWDI, Seoul.

Lee, Mijeong 1998 *Women's Education, Work and Marriage in Korea*, Seoul National University Press, Seoul.

Lett, D. 1997 'In pursuit of status: the lives of Korean middle-class women,' *Korean Culture Through Women's Eyes*, Asian Center for Women's Studies, Seoul.

Louie, M. Ching 1992 'Organising to answer the needs of Korean rape victims,' *New Directions for Women*, September, pp. 26–28.

Moon, Katherine H.S. 1999 'South Korean movement against militarized sexual labour,' *Asian Survey*, Vol. XXXIX, No. 2, pp. 310–27.

Park, Kyung-Ae 1999 'Political representation and South Korean women,' *Journal of Asian Studies*, vol. 58, no. 2, pp. 432–48.

Republic of Korea (ROK) 1998 *Fourth Periodic Report of States of the Convention on the Elimination of All Forms of Discrimination against Women, 1994—1997*, Presidential Commission on Women's Affairs, Seoul.

Roh, Mihye 1991 *The Status of Korean Women Today*, KWDI, Seoul.

Shim, Young-hee 1998 'Gender and body politics in Korea,' *Asian Women*, vol. 6, pp. 19–57.

Soh, Chunghee Sarah 1993 *Women in Korean Politics*, Westview Press, Boulder.

Spencer, F. 1988 *Yogong: Factory Girl*, Royal Asiatic Society, Seoul.

Sturdevant, Saundra ed. 1992 *Let The Good Times Roll*, New Press, New York.

Yu, E. and Phillips, E. eds. 1987 *Korean Women in Transition*, California State University, Los Angeles.

(See also the journals *Asian Women*, Sookmyung Women's University Press and *Asian Journal of Women's Studies*, Ewha Women's University Press)

9 Breaking the patriarchal paradigm: Chinese women in Hong Kong

C. Tang, W.T. Au, Y.P. Chung and H.Y. Ngo

The Chinese University of Hong Kong
Department of Psychology
Department of Management
Faculty of Education
Gender Research Programme

In the decades since 1970, the status of women relative to men in Hong Kong has undergone rapid change and consequently there have also been important shifts in gender relations (Cheung 1997; Pearson and Leung 1995; Tang et al. 1999; Westwood et al. 1995). This chapter summarises trends in the major indicators of women's status in Hong Kong since the 1970s and draws on various sources that focus on the divergent experiences of women in their quest for equality. These indicators include the demographic structure of Hong Kong, education, work, income, political participation, public perceptions of gender stereotypes, violence against women, and the women's movement. The chapter argues that although Hong Kong women have made considerable progress in the legislative and political arenas, the attitudes and behaviours dominating their day-to-day lives bear witness to the resilience of patriarchal values within the modern polity.

It is necessary to map out the traditional cultural constructions of women in Hong Kong as a basis for measuring more contemporary configurations. According to traditional Chinese culture, womanhood is largely defined by qualities of submissiveness, dependence and self-sacrifice. These values are encapsulated in the Chinese character for woman (*funü*) that depicts a kneeling woman holding a broomstick. This 'model' woman practiced the key Confucian maxim of 'the three obediences and the four virtues' (*san cong si de*). That is, a virtuous woman should be obedient to her father before marriage, to her husband after marriage and to her son on the death of her husband. She should also strive to be a 'virtuous wife and a good mother' (*xiang qi liang mu*). The proper traditional Chinese woman obeyed men at each phase of her life, confined herself to the domestic sphere, and certainly did not question or challenge the superior status of men. Confucianism was fundamentally patrilineal. Both inheritance and ancestor worship privileged sons and stressed their critical roles in the continuance, survival and spiritual endurance of the family line. Consequently, Chinese families have traditionally had a strong preference for sons over daughters. Daughters were regarded as temporary members of their natal families who would leave to join another patriline on marriage so they were often not provided with education or skills that would enable them to live independently. Chastity was required of women throughout their lives while no such restrictions applied to men. In traditional China, men were allowed to keep concubines while women had to be faithful to their husbands until death and often were prohibited or discouraged from remarrying as widows.

Despite rapid social change and westernisation, remnants of traditional Chinese conceptions of womanhood continue to exert an influence on the behaviour and attitudes of Hong Kong people (Yip 1997). Efforts to promote women's status in Hong Kong—such as the anti-slavery, anti-prostitution, and anti-footbinding campaigns of the 1920s and 1930s, and the debates over women's inheritance rights in rural Hong Kong in the 1990s—have been met with scepticism and hostility from both men and women (Choi 1995; Hoe 1991, 1996). However, Yip (1997) noted that there is an emerging counter narrative led by local young educated women, which is challenging both the remnants of the colonial legal system and the persistent Chinese patriarchal social system.

The following sections provide an overview of the changes to women's status in Hong Kong that have resulted from the social, economic and political changes of the past three decades. As well as summarizing the various key indicators of women's status it will also give some insights into the day-to-day experiences of women in contemporary Hong Kong.

Population and demographics

There is a close association between various aspects of women's status in society and the demographic patterns of fertility, mortality, and migration. In particular, the fertility behaviour of women, including the timing and number of children, has an important bearing on their health, educational opportunities, employment, and their roles in marriage and the family. Thus, demographic patterns and trends are barometers for the assessment of gender equality in a particular historical moment and a specific cultural context. Our reading of the demographic evidence reveals an optimistic picture as women are more able to participate in a number of activities outside the domestic sphere on the road to self-fulfilment.

Hong Kong's population at the start of this century had a skewed distribution with almost two times more men than women. This imbalance was the result of the 'immigrant' nature of Hong Kong's evolution—most of its residents had migrated from China where men have routinely had greater mobility than have women. There has been a progressive equalisation of the gender ratio since the 1960s. Census data from 1996 showed that men and women now constitute 49.99 per cent and 50.01 per cent of the total Hong Kong population. This is the first time that women outnumber men in the history of Hong Kong, particularly for people aged 20–39 and 65 and above. This substantial increase in the number of women who are in their childbearing age is probably due to the increasing number of men marrying women across the border in mainland China. As is the case in other developed countries, the greater number of elderly women than elderly men is related to the longer life expectancy of women over men—currently 81.8 and 78.5 years respectively in Hong Kong.

The marriage and fertility patterns of Hong Kong women have undergone similar changes to those found in other developed countries. Over the last three decades, a greater proportion of women have delayed their marriage or parenthood, remained single or childless and greater numbers have sought divorce. In the 1996 Census, the crude marriage rate for women was 11.2 as compared to 19 per 1000 population in 1971. The average age of women in their first marriage has been delayed from 22.9 in 1971 to 26.9 in 1996; and their first birth postponed from 23.4 years in 1971 to 27.9 in 1991. Women are also having fewer children—average births per woman have decreased steadily from 3.0 in 1971 and have stabilised at 1.2 in the 1990s. Moreover, the crude divorce rate has also risen from 0.3 in the early 1970s to 1.5 per 1000 population in recent years. As will become clear in the section on women and employment below, these changes in reproductive and marital patterns have had a major impact on the participation of women in the labour force.

Education

For centuries, Chinese culture has placed a very high value on education for men while endorsing the axiom that it could only corrupt women. As a consequence, access to education in Hong Kong had been restricted to men until the twentieth century. In the earlier years of this century, education for women in the form of private tutoring was limited to daughters of very rich families or expatriate families with religious or diplomatic duties in Hong Kong. The extension of education to local women did not begin until the 1920s when religious or charitable organisations established a small number of schools for girls (Hoe 1996). Parents were reluctant to send daughters to these schools on the grounds that it was not necessary. It was felt that boys needed a good education so that they would be able to support a family, including the wife and elderly parents, once they reached adulthood. Since girls would leave home to enter another household there was no need to earn an income independent of their husbands'. On this reasoning, parents often kept their daughters at home to help with the domestic chores or the family business prior to their departure on marriage.

During the 1970s there was a marked expansion of basic education in Hong Kong. Free and compulsory education including six years of primary schooling was instituted in 1971 and later extended by three years to include an additional compulsory secondary education in 1978. Women were the prime beneficiaries of this policy since they were the group that had previously been under-represented at all levels of education. As a result of this significant change in education policy the adult literacy rate, (defined as the proportion of individuals aged 15 or above achieving beyond kindergarten education) has greatly improved for women since 1970s. Only half of the women in Hong Kong were literate in 1971, but by 1996 this figure had increased to 86.6 per cent. The female to male literacy ratio showed an increase from .71 in 1971 to .91 in 1996. The growth of tertiary education in the 1990s has also encouraged more women to attend higher education than in earlier years. Only 2.8 per cent of the women aged 15 or above had completed tertiary education in 1971, but this figure had increased to 13.3 per cent in 1996. More importantly, the male advantage in higher education seems to have disappeared, as the ratio of female to male full-time tertiary education enrolment has increased from .61 in 1981 to .95 in 1996. Overall the educational attainment of women in Hong Kong has shown significant improvement during the past three decades.

The 'common curriculum' and the 'comprehensive school' movements in the West aimed to ensure that all children experience curricula of equal pedagogical value in a bid to prevent a systematic concentration of children from a particular background in a disadvantaged or lower-valued stream. In Hong Kong, there are generally equal resources and common curriculum for all schools at the basic nine years of education particularly with the institution of free and compulsory schooling. However, gendered streaming is evident at the upper forms of secondary schools with boys concentrating in the 'science' streams and girls in the 'arts'. This pattern continues throughout higher education. At present, women greatly outnumber men in sub-degree programmes especially in the teacher and nursing training programmes. Women are concentrated in the comprehensive and liberal arts universities while men are concentrated in the science and technology universities. Even in the comprehensive universities, women tend to dominate in the arts, business, and social science faculties; whereas men comprise the majority in the science, engineering, and medical faculties.

Employment and income

Major indicators of women's status and role in the labour market include their level of participation, patterns of employment and unemployment, occupational segregation, and income differentials. According to the 1996 by-Census in Hong Kong, the working population amounts to 3.2 million people, being 62.8 per cent of the total population. Men and women respectively constitute 60.5 per cent and 39.5 per cent of the work force. Despite the growing number of women in the labour force since the 1970s, local researchers have argued that women continue to hold a disadvantaged position in the labour market (Ngo 1997; Westwood et al. 1995; Wong 1995).

The female labour force participation rate (LFPR) refers to the proportion of female workers to the female population aged 15 and above. Significant increases in the number of women workers in the 1960s were possible with the blooming of the manufacturing and electronic industries in Hong Kong. However, the female LFPR has shown very little change since then, only moving from 42.8 per cent in 1971 to 48 per cent in 1996. The current overall female LFPR is comparable to those in the developed countries such as Britain and

Japan, and can be attributed to the following social and economic changes in the recent years: growth in the service sector and in white-collar occupations; an increase in wages for women; a decline in the fertility rate; the expansion of educational opportunities for women; attitudinal changes towards women working outside of home; mechanisation of domestic chores; and the increasing financial burden of the family as it strives to keep up with the rising living standards in Hong Kong (Ngo 1997).

Despite the stabilisation of female LFPR in the recent decades, the social and demographic composition of the female labour force has undergone significant changes. Young women, especially those aged between 25 to 39 accounted for most of the increases in female LFPR since 1980, and by 1996 over 55 per cent of all working women are less than 35-years-old. In particular, almost 4 out 5 women in the age group of 20–29 have joined the labour force. An increase in women's educational attainment since 1970s has enabled these young women to enter a broader range of jobs, particularly those relatively well-paid positions that require university degrees. On the other hand, there has been a drop in labour force participation among older women. These women are relatively less well-educated and deficient in their human capital, and thus, are disadvantaged in the labour market. Most of them enter the labour market because of economic necessity. In the past when they were young, they were typically employed as semi-skilled workers in the light manufacturing industries such as garment, textiles, and electronics. The industrial development in Hong Kong during the 1960s and early 1970s provided them with many job opportunities in the factories. However, their employment situation has deteriorated since 1980s owing to the restructuring of industries in Hong Kong and relocation of factories to mainland China. Under these unfavourable conditions, many of them have lost their jobs and are reluctantly leaving the labour market.

There is a direct correlation between the level of a woman's education and the likelihood of her participating in the labour force. In 1991, women with primary education only had a participation rate of 37 per cent, whereas the rate for those with tertiary education was 68.4 per cent. Women's marital status and family life-cycle stages also affects their labour force participation, because their decision to work is often contingent on childcare and domestic responsibilities. In general, married women, particularly those with children, are less likely to join the labour market. In 1996, only 40.7 per cent of the married women joined the labour force—eight points lower than the overall female LFPR of 48 per cent. However, the male LFPR shows little or no alteration regardless of marital status, level of education or the responsibilities of parenthood.

Women were more represented in the manufacturing sector than men in the 1970s and early 1980s. However, the industrial structure of Hong Kong has undergone significant changes during the last two decades because of the economic transformation of the economy. The manufacturing sector has contracted while the service sector has expanded dramatically. Currently, less than 20 per cent of the workforce are employed in manufacturing as compared to 41.3 per cent in 1981. Thus, there is a marked reduction of female workers in the manufacturing industry, while about 80 per cent of women are now employed in the service sector. In the last three decades, there has been an increase in women's representation in managerial and administrative, professional and associate professional occupations; although men still greatly outnumber women in these occupations. Young, educated women have made inroads into the better-paid and higher-status jobs that used to be dominated by men. The process of 'feminisation' has accelerated in these fast-growing occupation sectors in recent years. On other hand, there has been a drastic drift of blue-collar women out of the industrial employment since the mid-1980s, as factories have been relocated to mainland China with a large number of lower-skilled manufacturing jobs disappearing from the Hong Kong economy. It is mainly the middle-aged women who concentrated in this sector who have found themselves unemployed as a result of this economic shift.

Occupational segregation by sex is a pervasive and persistent feature of industrial societies resulting in negative consequences for women in terms of the type and quality of work assigned to them. The segregation of men and women in different occupations is called horizontal segregation, while segregation within the same occupation is termed vertical segregation. Vertical segregation by sex is usually represented by a gender gap in income, a topic discussed in the next section. Horizontal segregation by sex can be reflected by the Index of Segregation that tells the proportion of men (or women) that would have to change their occupations in order for the occupational distribution to be equal for the two genders. Recent figures indicate that there is little change in this index in Hong Kong over recent decades, suggesting that obvious occupational segregation based on gender stereotypes still persists despite an increase in women's educational attainment (Chan and Ng 1994). Women greatly outnumber men in clerical work since the duties involved coincide with the perceived traditional role of women as ancillary supporters of a male leadership. On the other hand, the trades are largely reserved for men because these jobs require skills and technical knowledge—qualities that women supposedly lack. Similarly, men dominate the professional and managerial sectors. Women are not culturally constructed as leaders nor are they regarded as possessing problem-solving abilities. Because the skills associated with masculinity carry more prestige, or cultural capital, than those of women, occupations designated as 'women's work' are under-valued and paid less than occupations designated as 'men's work'.

There is a close correlation between the level of an individual's education and his or her income. Generally speaking, higher educational attainment equates to higher income. However, throughout the world, women's pay tends to be lower than that of men even when both have similar qualifications and are employed in comparable jobs. In other words, the rate of payoff for each additional year of education is different for men and women. Chung (1996) indicated that a woman's rate of return or 'payoff' to education has been consistently lower than that of men in Hong Kong in the past three decades. This means that education for women has a less favourable effect than it does for men. He argued that there are two possible explanations for this phenomenon. First, the quality of education may be different even though the level of education is the same because women tend to concentrate in the Arts, Business, and Social Science fields of study, while men dominate the Science, Engineering, and Medical fields. Second, the labour market discriminates against women, valuing the education of women less than that of men.

The gender wage differential in Hong Kong compares favourably with that of other Asian countries such as Japan and South Korea. It has also narrowed over the past few years. In 1996, an average working woman earned about 76 per cent of the wage of an average working man from her main employment, as compared to 63 per cent in 1976, and 70 per cent in 1986. Such improvement is largely attributable to the increased education attainment of women, especially among younger women. It is noted that when young working adults aged 15–26 have educational attainment beyond secondary schools, the gender differentials in their income are small; however, the gender gap in income is the greatest when these young people have completed only below or at primary school level. Moreover, regardless of the educational level, the gender gap in income is still smaller for workers under 30 years, while the greatest gap is found in the middle-age group between 35–49 years. One main reason for this is women's heavy childcare and domestic responsibilities in that life cycle stage which may negatively affect their commitment at work and, in turn, their income attainment.

The income gender gap also varies by occupations and industries, being smallest in the white-collar occupations and greatest in the service and blue-collar jobs. In managerial and professional occupations, the gender gap in income has narrowed since the 1990s, but a wider gender gap is found in the elementary occupations. The manufacturing and service sectors, where most women work, also pay lower wages to women compared to men. For other industries such as transport, storage, communication, financing, insurance, real estate and business services, women's income is comparable to that of men.

Political participation

As senior government officials are involved in the making and implementation of government policies, the gender composition of the government directorate staff provides a good indicator of women's role and influence in the formal political system. In earlier times, men dominated the key directorate positions in the government. The consequence was that equal pay for men and women was not practised until 1973. Over the past three decades, the percentages of women in directorate posts have since increased sharply from 0.9 per cent in 1971 to 19.2 per cent in 1998. However, it was not until 1984 that the first woman was promoted to the post of a department director. Women soon made significant inroads into key government positions, particularly during the 1990s. At present, 4 out of the total 14 policy secretaries in the government are women; heading the civil service, judiciary, security, and treasury bureau.

The political developments of the past two decades (particularly decolonisation and democratisation) have provided more opportunities for Hong Kong citizens to participate in the political system than was previously possible. In addition, the social and economic transformation of the territory, such as the expansion of educational and employment opportunities for women and the improvement in women's status, are also likely to facilitate women's involvement in the public sphere (Manza and Brooks 1998). Indeed, there have been an increasing number of women standing for elections at various government levels since the 1970s. At present, women comprise 26.7 per cent of the Executive Council, 16.7 per cent of the Legislative Council, and 26 per cent of the Municipal Councils, as compared to 0 per cent, 3.8 per cent, and 11.5 per cent in the respective Councils in 1971. Despite the increasing visibility of women in the political system, Hong Kong women are still less likely to run for and hold elected offices than men at all levels of government.

They are also under-represented in official appointments, especially at the higher levels.

Several factors can account for the low rates of women's participation in politics. These include: (1) sex stereotypes and public attitudes towards women's role in politics, (2) women's limited career choice and preparation in politics, (3) women's domestic role and family demands, (4) sex discrimination, and (5) structure of the formal political system (McGlen and O'Conner 1995). Community surveys in Hong Kong also show that the public would like to have more female community group leaders and politicians, but they perceive men as more knowledgeable about politics and as more suitable political leaders than women (Tang et al. 1997). Women themselves isolate factors such as their inexperience in the dynamics of politics and political patronage, lack of time, and heavy domestic responsibilities as major impediments to their further participation in the political system (Association for the Advancement of Feminism 1985).

Perceptions of gender equality and the persistence of stereotypes

Local studies on attitudes and views about gender equality and sex-stereotypes show that Hong Kong people generally accept gender equality as a concept but still define women in terms of traditional roles. Choi, Au, Cheung, Tang, and Yik (1993) surveyed 849 Hong Kong college students and found that the students generally exhibited egalitarian attitudes towards both genders. They agreed that women are entitled to enjoy the same level of freedom and autonomy as men in dating, relationships, marriage and divorce, and employment conditions. However, both male and female college students upheld traditional views about the roles of women in the family and with regard to social morality. For example, they were more accepting of the practice of swearing and the use of obscene language from men than women, and they felt that women should not have intimate sexual intimate relationships before marriage. Similar findings were obtained from a large community sample with 2012 respondents across age groups (Cheung et al. 1994).

Despite the current trend towards an expansion of opportunities for women and a general rise in the status of women, remnants of Chinese patriarchal values persist in both the private and public spheres. Survey results reveal that people are ambivalent about women who have non-traditional as well as traditional roles. Within the private sphere, local researchers find that housework is not shared equally between spouses, but rather according to traditional gender roles. Moreover, men make the major decisions in family matters (Choi and Lee 1997; Chu and Leung 1995). In the workplace, Hong Kong people assign tasks based on job sex stereotyping and sex-typing, preferring men for 'masculine' jobs and women for 'feminine' jobs (Tang et al. 1999). The public attitude towards 'superwomen' who are successful in their careers is mixed. On the one hand, these women are described as achievement-oriented, dominant, rational, decisive, and competent; on the other, they are also criticised as lacking nurturing and domestic skills, and for being selfish and aggressive. In general, traditional gender attitudes are more salient in the private than the public spheres. A recent survey showed that people hold the most egalitarian attitudes towards men and women in the sphere of education, followed by the employment sphere, then marital and parental realms. Social morality was the topic that elicited the most traditional and least egalitarian attitudes (Tang et al. 1999).

Violence against women

The cultural and feminist perspectives suggest that violence against women (VAW) in Chinese societies is related to the cultural norms that permit such behaviours. The inherent gender inequality in the culture gives legitimacy to the perpetrators' actions, induces stigma and shame in victims, and promotes public's tolerance and acceptance of myths and stereotypes (Brownmiller 1975; Bograd 1990; Campbell 1992; Gallin 1992; Honig and Hershatter 1988; Levinson 1989). In Hong Kong, traditional Chinese values and conceptions of womanhood have exerted influence on the behaviour and mentality of its people. However, the rapid social and economic changes of Hong Kong in recent decades has necessitated the (re)definition of women's roles and status in the society which may impact on the occurrence of VAW. Women's increasing educational opportunities and the public's acceptance of greater flexibility of gender norms such as employment outside their homes, has inspired women to demand and expect to be treated with greater equality. A common feminist perspective argues that the greater demand for gender equality by women will elicit increases in the reporting and/or occurrences of VAW in the society (e.g. Brownmiller 1975; Fitzgerald 1993; Koss 1988).

Prevalence and incidence studies on VAW are difficult to conduct in Hong Kong for a number of reasons. There is no consensus on the behaviours that constitute VAW, there is no broadly accepted definition of VAW and there are no measures of sufficient local relevance or sensitivity for determining the incidence of VAW (Tang 1998; Tang and Cheung 1997; Tang et al. 1995). The tolerance of VAW in Hong Kong culture and the stigma attached to VAW victims makes accurate prevalence data difficult to obtain, as many cases are unreported. However, data based on official statistics, research reports, and victimisation studies on the prevalence of rape, wife abuse, sexual harassment, and female child sexual abuse have consistently shown an increasing trend in recent years. For example, figures from police reports showed that the number of cases for rape and indecent assault have increased from 772 in 1978 to 1188 in 1997. Tang and Davis (1996) conducted a study on cases of child abuse collated in the government Child Protective Registry and found an increase in female child sexual abuse from 4.1 per cent in 1979 to 17.9 per cent in 1995. A recent community survey also revealed that wife abuse is more prevalent than is commonly believed. About 67.2 per cent of women reported psychological abuse and 10 per cent experienced at least one incident of physical abuse by their husband during the surveyed year (Tang 1999). Sexual harassment was a taboo topic in Hong Kong during the early 1980s, but it has received increasing attention in recent years. The local Coalition against Sexual Abuse (1992) discovered that 86 per cent of their female respondents reported experiencing sexual harassment in the two years prior to the survey. The most common forms being obscene telephone calls, unsolicited bodily contact, and seductive attention. In another survey conducted on a university campus, 25 per cent of female students reported experiencing some form of sexual harassment, and 1 per cent were coerced into sexual activities by either teachers or peers (Tang et al. 1996).

In the past three decades the battles against VAW in Hong Kong have been fought with the concerted efforts of local governments, community organisations, women's groups, and academics. The War-on-Rape Campaign of 1977 was one of the first attempts. This campaign raised public awareness about rape in particular but also VAW in general. A crisis hotline for rape victims, a shelter for abused women, and a women's centre for promoting women's development have since been established. Similar campaigns, such as the 1990 Campaign against Sexual Violence and the 1997 Campaign on Violence against Women demonstrate the community's continuing efforts at fighting VAW. These campaigns often adopt multi-dimensional strategies involving public education, legal reforms, provision of support services, advocacy, and research.

Legislative and institutional changes are of vital importance in combating VAW. Since the War-on-Rape Campaign of the 1970s, women's groups have called for a review of all laws and legal procedures aimed at removing discrimination against VAW victims and women in general. They have been concerned to eliminate cumbersome and humiliating procedures in the reporting, investigation, and court hearings of VAW. Women activists have lobbied for the provision of services to victims and for the extension of compensation laws to VAW survivors. Their actions have resulted in the implementation of both broad and specific reforms. The adoption of the United Nations Convention on the Elimination of All Forms of Discrimination Against Women (CEDAW) and the enactment of the Sex Discrimination Ordinance (SDO) in 1995 were major victories for women in Hong Kong. As a result of these laws it unlawful to discriminate against women in any aspects of life, and sexual harassment is now legally defined and classified as a civil offence against individuals under the SDO.

Specific legal reforms in relation to VAW have been implemented to protect the rights of rape and child sexual abuse victims. These changes ensure that a rape victim's previous sexual history not be included in evidence at the trial for rape offence, and that publication of particulars about rape and child sexual abuse victims which could reveal their identifies are restricted. Measures have also been taken to reduce victims' humiliation, embarrassment, and trauma related to various court procedures. For example, court provisions are made for rape victims' testimony to be heard *in camera*; and recently, video-recording of the testimony of child sexual abuse victims is admissible in courts. Legal steps to protect victims of domestic violence are now available in the form of injunction and arrest where the courts can order abusive husbands to stop harassing and hurting their wives. New legislation to address the problems of stalking is currently being drafted to prevent the intimidation and harassment of VAW victims and women in general. Various government departments (e.g. Police and Social Welfare) have also devised their own internal operational guidelines on how to work with victims of rape, domestic violence, and child sexual abuse. Inter-departmental and multi-disciplinary working groups are often involved in the drafting of these guidelines as well as recommending legislative and institutional changes in the area.

While legal and procedural reforms are vital, broad changes in social attitudes must also occur in order to reduce VAW. As the status of women in society rises, the victims of VAW will feel less helpless and fearful when confronted with violence. In the past decades, various women's groups and feminist organisations have been formed to promote women's interests (Lai et al. 1997). Their roles in establishing pilot programs for research and in maintaining and operating services for VAW victims, such as rape_crisis hotlines and shelters for abused wives, are vital to the reduction of VAW in Hong Kong. These services are routinely under-funded and under-staffed. Many operate on short-term seeding funds from overseas or local charitable organisations. Those services that receive government funding are often sub-sections of other primary services such as family services, family planning, and youth programs. Thus, current services for VAW victims are mainly palliative and piecemeal, despite strenuous attempts to develop comprehensive programmes.

Hong Kong's women's movement

Researchers in Hong Kong have noted that while objective indicators of women's status in health, education, and employment rates have shown some improvement in the past three decades, specific measures to fight against the root cause of patriarchy have been slow (Lai, Au and Cheung 1997; Tsang 1995). Various reasons have been proposed to explain this inertia including: (1) the resilience of Chinese patriarchal values, especially the conception of ideal womanhood in regards to family duties and social morality, (2) the absence of a strong labour or civil rights movement, similar to those that gave momentum to the women's movements in the UK and US, (3) the perpetuation of the British Colonial government's *laissez-faire* attitude to social reform, (4) the marginalisation of women's issues in the 1990s as a result of the pressing political agenda of the transition of Hong Kong to Chinese rule.

There are currently over 200 local women's groups, and these can be classified into seven categories: women's studies groups, women's rights groups, service-related women's groups, grassroots-level women's groups, professional women's groups, foreign women's groups, and neighbourhood/social activities women's groups (Gender Research Programme 1989). In charting the trajectory of the women's movement in Hong Kong, researchers recommend including only those groups concerned primarily with the disadvantaged position of local women and the advocacy of changes in the gendered hierarchy in Hong Kong (Lai et al. 1997; Tsang 1995).

The women's movement in Hong Kong closely resembles that of the feminist movement in the West, and can be divided into three stages (Lai et al. 1997; Tsang 1995). The first stage includes the years after World War Two through the mid-1970s during which time activists focused on the more public and global forms of discrimination against women.

These included campaigns against prostitution, *muitsai* (women slave/servant) and the continued existence of concubinage (where husbands keep 'minor wives' as well as 'main wives'), as well as the gross disparity between men's earnings and those of women. These actions often represented the efforts of individuals, small groups of expatriate women or prominent local women rather than a solid campaign. The Hong Kong Council of Women, formed in 1947 and comprising mostly expatriate women, was one of few women's organisations that existed during this period.

The United Nation's International Women's Year of 1975 marked the beginning of the second stage of the women's movement in Hong Kong. This period of about ten years resembled the second-wave of Western feminism. The focus had sharpened to include the micro issues such as paid maternity leave, struggles against rape and wife-beating within the belief that women's individual rights and autonomy required support and protection. During this second stage, organised women's groups have sprung up to provide services for the disadvantaged, programmes for consciousness-raising and empowerment were launched, and platforms to lobby for various women's rights appeared. These organisations have developed distinct mandates and clear lines of representation in comparison to the previous period. With the growth in numbers of women's groups a greater diversity of approaches to solving women's problems emerged. In their efforts to improve women's status some groups targeted the provision of services to the disadvantaged, while others favoured campaigning for structural change in public institutions. For example, the 'Women's Centre' and 'Harmony House', formed respectively in 1981 and 1985 under the auspices of the Hong Kong Council of Women, started as service delivery organisations for women. Later both extended their services to become resource centres providing programmes for individual empowerment. The Association for the Advancement of Feminism, formed in 1984, has a distinctive mandate— it aims to dismantle capitalist patriarchy as a condition for bringing women's emancipation. In addition, some women's groups adopt the modest non-confrontational approach, while others welcome a more radical and critical appraisal of the existing system. Despite these differences, there seems to be a consensus that the promotion of women's status in Hong Kong needs the support and participation of the women at the grass-root level (Association for the Advancement of Feminism 1991; Ho 1990; Leung 1990).

The third stage of the women's movement (1986–present) has seen the proliferation of new groups with a strong grass-root basis and specific focus of concern. For example, the Hong Kong Women's Christian

Council formed in 1988 aims not only to redefine women's roles within the religious organisations and society at large, but also to promote women's rights as well as democracy in Hong Kong. The Hong Kong Women Workers Association founded in 1989 focuses on the marginalisation and exploitation of women workers, problems associated with the relocation of the manufacturing industry to mainland China, and unequal and poor employment conditions of women workers. These groups also form coalitions to lobby for women's rights in the political arena. For example, in 1991 they organised the Women Voters Development Plan to educate women voters and drafted a comprehensive Women's Joint Political Platform. In 1992 they campaigned for the establishment of a Women's Commission and the introduction of the United Nations Convention to Eliminate All Forms of Discrimination Against Women (CEDAW). In 1994 these groups rallied for rural women's right to inherit intestate land. They also prepared an alternative Hong Kong Report on Women and presented to the Fourth UN World Conference on Women in 1995. As a result of the concerted efforts of women's groups, the government passed the Sex Discrimination Ordinance in 1995 to prohibit discrimination based on sex, pregnancy, and marital status in the workplace, in education, and social life. The Equal Opportunities Commission was set up in the subsequent year to facilitate the implementation of the Ordinance as well as to promote education to raise public awareness regarding equality of opportunities between men and women. The Legislative Council in 1994 also passed laws to give rural women the right to inherit property.

As Lai et al. (1997, p. 301) summarise,

> the first phase of women's movement in Hong Kong is characterised by elitist women founding women's groups to offer services to the less fortunate; while the second phase is characterised by educated women initiating women's groups to raise women's awareness and to promote the fight for rights of women, then spreading the idea and action to women at the grassroots level.

Women's groups in Hong Kong have followed the approaches of localisation, diversification, co-operation, politicisation, and popularisation. To strengthen the women's movement, researchers and activists have suggested that these approaches should be continued. Women's groups should develop their local resources and take into consideration local socio-cultural factors when devising their future strategies. While allowing for pluralism and not insisting on a unified ideological orientation, women's groups have pledged to join together to call for changes in the local system and raise women's consciousness through popularising feminist ideals among the mass of women (Lai et al. 1997; Lam 1985; Mao 1988).

Conclusion

Objective indicators have shown that the status of women in Hong Kong has undergone important changes in the last three decades, with increases in women's level of educational attainment, rate of labour force participation, appointment to higher government positions, and election for public offices. On the other hand, traditional Chinese culture still exerts great influence in the private sphere and in the public conception of ideal womanhood. The persistence of gender segregation and discrimination at work, gender disparity in wages, and violence against women suggests that Hong Kong women continue to occupy a disadvantaged and inferior position in society despite improvements in various social fields. The extent to which the legal reforms introduced in the mid-1990s have affected the day-to-day life of Hong Kong women remains unclear at this stage. As many local feminist scholars have pointed out, women's status cannot be enhanced simply by increasing the visibility of women in formal institutional structures. These changes must be accompanied by increasing public consciousness about gender inequality before deep-seated problems will be solved. The journey to greater gender equality must be travelled with the conscious effort of organising, mobilising, and negotiation within women's groups as well as within the community at large.

References and recommended readings

Association for the Advancement of Feminism 1985 *A report on Hong Kong women's community participation*, Association for the Advancement of Feminism, Hong Kong.
—— 1991 *Feminist organisations in Hong Kong, fact sheet series 1*, Association for the Advancement of Feminism, Hong Kong.
Bograd, M. 1990 'Why we need gender to understand human violence?' *Journal of Interpersonal Violence*, vol. 5, pp. 132–35.
Brownmiller, S. 1975 *Against our will: men, women, and rape*, Simon and Schuster, New York.
Campbell, J.C. 1992 'Wife-beating: cultural contexts versus western social sciences,' *Sanctions and sanctuary: Cultural perspectives on the beating of wives*, eds A. C. Counts, J.K. Brown, and J.C. Campbell, Westview Press, Boulder.

Chan, K.W. and Ng, C.H. 1994 'Gender, class, and employment segregation,' *Inequalities and development: Social stratification in Chinese societies*, eds S.K. Lau, M.K. Lee, P.S. Wan, and S.L. Wong, Hong Kong Institute of Asia-Pacific Studies, CUHK, Hong Kong.

Cheung, F. ed. 1997 *EnGendering Hong Kong society: A gender perspective of women's status*, The Chinese University Press, Hong Kong.

Cheung, F., Ngo, H.Y., Lai, O.K., Lee, C., Ma, S. and Tam, M. 1994 *A survey of public's perception of equal opportunities for women and men 1993–94*, Report submitted to the City and New Territories Administration, Hong Kong Government.

Choi, P.K. 1995 'Identities and diversities: Hong Kong women's movement in 1980s and 1990s,' *Hong Kong Cultural Studies Bulletin*, vol. 4, pp. 95–103.

Choi, P.K., and Lee, C.K. 1997 'The hidden abode of domestic labour: The case of Hong Kong,' *EnGendering Hong Kong society: A gender perspective of women's status*, ed. F. Cheung, The Chinese University Press, Hong Kong.

Choi, P.K., Au, K.C., Cheung, F., Tang, C. and Yik, M. 1993 *Power and dignity: Sexual harassment on campus in Hong Kong*, Hong Kong Institute of Asia-Pacific Studies, CUHK, Hong Kong.

Chu, W.C. and Leung, S.W. 1995 'Gender issues reconsidered: Insights from the study of housework sharing,' *Indicators of social development: Hong Kong, 1993*, eds S.K. Lau, M.K. Lee, P.S. Wan, and S.L. Wong, Hong Kong Institute of Asia-Pacific Studies, CUHK, Hong Kong.

Chung, Y.P. 1996 'Gender earnings differentials in Hong Kong: The effect of the state, education, and employment,' *Economics of Education Review*, vol. 15, no. 3, pp. 231–44.

Coalition Against Sexual Abuse 1992 *A survey report on women's experience of sexual harassment*, Coalition Against Sexual Abuse, Hong Kong.

Fitzgerald, L.F. 1993 'Sexual harassment: violence against women in the workplace,' *American Psychologist*, vol. 48, pp. 1070–76.

Gallin, R. 1992 'Wife abuse in the context of development and change: a Chinese Taiwanese case,' *Sanctions and sanctuary: Cultural perspectives on the beating of wives*, eds D.A. Counts, J.K. Brown, and J.C. Campbell, Westview Press, Boulder.

Gender Research Programme 1989 *Hong Kong women's organisation bulletin*, The Chinese University of Hong Kong, Hong Kong.

Ho, C. 1990 'Opportunities and challenges: the role of feminists for social change in Hong Kong,' *Bridges of power—women's multicultural alliances*, eds L. Albrecht and R.M. Brewer, New Society Publisher Philadelphia.

Hoe, S. 1991 *The private life of old Hong Kong: Expatriate women in the British colony*, Oxford University Press, Hong Kong.

—— 1996 *Chinese footprints: Exploring women's history in China, Hong Kong, and Macau*, Roundhouse Publications Asia, Hong Kong.

Hong Kong Census and Statistics Department 1971–1997 *Hong Kong Annual Digest of Statistics*, Hong Kong Census and Statistics Department, Hong Kong.

Honig, E. and Hershatter, G. 1988 'Violence against women,' *Personal voices: Chinese women in the 1980's*, eds E. Honig and G. Hershatter, Stanford University Press, Stanford.

Koss, M.P. 1988 'Hidden rape: sexual aggression and victimisation in a national sample of students in higher education,' *Rape and sexual assault*, ed. A.W. Burgess, Garland Publishing, New York.

Lai, B., Au, K. and Cheung, F. 1997 'Women's concern groups in Hong Kong,' *EnGendering Hong Kong society: A gender perspective of women's status*, ed. F. Cheung, The Chinese University Press, Hong Kong.

Lam, T.Y. 1985 'Women and development: the case of Hong Kong,' *Hong Kong Young Christian Women Association*. Paper prepared for World YWCA conference, YWCA, Hong Kong.

Leung, L.C. 1990 'Yesterday, today and tomorrow—advancement of women and women's movement,' *Annual Report 1988–1989*, Association for the Advancement of Feminism, Hong Kong.

Levinson, D. 1989 *Family violence in cross-cultural perspectives*, Sage, Newbury Park, CA.

Manza, J. and Brooks, C. 1998 'The gender gap in US presidential elections: When? Why? Implications?' *American Journal of Sociology*, vol. 103, no. 5, pp. 1235–66.

Mao, T.Y. 1988 'Women's movement in democracy,' *Women*, vol. 4, p. 8.

McGlen, N.E. and O'Conner, K. 1995 *Women, Politics, and American Society*, Prentice Hall, New Jersey.

Ngo, H.Y. 1997 'Women and employment in Asian newly-industrialised countries,' *International Journal of Employment Studies*, vol. 5, pp. 67–93.

Pearson, V. and Leung, B. 1995 *Women in Hong Kong*, Oxford University Press, Hong Kong.

Tang, C. 1998 'Psychological abuse of Chinese wives,' *Journal of Family Violence*, vol. 13, pp. 299–314.

—— 1999 'Wife abuse in Hong Kong Chinese families: a community survey,' *Journal of Family Violence*, vol. 14, no. 2, pp. 173–91.

Tang, C. and Cheung, F. 1997 'Effects of gender and profession type on definitions of violence against women in Hong Kong,' *Sex Roles: A Journal of Research*, vol. 36, pp. 837–49.

Tang, C. and Davis, C. 1996 'Child abuse in Hong Kong revisited after 15 years: Characteristics of victims and abusers,' *Child Abuse & Neglect*, vol. 20, pp. 1201–206.

Tang, C., Au, W., Chung, Y.P. and Ngo, H.Y. 1999 *Statistical analysis on Census data on gender and disability*, Final report submitted to the Equal Opportunities Commission of Hong Kong.

Tang, C., Lee, E., Ma, E., Ngo, H., Lee, M., and Wan, P. 1997 *A baseline survey of equal opportunities on the basis of gender in Hong Kong*, Report submitted to the Equal Opportunities Commission, Hong Kong.

Tang, C., Yik, M., Cheung, F., Choi, P., and Au, K. 1995 'How do Chinese college students define sexual harassment?' *Journal of Interpersonal Violence*, vol. 10, no. 4, pp. 503–15.

—— 1996 'Sexual harassment of Chinese college students,' *Archives of Sexual Behavior*, vol. 25, no. 2, pp. 201–215.

Tsang, G.Y. 1995 'The women's movement at the crossroads,' *Women in Hong Kong*, eds V. Pearson and B. Leung, Oxford University Press, Hong Kong.

Westwood, R., Mehrain, T., and Cheung, F. 1995 *Gender and society in Hong Kong: A statistical profile*, Hong Kong Institute of Asia-Pacific Studies, CUHK, Hong Kong.

Wong, W.P. 1995 'Women and work: Opportunities and experiences,' *Women in Hong Kong*, eds V. Pearson and B. Leung, Oxford University Press, Hong Kong.

Yip, H.M. 1997 'Women and cultural tradition in Hong Kong,' *EnGendering Hong Kong society: A gender perspective of women's status*, ed. F. Cheung, The Chinese University Press, Hong Kong.

10 Being women in Japan, 1970–2000

Elise K. Tipton

School of Asian Studies
University of Sydney

The women's liberation movement in the United States of the late 1960s and early 1970s had more than a ripple effect on women in Japan as well as other countries like Australia. It stimulated a second wave of feminism in the post-World War Two period consisting of a proliferation of women's groups and organizations demanding equality in employment opportunities and pay, sexual liberation, reproductive rights, and equal political representation. Although membership in women's groups and activities declined during the 1980s, an Equal Employment Opportunity Law was passed in 1985, a majority of girl high school graduates proceeded to tertiary education and more than half of all married women could be found in the paid workforce. During the early 1990s '*onna no jidai*' (the era of women) became a catchphrase connoting freedom, affluence and independence achieved by women. And most recently, in the late 1990s the phenomena of 'yellow cabs' and schoolgirl prostitution suggest to some sexual liberation and empowerment for the younger generation of women. Does this mean that during the past three decades Japanese women have abandoned the ideal of 'good wife, wise mother' (*ryōsai kenbo*) that was dominant since the beginning of the century?

This is not just a rhetorical question, and the answer is not a simple 'yes' or 'no'. In this essay I want to convey the complexity of an answer to the question. On the one hand, there are commonalities among all or at least most Japanese women—factors that affect all women because they are women. On the other hand, Japanese women are not all alike and their experiences have been diverse due to differences in class, generation or age, geography (regional as well as urban vs rural), ethnicity and education. By looking at four areas of activity—the home, the workplace, the public arena and the world of popular culture—we will see that the range of options for women has widened during the past three decades. However, we will also see that the patriarchal underpinnings of social, economic and political institutions and practices remain firmly entrenched to perpetuate the sexual division of labour. These institutions and practices, both informally and formally, act as powerful influences on women's choices.

At the same time, while still generally favouring men, the messages that these institutions and practices send to women are not always consistent or uniform. These contradictions open up a space in which women are able to try to accommodate their individual needs and desires to the state's and society's expectations. The state, for example, promotes an image of women that is oriented contradictorily to both production and reproduction while the media encourages women to be consumers. Women may respond in different ways to these varied and sometimes contradictory conceptions of their proper role. However, I have said 'accommodate' to indicate that radical feminism has not been widely accepted by Japanese women (not that it has in any society) and to suggest that the ideology placing women primarily in nurturing roles has in many if not most cases been internalised.

The home: women's domain?

Some scholars, such as Sumiko Iwao (1993), as well as most Japanese men and the media, represent the home as a sphere where Japanese women enjoy dominant status and power. In most Japanese families the husband hands over his pay packet to his wife who then gives him 'an allowance' for pocket money and generally takes charge of the day-to-day management of the household's activities and expenses. She is also fully responsible for the rearing and education of the children. The images of 'the professional housewife' and 'education mama' which have emerged in the post-World War Two period indicate the complete devotion and skill required for success in these endeavours as well as the high social value placed on women's role as wives and mothers.

The home and domestic responsibilities have been the centre of Japanese women's activities since the 1890s, but being 'good wives and wise mothers' was not in fact the 'traditional' ideal for women. In premodern times the family was a unit of production as well as reproduction, and most Japanese women worked on the family farm or in the family business as well as being responsible for household tasks. Moreover, mothers did not spend most of their time in child-rearing, nor did they make important decisions regarding their children's education. Mothers-in-law or older children took over the former while fathers exercised authority for the latter. It was only in samurai families that women confined themselves to domestic tasks. In the 1890s and early twentieth century, when the patriarchal family became the foundation for the Meiji family-state ideology, the government began to disseminate the samurai ideal of 'good wife, wise mother' to middle-class women.

It was only later in the twentieth century that this ideal spread to other classes, and only post-World War Two affluence made it possible for a majority of Japanese women to devote themselves exclusively to being wives and mothers. Ironically, although Occupation democratisation discredited the 'good wife, wise mother' slogan and produced constitutional provisions for equality of the sexes, the affluence accompanying the 'economic miracle' of the 1960s enabled reinforcement of the sexual division of labour. So did the demands of corporate employers on the time and loyalty of male employees, keeping 'salarymen' husbands/fathers away from their families and household tasks and responsibilities. Surveys in the early 1990s revealed that Japanese men spent only one minute a day on childcare and eight to eleven minutes a day on housework (Diggs 1998, p. 81). The 1998 White Paper on Women reported an increase, but still only 20 minutes a day on housework, despite the increase in number of married women in the workforce over the past three decades.

These survey results indicate both the costs and benefits of the sexual division of labour. On the one hand, control over family financial planning may raise women's self-esteem and sense of independence, and government policy as well as society as a whole encourages motherhood and women as nurturers and household managers. The postwar conception of housewifery and motherhood is a demanding one whose success brings wide approbation. The phrase 'professional housewife' implies the efficiency, training, commitment and creativity with which Japanese wives are expected to apply to household tasks. Both the state and business have recognized the importance of Japanese housewives for the nation's economic growth. Without such full-time commitment from wives and their careful financial management, companies would not have been able to demand that husbands spend long hours at their jobs, or to count on a high personal savings rate for investment capital.

Self-sacrificing devotion is also expected in the nurturing and education of children. During the postwar period achievement in formal education, especially at university level, became increasingly the means to career success. Intensified competition to get into the most prestigious universities led to after-school 'cram schools', 'examination hell' and pressure on younger students to gain entry to the top middle schools and high schools acting as 'feeders' to the best universities. Japanese mothers have been given the entire responsibility for their children's success (or failure) in this competition, and for most women who live in urban areas this is carried out without help from the extended family. Mothers are expected to spend virtually all their waking and sleeping hours with their child during infancy and preschool years, then as many hours as possible during the school years, providing emotional support as well as resourceful devices for teaching both the social and academic skills that are required for success in school and later life.

In a revealing study of a middle-class nursery school in Tokyo during the late 1980s, Anne Allison (1996) demonstrates how the school managed, shaped and monitored women's behaviour so that they would assist their children in adapting to school. Even during summer vacation mothers were expected to supervise their children's activities to keep them practicing skills they were learning at school and to maintain school routines and schedules at home. Mothers' diligence was in turn monitored by the school through their being given a calendar on which to chart their children's activities during the break. Although some of the women in Allison's study expressed concerns and doubts about Japan's educational system, few questioned the role they were expected to play in helping their children to perform.

It goes without saying in Japan that motherhood means marriage. Single mothers remain stigmatised, and the comparatively small but increasing number of teenage pregnancies since the 1980s has become a social concern. From birth girls are socialised to make marriage and motherhood their primary goals, as is strikingly evident in the pattern of girls' education. Girls since the Meiji period have been required to complete the same number of compulsory school years as boys, and the 1946 Constitution made education for both girls and boys a basic right. In 1970 82.7 per cent of females continued on from lower to upper secondary school (up from 55.9 per cent in 1960), and by the end of the decade this proportion reached 95 per cent, exceeding that of boys (Fujimura-Fanselow and Kameda 1995, pp. 45–46; Hara 1995, p. 104). Dramatic growth in female participation in post-secondary education followed this trend at secondary school level with enrolments rising from 18 per cent of high school graduates in 1970 to 39.2 per cent in 1991 (Fujimura-Fanselow and Kameda 1995, p. 45).

While these statistics reflect a change in social attitudes toward acceptance of the desirability of providing higher education for women and a growth in incomes enabling families to educate daughters as well as sons, the education received by girls after lower secondary level differs from that of boys. Although more girls than boys continue on from lower to upper secondary school, fewer girls attempt to enter the most competitive high schools that will prepare them for entrance into a four-year university. In 1996 females made up only 22.9 per cent of four-year university students. Rather, the majority aim for the less rigorous, though expensive, junior colleges that generally do not require entrance examinations. These less ambitious goals appear to be formed during the lower secondary school years, for university aspirations were approximately the same for boys and girls in third grade according to one survey conducted in 1985 (Fujimura-Fanselow and Kameda 1995, p. 49). The select minority of females who do obtain a four-year university degree tend to come from wealthy families where the parents themselves have strong educational backgrounds.

A gendered approach to curriculum and school practices as well as parental attitudes and socioeconomic level contributes to these differences in educational aspirations. A revealing illustration of the continued aim of educating girls to become good wives and wise mothers was the introduction of home economics as a compulsory subject for girls only in upper secondary schools in 1973. This requirement finally changed in 1994 to include boys as well as girls. In addition, gender biases pervade textbooks that are predominantly written by males. Despite the efforts made by women's groups in the late 1970s and 1980s to eliminate gender stereotyping in textbooks, a 1989 study by the League of Japanese Lawyers found that although more males were depicted in home economics textbooks than earlier, they were pictured in supervisory roles. Females were pictured as doing the actual cooking or laundry. Other customary practices in everyday school life reinforce differences between the sexes and privilege boys over girls, for example, separating boys' and girls' roll lists and calling the boys' roll first.

Despite the marriage-motherhood oriented socialisation that girls receive, there are indications that many young women are delaying and limiting, though not rejecting, the burdens of being wives and mothers.

Women in their early twenties undergo intense pressure from family and friends as well as society at large to marry before they reach twenty-five. A common joke refers to them as 'Christmas cakes', meaning that like Christmas cakes, they will become too old and stale after the twenty-fifth. Despite all this pressure, in the 1990s women's average age at first marriage rose to twenty-six for the first time. Rising levels of education may be partly responsible for more women wanting to pursue careers, but surveys show that most Japanese women still make marriage and motherhood their primary goals. Increasingly, however, they are reluctant to give up the independence and comfortable lifestyle that their jobs as single women provide, and changing views of marriage toward a preference for 'love marriages' make women more choosy about a prospective husband. Since the 1970s when images of 'the new family' appeared, young people hope to marry for love or companionship and expect to spend their leisure time together, which was not the custom in earlier times. Rising divorce rates, especially among women in their forties and fifties and in spite of laws which make divorce financially difficult for women, suggest a gradual shift in women's expectations of marriage. In contrast to press reports in the 1970s, newspapers in the 1990s reported that a majority of divorcees would like to remarry, but only if they could do so for companionship.

The vast majority of women who still do marry are having fewer children. In 1989 newspapers headlined the '1.57 shock', referring to a new low in the birthrate. The birthrate has continued to decline further below replacement level since then. This trend began in the late 1950s after legalisation of abortion in 1948 and a government-sponsored family planning program encouraging contraceptive use in the mid-1950s. Government support for birth control at that time arose out of concern about 'overpopulation' in postwar economic conditions of devastation and poverty. Even as early as the mid-1960s, however, Prime Minister Sato began encouraging women to have more babies to provide the workforce for sustaining economic growth. In the 1980s the government faced the prospect of expanding welfare expenditures accompanying a rapidly aging population as well as a continuing labour shortage. Officials again urged women to have more children and to fulfil their nurturing role as care-givers of elderly relatives. These interests lie behind the repeated rejection until 1999 of recommendations to legalise the contraceptive pill, even in the face of lobbying by large-scale pharmaceutical companies and a reversal of attitudes by medical practitioners' organizations in the mid 1990s. In practice, middle-aged women provide most of the care for the elderly, including the physically or mentally impaired. Cultural norms as well as government policies favour such home care. However, younger women have not responded to the government's calls to raise the birthrate. The costs of education, limited housing space and more recently the long recession help to explain the low birthrate, but the all-encompassing nature of child-rearing may also encourage women to have a small number of children. Many express a relief when their children reach school age since this gives them some time for themselves.

For women in the middle and upper classes the school years of their one or two children can indeed bring time to enjoy hobbies, educational pursuits, sports and other leisure activities with female friends, while time-saving household appliances and supermarkets still enable them to keep a good home. And once their children finish schooling these women are relieved further of the time-consuming responsibility of assisting them on the ladder to success. Travel can then be added to the range of possible activities to keep women busy. No wonder that the majority of women would like to become full-time housewives and that Japanese men envy their lifestyle! However, the proportion of wives over the age of 35 who do not work has been declining. By the mid-1980s they made up only 30 per cent of all married women (Ueno 1994, p. 28). Consequently, while the state and society may still project an ideal of 'women's place is in the home', the reality is that the majority of Japanese women do not make the home their permanent workplace after they marry.

The paid workplace: separate and unequal

While the proportion of full-time housewives has been on the decline since the 1970s, the proportion of women who have returned to work after an interruption has 'gone from near invisibility to being an overwhelming majority' (Ueno 1994, p. 28). As will become clear, the primary motivation for returning to the paid workforce is not the desire to work and pursue career goals, but economic necessity 'to supplement household income'. Women's options for paid work have become more varied with restructuring of the economy in the postindustrial age, an ongoing labour shortage and attitudinal changes owed in no small part to the post-1970s women's movement. Nevertheless, the persistence of the 'good wife, wise mother' ideal has meant that state policies and corporate structures and practices treat women's labour as supplementary labour, which is therefore cheaper and disposable. Consequently, despite passage of the Equal Employment Opportunity

Law (EEOL) in 1985, gendered inequalities still abound in the workplace.

Government encouragement of married women entering the workforce began in the middle of the 1960s when a shortage of workers developed with rapid economic growth. However, it only promoted part-time work that would not interfere with women's 'family responsibilities' and especially their child-rearing responsibilities. Ambivalence about married women entering the labour force was indicated in a government white paper on child welfare at about the same time which blamed 'women's increased penetration of the workforce' for a perceived decline in the level of nurturing (Buckley 1993, p. 351). Meanwhile, tax incentives discouraged women from reentering the labour force on a full-time basis after their child-rearing years by allowing husbands to continue to claim their wives as dependents if they earned less than one million yen. The 1972 Working Women's Welfare Law assumed that women would need help to 'harmonise' their home and work responsibilities (Uno 1993, p. 305). Superannuation policies have also discriminated against full-time working wives.

The pattern of women's employment consequently developed into an 'M' curve, with the first peak of employment in the years before marriage and child-rearing and the second in middle age after child-rearing responsibilities decline. Reentry into the labour force on a part-time basis, however, means that women workers cannot enjoy the benefits of permanent full-time employees, such as retirement pensions, even though their work hours may run up to 35 hours per week. Their hours and jobs have been the first to be cut back in times of recession such as the one which began in the early 1990s.

The EEOL of 1985 supposedly ended discrimination against women, but because it lacks penalties for infringement, it has had little impact on improving women's career opportunities. The ineffectiveness of the law derives from the fact that it was primarily intended, according to the Ministry of Labour, 'to improve working women's welfare and to promote measures to enable them to harmonise work and family roles'. It was not designed to recognise women's fundamental right to work without discrimination and unfair treatment (Watabe-Dawson 1997, p. 42). Although women activists since the early 1970s had pushed for equality in the workplace, the law was a response to international pressure—it enabled Japan to ratify the United Nations' Convention on the Elimination of All Forms of Discrimination against Women—and businesses' need for more young qualified workers for the rapidly growing service industry. The law prohibits discrimination in training, fringe benefits, retirement age, resignation and dismissal, for which violators can be brought to court, but only exhorts employers to 'endeavour' to avoid discrimination in recruitment, hiring, job assignment and promotion. A revision of the law, coming into effect in April 1999, stiffened these 'endeavour' categories to 'prohibitions', but there still remain many formal as well as informal obstacles to achieving women's equality in the workplace.

Large companies responded to the EEOL by redeveloping a two-track recruitment and promotion system in which a recruit chooses to apply for either the managerial or the clerical track. Only the managerial track leads to top level positions in the company, but while theoretically open to both sexes, in practice male full-time employees automatically enter the managerial track whereas most women enter the clerical track. Even ten years after the passage of the EEOL only 1.2 per cent of women workers were at the department head level (Watabe-Dawson 1997, p. 41), and the majority of these worked for small or medium-sized companies. Company policies, such as interviewing women applicants only after all qualified male applicants are placed, have continued to discriminate against women in both direct and indirect ways, and the earnings gap between men and women did not narrow in the decade after passage of the EEOL. Discriminatory recruiting practices became notable during the 1990s recession as female college and university graduates found it more difficult to find jobs than male graduates. Informal practices have also continued to encourage women to resign upon marriage or childbirth.

Moreover, the number of women applying for the managerial track has remained low because it more or less forces women to choose between marriage and a male-type career requiring long hours and job transfers. Not surprisingly, few choose the latter. Even in the department store industry that promotes more women to managerial levels than other industries, Millie Creighton (1996) found that most department managers in her study had never been married. The corporate management practice of entertaining middle- and upper-level executives in hostess clubs at night also makes it difficult for women with families to develop the networks necessary for promotion. The masculine orientation of such corporation-sponsored recreation sends the message to women that work as a full-time career is for men (Allison 1994).

The M-curve pattern of women's employment therefore has continued from the mid 1970s to the present, but with ever increasing numbers of married women in their late 30s and 40s reentering the workforce as part-time employees. Thirty-nine per cent of all employees are now women, but 70 per cent of these are part-time workers (Hisano and Endo 1998, p. 2). The majority of married women who have returned to work have done so to supplement the family income in order to achieve or maintain a certain standard of living or to accumulate savings for their children's education. And while part-time work has been assumed, and justified in company rhetoric, to allow women to continue to fulfil their household and child-rearing responsibilities, in fact since the 1980s it has come to require almost as many hours as so-called full-time work. The definition of part-time work is therefore not based on the number of hours worked, but the treatment and lack of benefits going with the job. Part-timers do not, for example, qualify for company pensions or paid vacations, and they receive smaller bonuses.

Part-time women workers still have primary responsibility for household tasks, but despite the stress created by trying to fulfil both work and domestic responsibilities, many women recently surveyed did not try to lessen the time spent on housework. Rather, they tried to 'prove' to their families that working would not inconvenience the household. 'Once I decided to continue working I didn't want to cause my family any inconvenience so I decided not to slacken on housework ... ' (Broadbent and Morris-Suzuki 1998, p. 17). A number of women expressed the desire to avoid neighbours' as well as family members' criticism for failure to perform wifely duties. Carrying out the role of wife and mother thus has continued to be important to women as well as to society as a whole.

Women in the public arena

The continued primacy of a domestic role for women is reflected in the nature of women's participation in public activities and organizations as well as the workplace. In the 1946 election 39 women won seats in the Diet as millions of newly enfranchised women went to the polls for the first time. These numbers, however, have never been repeated, so that women remain under-represented in national politics, the lowest in fact among industrialised nations according to a 1991 survey (Kubo and Gelb 1994, p. 120). Despite the demands of the women's movement since the second wave of the 1970s, on average women have made up only 2 per cent of the more powerful House of Representatives in the Diet. Movements where women have been more prominent include environmental citizens' movements, the consumer movement and the peace movement, all of which can be seen as extensions of women's traditional areas of responsibility.

The low level of women's participation in politics has a long historical background dating back to premodern times, but even in the Meiji period

(1868–1912) when modernisation began, the state reinforced tradition with legal prohibitions against women's participation in political activities of any kind, including attendance at political meetings. Feminist groups in the 1920s gained some concessions and won support in the lower house of the Diet for women's suffrage, but the conservative upper House of Peers blocked enfranchisement.

The end of the war and the American Occupation finally brought women the vote and equality in the constitution, but until the 1980s social attitudes as well as the structures and operations of the major political parties worked against women's political activism. Susan Pharr's 1981 study of women in politics found that Japanese people considered it unacceptable for women to run for political office because it was seen as inappropriate to fulfilling women's domestic role and responsibilities. Several local politicians interviewed mentioned that their husbands had initially opposed their entry into electoral politics. The major parties and campaign practices have also made it difficult for women to stand as candidates. Although women comprise a substantial percentage of party members (40 per cent of the dominant Liberal-Democratic Party was female in the early 1990s), few are nominated to run for election. Instead they are expected to carry out support activities, such as preparing meals and making telephone calls for male candidates. The parties make up a party list of their candidates and provide financial support for expensive campaigns based on the member's ability to sign up new party members who pay a membership fee and on his or her standing within one of the main party factions. Traditional family and party roles make it difficult for women to obtain these prerequisites, so women candidates usually end up low on the party list.

Since the 1980s, however, there have been some indications that attitudinal changes and experience in local community-based movements lie behind an increase in the number of women candidates running for office. The 1997 White Paper on Women reported that in 1974 51.6 per cent of female respondents expressed 'some' interest in politics compared to only 35 per cent in 1951. In 1991 this group had grown to only 52.3 per cent, but the proportion expressing 'great' interest had risen from 5.6 to 8.2 per cent (Sōrifu 1997, p. 20). Inauguration of a new column in 1990 entitled 'From "*okusan*" to "*sotosan*"' in the women's magazine *Wife* suggested the increasing involvement of housewives in activities outside the home (Sato 1995, p. 366). The term '*okusan*', literally meaning 'the person who resides in the inner part [of the house]', in the past was an honorific one used to refer to middle- and upper-class wives who could afford to be full-time housewives. But in the post-World War Two period it has come to refer to all housewives.

Coining of the term '*sotosan*', meaning 'the person who is outside', refers to housewives of the 1990s who are no longer content to stay at home. A decline in the percentage of 'hobby' courses offered at civic and women's centres and a parallel increase in courses on 'women's issues and women's history' reflects the heightened consciousness among ordinary Japanese women about issues concerning their gender that occurred in the 1970s and 1980s.

According to the director of the Kanagawa Prefectural Women's Centre,

> Up until the beginning of the 1980s, there were very few opportunities available to college-educated women who had given up careers to become wives and mothers to re-enter the job market. Many of these women, therefore, directed their time, energy and talents into involvement in local community movements and in self-study programs (Quoted in Sato 1995, p. 367).

Women took part in many different local community causes, but were especially active in movements related to the environment, consumer interests, welfare of children and the elderly, and cultural projects such as establishment of libraries, civic centres and women's centres. These causes were added to women's large involvement in the peace movement since the end of World War Two. Their experience in these local movements seems to have led to recognition of the necessity of bringing political pressure to bear on the government in order to achieve solutions. A striking example of this new political strategy was the movement led by women to oppose destruction of the forests of Ikego in Kanagawa Prefecture south of Tokyo for construction of housing for American military personnel stationed nearby. Frustrated by the government's refusal to listen to them, the women ran their own representatives for the local city assembly in 1986. Although they did not win a majority, the top four candidates elected to the assembly were women activists from the movement. The following year 31 women affiliated with Seikatsu Club Seikyō, a nationwide network for improving life through cooperatives providing organically grown food, won seats in city assemblies in the greater Tokyo area.

The emergence of the charismatic Doi Takako as the first woman leader of the main opposition party, the Social Democratic Party of Japan, in the late 1980s seemed to signal a new era of political participation for women. The election of 22 women to the House of Councillors in 1989, up from 10 or fewer in previous elections, was touted in the media as 'the Madonna phenomenon'. Opposition to the new consumption tax and dissatisfaction with the handling of the Recruit political scandal had drawn support for women candidates from the four main opposition parties. Subsequent elections have not resulted in further large advances, however, so that Japanese women still remain under-represented compared to women in other countries. With women constituting only 2.34 per cent in the House of Representatives in 1992, Japan ranked 110 out of 131 countries surveyed. Representation in prefectural assemblies was no higher (Sato 1995, p. 370). Nevertheless, developments since the 1980s demonstrate a new political awareness on the part of ordinary Japanese housewives.

Besides their experiences in the workplace and community-based movements, this awareness can be attributed to the second wave of the women's movement that began in the late 1960s and early 1970s. At a 1970 demonstration a banner asking 'Mother, is marriage really bliss?' heralded the movement's rejection of domesticity as women's fate. Another banner declaring 'Let's Examine Our Feminine Consciousness' indicated the movement's emphasis on consciousness-raising among individual women as a means to recognizing the dual oppression of class and patriarchy. This mirrored the methods stressed by the women's liberation movement in the USA, as did another new emphasis on sexual liberation. But while the new feminist movement in Japan owed much of its stimulus and rhetoric to Western feminist developments, it also grew out of indigenous Japanese conditions. In particular, many of the feminists of the 1970s came out of the New Left movements of the late 1960s that had opposed the Vietnam War and the bureaucratic and technological aspects of modern capitalist society. Women activists in those movements were dissatisfied with the sexist discriminatory treatment they received from male activists that relegated them to traditional female jobs like typing and denied them access to decision-making positions. The new feminist movement also attacked the cultural values associated with the 'economic miracle' of the 1960s that undervalued women because they were less productive than men due their reproductive roles. Numerous women's liberation groups were formed which sought to widen cooperation among women and to develop women's independence from men.

The movement began to shift its focus from consciousness-raising to action on specific social issues when the numerous diverse groups came together in 1972 to fight successfully against a proposed revision of the Eugenic Protection Law which would have eliminated economic reasons as legitimate grounds for an abortion. The International Women's Year Action Group, formed in 1975, most clearly represented this shift to action on concrete issues:

'Act, act, act' is the most conspicuous characteristic of our activities. We go to the Diet to eliminate sex discrimination in politics. We go to NHK [Japan Broadcasting Corporation] to protest against sexist programs. We go to law courts to support any woman who sues for sexual discrimination. We telephone, write letters, send telegrams, and set up signature-seeking campaigns in order to make society free of sex discrimination (Quoted in Tanaka 1995, p. 348).

Most of the activists emerging at this time were older professionals with some access to the political establishment. Their social backgrounds and international pressure sparking media attention helped to counter negative public attitudes towards the women's liberation movement. United Nations sponsorship of the International Women's Year in 1975 and inauguration of the UN Decade for Women also forced the Japanese government to initiate policies to end sex discrimination.

During the 1980s and 1990s the feminist movement became more diverse and decentralised as different groups focused on specific issues and feminist debates arose among academics in the new field of women's studies. These trends have been viewed positively by some feminists, negatively by others. The diverse groups came together again successfully against further attempts to revise the Eugenic Protection Law, but could not unite on other issues, notably on whether to eliminate protective measures for women, such as limits on overtime work, from the Labour Standards Law. Some feminists also blame the lack of cooperation among feminist groups for the ineffectiveness of the EEOL. Even the legitimisation of women's studies and small gains in politics and government-sponsored programs have received criticism from some groups as mere 'assimilation' into the existing system rather than significant steps toward transforming it (e.g. Tanaka 1995, pp. 350–51).

Women as subject and object in the world of popular culture

Some of those who see the situation of Japanese women in the 1990s as worse than in the previous decade (e.g. Tanaka 1995; Suzuki 1995; Funabashi 1995) are thinking of the image and role of women in popular and consumer culture as well as in the workplace. Again, the continued conception of women in reproductive roles has shaped both the products and images offered to women by the popular culture industry and the leisure and consumption patterns chosen by women themselves. At the same time, although choices available to women remain limited, they have become more numerous and diverse as women's purchasing power has grown.

Since sellers focus on women as consumers, women's contribution to Japan's high household savings rate is probably less widely known. This would especially come as a surprise in overseas tourist destinations where Japanese women have a reputation for buying high-priced designer clothes and accessories. Most of these women are young single women in their early twenties who are not only big spenders, but big savers as well. They are at a period in their life when they are most free of responsibilities and have the most income at their disposal. Although information on gender differences is limited, it seems that young single working women are even more consumption-oriented than young working men. For example, they are more than twice as likely to travel abroad for pleasure than are single working men and generally spend more time and money on recreation. These gender differences became more pronounced during the 1980s as the consumption expenditures of single women under the age of 30 increased 15.8 per cent, while that of single men increased only 2 per cent. The biggest increases for young single women were in spending on sports, hobbies and lessons (e.g. English conversation and cooking), while for single men they were for accessories such as watches and non-alcoholic beverages. The soccer boom of the 1990s, for example, owed much to the Japan Football League's successful attempt to draw women fans into the sport (Watts 1998). At the same time, young single women in the early 1990s saved 1.9 times as much as single men, as much as 21.4 per cent of their income even in expensive Tokyo (Horioka 1993, p. 288).

Both the high savings and consumption rates of young single women are attributable to the persistence of the expectation that they will eventually become good wives and wise mothers. Since the 1970s the majority of them would have full-time work (three-quarters of 20–24 year-olds in 1991), often as 'office ladies' in non-career clerical and service positions. Typically, they would live with their parents, and some employers would even require this to ensure the respectability of their employees. Contributing only nominal amounts toward food expenses, young working women are able to spend large amounts on travel and recreation, yet still save 20 to 30 per cent of their income, most commonly for marriage and travel.

The retailing, entertainment and travel industries have understandably targeted this group with its large disposable income. By looking at advertising and the mass media we can see that the products and styles being sold to women present somewhat contradictory role models. Most still reinforce the image of women as cute (*kawaii*), childlike, and by extension subordinate and powerless, but in the 1990s some new images of aggressive, dominating women have appeared. New types of women's magazines emerged in the 1970s that responded to the increase in young, educated working women and marked the beginning of the consumer culture more generally in Japan. These magazines, including the still popular *An An* and *Non-No*, carried features on tourism and food as well as fashion. The proportion of advertisements in these magazines increased greatly during the 1980s (up to 54.4 per cent of *An An* in 1986), and with print runs in the hundreds of thousands and even over a million, women's magazines have become a major advertising medium. Though it is difficult to determine whether the magazines created or were responding to increased demand among readers, they began to carry detailed illustrated tourist maps and articles about foreign cities at the same time as the beginning of the travel boom among young women. And while women's magazines everywhere provide models of behaviour and style for their readers, Japanese women's magazines are notably prescriptive in their language, often adopting classroom phrases and tone, such as: "The theme of the second lesson knitwear is how to improve the neckline ... You must graduate from round collars ... (Quoted from *JJ* in Tanaka 1998, p. 119)." Or, "Those who are in the senior grade could give it a finishing touch with a purple scarf (Quoted from *25 ans* in Tanaka 1998, p. 120)."

Articles and advertisements often provide advice on how to look 'intelligent' (*chiteki*), but intelligence seems to be manifested in choice of clothing, make-up and fashion style. For example, Princess Masako, a graduate of Harvard University and an official in the Foreign Service before marrying the crown prince, featured in an article as a model of intelligence. A make-up artist noted that the princess demonstrated that outside appearance alone does not create true beauty, but nevertheless went on to say that she was 'intelligent indeed' because she wore grey eye shadow contrasting with a deep raspberry-pink lipstick. Furthermore, her hairdresser commented that the princess manifested her intelligence in her hair-style. Intelligence in a woman therefore seems to have more to do with appearance than mental capacities (Tanaka 1998, p. 124).

Television, also a pervasive source of role models for women, provides another reason for feminists' pessimism. Although the number of women employees has increased since the 1980s, the broadcasting industry remains male-dominated, and this is reflected in program content (Suzuki 1995). The government-funded NHK emphasises self-improvement content in its programs aimed at women, having motives that are less commercial than those of women's magazines or private broadcasting companies. Its immensely popular serialised 'morning dramas' explicitly and implicitly promote the ideal of women working outside the home but simultaneously support traditional values of self-sacrifice and loyalty to the family (Harvey 1998). Commercial channels chase high ratings more crassly, exploiting women's sexuality to an even greater extent in the 1990s than in previous decades.

Women's organizations have criticised the representation of women in the mass media, opposing not only sex stereotyping, but also the spread of pornography and the more general commercialisation of sex since the beginning of the 1990s. These trends certainly characterise the mass circulation *manga* (comics and their animated video and movie versions) aimed at male readers and viewers. In comparison, *manga* written for young women exhibit characteristics which both preserve and subvert traditional female roles. They now place less emphasis on virginity, but marriage is still presented as the ideal for women, and passivity and self-sacrifice remain virtues to emulate. This even applies to the young fantasy heroines with supernatural powers who began to appear in the mid-1970s and 1980s. The popular schoolgirl heroines of the 1990s' *Sailor Moon* are more aggressive and violent, but psychologically less complex than earlier characters, and the merchandising accompanying the series is far more extensive. The emergence of these young heroines parallels the image of the adult 'cyborg woman' which rose to prominence in fantasy and science fiction works in the 1990s. These women contrast sharply with the stereotypical image of passive Japanese women not only in their aggressiveness and use of violence, but also their use of futuristic technology (Napier 1998).

The adolescent romantic themes appearing in young women's *manga* do not disturb feminists as much as the actual sexual behaviour of schoolgirls and young single women tourists. In the 1970s feminists campaigned against Japanese men's sex tours to foreign destinations in Asia, but in the 1990s attention has also been directed to 'yellow cabs' and schoolgirls' participation in the commodification of sex (e.g. Kanai 1996, p. 18; McGregor 1996). How extensive the behaviour is in reality is unclear. However, the media abounds with stories about '*enjo kōsai*', high school girls engaging in phone sex or selling their used uniforms and underwear in stores to earn pocket money to purchase expensive brand-name products. Equally common are tales of women tourists who pick up foreign men for sex in places like Bali and Hawaii (though the term 'yellow cab' originated from behaviour observed in New York). Some may argue that these phenomena constitute sexual self-determination, but as the prominent feminist academic Ueno Chizuko has observed, while perhaps indicating that Japanese women have achieved equality in the bedroom, they still have not achieved equality in the workplace. Even equality in the bedroom is questionable considering the exploitation of women in the sex industry. This ranges from high class hostess bars where hostesses massage salarymen's egos more than their bodies to brothels where foreign Asian women have often been lured by false promises to become virtually imprisoned prostitutes (Matsui 1995; Murata 1996).

Conclusion

How can we assess the developments in Japanese women's role and status since the 1970s? The picture is a mixed one, in large part because Japanese women themselves have become more diverse. On the whole, there is no doubt that Japanese women are now able to choose and enjoy a greater variety of lifestyles, owing to higher levels of education, greater affluence accompanying structural changes in the economy and overall economic growth, and attitudinal changes accepting the idea of equal access to education and employment. The women's movement and international pressures since the 1970s have contributed actively to these changes. Nevertheless, as evident in the discussions of women's role in the workplace, politics and popular culture, inequality and discrimination remain pervasive in Japanese society because of persisting assumptions about the sexual division of labour. These assumptions position women primarily in nurturing, reproductive roles even outside the home. They persist among women as well as men as a result of myriad factors, including: childhood socialisation, educational practices and content, corporate practices and structures, state ideological and economic goals, mass media representations and the values of consumer culture. The recession of the 1990s exposed this reality, taking back the promises of gains in politics and employment made during the late 1980s. Many Japanese feminists also look gloomily at the lack of unity and support for feminist causes among the younger generation of women.

Even as feminists point out the many obstacles and constraints to progress toward equality, however, they also note portents of change in the new attitudes toward work and leisure among young men as well as women that have surfaced in the 1990s. With Japan's aging population, business and the state may put a higher value on the talents and contributions that women can make, and with increasing financial independence may come power. But perhaps these are just the product of wishful thinking, for achievement of equality for women will require transformation of deeply rooted social structures and male-dominated

institutions. Whether this calls for optimism or pessimism depends in the
end on one's assessment of this possibility in the near or distant future.

References and recommended readings

Allison, Anne 1994 *Nightwork*, University of Chicago Press, Chicago.
—— 1996 'Producing mothers,' *Re-Imaging Japanese Women*, ed. A. Imamura,
University of California Press, Berkeley.
AMPO—*Japan Asia Quarterly Review* ed. 1996 *Voices from the Japanese Women's
Movement*, M.E. Sharpe, Armonk, N.Y.
Broadbent, Kaye and Morris-Suzuki, Tessa 1998 'Women and industrialisation in Japan.'
Paper presented at 'Costed, Not Valued: Women Workers in Industrialising Asia'
Conference, University of New England, Armidale, Australia
Buckley, Sandra 1993 'Altered states: the body politics of "being woman",' *Postwar
Japan as History*, ed. A Gordon, University of California Press, Berkeley.
—— 1994 'A short history of the feminist movement in japan,' *Women of Japan and
Korea*, eds J. Gelb and M. Palley, Temple University Press, Philadelphia.
Creighton, Millie 1996 'Marriage, motherhood, and career management in a Japanese
"counter culture",' *Re-Imaging Japanese Women*, ed. A. Imamura, University of
California Press, Berkeley.
Diggs, Nancy 1998 *Steel Butterflies: Japanese Women and the American Experience*,
State University of New York Press, Albany.
Ehara Yumiko ed. 1990 *Feminizumu ronsō: nanajūnendai kara kyūjūnendai*, Keiso
Shobō, Tokyo.
Fujimura-Fanselow, K. and Kameda, A. 1994 'Women's education and gender roles in
Japan,' *Women of Japan and Korea*, eds J. Gelb and M. Palley, Temple
University Press, Philadelphia.
—— eds 1995 *Japanese Women: New Feminist Perspectives on the Past, Present, and
Future*, Feminist Press, New York.
Funabashi, Kuniko 1995 'Pornographic culture and sexual violence,' *Japanese Women:
New Feminist Perspectives on the Past, Present, and Future*, eds K. Fujimura-
Fanselow and A. Kameda, Feminist Press, New York.
Gelb, Joyce and Palley, Marian eds 1994 *Women of Japan and Korea*, Temple
University Press, Philadelphia.
Gordon, Andrew ed. 1993 *Postwar Japan as History*, University of California Press,
Berkeley.
Hara, Kimi 1995 'Challenges to education for girls and women in modern Japan: past
and present,' *Japanese Women: New Feminist Perspectives on the Past, Present,
and Future*, eds K. Fujimura-Fanselow and A. Kameda, Feminist Press, New
York.

Harvey, Paul 1998 'Nonchan's Dream: NHK Morning Serialized Television Novels,' *The Worlds of Japanese Popular Culture: Gender, Shifting Boundaries and Global Cultures*, ed. D. P. Martinez, Cambridge University Press, Cambridge.

Hisano, Kunio and Yuji Endo 1998 'Industrialization and women's economic participation in Japan.' Paper presented at 'Costed, Not Valued: Women Workers in Industrialising Asia' Conference, University of New England, Armidale, Australia.

Horioka, Charles 1993 'Consuming and saving,' *Postwar Japan as History*, ed. A. Gordon, University of California Press, Berkeley.

Imamura, Anne ed. 1996 *Re-Imaging Japanese Women*, University of California Press Berkeley.

Iwao, Sumiko 1993 *The Japanese Woman: Traditional Image and Changing Reality*, Free Press, New York.

Joseishi Sogo Kenkyūkai ed. 1990 *Nihon josei seikatsushi*, University of Tokyo Press, Tokyo.

Kameda, Atsuko 1995 'Sexism and gender stereotyping in schools,' *Japanese Women: New Feminist Perspectives on the Past, Present, and Future* eds K. Fujimura-Fanselow and A. Kameda, Feminist Press, New York.

Kanai, Yoshiko 1996 'Issues for Japanese feminism,' *Voices from the Japanese Women's Movement*, ed. AMPO—*Japan Asia Quarterly Review*, M.E. Sharpe, Armonk.

Kawashima, Yoko 1995 'Female workers: an overview of past and current trends,' *Japanese Women: New Feminist Perspectives on the Past, Present, and Future*, eds K. Fujimura-Fanselow and A. Kameda, Feminist Press, New York.

Kubo, Kimiko and Gelb, Joyce 1994 'Obstacles and opportunities: women and political participation in Japan,' *Women of Japan and Korea*, eds J. Gelb and M. Palley, Temple University Press, Philadelphia.

Martinez, D.P. 1998 *The Worlds of Japanese Popular Culture: Gender, Shifting Boundaries and Global Cultures*, Cambridge University Press, Cambridge.

Matsui, Yayori 1995 'The plight of Asian migrant women working in Japan's sex industry,' *Japanese Women: New Feminist Perspectives on the Past, Present, and Future*, eds K. Fujimura-Fanselow and A. Kameda, Feminist Press, New York.

McGregor, Richard 1996 *Japan Swings: Politics, Culture and Sex in the New Japan*, Allen and Unwin, Sydney.

Murata, Noriko 1996 'The trafficking of women,' *Voices from the Japanese Women's Movement,* ed. AMPO—*Japan Asia Quarterly Review*, M.E. Sharpe, Armonk.

Napier, Susan 1998 'Vampires, psychic girls, flying women and sailor scouts: four faces of the young female in Japanese popular culture,' *The Worlds of Japanese Popular Culture: Gender, Shifting Boundaries and Global Cultures*, ed. D. P. Martinez, Cambridge University Press, Cambridge.

Pharr, Susan 1981 *Political Women in Japan: The Search for a Place in Political Life*, University of California Press, Berkeley.

Sato, Yoko 1995 'From the home to the political arena,' *Japanese Women: New Feminist Perspectives on the Past, Present, and Future*, eds K. Fujimura-Fanselow and A. Kameda, Feminist Press, New York.

Shinotsuka, Eiko 1994 'Women workers in Japan: past, present, future,' *Women of Japan and Korea*, eds J. Gelb and M. Palley, Temple University Press, Philadelphia.

Sōrifu (Prime Minister's Office) 1997 *Josei hakusho* in Nihon Jōhō Kyōiku Kenkyūkai, ed. *Nihon no hakusho*, Seibunsha, Tokyo.

Suzuki, Midori Fukunishi 1995 'Women and television: portrayal of women in the mass media,' *Japanese Women: New Feminist Perspectives on the Past, Present, and Future*, eds K. Fujimura-Fanselow and A. Kameda, Feminist Press, New York.

Takenaka, Emiko 1989 *Sengo joshi rōdōshiron*, Yuhikaku, Tokyo.

Tanaka, Kazuko 1995 'The new feminist movement in Japan, 1970–1990,' *Japanese Women: New Feminist Perspectives on the Past, Present, and Future*, eds K. Fujimura-Fanselow and A. Kameda, Feminist Press, New York.

—— 1995a 'Work, education, and the family,' *Japanese Women: New Feminist Perspectives on the Past, Present, and Future*, eds K. Fujimura-Fanselow and A. Kameda, Feminist Press, New York.

Tanaka, Keiko 1998 'Japanese women's magazines: the language of aspiration,' *The Worlds of Japanese Popular Culture: Gender, Shifting Boundaries and Global Cultures*, ed. D. P. Martinez, Cambridge University Press, Cambridge.

Ueno, Chizuko 1994 'Women and the family in transition in postindustrial Japan,' *Women of Japan and Korea*, eds J. Gelb and M. Palley, Temple University Press, Philadelphia.

Uno, Kathleen 1993 'The death of "good wife, wise mother"?' *Postwar Japan as History*, ed. A. Gordon, University of California Press, Berkeley.

Watabe-Dawson, Madoka 1997 'An overview: status of working women in Japan under the Equal Employment Opportunity Law of 1985,' *Waseda Journal of Asian Studies*, vol. 19, pp. 41–63.

Watts, Jonathan 1998 'Soccer *shinhatsubai*: What are Japanese consumers making of the J. League?' *The Worlds of Japanese Popular Culture: Gender, Shifting Boundaries and Global Cultures*, ed. D. P. Martinez, Cambridge University Press, Cambridge.

Yunomae, Tomoko 1996 'Commodified sex: Japan's pornographic culture,' *Voices from the Japanese Women's Movement*, ed. AMPO—*Japan Asia Quarterly Review*, M.E. Sharpe, Armonk.

11 Women in Taiwan: linking economic prosperity and women's progress

Lan-Hung Nora Chiang

Department of Geography
National Taiwan University

Over the thirty years since 1970, Taiwan, Republic of China, has undergone tremendous political, economic and social change. It has progressed from a nation governed by strict martial law to a vibrant democracy. In the 1990s Taiwan has gained notable economic and political influence in the Asia-Pacific region. Rapid post-war industrialisation resulted in Taiwan's per capita income growing 69 times from US$186 in 1952 to US$12 838 in 1996. There has been a concomitant rise in the education standards of the population with the percentage of citizens completing university education increasing 7.2 times, from 1.4 per cent in 1952 to 10.1 per cent in 1994. The Republic of China on Taiwan has moved into the ranks of the world's 'developed' countries in the space of a few decades. However, in 1971 Taiwan faced a significant deterioration in its international position when its seat as 'China' within the UN passed to the People's Republic of China (PRC) on the mainland. This has left Taiwan in theoretical political and economic isolation for the succeeding years since it is not recognised by the UN and has diplomatic relations with only twenty-two nations around the world. In practical terms, however, Taiwan remains an important economic force within the world and the standard of living of its population has improved dramatically.

The social and economic position of women has improved in tandem with these national successes but the Confucian cultural norms of the overwhelmingly Chinese population of the island still pose certain challenges to the status of women. Women still perform traditional roles in the family and fulfil limiting gender specific social expectations with regards to behaviour and employment. Although women have had constitutionally guaranteed equality with men since 1947 only small numbers of women attain high levels of social, economic or political participation. In each of these important aspects there is room for improvement. The empowerment of Taiwan's women will require substantial effort on the part of governments, NGOs, women's groups and educational institutions. More education on gender equity, greater sensitivity to gender at an institutional level, and broad legal reforms that eliminate a wide range of discriminatory practices are required to create more opportunities for women. This chapter argues that although there have been substantial improvements in the status and well-being of women in Taiwan during the years from 1970 to 2000, these improvements have been inadvertent results of the general rise in the standard of living for all Taiwanese and a general liberalising of the political arena rather than the result of conscious interventionist social planning or agitation by Taiwan's women's movement. Progress towards improving the status of women in Taiwan can almost be considered an inadvertent consequence of national development rather than a central concern of social and political planners.

Women and family planning

In 1996 women comprised 48.4 per cent of Taiwan's 21 357 431 population. In the decades since World War Two, these women have experienced a major shift in their life cycles as a result of a decline in birth-rate. The birth rate started to fall in the late 1950s and continued to drop when an intensive island-wide family planning program was officially implemented in 1968. In the 1980s Taiwan had completed the demographic transition in respect to fertility expected of developed countries (Chang 1994). The rate of natural increase stayed at 2.5 per cent in the 1960s, declined to 2 per cent in the 1970s, and was under 1 per cent through the 1990s. For individual women this change had direct effects on their lives—the total fertility rate decreased from 6.01 births per women in 1950 to 1.77 in 1995. Taiwan's net reproduction rate was as high as 2.84 in 1956, fell to below 1 in 1984 and reached 0.78 in 1989. Family size in Taiwan had shrunk over the course of a few decades and consequently the roles performed by women have altered. Opportunities for employment outside the home have expanded as domestic duties and childcare responsibilities have diminished. This successful Family Planning Program has attracted international attention. In 1987 the Population Crisis Committee of the USA rated Taiwan as the best performer in 90 developing countries and in 1992 as the top performer amongst 120 developing and developed countries.

Taiwan's family planning program was eugenicist in philosophy. Aiming to improve the quality of the population, the government focussed its population control campaigns on those groups identified as 'problematic'. Psychiatric patients, disabled persons and people from lower incomes were special target groups along with residents of the remote mountain regions where family-sizes were generally larger. This emphasis on 'quality' continued into 1984 when it became apparent that the net reproduction rate had fallen under 1 per cent. Government planners felt that a further decline in fertility was undesirable and that while the 'two child family' should continue to be promoted as the norm, greater emphasis should be placed on the quality rather than quantity of children. To this end the population policies were directed at achieving 'a reasonable growth in the population' and 'desirable' young couples were encouraged to marry and have children. This new perspective aimed to increase fertility levels among 'preferred' couples to ensure the emergence of a youthful and vigorous work-force and alleviate the anticipated problems of Taiwan's ageing population. The anti-natal philosophy of the population policy prior to the mid-1980s changed to become selectively pro-natal once the government felt that the demographic transition to 'developed' nation status had been achieved.

The decrease in family size that has occurred as a result of this decline in fertility has highlighted the prevalence of the Confucian preference for sons. Despite Taiwan's wealth and modernity Confucian values prevail: sons carry the family name, their privileges are protected by family law, they are expected to inherit family property and provide economic support for their parents (see Holton 1995). Under current cultural norms, it is extremely rare for elderly parents to live with their married daughters who are traditionally regarded as 'spilled water' once they are married. According to Chang's 1994 study, 70 per cent of the aged lived with married sons while no more than 5 per cent stayed with married daughters. The population's compliance with population control policies has been high but the Confucian preference for sons affects the manner of compliance in quite distinct ways.

Chang's 1993 study has shown that pre-natal sex determination technologies, such as ultra-sound and amniocentesis, have been used in conjunction with induced abortion to guarantee the birth of a son particularly where the child is the third or fourth in a family. The sex ratio at birth for first born children has been stable and is around 105 boys to 100 girls, but the sex ratio of births for third and fourth children shows an increase in births of boys. Boy-preference in Taiwan is comparable to other countries with Confucian values such as Korea. The sex ratio in Korea also tends to be very high with fourth and fifth births (Park and Cho 1994). Thus, son-preference may actually have an impact on family size. The earlier a couple has a son the earlier they stop having children (Hsieh and Cheng 1998). Ironically, people acknowledge that daughters and daughters-in-law are more likely to perform filial duties, such as caring for ailing parents, than sons. Son-preference clearly relates to a cultural concern for continuing the patriline that reaches beyond the life-span of the individual parents.

Women's educational attainment

In the post-war period, Taiwanese educational standards have risen considerably and the inequality between the levels of men's and women's education has decreased. Educational advancement has been a critical factor in the gradual improvement of the status of women in recent decades. In 1991, Taiwan recorded a literacy rate of 93.24 per cent. The illiterate population is concentrated in people above 65 years of age of whom 28.8 per cent are males and 71.2 per cent are females (Ministry of Education 1991). These figures demonstrate both the vast improvement in literacy over the past few decades and the improvement in women's access to education since there is no significant difference in the literacy rate between men and women below the age of 65.

Table 11.1:   Educational attainment of population aged 6 and over (%)

	1980		1985		1990		1993	
	M	F	M	F	M	F	M	F
First level (6–11 years)	50.64	48.27	43.59	44.93	36.11	38.98	31.18	34.19
Second level (12–17 years)	29.72	18.07	37.08	26.32	44.33	35.53	48.01	40.79
Third level (18–21 years)	11.11	5.32	13.26	7.24	15.05	9.43	16.90	11.39

Source: DGBAS (1997b, pp. 88–89)

Nonetheless, Table 11.1 demonstrates that while there have been educational improvements for women there are still sharp inequalities. A significant but slowly .declining gap is evident between men and women's educational attainment at both secondary and university levels across all the survey years. The only level that women dominate is that group where First Level education was the highest educational standard attained. However, the Table also demonstrates that younger Taiwanese women have many more opportunities for education than did their grandmothers and mothers. The poorly educated section of the population is concentrated among the elderly and so the percentage of all citizens with only primary school education has declined rapidly as this section of the population diminishes.

The improvement in access to education for women over the generations is the result of several factors. Recent economic growth, together with reduced family size, the introduction of free education up to junior high school, and changing attitudes on the part of both parents and women themselves, have all contributed. A more equal pattern of educational attainment is common in urban Taiwan where there is a concentration of wealth, good schools, and modern attitudes. However, in rural Taiwan the preference for men inherent in patrilineal societies still influences many familial decisions about schooling. Sons usually enjoy a higher priority than daughters in family resource allocation particularly in straightened financial circumstances. Nonetheless, the gap in educational achievement is closing. In 1950, female students at the college and university levels occupied only 10.89 per cent. In 1980, women amounted to 42.2 per cent at the undergraduate level and 20.4 per cent at the graduate level. This has increased to 46 per cent and 25.45

Table 11.2:   Students of colleges in National Taiwan University by sex, 1997 [raw numbers (%)]

Colleges	Undergraduate		Masters		PhD	
	M	F	M	F	M	F
Arts	391	1328	147	207	69	63
	(22.7)	(77.3)	(41.5)	(58.5)	(52.3)	(47.7)
Science	1091	692	411	195	288	86
	(61.2)	(38.8)	(67.8)	(32.2)	(77.0	(23)
Law	948	1514	281	227	104	38
	(38.5)	(61.5)	(55.3)	(44.7)	(73.2)	(26.8)
Medicine	1034	875	126	234	168	87
	(54.2)	(46.8)	(35.0)	(65.0)	(65.9)	(34.1)
Engineering	1688	295	1169	170	454	43
	(85.1)	(14.9)	(87.3)	(12.7)	(91.3)	(8.7)
Electrical Eng.	602	57	361	17	291	6
	(91.4)	(8.6)	(95.5)	(4.5)	(98.0)	2.0)
Agriculture	1178	1100	425	298	243	95
	(51.7)	(48.3)	(58.8)	(41.2)	(71.9)	(28.1)
Management	1047	1218	301	146	100	37
	(46.2)	(53.8)	(67.3)	(32.7)	(73.0)	(27.0)
Public Health	49	126	64	108	39	35
	(28.0)	(72.0)	(37.2)	(62.8)	(52.7)	(47.3)
Evening	456	651	—	—	—	—
Section	41.2)	(58.8)				
Total	8484	7856	3285	1602	1756	1282
	(52.0)	(48.0)	(67.2)	(32.8)	(57.8)	(42.2)

Source: National Taiwan University (1997, pp. 70–71)

per cent respectively in 1990, and 48.08 per cent and 28.9 per cent in 1997.

At the same time, women university students are overwhelmingly concentrated in the humanities and liberal arts and are disproportionately enrolled in vocational schools and colleges or in teaching colleges. This leads to the conclusion that while rapid development has provided improved educational opportunities for women, other social and cultural factors perpetuate differences in the type and quality of education received by men and women. There is a consistent concentration of men in traditionally 'male' oriented subjects, such as science and engineering, while females are concentrated in traditionally 'female' subjects such as arts. At the National Taiwan University, female undergraduate students are concentrated in the faculties of Arts (77.3 per cent), Public Health (72.0 per cent), Law (61.5 per cent), and Management (53.8 per cent) (Table 11.2).

The economic achievements of women in Taiwan

Since the 1970s, as is typical in newly industrialising economies, the distribution of both male and female employment has shifted from a concentration in agriculture to manufacturing. In 1995, manufacturing, commerce and services employed the largest proportion of men and women amounting to 37.21 per cent and 31.89 per cent respectively (Table 11.3). The role played by women in effecting this sectoral shift is representative of industrialisation throughout Asia. In the 1970s, young and unmarried women factory workers supplied cheap, semi-skilled and unskilled labour to the new factories and workshops (Arrigo 1980). The development of light industry brought a massive migration of young women from rural locations to urban and industrialised suburban areas and to export processing zones. With the accompanying decline in fertility, the pool of young female workers soon began to contract, while married women who had completed child-bearing began to enter or re-enter the labour force. As household expenses increase, married women are expected to join the labour force to supplement family income or to improve the family's quality of life. Lu's 1995 study found that the labour participation rate among married women increased rapidly between 1980 and 1990 and noted that they were more likely to choose formal employment rather than informal employment such as work in the family business or work without a formal contract.

Another important sectoral shift occurred in the early 1980s opening further opportunities for women in the workforce—the number of white-collar jobs exceeded blue-collar jobs. In the years since 1980, women have become increasingly employed in white-collar jobs. In 1982, white-collar employment exceeded blue-collar for women for the first time, and women's participation in the tertiary sector (retail businesses, social services, insurance, and commerce) grew considerably.

Table 11.3:   **Industry of employed persons in Taiwan area by sex (%)**

	1980		1985		1990		1995	
Industries	M	F	M	F	M	F	M	F
Agriculture, Forestry, Fishing, Animal Husbandry	13.4	6.06	12.0	5.40	9.03	3.82	7.56	2.99
Mining, Quarrying	0.72	0.13	0.41	0.06	0.20	0.04	0.14	0.03
Manufacturing	19.6	13.2	19.3	14.3	18.8	13.1	16.1	10.9
Electricity, Gas, Water	0.37	0.04	0.40	0.06	0.38	0.06	0.34	0.06
Construction	7.73	0.65	6.34	0.62	7.28	0.84	9.66	1.43
Commerce	10.1	6.02	10.4	7.44	11.0	8.53	11.3	9.92
Transport, Storage, Communication	4.39	0.67	4.42	0.75	4.45	0.88	4.29	0.89
Finance/Business Services	1.40	0.92	1.52	1.18	2.28	2.17	2.94	2.97
Social, Personal, Community Services	6.08	4.77	6.05	5.49	6.43	6.82	6.80	8.10
Public Administration	2.67	0.91	2.56	1.14	2.51	1.21	2.24	1.26

Source: DGBAS (1996)

Increasingly, women have entered professions long dominated by men, becoming lawyers, chemists, engineers, architects, and computer scientists. This trend reflects the expansion in the diversity of careers available to women. It is anticipated that, in the near future, the percentage of female government employees will grow even higher due to the fact that women have normally performed better than men in the civil service examinations. Chang (1993) noted that in 1950, only 8 out of 216 people who passed the advanced level public service examination were women but in 1992 this figure had improved to 4108 (58.7 per cent) out of a total of 6995 successful candidates. For the ordinary level public service examination, only 2 out of 215 who passed in 1950 were females, while in 1992 the figure was 4888 (81.22 per cent).

In sum, the female labour force has expanded considerably since 1970 because of a set of interrelated factors: the strong demand of industrialisation for unskilled labour in the early development period; increases in urban tertiary employment; a rise in women's overall educational level; technological advances that simplified housework; and

Table 11.4:   Labour force participation rates in Taiwan by sex (%)

Year	Male	Female	Year	Male	Female
1972	77.16	37.07	1985	75.47	43.46
1973	77.13	41.53	1986	75.15	45.51
1974	78.24	40.22	1987	75.24	46.54
1975	77.61	38.56	1988	74.83	45.56
1976	77.20	37.56	1989	74.92	45.35
1977	77.79	39.27	1990	73.96	44.50
1978	77.96	39.16	1991	73.08	44.39
1979	77.92	39.21	1992	73.77	44.32
1980	77.11	39.25	1993	72.67	44.89
1981	76.78	38.76	1994	72.44	45.40
1982	76.47	39.30	1995	72.03	45.34
1983	76.36	42.12	1996	71.13	45.76
1984	76.11	43.30	1997	71.09	45.64

Source: Council for Economic Planning and Development (1998)

family planning which has given women the choice of fewer children and longer working years. However, many problems for improved female employment remain unresolved.

Discriminatory practices inhibiting the employment prospects of married women persist into the present. Some companies encourage women to leave work on marriage or childbirth to avoid paying maternity leave. To this end, employers will give small amounts of money to the displaced worker as 'dowry supplement' or 'birth supplement'. It is difficult for women to re-enter the workforce after a break since employers show marked preferences for younger women in part because they are perceived to be easier to control. Despite laws to protect women from discrimination, employers' practices are often unfavourable towards women who are married or pregnant.

Despite the improvements in educational attainment, employment rates have increased rather slowly since 1990. This disparity can be explained by the aspirations by women for higher education but it may also be due to the reluctance or inability of married women to gain employment, particularly in the formal labour market. As is clear from Table 11.4 a clear gender discrepancy exists in formal labour market participation. Moreover, even among that proportion of the population with higher education because women are concentrated in the social rather than the physical sciences, they are over-represented in the lower-paid teaching and clerical professions and considerably under-represented in the higher paid professions like engineering, architecture, and medicine.

Job advertisements send out clear messages that segregate the labour force by gender. Male applicants are preferred in administrative positions requiring leadership skills, and in areas requiring professional training and technical skills; while jobs requiring clerical skills and good appearances specifically advertise for female applicants. This custom limits the career potential of women and partly explains the fact that women currently earn 60 per cent of the male wage. Women are concentrated in the lower rungs of the occupational ladder and receive less on-the-job training and promotion opportunities than men. They often had shorter or interrupted employment records because of family responsibilities. As a result, women are under-represented among the top level of managerial and administrative personnel (only 10 per cent of top positions were held by women in 1996) while their numbers in clerical and sales sectors have grown significantly.

Overwhelmingly, women perform all domestic chores and consequently women in paid employment carry the double burden of labouring both in and outside the home. While their husbands socialise after work and their high-school children are studying to survive Taiwan's tough examination system, women remain solely responsible for household tasks, maintaining family well-being and often also looking after elderly parents-in-law. Childcare services are limited and those that exist have not been designed to give equal responsibility to both parents. The restrictive quotas of visas for overseas workers in Taiwan has prevented middle-class women from hiring foreign domestic help as is common in Hong Kong.

The problem of balancing work and family is constant for Taiwanese women. Young married women still often feel that they are forced to choose between 'the fish or the bear palm'—give up one to have the other—others embark on the difficult task of balancing responsibilities to both. Recent research on family values of married women (Hsieh and Wang 1995) shows that women place the highest priority on family life and identify the family as the place where they hope to obtain their greatest sense of fulfilment. However, these family responsibilities are fulfilled at the expense of pursuing self-interest in work, recreation, and other personal life goals.

Political and social participation

With advancements in both education and employment since 1970 one would expect Taiwanese women to have an increasing interest in participating in politics. The Constitution of the Republic of China, promulgated in 1947, reserved a set minimum quota of 10 per cent of seats for women (Edwards 1999). Ironically, the need for the reserved-seats system is being questioned, not only by conservatives but also by many women voters and politicians in Taiwan. Theoretically, this quota should provide a platform for guaranteeing women an opportunity to enter electoral politics. However, in actual political practice, the implemented quota system has turned the floor into a ceiling (Chou, Clark and Clark 1990).

Since 1960 female political leaders have formed a very small minority, amounting to less than 20 per cent at all levels of the central government. Currently, the highest ranked woman in Taiwan is the Director of the Council for Cultural Affairs and recently, the Minister of Law. Out of twenty-one Counties and Cities, only three (Taoyuan County, Chia-yi City, and Taichung City) are headed by women. The low representation of women in the political leadership is partly a result of the differences in gender socialisation and partly a consequence of the political system. Male students, for example, were much more likely to participate in politics than females by attending political rallies, speeches, or other campaign activities, and males expressed more interest in seeking political office in the future. In patterns of voting, women tended to vote in accordance with their family's decisions and desire, while male voters were more concerned with candidates' issue positions and with their past performance in politics.

Though not as visible as political participation, women's participation in community activities has expanded and taken new directions. While some are recreational, social and self-educational in their objectives, others provide either resources or help to address social problems and have a broad goal of elevating women's status in society. Women's activities have ranged from traditional ones such as home improvement (flower-arrangement, cooking), or service to society, to the encouragement of personal growth, prevention of violence against women, and support of environmental and consumer movements.

The most significant feminist organisation is the 'Awakening' society. It was founded in 1982 by university educated women and represents the second wave (1975–present) of Taiwan's feminist movement. This group aims to raise women's consciousness on the one hand and lobby the government for better rights for women on the other. It was the first women's organisation to explicitly identify as 'feminist'. The so called first wave of Taiwanese feminism (between 1971–1975) was almost a 'one woman crusade' led by Lu Hsiu-lien. The term 'feminism' was introduced to Taiwan by Lu in 1971, but restrictions on the formation of political groups under Taiwan's 'Wartime non-governmental organisation law' prevented Lu from forming her planned feminist organisation. Taiwan was still officially in a state of war with the Communist led People's Republic of China and martial law had been imposed. Freedom of speech and association were severely limited, delaying the development of an independent women's movement until 1986 after martial law was lifted. Nonetheless, Lu challenged the double standard of chastity, female subservience to males and spoke for legalisation of abortion. She stressed the importance for women to have the right to decide on the number of children to have and to carry their own family names after marriage. Each of these ideas ran contrary to the ideology of the ruling Kuomintang (KMT—Nationalist Party), which adopted a conservative line on gender issues. In the late 1970s Lu was jailed for her outspoken political views. Five years later, on her release, Lu recommenced her feminist and political activities. The bigger second wave of women's activism originated with her crusade since the core of the 'Awakening' society was comprised of Lu's followers (see Ku 1989).

Non-feminist women's associations that functioned during the period of martial law were conservative in outlook and agenda and had the direct support of the KMT. These earlier women's organisations emphasised family values and engaged in philanthropic work to reach the poor and disadvantaged. They were also active in providing occupational skills for women who wanted to supplement the family income with a part-time job or sideline income-generating industry. These traditional women's organisations include the KMT's Central Women's Committee that has an extensive network across the whole island. Together with provincial women's organisations, they effectively lobbied women's votes for KMT and generally supported KMT politicians at the various elections. Other women's organisations remain small in scale and include religious and professional groups and branches of international organisations.

In 1985, the closing year of the UN's Decade for Women, martial law was lifted and less than two years later, in 1987, the first legal opposition party, Democratic Progressive Party, was formed. The relaxation in political control released a torrent of political activities. Social movements of various kinds flourished, a host of different women's organisations included. Democratisation led to greater freedom in public communication and soon women gathered to form small groups based on mutual interests. Groups of urban middle-class women, some of whom were educated abroad, addressed issues such as prostitution, gender stereotypes in textbooks, environmental protection and consumer rights. For instance, 'Warm Life' is a women's organisation that provides moral support and psychological counselling to those in need. The 'Homemaker's Union and Foundation' established in 1989 has become not only a leading group on environmental protection, but it also inspired a large number of women to participate in various social movements. The women's movement, lead by NGOs, thus reached a new phase emphasising the individual and supporting disadvantaged women, such as young prostitutes, battered wives and comfort women who were victimised during World War Two. Women's activities, often led by middle-class women in Taipei are spreading out to other counties and cities on the island. Contacts with international women's groups are increasing through visits and conferences, such as the International Environmental Education Seminar held by the Pan-Pacific and Southeast Asia Women's Association in 1993 (Chiang 1993), and the East Asian Women's Forum. Nonetheless, Taiwan's diplomatic isolation from the international community still presents barriers to the further integration of Taiwan's women's movement into the global arena. For example, Taiwanese activists were prevented from attending the UN's Fourth World Conference on Women in 1995 held in Beijing. From Beijing's point of view, Taiwanese women were represented by delegates from the People's Republic of China (Waldon 1995).

Academic interest in gender and women's rights and status also grew rapidly in the years after the lifting of martial law. The Women's Research Program at the Population Studies Centre of National Taiwan University pre-empted the wave of democratisation and was established in 1985 with four years seed-funding from the Asia Foundation. From January 1999 its parent-body was renamed the Population and Gender Studies Centre in recognition of its status in the institution. Its activities have included the organising of seminars on issues of gender education, health, employment, history, and research methodology. The Centre has published a substantial body of literature on women in Taiwan in the form of journals, newsletters, discussion papers and monographs. The most recent publications include an annotated bibliography on women's research in both Chinese and English—this important volume involved the co-operation of a host of scholars (Women's Research Program 1992). The Centre has supported young scholars to carry out women's research in Taiwan and teachers in other universities to develop curricula for teaching women's studies. A Women Studies Certificate Program was approved in 1998 enabling students who take a set number of courses on women studies in the University to receive a Certificate when they graduate. The course 'Gender Relations' had been offered for over ten years in 1999 and over 2000 students have undertaken the course during this time. Women's Studies has become a well-established field recognised in both the humanities and the social science in numerous universities on the island. In 1998 eighty courses on gender and women studies were offered at various universities and eight gender-related programs were in existence. The academic and political wings of the Taiwanese women's movement continue to grow and rise to new challenges.

Conclusion

The Republic of China on Taiwan has undergone significant economic and political changes during the post-war period. In the three decades from 1970, Taiwan has transformed from a poor agricultural society into a wealthy industrialised country that despite its relatively small population and international isolation maintains some of the highest foreign exchange reserves in the world. From the mid-1980s substantial political liberalisation has occurred lifting the weight of an authoritarian political system and allowing more freedom of expression and an open style of politics. Taiwan has become the world's eleventh largest trading nation and has maintained an upward economic growth rate despite the regional economic turmoil of the late 1990s. During the period of transformation the population has become better educated and well-informed. Women have seen an improvement in their lives as a result of this economic and political metamorphosis rather than as a result of any proactive political leadership by the ruling KMT. The challenge for Taiwan's women into the future will be mobilising themselves sufficiently to ensure that their now responsive democratically elected representatives are sensitive to the particular needs of women.

As patriarchal values dominate cultural norms, son-preference is still strong. Even though women have advanced significantly in educational levels, their social, economic and political participation is limited in an effort to prevent conflict with their traditional familial obligations. The dilemma of modern working women, who balance family responsibilities and professional careers, continues. Breakthroughs on these cultural and institutional fronts will require sustained group mobilisation to ensure that women have access to power and influence so that the necessary reforms are implemented.

A survey conducted by the Central Women's Committee in Taiwan in 1997 shows that women's priorities are: caring for their children's education, personal safety, marriage and the family. Fears about the rising crime rate have led many women to worry more about their roles as mothers and the responsibility for disciplining of children. A recent report on human right shows that while gains in women's rights have been made in the areas of personal freedom, education, work, marriage and family, and social participation; dissatisfaction with personal safety remains (Wang 1998). Women's issues are taken for granted, or ignored in the national agenda as reflected in the lack of political advocacy and coverage in the media. Gender stereotypes are still built on the traditional role of women as emotional supporters of successful men and 'normal' families.

As a whole, the modern Taiwanese woman sees herself as holding a better position in the family and in society than her mother and grandmother. Younger women who are well-educated and living in urban areas would take a modern outlook in life, enjoying an independence and autonomy which was not possible for their mothers born soon after World War Two. It is found that professional women tend to exert more influence in the family decision-making than women with non-professional jobs, especially in the management of finance (Yi and Chang 1995). They are the new generation who are conscious of their rights and obtain satisfaction from both work and family.

To improve the status of women, more egalitarian laws, stronger representation of women in politics and better support for working women should be introduced. Urbanisation has drastically reduced the number and power of extended families. Indeed, the prevalence of nuclear families has given women more autonomy within their immediate domestic environs. Increasingly, men have participated in child-minding and shared domestic responsibilities, since more women are income-earners. The notion of the 'new good man' who holds both traditional and modern values is popularised—these are men who accept their wives' employment or participation in society, share housework without fear that it diminishes their 'manliness', and interact with their children more than the older generation of men.

With the introduction of gender equity education by the Education Department 1997, it is hoped that both men and women are sensitised to new gender values. Empowering women would have to take many forms and all levels of government have to join the world order of action plans for women. It has been pointed out that the present social welfare approach towards women's rights should be replaced by a legal rights approach (Wang 1998). Since 1985, women studies in Taiwan has gone through a quiet revolution in the academic world leading to institutionalising a new body of knowledge in the university curriculum. The improvement of women's status in Taiwan has been due to socio-economic changes and the joint efforts of individuals in the feminist movement. The problems faced by Taiwan women are the common experiences of women in the developed world. Undoubtedly, more efforts should be made by the Taiwan government to enact better laws to protect the rights of women and to ensure women's stronger participation in development.

Note: This chapter was modified from a paper presented at the 6th Pacific Basin Symposium, Soka University and Thammasat University, March 4–6, 1998, Bangkok. An earlier version has been published under the title 'Women and Development in Taiwan' *Asian Journal for Women Studies* vol. 4, no. 4. The author wishes to thank the editors for their suggestions.

References and recommended readings

Arrigo, Linda Gail 1980 'The industrial workforce of young women in Taiwan,' *Bulletin of Concerned Asian Scholars*, vol. 12, no. 2, pp. 25–38.

Chang, Ming-Cheng 1993 'Sex preference and sex ratios at birth: the case of Taiwan.' Paper presented at the annual meeting of the ROC Population Association, Taipei, 5–7 February.

—— 1994 'Demographic change and family planning in Taiwan,' Research Report, Taiwan Provincial Institute of Family Planning, Taichung.

Chang, Po-ya 1993 'The new role of Taiwan's women in the future.' Paper Presented at International Conference on Women, Dec. 16–19, Taipei.

Chang, Ying-hwa 1994 'Household composition and attitudes of support for parents in a changing society: the case of Taiwan,' *Journal of Sociology*, National Taiwan University, vol. 23, pp. 1–34.

Cheung, Fanny M. 1997 *Engendering Hong Kong Society—A Gender Perspective of Women's Status*, The Chinese University Press, Hong Kong.

Chiang Lan-hung ed. 1993 *International Environmental Education Seminar for Women*, Pan Pacific and South East Asia Women's Association, ROC.

—— 1995 'Women's movement, women's studies,' *Asian Journal of Women's Studies*, vol. 1, pp. 152–59.

—— 1995a 'Women's studies in Taiwan: my personal experience as a woman scholar,' *Asian Journal of Women's Studies*, vol. 5, no. 2, pp. 100-109.

Chiang, Lan-hung and Ku, Yen-lin 1985 *Past and Current Status of Women in Taiwan*, Women's Research Program, Population Studies Center, Monograph no. 1, Taipei.

Chou Bih-er, Clark, Cal and Clark, Janet 1990 *Women in Taiwan Politics: Overcoming Barriers to Women's Participation in a Modernizing Society*, Lynne Rienner, Boulder.

Council for Economic Planning and Development (CEPD) 1998 *Quarterly Report on the Labor Force Market, 1972–1997*, CEPD, Taipei.

Directorate-General of Budget, Accounting and Statistics (DGBAS) 1997a *Yearbook of Manpower Survey Statistics*, Taiwan Area Directorate General of Budget Accounting Statistics, Taipei.

—— 1997b *Statistical Yearbook of the Republic of China*, 1997 Directorate General of Budget Accounting Statistics, Taipei.

Edwards, Louise 1999 'From gender equality to gender difference: feminist campaigns for quotas for women in politics 1936–1947,' *Twentieth Century China*, vol. xxiv, no. 2 (April), pp. 69–105.

Holton, Mandy, D. 1995 'Father knows best,' *Far Eastern Economic Review*, September 7, p. 49.

Hsieh, Yu-sheng and Cheng, Chi-chuan 1998 'Sex preference in family and reproductive behavior in Taiwan,' *Proceedings on Population and Related Problems at the Turn of the Century*, ROC Population Association, Taipei.

Hsieh Shiu-feng and Wang Li-rong 1995 *Family Values, Needs and Policies Technical Report*, National Science Council.

Ku Yen-lin 1989 'The feminist movement in Taiwan 1972–1987,' *Bulletin of Concerned Asian Scholars*, vol. 21, no. 1, pp. 12–22.

Liu Hsiu-lien, Annette 1994 'Women's liberation: the Taiwanese experiences,' *The Other Taiwan*, ed. M. A. Rubenstein, M.E. Sharpe, New York.

Lu, Yu-hsia 1995 'Changes in women's work patterns during Taiwan's economic development: 1980–1988,' *Families, Human Resources and Social Development* eds H. H. Nancy Chen, Yia-ling Liu and Mee-O Hsieh, Graduate Institute of Sociology, National Chengchi University, Taipei.

Ministry of Education 1991, 1997 *Educational Statistics of the Republic of China*, Ministry of Education, Taipei.

Ministry of Interior 1997 *Taiwan Demographic Fact Book*, Ministry of the Interior, Taipei.

Park, Chai Bin and N. H. Cho 1994 'Consequences of son preference in a low-fertility society: imbalance of the sex ratio at birth in Korea,' *Population and Development Review*, vol. 21, pp. 59–84.

National Taiwan University 1997 *Statistical Yearbook of National Taiwan University 1997*, National Taiwan University, Taipei.

Yi, Chin-Chun and Chang, Ying-Hwa 1995 'Change of family structure and marital power in Taiwan,' *Families, Human Resources and Social Development*, eds H. H. Nancy Chen, Yia-ling Liu and Mee-O Hsieh, Graduate Institute of Sociology, National Chengchi University, Taipei.

Waldon, Marjorie Joy 1995 'Exclusion of Taiwan activists diminishes impact of the UN Fourth Conference on Women,' *Bulletin of Concerned Asian Scholars*, vol. 27, no. 3, pp. 89–91.

Wang Li-Rong 1998 *The ROC Report on Women's Rights Indicators in 1998*, Human Rights Association of China, Taipei.

Women's Research Program 1992 *Research on Women in Taiwan—An Annotated Bibliography*, Women's Research Program, Population Studies Center, National Taiwan University, Taipei.

(See also the journals *Bulletin of Women and Gender Studies* and *Journal of Women and Gender Studies*, published by Population and Gender Studies Center, National Taiwan University)

12 Exploring women's status in contemporary Thailand

Bhassorn Limanonda

College of Population Studies
Chulalongkorn University

From a comparative perspective women in Thailand have suffered less discrimination than women in many other parts of Asia. Indeed, gender relations in three Thai Kingdoms of Sukhothai, Ayudhaya, and Ratanakosin provided a positive template for the inscribing of a better status for women in the twentieth century. Even in this context the improvement in the status of women since the 1970s has been dramatic. Women's activities have expanded in all spheres as a result of the economic growth of the nation and the accompanying social policy initiatives of successive governments, academic institutions and Non-Governmental Organisations (NGOs). The favourable cultural base upon which the current modernisation drive was built has enhanced efforts at developing gender equity in Thailand. This chapter explores changes in the position of women in Thai society over the past three decades through the prisms of four variables: official policies on women; health and reproduction; education and employment; and position in the family. It argues that although Thai women started the century in a comparatively favourable position relative to many other women in the region, some traditional problems faced by women have yet to be fully addressed and moreover, new problems continue to emerge as a result of

247

Thailand's economic and social development. It suggests that not all of these problems will be solved by economic growth alone. Thus, the roles of the National Commission for Women's Affairs (NCWA) and various NGOs are critical to ensure that both old and new forms of discrimination are addressed.

Thailand's first five-year national economic development plan of 1961–66 laid the groundwork for a remarkable transformation. Over a mere three decades Thailand has achieved an exceptional economic growth rate with an average of 7.8 per cent per annum since 1970. The structure of the economy shifted from a reliance on agriculture to the establishment of vibrant industrial and service sectors. The proportion of the population engaged in agriculture, both male and female, declined steadily between 1960–90. During these years economic development and social planning have produced significant improvements in family incomes, living conditions and general quality of life. The average per capita income reached 68 000 Baht (US$1700) in 1995 compared with only 2100 Baht (US$53) in 1961. Similarly, the number of people living in absolute poverty fell to around 14 per cent in 1992, far outstripping the Seventh National Plan's target of 20 per cent set for the end of 1996. Accompanying the industrialisation of the economy has been the development of social services and public utilities—electricity, water, and transport infrastructure have all been improved alongside the expansion in education and health services (NESDB 1997). These major structural changes have had a dramatic influence on the day-to-day lives of Thai women. Nonetheless, the need for gender specific policy initiatives remains crucial in ensuring women gain full benefit from these social and economic improvements.

Complicating the picture has been the instability of Thailand's governments over the past several decades. A Constitutional Monarchy since 1932, Thailand has moved between democratically elected governments and military dictatorships numerous times. At the close of the twentieth century Thailand has a democratically elected government committed to maintaining the stability of the nation despite the economic turmoil of 1997. The role of the military in national politics appears to be diminishing.

Cultural values and gender equity

As mentioned above, historically women in Thailand have not suffered the same degree of discrimination as many other women in the Asian region. For example, the strong preference for sons that prevails in many East and South Asian societies appears less pronounced among Thais. A daughter born into a Thai family is usually valued as much as a son. There are a number of cultural conditions that explain the reduced sex-bias among Thais.

Religious influences

Theravada Buddhism is the predominant religion in Thailand and it continues to exert a strong influence over social values, codes of ethics and day-to-day behaviour. Buddhist teachings include principles of 'hierarchical order' that influence 'superordinate and subordinate' social relationships, but the relative status of the individuals involved is normally defined by age (younger:older; children:parents:grandparents; younger sibling:older sibling) rather than sex (male:female) (Smith 1979; Pongphit 1988 cited in Limanonda 1996). This understanding of social hierarchies has helped minimise discrimination based on sex and has enabled women to hold higher places in the family than would be possible in a Confucian society, for example, where social hierarchies explicitly include sex (men over women) as well as age.

Religious practice has also supported the participation of women in worship. In Thai Buddhism a child should aim to gain spiritual merit for his/her parents in order to demonstrate gratitude to the parents for giving life to the child. Sons can perform this act of filial gratitude by joining monasteries and becoming monks. This avenue is not open to women but the exclusion of women does not imply that men have superior status to women. Daughters have other mechanisms for repaying debts of gratitude to parents that are equally as valid—they are simply different from those of sons.

A young daughter is valued as an important member of the Thai family for the domestic chores she performs—in particular caring for younger siblings. Daughters are generally considered to be better companions for parents since they are more inclined to spend time at home than sons. As a married woman she will control the family finances while engaging in paid employment outside the home. Moreover, it is normally daughters who care for elderly parents. If she is living away from home a daughter will commonly send money to support her parents (Prachuabmoh, Knodel and Alers 1974, p. 613; Prachuabmoh and Knodel 1977; Smith 1979; Rabibhadana 1984 cited in Limanonda 1996). Each of these practices enable women to repay debts of gratitude to parents and win merit points for the parents within the context of Theravada Buddhism. From this religious perspective, the heavy burden of domestic duties undertaken by the daughter of a family is recognised by her parents as being of considerable importance. Her status in the family remains comparatively high as a consequence since without the dedication of a daughter both the daily needs and the spiritual needs of the parents would not be met.

Family lineage, inheritance, and marriage system

Another factor explaining the low preference for sons in Thailand is that strong lineage connections are not valued as highly as they are in Confucian societies, such as China and Korea. Thai custom does not demand a male heir to perpetuate the family name and inherit family property. This cultural trait can be accounted for by the fact that traditionally people did not have family names—individuals were known only by their given names. The use of family names as surnames has only been adopted since the 1913 Royal Decree insisted that family names be used (Singholaka 1982). Even today few rural families can trace their ancestry back more than two or three generations (Limanonda 1996). Individual and community identities in Thailand do not revolve around the ability to trace ancestry as they do in Confucian cultures.

The long-term practice of bilateral inheritance is another cultural trait that reflects Thailand's traditional trend to gender equity. Normally, each child, regardless of sex received an equal share of parental land or property on the death of the parents. The child who has remained with the parents throughout their old age (this is usually the youngest daughter) typically receives the house and surrounding land as well as a little extra in recognition of the sacrifice she has made for her parents. The value of daughters to the welfare of the parents is recognised in their privileged access to continuity of family residence and land. In addition, marriage rituals and patterns of post-nuptial residence in Thailand indicate the importance of females in Thai society. Bride price is paid by the future husband to the bride's parents by way of demonstrating both respect and gratitude that her parents have consented to the union. There are no fixed customs dictating the residence of the new couple after marriage. Most commonly all married children except the youngest daughter establish independent households. The youngest daughter and her husband will live with the woman's parents, caring for them in old age and inheriting the house and land on the death of the parents. Consequently, unlike Confucian societies Thais do not rely predominantly on male heirs for old-age security. The practice of matrilocal post nuptial residence is more pronounced among rural residents while the neolocal and patrilocal post nuptial residences are more prevalent among the urban residents especially among ethnic Chinese (Limanonda 1992; 1995; 1996).

This cultural base provides the vital background to understanding the following discussion of the status of women in Thailand. Indicators commonly used to measure the status of women relative to men can vary considerably and global measures that fail to take into account cultural differences need to be treated with caution. Dixon (1976) stated that women's status could be measured in five major spheres: sexual relationships, reproduction, homemaking and childcare, economic production, and political decision making. Within these spheres Dixon argued that the degree of functional independence correlated to women's status. Curtin (1982) proposed that women's status in any given cultural setting could be viewed as a composite of a host of different, often interdependent, variables. Women's position in society relative to men could be illustrated by indices in at least five spheres: (1) politics and laws (2) education (3) the economy (4) social recognition and (5) power. Only a few years after Curtin proposed her scheme, the Economic and Social Commission for Asia and the Pacific (ESCAP) introduced a quantitative measure of the social position of women known as 'Measure of Status' (MS) in 1985. The MS comprises of five variables; life expectancy at birth, rates of contraceptive use, literacy rates, secondary school enrolment ratio, and female labour force participation (ESCAP 1985).

The following analysis of the status of women in Thailand draws on aspects of each of these models. It is clear from the data that the status of Thai women has improved since 1970 and that the roles played by women in Thailand's national development have broadened considerably. However, it is also evident that within this generally positive assessment, women from underprivileged or disadvantaged groups still face considerable difficulties. Besides the hardships inflicted by economic privations these women also face discrimination and oppression that places them in an inferior position relative to men of the same class and background.

Official policies on women: the evolution of strategic plans

In the 1940s the government began to address the problem of improving the status of Thai women. Thanpuying La-iad, the wife of the then Prime Minister Field Marshal Pibul Songgram, was instrumental in this early activism. It was at this time that both the philanthropic National Council of Women (under the patronage of the Queen) and the Women's Culture Club were established. These early women's associations were primarily active in charitable works and the promotion of women's social and family activities. Many laws were revised to eradicate institutionalised discrimination against women. Alimony provisions aimed at protecting women's livelihood after divorce were introduced and from this point on women were guaranteed equal opportunities to enter the public service (Ekchai 1984). In the decades following these initial reforms various professional women's groups, such as the Women's Lawyers Association of Thailand (WLAT), lobbied the government to include specific provisions guaranteeing gender equality in the National Constitution. By 1974 this victory was won and Section 28 of the 1974 document stated: 'All persons shall enjoy rights and liberties under the Constitution. Men and women have equal rights. Violation of the rights and liberties guaranteed in the Constitution shall not be permitted' (Branch 1982).

Since the 1970s Thailand's increasing involvement in global and regional bodies has also been a considerable influence on the improving status of women. In response to the UN's International Women's Year in 1975, and the UN's Decade for Women (1976–85), the Thai government established a National Executive Committee to implement strategies for achieving the UN's objectives. Consequently, the role of women in development received its most intense attention to date in the Fourth Five-Year National Economic and Social Development Plan of 1977–81. By 1979 these efforts had culminated in the drafting of the first strategic plan to deal specifically with women's status in national development. Called the Long-term Women's Development Plan it was designed to cover the years from 1982–2001 and its policies were to be integrated into each subsequent national five-year plan. The Fifth Five-year Plan of the period 1982–86 placed an explicit emphasis on women as a discrete target group in social development initiatives. In 1989, the 1982 Women's Development Plan was renamed the Prospective Plan of Policies for Women's Development and extended to cover the period from 1992–2011. This wide-ranging document, like its predecessor, provided guidelines for integrating issues of gender into subsequent national economic plans.

Accompanying these initiatives, and in line with the strategies for further work established by the UN's 1985 Nairobi Conference on Women, Thailand established the National Commission on Women's Affairs (NCWA) in 1989. The NCWA's tasks were to serve as a co-ordinating body and a centre for information exchange on women's development activities. The NCWA signed the Beijing Resolution of 1995 at the UN's Fourth Conference on Women and has been instrumental in determining strategies for the development of Thai women in the years 1995–2015 (NCWA 1985;1991;1994). The NGO sector has also been active with over ten major bodies working on women's development being established since the 1970s. For example, the Association for the Promotion of the Status of Women was formed to perform both research into discrimination against women and social work for disadvantaged women and children—including HIV/AIDS infected women and Buddhist nuns. The Gender and

Development Research Institute targets policy makers and development planners as well as grass-roots women in the attempt to ensure that development initiatives are gender sensitive and that dialogue between women and development planners is enhanced. The Foundation for Women aimed specifically to promote women's rights as promulgated in the United Nations Declaration in Human Rights but also undertook to provide support for women in distress and provide non-formal education support for women. The combined efforts of these various NGOs comprise the active body of the Thai women's movement.

Reproduction, sexuality and the changing demographic profile

Since the 1970s the Thai government has implemented a major population control plan which promoted the model 'two child family.' This campaign has had a dramatic impact on reproductive patterns and behaviour among Thai women. The percentage of women currently using contraceptives has dramatically increased from approximately 8 percent in late 1950s to 72 per cent in the latest Contraceptive Prevalence Survey 1996–97 (Bennett et al. 1990; NESDB 1994; Chamratrithirong et al. 1997). Fertility trends over the past four decades reflect the success of this policy. In the early 1960s the Total Fertility Rate (TFR) of Thai women was about 6.3; by 1991 this had fallen to 2.17 (Bennett et al. 1990; NESDB 1994). The TFR measures the average number of children that would be born alive to a woman during her lifetime. The latest Survey of Population Change (1995–96), noted that Thailand's TFR had continued to drop and was as low as 2.02. Another survey of 1996, the Contraceptive Prevalence Survey, indicated that the TFR was 1.98 with the urban TFR at 1.70 and the rural TFR at 2.08. This continuous decline is expected to slow by the turn of the century (Chamratrithirong et al. 1997). Over the past thirty years the families that Thai women manage have become considerably smaller. In 1996 the average ideal family size expressed by women of reproductive age was 2 children.

   These rapid changes in reproductive patterns are the result of two main factors: the government's strong commitment to, and the effective implementation of, the population program; the active roles played by Thai women as service providers and recipients in the population control program. Approximately 90 per cent of family planning acceptors in Thailand are women although regional differences in contraceptive use exist (NESDB 1994). For instance, in the North and Central areas of Thailand 84 per cent of couples use some form of contraception, compared to 77 per cent in the Northeast and only 60 per cent in the South. Women also play significant roles as service providers within the government's population program: women are variously physicians, trained nurses, health personnel, trained midwives and health volunteers and are stationed throughout the country. The full participation and co-operation of women in the population program has been central to its success (see Whittaker 2000).

The decline in fertility rates over recent decades has been matched by a similar decline in mortality rates. Improved health care services and the rapid socio-economic development of the period have reduced the mortality rate to the lowest ever (5–6:1000 population). Life expectancy has risen accordingly and currently the rate stands at 74.9 years for women and 69.9 for men (NSO 1997a). A major social policy implication of the comparative longevity of women is that there will be an increasing need for appropriate programs to care for large numbers of elderly women who were economically dependent on deceased male partners.

Despite the improved health conditions of the population in general, Thai women still face numerous gender specific health problems related to childbirth. Prime among these is maternal death caused by direct obstetric causes such as haemorrhage and anaemia. Maternal death resulting from malignant neoplasm is the second most frequent cause of death of women in Thailand. Abortion is illegal in Thailand (except in exceptional circumstances) nonetheless it is estimated that several thousand pregnancies are terminated each year despite the ban. The common perception is that many of those seeking abortions are young unmarried adolescent girls but poverty stricken farmers also seek abortions when contraception fails and economic pressures limit their ability to provide for another child (Whittaker 2000). Because there are no professional or controlled abortion services there is no accurate information on the number of terminations performed each year nor on the health status of women who undergo the illegal procedures. Social and religious taboos ensure that women who have undergone abortions remain silent. The National Commission on Women's Affairs (1994) has recently recommended that the issue of access to abortions should be discussed at a national level and that abortion law reform is a necessary and pressing matter. Rapid social and economic changes as well as alterations to the sexual behaviour of adolescents demand a re-examination of the ban on abortions.

As well as problems related to pregnancy and childbirth Thai women face a major threat from sexually transmitted diseases. There still a high incidence of Urinary Tract Infections among females although the decline in Sexually Transmitted Diseases (i.e. Gonorrhoea, Syphilis, Hemophilus Ducreyi, NSU) among both men and women provides some cause for optimism. Figures released in 1993 by the Thai Ministry of Public Health showed that out of the total infected persons, only 16 per cent were women. Among these infected women, the large majority of them (76 per cent) were those in reproductive ages. However, since the 1980s there has been a rapid rise in the number of people infected with a new sexually transmitted disease, HIV/AIDS. This disease presents a major threat to the Thai population and undermines the recent records of declining mortality rates. It is projected that the cumulative number of HIV infected persons in Thailand will exceed one million in 1999 (van Griensven and Suwanee 1998). The anticipated result of this epidemic is a rise in the mortality rate into the twenty-first century. In 1997 it was estimated that approximately 15 000–20 000 pregnant women are found to be HIV positive each year and about 4000–6000 of their babies will be born infected with the virus (NSO 1997a). The major source of HIV transmission in Thailand is through sexual contact between individuals who fail to practice 'safe sex' and who continue to have 'unprotected sex'. Young female adolescents are particularly vulnerable because, in a culture that values feminine modesty, they are the least likely to receive education about human sexuality and sexual health care. The relative ignorance of young girls about 'safe sex' and HIV is an issue of grave concern.

Education and employment

Traditionally, boys were sent to *wats* (monasteries) for a basic education while girls were kept at home and trained in domestic skills. This pattern changed in 1921 when the government implemented compulsory education for both boys and girls from the ages of 7–14. By 1932 the Constitution stipulated that all Thai citizens had the right to a minimum of four years public education. Since the 1960s there has been a dramatic increase in the numbers of students, both boys and girls, enrolled in all levels of education (primary to university). However, illiteracy rates remain consistently higher among women than men. In 1937, 85 per cent of women were illiterate compared to 57 per cent of men. By 1990 the illiteracy rates had dropped markedly but the sex disparity remains with 9 per cent of women and 5 per cent of men recorded as illiterate. Moreover, in the past three decades more women than men are reported to have received no education at all (Bavornsiri 1982; NSO 1997a).

After the age of twelve the number of children leaving formal schooling increases rapidly. By age fifteen approximately 66 per cent of all Thai youths had left school and by the age of 20 almost 90 per cent were no longer enrolled (NCWA 1994). The main reason for this rapid decline in school attendance is poverty but the absence of essential educational facilities and the ineffective enforcement of education laws compound the problem. Of those few Thai citizens who enter university there are almost equal numbers of men and women (NSO 1997a). This pattern of gender balance has been typical of the entire education spectrum since the 1980s indicating that sex discrimination is not the major factor in influencing the termination of a child's schooling—financial pressures remain paramount (NCWA 1994; NSO 1997a).

The experience of women in employment is not as cheerful. Although it is difficult to trace longitudinal trends accurately because the measures used to gather data have changed over time, there is a clear shift in the nature of women's participation in the national economy since the 1970s. Women have joined the wage-labour force in greater numbers than ever before with the expansion in jobs outside of the dominant agricultural sector. Traditionally agriculture was the main focus of economic activity for Thais and women were an integral part of the agricultural labour force. Women produced a considerable proportion of family and national income from their agricultural activities and played significant roles in marketing and selling the family produce and controlling the family finances (Chayovan et al. 1995). Census data indicates the expansion in the female labour force. In 1980, 44.4 per cent of the economically active persons (age 11 and over) were women and in 1990 this had increased to about 68 per cent (age 13 and over). This high participation rate does not necessarily equate to high wages since many of the women identified as 'engaged in employment' are working on family farms and remain unpaid for their labour.

The industrialisation of the economy is breaking the dominance of agriculture and this is affecting the nature of women's participation in the workforce. Data from the latest census (1990) indicates that women are increasingly finding employment in traditionally male dominated occupations and industries and are being paid a wage income directly and independently of their families. This economic freedom has reinforced the already relatively equal status of women and men in Thailand by providing young women with independent sources of income. Nonetheless over the entire period of 1970–96 the proportion of women engaged in unpaid family work was more than double that of the men. Women continue to concentrate in the agricultural sector (more than 50 percent of women are in this sector) with trades, service and professional sectors being the next largest employers of women. In contrast, the proportion of men categorised as employers, government employees and small businessmen was much higher than that of women. These figures indicate the continuing difficulty for women of gaining access to the wage sector of the economy. Those within this sector often find that, despite the legal guarantees of equal pay for equal work women usually receive on average lower pay than men who are engaged in the same time of work. Women continue to predominate in the lowest rungs of the salary or wage scales according to the National Statistical Office (NSO 1990b;1991;1997a). For example, in 1994 the average monthly per capita income by gender indicates that where women in urban areas earn 5669 Baht, men earn 8995 Baht. In rural areas women earn 1494 Baht compared to their male counterparts' 3238 Baht (NSO 1997a, p. 77).

Accurate figures on the work conditions for women are difficult to obtain and particularly little is known about those women workers in the informal sector. The work conditions of women migrants, slum-dwellers and sex workers are even more difficult to ascertain since their life-styles often preclude the government's statistics collectors' intervention. It is clear, nonetheless, that women workers in both the agricultural and industrial sectors face numerous health hazards as a direct consequence of their work environments. Pesticides and insecticides are routinely used without attention to safety precautions and, as the main component of the agricultural labour force, women are particularly vulnerable. Although women industrial workers are under the direct jurisdiction of the Labour Protection and Welfare Law, unlike their rural sisters, they too face deteriorating work conditions. Many women are routinely exposed to toxic substances in the textile industry such as lead, aluminium, and trichloroethylene. Reports of illness as a result of exposure to these toxins are common but the effects on their reproductive health and infant health are difficult to ascertain. The National Commission on Women's Affairs points to spontaneous abortion, abnormal birth outcomes and delayed physical and mental development of children as possible side-effects of a mother's exposure to industrial and agricultural toxins (NCWA, 1994).

The rapid industrialisation of the Thai economy over the past two decades coupled with the globalisation of the international labour market have combined to generate large numbers of Thai women migrating from their homes to other centres for employment (Mills 1999). Women comprised the majority of those entering the Bangkok metropolitan area as the opportunities in the service and industrial sectors expanded. Women were preferred employees for the new jobs such as clothing and shoe manufacturing, the sorting of transistors, the assembly of pocket calculators and the handling of microchips for computer components. Thai government planners note that in four out of seven geographical regions the net migration of the female population has been consistently higher than that of men since 1980. They predict that this trend will continue until 2010 (NESDB 1992). The majority of these female migrants move into the large urban centres, have no skills or training, many have little or no knowledge of city-life and even fewer have a network for social and moral support at their destinations. Some form of centrally organised labour advice is required to ensure that female migrants have knowledge of the nature of their employment, the likelihood of finding employment and the social conditions at their destination prior to their departure. Currently, female migrant-workers are placed in extremely vulnerable positions as they venture forth into jobs away from their family and community support.

The economic downturn since 1997 has also demonstrated that unskilled women workers remain the most disposable workers. They are often the first laid-off and few have access to severance or redundancy payments. Many of these women are single-parents or heads-of-households with a group of parents or children depending on their wage. The social security system in Thailand is currently too weak to provide support for these women and their families. Labour laws that guarantee severance pay or worker's compensation need to be introduced across all sectors of the economy to ensure that these, the most vulnerable of Thailand's industrial workers, are protected. In sum, employment for women in Thailand remains concentrated in the unskilled, or semi-skilled sectors and also in the informal agricultural sectors.

On the international arena, Thailand has exported large number of unskilled or semi-skilled workers to a range of nations since the 1970s. Most of these workers come from the poverty stricken North-eastern region of Thailand. Initially the main destination for these labour migrants was the Middle East but in the 1980s East and Southeast Asia became popular destinations (for example, Singapore and Brunei). The women who travel for work are primarily engaged in domestic work but a number of studies indicate that a certain proportion are employed in the entertainment industry, including prostitution. Destinations for these workers are diverse and include Taiwan, Japan, Hong Kong, Brunei, Malaysia, USA and Europe. Thai women in the overseas sex industry face considerable hardship and racism abounds. In Japan the problems is particularly acute and Thai sex-workers face accusations that they are spreading HIV/AIDS on a routine basis (Wongboonsin et al. 1997).

At home, prostitution remains a long-term, growing and unsolved problem. Economic hardship remains the predominant reason for women to enter the sex industry. Lack of education combines with diminishing economic opportunities to create considerable incentives for women to become prostitutes (see Cook 1998). Others are forced or lured into the profession by unscrupulous middle-men. Leaving their homes on the assumption that they will be working in factories, many girls find themselves tricked into prostitution instead. Some of the women travelling overseas do so illegally but the income they earn is generally sent home to support parents and siblings in desperate need. Needless to say the majority of these sex-workers work in adverse life-threatening circumstances. The illegal nature of the industry makes it very difficult to monitor numbers of women involved and the conditions under which they work. Prostitutes who face abuse or danger rarely seek legal protection precisely because of the illegal status of their work. While accurate numbers are impossible to gather, it is anticipated that the current economic downturn will cause more women to enter prostitution as alternative, legal means of employment diminish. Attempts to close the industry by law enforcement agencies have proved unsuccessful since the networks supporting the industry are complex and well entrenched. No single solution will solve this growing problem. The rapid spread of HIV/AIDS since the 1980s has meant that prostitution is now a major health public threat since it is regarded as being the major source of the spread of the disease.

At the other end of the professional spectrum, women's involvement in politics and government administration remains limited. Thai women were granted the right to vote in 1933 a year after the government system changed from an Absolute Monarchy to a Constitutional Monarchy. However, in the sixty years since then women's share of power at both a national level (as MPs or Senators) and at a local level (as council administrators) remains low. In the last general election held in 1996 on 5.6 per cent of elected MPs were women and only 8 per cent were appointed as Senators. The number of women working as administrators in the State Bureaucracy is increasing but the numbers are still extremely low. Until 1982, when the law was repealed, the Local Administration Act of 1914 prohibited women from holding administrative posts at both the provincial and local (district and village) levels. Soon after the revision of this law several hundred women were either elected or appointed to various administrative posts at the local level. In 1993 Thailand appointed its first woman Provincial Governor. Overall, in 1995 official statistics showed that women constituted 2.7 per cent of all Governors (out of 75 provinces), 0.1 per cent of all District Heads (out of 774 districts) and 0.2 per cent of Assistant District Heads (out of 7877 positions). Women's participation in the judiciary remains minimal at only 7 per cent of prosecutors, judges and judge-trainees (NCWA 1994; NSO 1997a).

Women's status in the family

Thai Family Law within the Civil Code contains many outright discriminatory items. For example, if a woman engaged to be married has sexual relations with a man other than her fiancé, her fiancé is entitled to terminate the engagement and seek compensation from the third party. An engaged woman does not have reciprocal rights. Similarly, if a spouse seeks a judicial divorce (as opposed to a divorce based on mutual consent), the husband is able to divorce his wife on the grounds of adultery but the wife cannot use this reason against her husband without proof that the husband has maintained and honoured the 'other woman' as his wife (NCWA 1995, p. 37). Consequently the National Commission on Women's Affairs 'Long-term Women's Development Plan (1992–2011)' proposed revisions to these laws to eradicate those aspects which implicitly promote double-standards in the treatment of women. The Plan was keen to ensure that the law affords women protection as wives and mothers and that men be encouraged to share a greater proportion of the childcare and household chores in their roles as fathers and husbands. The Plan stated that attention should be given to family laws that promote or the notion of shared responsibilities and shared loyalties between husbands and wives. Currently the marriage registration system affords women no protection from bigamous husbands, and neither do they provide women with protection against sexual abuse, sexual harassment, rape or domestic violence (NCWA 1994). Domestic violence (especially wife beating) is major family problem in Thai society but it remains underreported because of the social stigma attached to the victims and the perpetrators. One study on Status of Women and Fertility in Thailand conducted in 1993 interviewed 2800 women and found that one-fifth (approximately 600 women) reported having been beaten by their husbands. The highest concentration of women who had experienced domestic violence was in Bangkok. About 13 per cent of Bangkok women reported being beaten regularly and 47 per cent of these remained in the relationship within a submissive role, neither retaliating nor leaving (Chayovan et al. 1995).

Traditionally Thai customs have discouraged marriage at a young age and the impact of urbanisation and socio-economic development have reinforced this tendency leading to an increase in marriage age among Thais (Limanonda 1992). The last four census figures indicate that the age at first marriage for women has risen from 21.6 in 1960 to 23.5 in 1990. The age at first marriage of urban dwellers remains higher than that of rural dwellers. There has also been an increase in the proportion of the population that remain single for both men and women. Nonetheless marriage is still the overwhelming choice with only a small number of Thais remaining single by the age of 50 (Limanonda 1992; NSO 1960; 1970; 1980; 1990; 1996). The divorce rate is increasing especially in Bangkok where remarriage among younger divorcees is quite high.

This increase in the marriage dissolution rate has resulted in a growing number of female heads-of-households. From the 1994 Household Survey, out of the total 15.8 million households counted, 3.2 million households (about 20.1 per cent) were headed by women and these households had an average of 3.2 family members. The average age of these women heads was 51 years old. Sixty-six per cent of them had primary education while only 5.2 per cent attained university education (NSO 1997b). The low levels of education and income prevalent among these single female heads-of-households signifies a considerable burden for the women involved since they would most likely be the major provider of the economic and emotional needs of their household members.

Conclusion

Thai women have made considerable progress in the last thirty years. This results from Thailand's comparatively equitable cultural traditions as well as the rapid economic development of the nation since the 1970s. However, certain groups of women remain at a severe disadvantage compared to men and consequently their potential to contribute to national development is often ignored or overlooked. The continued existence of these weak points, given Thailand's favourable economic and cultural context, suggests that many opportunities for improving the status of Thai women have been missed. As greater numbers of women enter the administrative and political realms and with the continued support of international bodies like the UN, fewer opportunities should be missed in the future.

Over the past few decades numerous policies, programs and government initiatives have been implemented to address these problems but these have had mixed results. Greater co-operation between those involved (both Governmental organisations and non-Governmental organisations) in designing and implementing programs of action for women is required to achieve better results. Programs require constant monitoring and evaluation to allow for revision and improvement. It is important that both top-down (full support from authorities) and bottom-up approaches (participation of the grass-root level) are adopted. Moreover, research studies to gather current data on the role and status of women in Thailand's development are vital to the design and implementation of effective policies.

References and recommended readings

Bavornsiri, Varaporn 1982 'Role, status and problems of women in education,' *Women in Development: Implications for Population Dynamics in Thailand*, eds Piampiti Suchart and Prasitrathsin Suwanlee, Parbpim, Bangkok.
Bennett, Anthony et al. 1990 'How Thailand's family planning program reach replacement level. Fertility lessons learned,' *Occasional paper no. 4. Population Technical*

Assistant Project, Dual Associates and International Science and Technology Institute, Washington D.C.

Branch, Betty 1982 'Khunying Suphatra Singholka: Thailand's gentle equivalent of women's lib,' *SWADDI Magazine* (March–April, 1971) republished in *Women's Rights*, by Khunying Suphatra Singholka, pp. 67–Index.

Business and Professional Women Association of Thailand 1985 *The Women of Thailand.* A document prepared for The United Nations Decade for Women, 1985, Chulalongkorn University Press, Bangkok.

Chamratrithirong, Apichat et al. 1997 *Report on National Contraceptive Prevalence Survey 1996*, Institute for Population and Social Research, Mahidol University, Bangkok.

Chayovan, Napaporn, Malinee Wongsith, Vipan Prachuabmoh Ruffolo 1995 'A study on status of women and fertility in Thailand,' IPS Publication No. 229/95 (May), Institute of Population Studies, Chulalongkorn University, Bangkok.

Cook, Nerida 1998 ' "Dutiful daughters", estranged sisters: women in Thailand,' *Gender and Power in Affluent Asia*, eds K. Sen and M. Stivens, Routledge, London.

Curtin, Leslie B. 1982 'Status of women: a comparative analysis of twenty developing countries,' *Reports on the World Fertility Survey 5*, Population Reference Bureau, Washington D.C.

Dixon, Ruth B. 1976 'Measuring equality between the sexes,' *Journal of Social Issues*, vol. 32, no. 3, pp. 19–45.

Ekchai, Sanitsuda 1984 'Thanpuying La-iad: gone but not forever,' *Bangkok Post Outlook.*

ESCAP, General Demography Section 1985 'Measuring the status of women,' *Demography Notebook*, ESCAP, Bangkok.

Human Resource Planning Division, National Economic and Social Development Board 1994 *Thailand: National Report on Population and Development.* Prepared for the International Conference on Population and Development, Cairo, Egypt.

Limanonda, Bhassorn 1992 'Nuptiality patterns in Thailand: their implications for further fertility decline,' *Fertility Transitions, Family Structure, and Population Policy*, ed. Calvin Goldscheider, Westview, Boulder.

—— 1995 'Families in Thailand: beliefs and realities,' *Journal of Comparative Family Studies. Special Issue on Family in Asia: Beliefs and Realities*, vol. XXVI, no.1 (Spring), pp. 67–82.

—— 1996 'Preference for sex of children, determinants and implications. a case of Thailand.' A paper presented at the International Workshop on Fertility, Son Preference and Child Mortality of Koreans in Korea and China (November).

Mills, Mary Beth 1999 *Thai Women in the Global Labor Force: Consuming desires, contested selves*, Rutgers University Press, Piscataway.

National Commission on Women's Affairs (NCWA) 1985 *Women's Development in Thailand.* A report prepared by the National Committee for International Co-operation for the World Conference of the United Nations Decade for Women, Nairobi, Kenya (15–26 July), n.p., Bangkok.

—— 1991 *Policies and Long-Term Plans for Women's Development (1992–2011). Sub-Committee for Long-Term Plan for Women's Development* (Draft). Office of the Civil Service Commission Printing House, Bangkok.

—— 1994 *Thailand's Report on the Status of Women and Platform for Action 1994.* A report prepared for the Fourth World Conference on Women. Beijing, People's Republic of China (4–15 September, 1995).

—— 1995 *Thailand's Report on the Status of Women and Platform for Action 1994.* Prepared for the Fourth World Conference on Women, Beijing, People's Republic of China, Amarin, Bangkok.

National Committee for International Cooperation, Thailand National Commission on Women's Affairs 1985 *Women's Development in Thailand.* Prepared for the World Conference of the United Nations Decade for Women, Nairobi, Kenya.

National Economic and Social Development Board (NESDB) 1992 *Population Projections for Thailand 1980–2015*, NESDB, Bangkok.

—— 1994 *Thailand: National Report on Population and Development.* A Report prepared by Thailand Working Committee for preparation of the International Conference on Population and Development (September), NESDB, Bangkok.

—— 1997 *Summary of the Eight National Economic and Social Development Plans (1997–2001)*, Med Sai, Bangkok.

National Statistical Office (NSO) 1960,1970, 1980, 1990 *Thailand Population and Housing Census: Whole Kingdom.*

—— 1990b *Report of the Labor Force Survey: Whole Kingdom (Round 3, August 1988)*, Technique, Bangkok.

—— 1991 *Report of the Labor Force Survey: Whole Kingdom (Round 3, August 1989)*, Aksorn Thai, Bangkok.

—— 1992 *Survey of Migration into Surat Thani Province; Chiang Mai Province; Khon Kean Province 1989*, Cooperative Marketing and Purchasing Federation of Thailand, Bangkok.

—— 1995 *Report of the 1992 Migration Survey*, Ro So Po, Bangkok.

—— 1996 *Nuptiality of Thai Population: 1990 Population and Housing Census. Subject Report No. 4*, Arun, Bangkok.

—— 1997a *Statistical Booklet on Thai Women and Men*, National Statistical Office, Bangkok.

—— 1997b *Analysis of Households with Female Heads 1997*, Text and Journal, Bangkok.

Prachuabmoh, Visid, Knodel, John and Alers, J. Oskar 1974 'Preference for sons, desire for additional children and family planning in Thailand,' *Journal of Marriage and the Family* (August), pp. 601–614.

Prachuabmoh, Visid and Knodel, John 1977 'Preference for sex of children in Thailand: results from the second round of a national survey,' Paper no. 23, Institute of Population Studies, Chulalongkorn University, Bangkok.

Prasitrathsin, Suchart and Suwanlee Piampiti eds. 1982 *Women in Development: Implications for Population Dynamics in Thailand*, Parbpim, Bangkok.

Richter, Kerry and Napaporn Havanon 1995 *Women's Economic Contribution to Households in Thailand. Implication for National Development and Social Welfare,* Gender Press, Bangkok.

Singholaka, Supatra, Khunying 1982 *Women's Rights: History and Development of Women's Rights Movement,* Reun Keow, Bangkok.

Smith, Harold E. 1979 'The Thai rural family,' *The Family in Asia,* eds Man Singh and Parros D. Bardis, George Allen and Unwin, London.

Soonthornthada, Kusol, Orapin Pitakmahaket and Uraiwan Kanungsukkasem 1995 *Opinion of Bangkokians towards the Election of Female Representatives,* IPSR Report No. 194. Institute for Population and Social Research, Mahidol University, Bangkok.

Thai Studies 1996 *Women, Gender Relations and Development in Thai Society. (Theme V)* Proceedings of the 6th International Conference on Thai Studies, Chiang Mai (14–17 October).

Thomson, Suteera 1994 *Women Acting for Change: Towards an Equitable Society* (Thai translation by Metahnee Pongvej), Gender and Development Research Institute, Bangkok.

United Nations, ESCAP 1996 *Women in Thailand: A Country Profile, Statistical Profiles,* No. 5, United Nations, New York.

van Griensven, Frits and Suwanee Surasiengsunk 1998 'The use of mortality statistics as a proxy indicator for the impact of the HIV epidemic on the Thai population.' A paper prepared for the AIDS Co-ordination Unit of the Delegation of the European Commission to Thailand (January).

Whittaker, Andrea 2000 *Intimate Knowledge: Women and Their Health in North-east Thailand,* Allen and Unwin, Sydney.

Wongboonsin, Pacharavalai et al. 1997 *Human Resources Development and Migration Patterns among ASEAN Member States.* Working Paper for the AIPO ad-hoc committee on human resources development. Institute of Population Studies, Chulalongkorn University, Bangkok.

13 Militarism, civil war and women's status: a Burma case study

Janell Mills

Department of Economic History
University of Sydney

From a historical perspective, the status of women in Burma was high compared to that of women both in the west and elsewhere in Asia. Nonetheless, in the two most important national institutions—the government and Buddhism—Burmese men were privileged over women. Traditionally political power was a male preserve and membership of the Buddhist monk-hood an exclusively male privilege. Cultural concepts ensured official power gravitated to the male while Buddhist ideologies reaffirmed men's superior status in the hierarchy of rebirth. Despite this, women played critical roles in society, the economy and the household and in many areas enjoyed equality with men. These roles, however, were to be affected significantly by the military coup of 2 March 1962 that overturned the democratically elected government and entrenched the *Tatmadaw* (armed forces) in power. Consequently during the three decades from 1970 to 2000 Burmese women had to contend with an authoritarian, conservative, military and essentially masculine regime that gradually curtailed their customary independence and status.

The military junta introduced policies of socialism and isolationism. They presided over a declining economy and an increasingly impoverished population. In 1988 massive popular uprisings against the oppression and hardship inflicted by the government marked a turning point in Burma. The military authorities abandoned socialism for an 'Open Door' economic policy but accelerated their policies of repression and control. At the same time the uprisings produced a pro-democracy movement in Burma, headed by a woman, Aung San Suu Kyi. It was this development which charted new possibilities for women in Burma. Her leadership of the pro-democracy movement challenged and highlighted the militarisation and masculinisation of the symbols of power used to buttress the regime's control. It also contributed to the politicisation of other Burmese women, as the authoritarian regime of the *Tatmadaw* introduced policies that increased the repression of women, particularly women in Burma's ethnic minorities.

This chapter argues that the militarisation of Burma's government in the two periods 1962–88 and 1988–present writing 1999 meant that the Burmese state became more masculine. Male symbols were strengthened with the domination of the dynamics of power by military might and men in uniform. This process undermined the fabric of Burma's traditional values and society and had a particularly detrimental impact on women's lives as their customary independence and status was eroded. As the *Tatmadaw* leadership attempted to regiment the whole of Burma into one hierarchy of command, the pro-democracy movement under the leadership of Aung San Suu Kyi offered an alternative path of liberty, equality and diversity. As the 'space' ascribed for women in Burma was reduced, it was a woman leader who demanded an equal 'space' not only for women but for all members of the community that is modern Burma.

After the 1962 coup Burma's social and economic structures declined. In the middle of the twentieth century Burma had been a country rich in natural resources and recognised as the rice bowl of Asia because of its productive agricultural sector. By 1987 Burma was classified as a Least Developed Country (LDC), a United Nations classification reserved for the poorest countries of the world. This poverty was remarkable given the economic growth of Burma's Southeast Asian neighbours over the same period. The average annual growth rate of the economy from 1960 to 1973 was 2.9 per cent (compared to 7.9 per cent and 6.5 per cent over the same period for Thailand and Malaysia respectively) (FEER 1977, p. 14). In 1988 the real growth rate in the economy was an estimated 3.2 per cent (FEER 1990, p. 6). It grew to 5.8 per cent in 1996–97 with the changed economic policy (FEER 1998, p. 91) but fell to less than an estimated 2 per cent in 1998 (Seekins 1999, p. 14). A cautionary note is warranted here. Due to the government's deliberate distortion of data for propaganda purposes or incapacity to collect and collate it, official statistics on modern Burma should be treated with discretion.

Geographically, Burma is the largest of the mainland Southeast Asian states but comparatively lightly populated with approximately 46 million people. The largest ethnic group is the Burmans—constituting between 66 and 75 per cent of the population. Buddhist in religion and Burmese in language, the Burmans live in the rich agricultural regions of the central river valleys and coastal flats. The major towns and cities of Burma are also in the Burman areas. The rest of Burma's population is comprised of a mosaic of ethnic minorities who speak over 100 different languages. The largest of these include the Shan, Karen, Kachin and Chin (Smith 1991, pp. 27–39; Steinberg 1985, pp. 125–26). These minority groups live mainly in the hills and mountainous border regions of the country.

Women in monarchic Burma: pre-1886

Documentary evidence of the freedom and economic independence enjoyed by women in Burma in the past is found in numerous temple inscriptions and chronicles of the Pagan era of the 11th–13th centuries (Luce 1940, p. 327, 329). Later European commentators also note the favourable status of Burma's women. In 1826 one wrote:

> The female branches of the family are not recluses here, neither are they reserved or shy in their manners; they form a constituent part of domestic and public society. The wife of a judge or governor is often seen at his side, assisting in the decision of cases; and the wives of viceroys and other high officers are often permitted to hold their own courts, and decide independently on petitions presented to them. Women of all ranks enjoy a high degree of freedom and appear abroad unveiled whenever they choose (quoted in Spiro 1997, p. 13)

Some fifty years later another writer noted:

> All the money and possessions which a girl brings with her on marriage are kept carefully separate for the benefit of her children or heirs, and she carries her property away with her if she is divorced, besides anything she may have added to it in the interim by her own trading or by inheritance. Thus a married woman is

much more independent than any European even in the most advanced states (Shwe Yoe 1882, p. 52).

Women inherited the family estate equally with their brothers and were the main traders in local shops and bazaars. They had responsibility for family finances and household matters but could also work in the paddy fields, at light tasks of transplanting and weeding, and helped the men with harvest. Marriage could be arranged but was entered into freely. Women did not change their names upon marriage and were as able to initiate divorce as men with little or no resulting stigma.

Women could also hold positions of power, a few reigning as queens in the early kingdoms, the latest and most famous being the fifteenth century Queen Shin Saw Pyu of the Pegu dynasty. More commonly women could be heads of villages, some inheriting the position through the female line, possibly indicating an early matriarchal tradition in Burma (Mi Mi Khaing 1984, pp. 7–8). Most women holding political power derived it from their relationships with men—as wives or daughters, the latter succeeding their fathers to hereditary positions in the absence of male heirs. This was the route by which Queen Shin Saw Pyu came to the throne.

Much of the high social status and considerable economic autonomy held by women in Burma were due to customary practice rather than strictly legal prescription. The anthropologist Melford Spiro has called these extra-structural or informal rights (Spiro 1997, p. 13). Though the formal laws of the country were based on the Hindu *Dhammathats* (sacred law books), their distinct bias against women was either ignored or only partially implemented. However, Burmese ambivalence about women was evident in an old proverb that listed a thief, the bough of a tree, a ruler and a woman among 'things not to be trusted' (quoted in Cady 1958, p. 61). Burmese rituals also point to the subordination of women. Male and female clothing was washed and dried separately to prevent the pollution of the former and a woman could not be elevated physically above her husband. In public women were expected to defer to men, a wife always walking behind her husband who was the formal head of the family. Adultery on the part of a woman entitled the husband to divorce whereas adultery on the part of a man did not carry the same sanction. Rape, however, was a recognised crime carrying the penalty of forfeiture of all property (Gledhill 1962, p. 181; Mi Mi Khaing 1965, pp. 110–11). Women allegedly prayed to be reborn in a future life as men and the birth of a son was regarded as a great privilege. Nonetheless, the birth of a daughter was also welcomed because it was recognised by both parents that a daughter would remain closer to her parents in later life (Spiro 1977, p. 260; Khin Myo Chit 1969, p. 135).

The inferior status of women in Burma was particularly apparent when we consider their roles in two important arenas—government and Buddhism. According to Spiro, 'By cultural prescription, the exercise of authority (*awza*) is a male prerogative, so that any social status endowed with authority is, by cultural ascription, a male monopoly' (1997, p. 13). The basic premise that men were inherently superior to women was thus embedded in Burmese culture. It was believed that men possessed an innate spiritual quality, known as *hpoun*, explained by Mi Mi Khaing as 'the nobility' or 'glory' of manhood (1946, p. 39) and elsewhere as male 'power-aura' (Yawnghwe 1997, p. 75). Lacking this attribute, women were regarded and indeed regarded themselves, as inferior (Spiro 1977, pp. 259–60).

Within Burmese society monks are granted the most prestigious social status. Called *hpoungyi*, (literally 'great *hpoun*' or 'great glory'), a monk is therefore perceived as epitomising and embodying *hpoun*. Since *hpoun* is a male quality, only men were eligible to be *hpoungyi*. Women could become nuns (*thilashins*, literally 'keepers of the precepts') but this did not attract the same veneration as being a monk. Nevertheless over the centuries *thilashins* acted as teachers of Buddhism to women and girls, some achieving considerable prominence. Such was Saya Kin. She taught the women of the court of Mindon (1853–78) and established cloisters at Sagaing, not far from the then capital of Mandalay (Mi Mi Khaing 1984, pp. 79–80). *Thilashins*, however, were not part of the formal *sangha* (monastic order) and were never as numerically significant as the *hpoungyi*. For most women the path to achieving Buddhist merit was through serving the Buddha in a lay capacity. As women they were excluded from the noviciate to which all young Buddhist males were required to enter for a time and were thus also excluded from the *sangha*. An integral institution of Burmese society, the *sangha* provided a rudimentary education for all those recruited to it—all Burmese Buddhist males. Consequently, education for men was culturally embedded in the institutional structures of the society. For women, education was possible but it was informal, far from universal and confined almost entirely to women in the official class. It was provided through the family and in *thilashin* or lay private schools (Malcom 1840, p. 59, 72; Mi Mi Khaing 1984, p. 101).

Despite the restrictions on women's access to formal power, women could still exercise political influence and informal power through their male connections. Indeed, wives were often regarded as more powerful than their husbands who held the political office. The chief queen of the last king of Burma, Supayalat, was widely believed to exert paramount influence over the king, Thibaw. The wives of officials at every level of government were also regarded as powerful figures. Similarly, within the family, regardless of the formal position of superiority held by the husband, the wife was commonly recognised as wielding the actual day-to-day power (Spiro 1997, pp. 15–16).

Women in the colonial period (1886–1948)

In 1886 Burma lost her independence and became an adjunct of British India. The colonial government provided girls with the chance for formal government or missionary (proselytising and non-proselytising) sponsored education. The colonial education system still gave priority to the education of boys, as did the Buddhist monastic system, because boys were seen as future civil servants in the exclusively male administrative system. Nonetheless, the number of girls receiving a formal education increased by a factor of sixteen in the half century between 1885–86 and 1935–36 (Mi Mi Khaing 1984, p. 103). The need for female teachers and increasing job opportunities in the expanding commercial sector, largely in family-run businesses, ensured the continued expansion of education for girls. A number of women writers emerged, such as Khin Myo Chit, Shwe Gu May Hnin and Kyi Aye. These made significant contributions to early Burmese modern literature. A few privileged women were educated overseas and entered professions such as law but most women continued to follow the time-honoured occupations of working in the home and in the bazaars. At a time when foreign interests increasingly dominated the economy, Burmese women held their own by remaining the main force in the country's petty bazaar trade (Nisbet 1901, pp. 450–51).

In the early twentieth century when women in the West were engaged in their historic push for emancipation, Burmese women were involved in the nationalist movement striving for Burma's independence. They did not conceive of the need for a struggle against Burmese men—their concerns were overwhelmingly nationalist. Mi Mi Khaing suggested that the traditional advantages that gave Burmese women near parity with men, dulled their 'spirit to seek new fields to conquer [and] challenge the traditional concept of male *hpon* [sic] and prestige' (1984, p. 26). More as a part of their nationalist agenda than as a feminist gesture, women demonstrated in 1927 against a clause preventing them from standing for election to the Legislative Council. As a result, the first woman was elected in 1929 (Mya Sein 1958, pp. 25–26). The constitution of 1935 enfranchised females over 21, provided they were literate and one woman, Daw Hnin Mya, was elected to the Legislative Assembly in 1936 (Mi Mi Khaing 1984, p. 157; Donnison 1970, p. 115). Another woman, the scholar and author Daw Mya Sein, daughter of a distinguished jurist and scholar, was chosen to represent Burmese women at a special Burma Round Table Conference in London in 1931 and later lead a delegation to China.

Although female students participated in the student strikes against the colonial government it was still men who both predominated and led the nationalist movement. Women members of the *Dobama Asi-ayone* (We Burmans Society), such as Thakin-ma Ma Aye and Thakin-ma Daw Say, played prominent roles in the strikes on the oil fields in 1938. But for the most part the various women's organisations, such as the *Konmari* association, played only supporting roles in the nationalist struggle. They focussed primarily on promoting and preserving traditional culture and values (Hla Hla Moe 1998, pp. 62–63).

Women in independent Burma: parliamentary period (1948–62)

Burma regained her status as an independent country in early 1948 but this transition did not result in a dramatic improvement in the position of women. The first constitution confirmed equal rights for women in political, social, and economic affairs but this early post-independence period saw no progress in the dismantling of the traditional connection between masculinity and authority to rule. Moreover, the turmoil of World War Two, which included a period under Japanese occupation, created an atmosphere fostering military values and military leadership. Not long after hostilities ceased and Burma was preparing for independence, the young nationalist leader and provisional Prime Minister, General Aung San, was assassinated in mid July 1947. Despite his military background, Aung San had emerged as committed to democratic government and opposed to the fascist, militaristic elements already present in Burma (Silverstein 1993, p. 156). The stability of the new nation was tested with his assassination. Aung San was succeeded by U Nu, a devout Buddhist, and the assassins were tried and convicted. Nonetheless the country slid into civil war as the Communists and various ethnic minorities challenged the new state. Soon after the Chinese Nationalist forces also threatened Burma's borders. This combination of internal and external threats heightened the importance of the defence forces as custodians of the integrity of the nation state.

With these pressures on the new state there was little opportunity for rational dismantling of masculine privilege. Although a small number of women's units were formed within the armed forces (Maung Maung 1974, pp. 101–10) their existence did not challenge the overarching male power structures of the country. University education continued to open professions such as law and medicine to select groups but, for the most part, women still gravitated to their customary occupations. This meant they continued to work in the home or the family fields, trade in the bazaars, work in light industry or serve as teachers. Voluntary welfare work was also encouraged as a suitable occupation for women by the new government through the national Council of Women in Burma which provided a number of maternity and child welfare centres. At this stage nursing itself did not attract many recruits from the ethnic Burman population, despite an acute shortage of nurses. This was because the profession was associated with the Christian communities, in decline since independence in 1948.

Men continued to dominate the political scene. Only one woman, Mrs Ba Maung Chain, served briefly (1952–53) in the cabinet as minister for the Karen State (no woman has served as minister since) and there was only a handful of women amongst the members of the first Constituent Assembly (Tinker 1967, p. 26). Some of these women attained their positions through the status of their husbands, for example, the widow of the assassinated Aung San, Daw Khin Kyi, became the local representative in Aung San's electorate after his death. Daw Khin Kyi, an ethnic Burman, had been active in public life before her husband's death. A teacher and strong advocate of nursing among the Burmans, she had worked with the Burmese resistance during the war (Ang 1998, p. 5, 12). In 1960 Daw Khin Kyi became Burma's first woman ambassador.

Women in the first period of military rule (1962–88)

Burma's fragile parliamentary democracy came to an end with a military coup, led by General Ne Win, in March 1962. This shift to military rule brought significant changes to all levels and sectors of society. *Tatmadaw* rule in Burma condensed a narrow, nationalist and masculine ethos within Burma's power structures. With a rank and file composed largely of ethnic Burmans from predominantly rural backgrounds, the *Tatmadaw* leadership focussed on preserving 'traditional' Burman cultural values, emphasising the integrity of the Burman ethnic majority while suppressing pluralist features present in society. The official ideology of the military regime, entitled *The Burmese Way to Socialism*, was to achieve a new economic order, an egalitarian utopia, as well as national self sufficiency. What also characterised this conservative nationalist regime was a growing xenophobia so that Burma was increasingly isolated from the international community as its military rulers attempted to protect it from contamination by the outside world.

The relentless rigidity of the soldier-socialists in enforcing the new economic order saw the economy falter and the standard of living decline. As a result of nationalisation, most of the important non-indigenous business people left the country. Many of the new managers were soldiers with little or no knowledge of the industries they headed. Output fell and both unemployment and prices rose. State intervention in agriculture was equally disastrous. The shortage of consumer goods gave rise to corruption and generated a thriving black market that undermined both public and private morality. Inflation and shortages of basic foods such as rice caused greatest hardship in Burma's cities and towns and led to riots in 1974 and 1975.

The nationalist agenda of the *Tatmadaw* required raising the education standard nationally and this was to bring some benefits to women. Education was both nationalised and Burmanised. All non-public education was eliminated and the Burmese language made the only medium of instruction. The public education programme begun by the previous regime was expanded so that literacy at least in the Burman areas of the country improved significantly, particularly amongst the female population. Between the two census years of 1973 and 1983 female literacy increased by over 12 per cent. The male literacy rate was higher than that for females but the gender gap had narrowed considerably. At primary school level almost equal numbers of boys and girls attended but by secondary school boys significantly outnumbered girls and this continued at tertiary level (Maung 1997, pp. 21–22; Mi Mi Khaing 1984, p. 107, 160).

Women's health also improved largely due to the expansion of public health services the *Tatmadaw* government regarded as part of their nationalist obligations. This was in spite of budgetary restraints imposed by the continuing high level of defence expenditure. Health services had been reduced to a pitiful level during the war years of 1942–45 and the immediate period after but between 1953 and 1976 the available health statistics reveal growth in the number of health personnel and institutions. In that period life expectancy in urban areas rose from 34.5 years to 57.5 years as the number of doctors nearly tripled, the number of nurses rose from 530 to 3801 and that of midwives increased from 1740 to 10 140. In rural areas volunteer health workers began to provide simple health services, sometimes using indigenous medicines. Also

contributing to this improvement was the diffusion of health knowledge
and the practice of modern hygiene because of the progress made in
basic literacy and education. The consequence of all this was a
significant decline in infant, child and maternal mortality though little
changed in remote regional areas (Maung 1990, pp. 18–21, 24).

The deterioration of the economy in combination with rising
community health and education standards resulted in an increase in
women's participation in the paid labour force. The share of women in
the work force rose from 33 per cent to 36 per cent between 1973 and
1983, the greatest increase being among those aged between twenty and
forty years old. For these women there was no counterpart to the jobs
growth in manufacturing in neighbouring Thailand through multinational
industrial activities. In Burma the number of women working in that
sector shrank, reflecting its overall decline. Between 1973 and 1983, the
greatest employment growth for women were in nursing, teaching,
clerical and other service jobs as well as agriculture. The increased
participation in the labour force of women of all ages, including those
over 55 years of age, indicated rising economic pressures as well as
increased education. The growth of female employment in agriculture
reflected the withdrawal of child labour for schooling and was consistent
with the low rate of agricultural mechanisation (Maung 1997, p. 33, 64,
67, 77). While women held responsible jobs as doctors, lawyers, and
academics—jobs of considerable status—they were largely functional
and administrative positions carrying no real power. Many women
turned to bazaar trading to eke out a living or supplement meagre family
incomes. Some became involved in the black market. The stagnating
economy produced few job opportunities for the growing population and
unemployment and underemployment were endemic. Consequently the
educated began to emigrate.

Doctrinaire socialist rigidity, economic incompetence and
administrative mismanagement were not the only reasons for the
economic malaise. The continued unrest in the borderlands by minority
insurgents, alienated by the Burmanisation of the regime, as well as
sporadic protests in the lowlands drained crucial government funding
into the military sector. In the 1970s and 1980s an estimated 50 per cent
of annual government expenditure was spent on the military (Bray 1995,
pp. 27–28). This remained predominantly a male organisation with
female personnel in the armed forces in 1983 limited to about 500,
representing less than one per cent of all three services. They were
assigned primarily to medical and clerical duties. None had combat roles
(Andrew Selth, personal communication, 27.5.99).

To outsiders, Burma seemed a state and society 'set in aspic'—
continually engaged in conflict, untouched by change and isolated from
modern economic development (Steinberg, quoted by Mi Mi Khaing
1984, p. 180). It was still a deeply conservative society with a
predominantly agrarian economic base and relatively low rate of
urbanisation. In keeping with this there was a revival of the institution of
the *thilashins* (nuns), which had declined during the colonial period.
Though exact numbers are not known there were more than 8700 in
1961. The main *thilashin* centre in Burma was Sagaing where there were
over one hundred cloisters in the 1980s. Parents turned to the *thilashins*
to check undesirable outside influences undermining the traditional
values they wanted for their daughters. Some cloisters cared for orphans
or did other welfare work, sometimes with the support of government
departments. Some became known for their Buddhist scholarship and
attracted students from abroad (Mi Mi Khaing 1984, pp. 80–86).

In the political arena male dominance not only continued but it was
further entrenched. In 1974 a new constitution was promulgated that
established Burma as a one party state. The army remained the dominant
influence, though Ne Win formally resigned from the army to become
president. Only three of the 97 members of the drafting commission were
women though their rights to political, economic and social equality
were constitutionally guaranteed. By the 1980s less than three per cent of
members of the *Pyithu Hluttaw* (People's National Assembly) were
women and there were no women at all amongst the Secretariat or
officials in general administration. All organisations had to be registered
with the government and independent women's organisations were
discouraged. Mi Mi Khaing recognised that the low level of female
participation in politics was also common in developed countries, such
as the USA and France, but she noted:

> What is extraordinary here are two points of difference. Women in
> Burma have been going about freely in the public places of trade
> and manufacture for centuries. Yet they have made hardly any
> inroads into the posts of government, politics or some professions.
> The second extraordinary point is that the reasons given for their
> inactivity in these spheres, which, elsewhere are rejected as
> discrimination disguised as protectiveness, neither needed nor
> desired by the women themselves—these reasons are here accepted
> by women in Burma in general as being sound ones (1984, p. 150).

Women in Burma after 1988

1988 was a turning point in the history of Burma. It signified the end of public tolerance of the existing government and this in turn altered the logic and mechanisms of military governance in Burma. It also led women in Burma to reposition themselves more clearly in relation to the regime. The process altered their status as well as their self-perception. This leads to the question of why the crisis of 1988 occurred? Minor modifications to the isolationist economic policies of the 'Burmese Way to Socialism' had generated some slight improvements in the economy during the late 1970s and early 1980s but these gains were only temporary. By the mid-1980s the economy had resumed its downward spiral. In urban areas, where people could not rely on the land to provide basic food-stuffs, the ballooning black-market, growing corruption and inflation made life particularly hard. The government's handling of the latest economic crisis was inept but it was the brutality of police response to a student demonstration that sparked mass uprisings in all of Burma's major centres. In the authorities' ruthless and savage reaction, thousands of people lost their lives (Lintner 1990, pp. 2–6, 96–129; Guyot 1989, pp. 122–24). Nonetheless that these uprisings had occurred at all was significant. Prior to these events of 1988 'there had never been an attempt in the entire history of Burma to control the misrule of the men in power by public revolt' (Maung Maung Gyi 1983, p. 196). There had been demonstrations by students and workers in the past, all savagely suppressed but these were sporadic incidents confined to one or two localities. The uprisings of 1988 were much more than that and indicated a general collapse of power as well as the awe supporting that power.

The spreading turmoil caused the collapse of one party rule, the formal retirement from politics of Ne Win (though he was believed to remain at the real centre of power), and the resumption of direct control of government by the *Tatmadaw*. It set up the transitional State Law and Order Restoration Council (SLORC), the name signalling its intent, and Burma was renamed Myanmar, the historic ethnic Burman name for Burma (Smith 1991, p. 21). The SLORC was not the only new political force established in 1988. From the uprisings of that year the first organs of popular opposition emerged when a number of parties were formed. Among these was the National League for Democracy (NLD) which soon gained pre-eminence. One of the NLD leaders was Daw Aung San Suu Kyi, the daughter of Burma's national hero, General Aung San. She rapidly emerged as the focal point of the new opposition. Her birthright and political debut at the time of Ne Win's resignation brought into question the continued legitimacy of the old order just as her female gender and personal experience introduced the possibility for a different and democratic direction for Burma's political development.

Under the SLORC women's issues were initially disregarded on the grounds that women had no special problems. According to Khin Nyunt, secretary to the SLORC, women in Burma faced 'no restrictions, enjoying equal status and equal rights' (Documentation and Research Centre 1997, p. 23). In the absence of any direct policy initiatives regarding women by the SLORC, the impact of the new regime on women was felt primarily through its concern to maintain military, economic and political domination of the nation. Apart from increasing political coercion and surveillance of the people, the major initiative of the SLORC regime was the abandonment of the 'Burmese Way to Socialism' and the introduction of an 'Open Door' economic policy. International trade and foreign investment restrictions were lifted and for a short time the economy improved. Indeed, Burmese government reports indicate that in 1992–93 the economy grew by 10.9 per cent and in 1993–94 by 5.8 per cent. These were impressive results but, as John Bray noted, official Burmese statistics should be treated with considerable caution (Bray 1995, p. 29). All the same, an improvement in living standards was apparent in the cities of Rangoon and Mandalay, where large-scale construction of roads and buildings was underway and imported consumer goods were widely available. Outside these two cities, however, inflation was still running at 30 per cent (1993–94) and poverty and hardship remained the norm. Rural dwellers were subject to arbitrary increases in taxes and were often forced into performing compulsory labouring on infrastructure projects, such as road construction. These additional forms of 'taxation' represented the regime's willingness to exploit its most vulnerable citizens.

The reforms opening the economy had created the conditions for a growing visibility in the disparity in wealth between 'haves' and 'have-nots'. In the past the small group connected to the military junta had accumulated wealth but in the austere socialist Burma prior to 1988 it was concealed from public view. After 1988 the previous moral sanction against flaunting one's wealth was removed but it did not change the fact that wealth and prosperity still depended on personal connections to people in power. The *Tatmadaw* remained in control of significant economic enterprises after 1988 through bodies such as the Union of Myanmar Economic Holdings Limited, just as they had controlled all state economic enterprises before 1988. This centralisation of economic and political power gave considerable economic power to the wives and daughters of high-ranking government and military officials. In particular, their privileged access to restricted goods made them key players in the black market (Mya Maung 1991, p. 135). One woman, in particular, stood out in this context and that was Sanda Win, daughter of the military strong-man, Ne Win, and an army major in the medical corps. She accumulated great wealth as well as wielding formidable power (Lintner 1990, p. 188; Williams 1998, pp. 185–88). Occasionally, the illegal activities of wives would be used to discredit their powerful spouses. One example of this was the dismissal of Tin U, chief of the National Intelligence Bureau, in 1983, allegedly because of his wife's rampant black marketeering (Lintner 1990, p. 65).

In 1993 the connection between these privileged businesswomen and the military junta was institutionalised when the previously independent Myanmar Women's Entrepreneurial Association was forced under the umbrella of the Union Solidarity and Development Association (USDA). This was a social organisation developed and closely controlled by the SLORC as a vehicle to create and foster a privileged and loyal constituency (East Asia Analytical Unit 1997, p. 102, 107; Documentation and Research Centre 1997, pp. 24–25). This annexation of Burma's peak independent businesswomen's group by the SLORC effectively increased the difficulties for those women without close links with the regime. Their prospects diminished further, when in 1995 the economy faltered again as economic management by the SLORC proved as inept as that of socialist Burma.

By 1997 when the currency and stock-market crisis hit Southeast Asia, it was clear that the Open Door policy was achieving minimal results. An internal power shuffle led to the SLORC transforming itself into the State Peace and Development Council (SPDC) in November 1997. Despite the apparent commitment to peace and development, rather than pacification and harsh law, the international community grew increasingly concerned about political instability in Burma and the regime's flagrant abuses of human rights. Only companies prepared to face international criticism for their 'dealing with dictators' were prepared to invest in the country despite the fact that Burma gained membership of ASEAN in July of the same year.

Consequently, foreign investment remained limited and employment growth in the manufacturing sector, one holding significant potential to employ women, was low (Lintner 1997, p. 61). Another likely source of employment for women was the hospitality and service sector but with continuing unrest and international ostracism, tourism failed to flourish. Consequently, the late 1980s and early 1990s saw a significant outflow of women from Burma to neighbouring Thailand and other countries in search of employment. For the most part these women worked illegally.

Some became domestic workers, others laboured in the construction industry, but the majority found themselves working in the sex industry. Trapped by a lack of education, skills, and illegal status, they found the Thai sex industry a source of jobs but also one exposing them to danger and abuse. This included the possibility of being trafficked to a third country. According to the Thailand Special Branch Police Bureau of the 300 000 foreign victims a year passing through Thailand en route to a third country, the largest number came from Burma (ALTSEAN Burma 1999, p. 16). The Burmese government, unlike some others, provided no legal protection for its citizens working abroad.

Although women with low levels of education were more often those who sought work overseas, the tight control the junta exercised over employment meant many educated women continued to emigrate. Under the SLORC regime, education was no guarantee of a job—especially for women. As had been the case under the previous military leadership of Ne Win, army officers with little education dominated most of the important government positions. In this situation educated men found themselves without access to work. For educated women the situation was much more desperate. Despite the fact that the number of women graduating from tertiary institutions was consistently high, unemployment among this group was so common that Burmese women doctors could be found washing dishes in Japan and serving as domestic workers in Bangkok (Konmari 1998, pp. 70–71). This trend, coupled with an atrophying education system triggered by reduced government funding and periodic shutdowns in response to student protests, undermined the social fabric and human infrastructure of the country.

The continued harsh economic climate began to have a detrimental impact on the physical health and welfare of the population. Most vulnerable were women and children. Since the 1980s it was obvious that food supplies were becoming inadequate. Consequently, malnutrition was increasingly common. Because of the cultural deference of Burmese women to men, women would do without rather than deprive their men. This affected female and infant health. Serious deficiencies of iron and iodine amongst pregnant women reduced the live birth rate and birth weights of those born. Inevitably these children suffered retarded development as a result of their *in utero* malnutrition (WHO 1985, pp. 76–77). According to a 1998 UNICEF report the infant mortality rate was 105 per 1000 births, the highest in the region, and the maternal mortality rate was 580 per 100 000 live births. The figures varied within the country—the more remote regions with high concentrations of non-Burmans had higher than average rates on both counts (Chelala 1998, pp. 30–32). Contributing to the poor health of

Burma's women was the large number of illicit abortions, the result of the absence of official family planning programmes. Abortion is illegal in Burma and although sterilisation was permitted on medical grounds, deep cultural inhibitions by Buddhist doctors and patients alike ensured the incidence of both was low. However, in times of economic hardship the rate of abortion increases (see Allott 1994, pp. 111–19). The government's reluctance to institute formal family planning stemmed from its belief that a reduction in birth rates would reduce the labour force available for seasonal chores. Moreover, Burma's leaders feared that a reduced Burmese population made the country vulnerable to its large and populous neighbours of China and Bangladesh.

The health of Burma's women was also affected by the spread of HIV/AIDS. The Open Door policy legalising cross-border trade with Thailand also opened the country to a major health threat as the main route for transmission was through the Burmese sex-workers returning from Thailand. Unscrupulous Thai dealers had recruited many of these women and girls with false promises of jobs in factories. Instead they found themselves in virtual sex-slavery within the booming Thai sex tourist trade. Women and girls from the ethnic minorities living near the border were particularly vulnerable to this form of trickery. With the collusion of police and military personnel in both Burma and Thailand young women were being sold into forced prostitution, sometimes by their parents, to work in border towns such as Ranong, Chiang Mai, Mae Sai and Kanchanaburi. The 'sale' of many of these women and girls amounted to a modern form of slavery or debt-bondage in often appalling employment conditions. As the fear of contamination among customers in Thailand increased, girls from remote villages were targeted because traffickers believed them to be unexposed to the virus. Usually these were illiterate tribal girls, some as young as thirteen. In 1992 an estimated minimum 40 000 Burmese women and girls were traded into Thai brothels and exposed to physical confinement, rape, mutilation, and murder as well as infection from HIV/AIDS (Documentation and Research Centre 1997, p. 41). According to one estimate the rate of infection among Burmese women and girls in the sex trade in Thailand was roughly three times that existing among Thai prostitutes which was said to be over 21 per cent (Asia Watch 1993, p. 125). Women who escaped sex enslavement in Thailand faced the prospect of imprisonment in Burma on their return because of their unauthorised emigration and participation in illegal prostitution. In Burma itself, despite a prohibition on prostitution, economic hardship contributed to a rising incidence of prostitution. The lack of sex instruction, inadequate treatment facilities, and rising intravenous drug consumption meant HIV/AIDS posed a major health hazard to the people of Burma.

The increased trafficking in women coincided with a renewed effort by the military junta to end the decades-old ethnic insurgency in the borderlands. Military spending increased as spending on health and education fell. Between 1988 and 1992 the number of men in the armed forces rose by more than 60 per cent. Expenditure on health care fell from 2.6 per cent in 1992–93 to 1.6 per cent in 1994–95 while the education budgets fell from 5.9 per cent to 5 per cent (Bray 1995, pp. 27–28; Selth 1996, p. 19). The increased military activity on the border included use of the strategy of the 'four cuts' (*pya ley pya*), developed originally in the campaigns of 1963. The strategy involved cutting the rebel armies' food, funds, intelligence and recruits. Entire villages were forcibly removed along the Burmese side of the Thai border and a scorched earth policy transformed previously populated areas into 'no-man's lands' (Smith 1991, pp. 258–61, 307, 408). In 1991, 80 000 Palaung of Shan State were shifted into relocation zones; and a year later 20 000 Karenni received the same treatment as well as thousands in Karen and Mon States. In 1992, the policy led to the flight into Thailand of villagers from these two states at the rate of 1200 a month (Asia Watch 1993, p. 11; Clements and Kean 1994, p. 63). More than 225 000 Muslim Rohingyas were also driven from Arakan into Bangladesh (Clements and Kean 1994, p. 69). Renewed *Tatmadaw* attacks on the minority peoples in 1997 brought the number of refugees in Thailand to over 115 000 (Apple 1998, p. 9).

While all members of these communities bore the brunt of these tactics, for women there were new horrors. Those herded into the new settlement camps were conscripted as forced labourers for development projects and as porters for military manoeuvres. All community members were liable for this but when no men were available the military seized those remaining—women, children, the old and infirm. Pregnant women were not spared. It is not unusual for uneducated women in Burma to work on construction sites at the lighter tasks of fetching and carrying. However, during the bitter border wars, the military required them to do hard physical labour in poor conditions without pay or medical treatment, or alternatively to carry supplies or ammunition to the front. In battle they were sometimes used as human shields. Vulnerable and defenceless against armed soldiers, they were also subjected to rape and gang rape. Any who resisted this assertion of male power were killed.

While forced labour was not confined exclusively to the border areas, conditions were undoubtedly worse there, particularly in the Mon-Karen areas that had been in the throes of insurgency for decades. This was the area where the new Ye to Tavoy railway was being built in conditions and circumstances not so different from those faced by Allied soldiers half a century before. The systematic abuse of women in these areas and of the Rohingya women in Arakan echoed the 'ethnic cleansing' underway at the same time in former Yugoslavia. Rape by the Burmese military against ethnic minority women had become 'an intrinsic component of the conflict in Burma' as well as a new process of Burmanisation (Apple 1998, p. 4, 18, 41).

The women who escaped successfully across the borders were subjected to the miseries of dislocation with its attendant insecurities and vulnerability. In late 1995 Burma's total refugee population in Thailand, Bangladesh and other countries amounted to nearly 400 000. Of these more than 80 per cent were women and children. In Thailand not only were they vulnerable to continued *Tatmadaw* attack from Burma, they were also exposed to exploitation by the Thai authorities, especially as Thailand was not party to the UN Convention relating to the Status of Refugees. They also faced the prospect of being forced back into Burma. In Bangladesh though they received more government and UN assistance, disease and starvation stalked the camps. The effect of the civil war on women was summed up in one report:

> Many women who have taken no part in conflicts are being murdered, raped and mutilated. Others have endured the loneliness and vulnerability of separation and bereavement. Hardship and deprivation face women who have to support a family alone, in an economy itself distorted by the violence. These women have lost their homes, their possessions, their family and they are struggling for their daily survival in a strange place. For them, to work actively to upgrade their political, economic and social position is impossible (Documentation and Research Centre 1997, p. 40).

Women political activists who chose to remain in Burma suffered continual harassment. In the 1988 uprising girls and women became victims of *Tatmadaw* brutality. Some female student demonstrators were beaten and gang raped, some so traumatised they entered Buddhist nunneries. Others committed suicide (Lintner 1990, pp. 70–71). Once the SLORC seized power, life became even more dangerous for opponents of the regime. Although it agreed to UN sponsored multi-party elections in 1990, the SLORC engaged in a campaign of suppressing the opposition parties. Despite this repression the SLORC still lost in an electoral land-slide. Dismissing these results, the SLORC refused to hand over power. It also reinterpreted the law in its favour so that any opposition to its continued rule was unlawful (East Asia Analytical Unit

1997, p. 106). As a consequence, critics of the SLORC were branded criminals and faced prosecution, torture, and imprisonment.

A number of politically prominent women were incarcerated with punitively long prison sentences. Daw San San Win, an advocate and NLD candidate, was sentenced to twenty-five years imprisonment, her crime—attending a 'clandestine meeting to form a temporary government' in 1990. Daw Cho Cho Kyaw Nyein, General Secretary of the Anti Fascist Peoples Freedom League (AFPFL) and daughter of one of the founders of this party in the 1950s, was sentenced to seven years imprisonment for carrying out 'activities to cause unrest and instability'. Ma Thida, a medical doctor, short story writer and close associate of Aung San Suu Kyi, was sentenced to twenty years for contact with illegal organisations and distributing anti-SLORC leaflets (Burma Information Group 1994, pp. 4–11). Various female writers and intellectuals were also censored or banned from publication. San San Nweh, journalist, author, and poet, was detained in 1988–89 and after her release with her work banned from publication, she had to maintain her family by trading (Allott 1994, p. 78, 124). Despite these examples, the number of politically active women was relatively small compared to the number of men. In the 1990 elections of 2296 candidates, 84 were women and out of the 485 members elected fourteen were women. These results did not reflect the fact that approximately half the nation's voters were women. The fourteen elected were all from the NLD which won 80 per cent of the seats, whereas the military won only 10 per cent (Aung San Suu Kyi 1997, p. 61).

The co-founder and secretary-general of the NLD, Aung San Suu Kyi, was not among this group of fourteen women. She had been placed under house arrest in 1989 under the law that classified her as a subversive and therefore a threat to the state. Released in 1995, but constantly subjected to harassment and denigration by the military authorities, Aung San Suu Kyi nevertheless remained a powerful political figure. Her initial rapid ascendancy to political prominence owed much to her identification with her father, Aung San, so that she conformed to the traditional pattern of women's attaining power in Burma. Linking her crusade to her father's political beliefs, she said: 'I could not, as my father's daughter, remain indifferent to what was going on' (Aung San Suu Kyi 1997b, p . xiv). Elsewhere she wrote:

> My father didn't build up the Burmese army in order to oppress the people—He made many speeches where he specifically said, don't start oppressing the people just because you have weapons. You are

to serve the country. You are for the country, the country is not for
you (1991, p. 274).

During the first year of her political career she rapidly won respect in her
own right through her display of cool courage in the line of fire, her
charisma, her eloquence, her vision and her political tactics. These
strategies were based on the non-violence and civil disobedience earlier
employed by Mahatma Gandhi and Martin Luther King, concepts also
compatible with Buddhism. Waging her campaign as one of 'freedom
from fear,' she stressed the need for self-responsibility, for self-esteem
and courageous action.

Her vision for Burma was based on the universal ideals of liberalism,
humanism, and Buddhism with democracy the main goal. Utilising
traditional Burmese and Buddhist terms, she spoke of the just ruler
(*dhammaraja*) and the importance of the ruler's providing welfare and
not opposing the people's will (*avirodha*) (Gravers 1993, pp. 73–74). She
spoke also of the importance of *metta* (loving kindness) and *thissa* (truth)
as more powerful than coercion (Aung San Suu Kyi 1997, p. 17). Though
her use of such traditional terms, particularly that of *dhammaraja*, with
its suggestion of authoritarianism sits uneasily with the concept of
democracy, she explained the need to use these terms because most
Burmese people were unfamiliar with modern political terms. How she
would address the question of Burmese nationalism and the ethnic
minorities was also not clear. Nonetheless, her vision for Burma offered a
real alternative to the regimented and repressive regime of the *Tatmadaw*.

Some sceptics dismissed her as a mere woman and rationalised her
politicisation as an accident of fate but when she was awarded the Nobel
Peace Prize in 1991, they were won over. She herself had not infused the
pro-democracy movement with a feminist perspective but her gender
became an important attribute of her leadership which others noted. Her
compassion, her stance against corruption and brutality and even her
broad education stood as stark alternatives to the narrow male military
cult of power and of the violence that steadily permeated all levels of
society. Appearing as a physically frail woman, she projected a powerful
symbolic contrast to the violent and aggressive image of the military men
in power. Courageous enough to criticise General Ne Win in public, she
broke new ground by presenting a model of the fearlessness she was
promoting and transformed the feminine role from passivity to
assertiveness (Aung San Suu Kyi 1997, p. 63; May Pyone Aung 1998,
pp. 31–33).

Despite the passage of years of restriction, ongoing harassment by the
authorities, and their relentless exclusion of her from power or dialogue,

the momentum of her message was maintained mainly by her weekend public speeches from her home when crowds of several thousands would attend. Indeed, it was a measure of the success of Aung San Suu Kyi in countering the *Tatmadaw* regime that it eventually moved to establish women's organisations to counter her leadership and role model. An All Women's Affairs Committee was set up under the Ministry of Social Welfare headed by a brigadier, while General Khin Nyunt headed the Myanmar Maternal and Child Welfare Association (MMCWA). His wife was vice chairman. Beyond Rangoon, MMCWA leadership was a spousal mirror of the junta's military and political command, typical of the intense centralisation of power characteristic of the regime. Wives also were designated only by their husbands' names rather than their own. One critic referred to this trend as 'guided feminism'. She noted;

> If guided feminism means a gradual improvement of women's status, such an objective might be regarded as better than nothing. But these women's organisations are preoccupied with beauty contests, flower shows and fashion galas (May Pyone Aung 1998a).

A further indication of the generals' reaction to Aung San Suu Kyi's presence would seem to be the clause in the constitution drafted by the National Convention requiring all presidential candidates to have served in the armed forces with full combat experience. This effectively ruled out Burmese women as the comparatively few in the armed forces (an estimated 1–2 per cent or about 3000 to 4000) did not perform combat roles (Selth, personal communication, 27.5.99).

Despite the extreme conservatism of the male leaders of the regime, statistically the number of women prominent in political life in Burma remained low. The number who became members of the All Burma Students' Democratic Front in 1988 was approximately 200, compared with 2500 men among whom old attitudes changed only slowly (Ngu Wa 1998, p. 81; Khin Htay Kyu 1998, pp. 89–92; Mi Sue Pwint 1997, p. 67). The situation was no different amongst the ethnic minorities (cf. Nang Mo Ngem Hom 1998, pp. 83–86) although *Tatmadaw* terrorism served to politicise women. Overseas experience of equal opportunities for women also impressed those in exile so that there was growing awareness of the need to engage in political struggle. One Chin girl noted: 'We have to build our nation. We need to start in the family and extend to the nation. Chin women need to get education to make progress' (Van Sui Chin 1998, pp. 12–13). A Burman girl expressed a similar sentiment:

I think that nobody can deny that women suffer so much more than men under our military dictatorship; that women are doubly burdened by the restrictions of our traditional culture. If my sisters are committed, educate themselves and are provided with the same opportunities as men, my sisters and I will be able to actively and positively strive for a genuinely peaceful Burma (Khin Htay Kyu 1998, p. 93).

At the same time that women were seeing the need to get involved in radical politics, Burmese men were beginning to acknowledge the advantages of including women in the power structure. They saw how women's management, entrepreneurial and administrative skills, honed by years in managing households and bazaar finances, could be used for the wider good. They also saw the leadership potential of women. The Shan activist, Eugene Thaike Yawnghwe (1998, p. 76) argued against the empty myth of the 'imagined' superiority of men and the imposed 'inferiority' of women. However, he also stressed that,

the women of Burma must themselves break the chains of political paralysis which centuries of brain-washing have imposed [upon] them and have thus, [sic] kept them from leadership roles in public political life. They must realise that it is their exclusion from politics and public life, which has made it possible for men to make an unholy mess of everyone's life in Burma.

Conclusion (written June 1999)

Nearly two decades ago, Mi Mi Khaing wrote that Burmese women generally refrained from political and administrative activities until 'times have been critical and the need has arisen, [then] they will act, organise and associate—something which they do only with religious and national need as inspiration' (1984, p. 159). Undoubtedly Burma is experiencing such critical times. Nonetheless, although Aung San Suu Kyi stands as a powerful model of female leadership, the tactics of the *Tatmadaw* have ensured that she remains without formal power despite the overwhelming victory of the NLD in the 1990 election. Other women are being politicised, some mobilising in women's organisations, mainly on the periphery of Burma or beyond. What seems required is a national reassessment of the fundamental cultural values of Burmese society to provide new scope for women in Burma. The current climate merely entrenches asinine male arrogance as expressed in the old Burmese proverb—'Day will not break for the hen's cackle, only for the cock's crow' (*kjè ma tun hljin mou ma lin*). However, undoubtedly more people of both sexes are coming to realise that men and women should contribute equally to shaping the future. Unfortunately until the narrow male military culture that has evolved over the last four decades no longer dominates and distorts Burmese society the opportunity for this to occur in the near future seems remote.

The author wishes to acknowledge the advice of Daw Ida Pay but responsibility for the content rests with the author.

References and recommended readings

All Burma Students Democratic Front in conjunction with Alternative ASEAN Network on Burma (ALTSEAN Burma) 1997 *Burma and the Role of Women*, (revised edition) ALTSEAN Burma, Bangkok.

Apple, Betsy 1998 *School for Rape*, (revised edition) Earthrights International, United States and Thailand.

Allott, Anna J. 1994 *Inked Over, Ripped Out: Burmese Storytellers and the Censors*, Silkworm Books, Chieng Mai.

Alternative ASEAN Network on Burma (ALTSEAN Burma) 1998 *Burma: Voices of Women in the Struggle*, ALTSEAN Burma, Bangkok.

—— 1999 *Report Card The Situation of Women in Burma*, prepared for the 55th session of the United Nations Commission on Human Rights, ALTSEAN Burma, Bangkok.

Ang Chin Geok 1998 *Aung San Kyi towards a new freedom*, Prentice Hall, Sydney.

Asia Watch and The Women's Rights Project 1993 *A Modern Form of Slavery Trafficking of Burmese Women and Girls into Brothels in Thailand*, Human Rights Watch, New York, Washington, Los Angeles, London.

Aung San Suu Kyi 1991 *Freedom from Fear and Other Writings*, foreword by Vaclav Havel, ed. and introd. by Michael Aris, Penguin Books, Harmondsworth.

—— 1997 *Letters from Burma*, introd. by Fergal Keane, Penguin Books, Harmondsworth.

—— 1997a 'Opening keynote address to the NGO forum on women (Beijing August 31, 1995),' *Burma and the Role of Women*, rev. ed., All Burma Students Democatic Front in conjunction with Alternative ASEAN Network on Burma, Bangkok.

—— 1997b *The Voice of Hope—Conversations with Alan Clements*, with contributions by U Kyi Maung and U Tin U, Penguin Books, Harmondsworth.

Bray, John 1995 *Burma The Politics of Constructive Engagement*, The Royal Institute of International Affairs, London.

Burma Information Group 1994 *Women in Politics*, Burma Information Group, Silver Spring.

Cady, J. F. 1958 *A History of Modern Burma*, Cornell University Press, Ithaca.

Chelala, Dr Cesar 1998 'What's ailing Burma? The state of women and children's health,' *Burma*, vol.V, no. 2, pp. 28–37.

Clements, Alan and Kean, Leslie 1994 *Burma's Revolution of the Spirit: The Struggle for Democratic Freedom and Dignity*, Aperture Foundation, New York.

Documentation and Research Centre, All Burma Students' Democratic Front 1997 'Burma and the role of women,' *Burma and the Role of Women*, rev. ed., All Burma Students' Democratic Front in conjunction with Alternative ASEAN Network on Burma, Bangkok.

Donnison, F.S.V. 1970 *Burma*, Ernest Benn, London.

East Asia Analytical Unit 1997 *The New ASEANS Vietnam, Burma, Cambodia and Laos*, Department of Foreign Affairs, Commonwealth of Australia, Canberra.

Far Eastern Economic Review (FEER) 1977, 1990, 1998 *Asia Yearbook* FEER, Hong Kong.

Gledhill, Alan 1962 'Burmese law in the nineteenth century, with special reference to the position of women,' *Journal of World History*, vol. 7, no.1, pp. 172–93.

Gravers, Mikael 1993 *Nationalism as Political Paranoia in Burma An Essay on the Historical Practice of Power*, Nordic Institute of Asian Studies, Copenhagen.

Guyot, James F. 1989 'Burma in 1988—*Perestroika* with a military face,' *Southeast Asian Affairs*, pp. 107–133.

Hla Hla Moe, Daw 1998 'The voices of women in our struggle,' *Burma: Voices of Women in the Struggle*, ed. ALTSEAN Burma, Bangkok.

Khin Htay Kyu 1998 'A border incident,' *Burma: Voices of Women in the Struggle*, ed. ALTSEAN Burma, Bangkok.

Khin Myo Chit 1969 'Our son's Shinpyu,' *We the Burmese: Voices from Burma*, ed. Helen Trager, Frederick A. Praeger, New York.

—— 1978 *Colourful Burma*, U Thein Tan, Rangoon.

Konmari 1998 'The status of Burmese women: a comparative essay,' *Burma: Voices of Women in the Struggle*, ed. ALTSEAN Burma, Bangkok.

Lintner, Bertil 1990 *Outrage: Burma's Struggle for Democracy*, White Lotus, London and Bangkok.

—— 1997 'Paper Tiger,' *Far Eastern Economic Review*, August 7, pp. 60–61.

Luce, G. 1940 'Economic life of the early Burman,' *Journal of the Burma Research Society*, vol. 30, pt. i, April, pp. 283–337.

Malcom, Howard 1840 *Travels in the Burman Empire*, William and Robert Chambers, Edinburgh.

Maung Maung 1974 *To a Soldier Son*, U Htin Gyi, Rangoon.

Maung Maung Gyi 1983 *Burmese Political Values—the Socio-Political Roots of Authoritarianism*, Praeger, New York.

Maung, M. Ismael Khin 1990 *Estimates of Burma's Mortality, Age Structure, and Fertility, 1973–83*, Papers of the East–West Population Institute, no. 116, East–West Center, Honolulu.

―― 1997 *The Myanmar Labour Force Growth and Change, 1973–83*, Institute of Southeast Asian Studies, Occasional Paper No. 94, Singapore.

May Pyone Aung 1998 'Aung San Suu Kyi: our leader,' *Burma: Voices of Women in the Struggle*, ALTSEAN Burma, Bangkok.

―― 1998a 'Unsung heroes in an unfinished struggle,' *Bangkok Post*, 19 June.

Mi Mi Khaing 1946 *Burmese Family* Longmans, Green & Co, London, New York, Toronto.

―― 1965 'Burma: balance and harmony,' *Women in the New Asia*, ed. Barbara E. Ward, UNESCO, Paris.

―― 1984 *The World of Burmese Women*, Zed Books, London.

Mi Sue Pwint 1997 'The plight of Burmese women,' *Burma and the Role of Women*, rev. ed., All Burma Students Democratic Front in conjunction with Alternative ASEAN Network on Burma, Bangkok.

Mya Maung 1991 *The Burma Road to Poverty*, Praeger, New York.

Mya Sein, Daw 1958 'The women of Burma: a tradition of hard work and independence,' Perspective of Burma, *Atlantic Monthly*, supplement, pp. 24–27.

Nang Mo Ngem Hom 1998 'My life as a woman soldier,' *Burma: Voices of Women in the Struggle*, ed. ALTSEAN Burma, Bangkok.

Ngu Wa 1998 'A woman's struggle,' *Burma: Voices of Women in the Struggle*, ed. ALTSEAN Burma, Bangkok.

Nisbet, John 1901 *Burma under British Rule*, 2 vols, Archibold Constable, Westminster.

Seekins, Donald 1999 'Burma in 1998 little to celebrate,' *Asian Survey*, vol. 39, no.1 (January–February), pp. 12–19.

Selth, Andrew 1996 *Transforming the Tatmadaw: the Burmese Armed Forces since 1988*, Strategic and Defence Studies Centre, Research School of Pacific and Asian Studies, Australian National University, Canberra.

Shway Yoe 1882, rpt.1963 *The Burman His Life and Notions*, W.W. Norton, New York.

Silverstein, Josef ed. 1993 *The Political Legacy of Aung San*, Southeast Asia Programme, Cornell University, Ithaca.

Smith, Martin 1991 *Burma: Insurgency and the Politics of Ethnicity*, Zed Books, London.

Spiro, Melford E. 1977 *Kinship and Marriage in Burma a cultural and psychodynamic analysis*, University of California Press, Berkeley.

―― 1997 *Gender Ideology and Psychological Reality An Essay of Cultural Reproduction*, Yale University Press, New Haven.

Steinberg, David 1985 'Burma in 1984: unanswered questions, unanswered issues,' *Southeast Asian Affairs*, pp. 111–27.

Tinker, Hugh 1967 *The Union of Burma: A Study of the First Years of Independence*, 4th ed., Oxford University Press, London.

Van Sui Chin 1998 'A Chin woman's story,' *Burma: Voices of Women in the Struggle*, ed. ALTSEAN Burma, Bangkok.

Williams, Louise 1998 *Wives, Mistresses and Matriarchs: Asian Women Today*, Allen and Unwin, Sydney.

World Health Organization (WHO) 1985 *Health Care in South-East Asia*, WHO Regional Publication, South-East Asia Series No.14, New Delhi.

Yawnghwe, Eugene Thaike 1997 'The women of Burma: holding up two-thirds of the sky,' *Burma and the Role of Women*, rev. ed., All Burma Students Democratic Front in conjunction with Alternative ASEAN Network on Burma, Bangkok.

14 Re-gendering Vietnam: from militant to market socialism

Esta Ungar

Department of History
University of Western Australia

The two most pronounced changes in gender relations in modern Vietnamese history occurred in two stages. First, when the socialist system was established (in the north from 1954 and then throughout the country from 1975), and second, from 1986 to the present, when the Vietnamese Communist Party (VCP) declared a new economic program along the lines of a market economy. Born out of war with the French, Socialist Vietnam developed a state structure while at war with the USA and its client regimes in the south. It declared a socialist ideology based on reducing traditional class and gender divisions. Socialist ideology, combined with wartime policies, led to what I term below a 'de-gendering' of the economic and political sphere up to 1973. After 1973, in a period of relative peace, the state reaffirmed socialist principles, at the same time retreating from the policies of gender equality pursued earlier, particularly in the political and social spheres. In economic terms it remained committed to gender equality, especially in agricultural work at the commune level.

My argument is that a 'de-gendering' of Vietnamese society, and a partial move away from traditional Confucian values, took place in the period up to 1972 and that after the war a 're-gendering' of society began to occur. This has happened in two phases: (1) from 1975–86, the period of socialist re-unification and (2) from 1987 to the present, the period of 'market socialism'. For women the wartime period led to a de-feminisation as they took up the roles of agricultural producers and defenders of the nation at home while men responded to the military challenge by leaving home to join the army. In the aftermath of the war women were encouraged to turn their energies to restoring family life and to leave public positions to their returning men-folk. However, the return of women to more traditional roles saw little change in the scope of their economic activities.

This chapter examines the sphere of gender relations mandated by the state, with particular attention to shifts in the gender division of labour (particularly in the agricultural sector of the economy) and the relationship between the growing involvement of women in wartime economic production and their participation in politics. It then summarises other critical factors affecting women both in terms of their self-image and social roles. These factors include societal attitudes, health and education.

For the period from 1987 to the present, I argue that economic policy and related market changes have led to an increasing gap between urban and rural areas. This has led to sharply divergent trends in gender relations: on the one hand, a re-Confucianising of gender relations in the countryside and on the other, a 'bourgeoisification' in the cities. In the urban areas the trend is toward a re-feminisation of women's image, combining bourgeois 'capitalist' signs with a modified Confucian family system. I will conclude by raising potential consequences of these developments for women.

The pre-1973 period

The historical pattern of gender relations in Vietnam plays a crucial part in understanding women today. Gender relations in Vietnam bear a distinct similarity to those in China. Chinese Confucianism was adapted as the ideology of the Vietnamese nation in the fifteenth century, and the shared heritage of socialism after 1954 has strengthened these connections. Even today, gender relationships in Vietnam may generally be characterised as Confucian relationships. They are based on the superiority of the male line and the subordination of the female line within the family. Prior to the spread of socialist doctrines in the northern countryside from 1947 onward, these teachings were accepted as the natural state of human affairs. Thus, the celebrated eighteenth-century heroine of Vietnamese literature, Kieu, sells herself out of filial loyalty to redeem her father (Nguyen 1973). However the Confucian system, as it developed in Vietnam, diverged somewhat from its Chinese origins. A certain ambiguity existed between the Confucian ideal of the obedient wife and other Vietnamese traditions. The pre-Confucian custom of bilateral kinship and the right to inheritance by the female line enshrined in Vietnamese written law in the fifteenth-century disregarded Confucian dictates. Throughout history the Vietnamese kingdoms in the northern part of present-day Vietnam fended off periodic threats from China. Vietnamese heroines, like the Trung sisters, led campaigns against invaders astride their war elephants and are enshrined in temples and myths.

Up to 1947, however, women outside the urban middle and upper classes rarely learned to read and write. Peasants of either sex were generally illiterate and the Confucian ideal of patriarchal family and submissive young wife, or wives, with numerous children was the norm. Gender relations remained within rather fixed boundaries. In 1945 the VCP under a United Front ushered in a new era, defeating the French colonisers in a war which lasted from 1945 to 1954. The VCP took socialist ideology into the countryside as part of its strategy of guerrilla warfare. Ho Chi Minh, VCP leader and later president, embarked on a campaign to expand adult literacy and to educate the children of peasants and workers. The literacy movement, aided by the use of the national language written in the Roman alphabet, helped to raise the self-esteem of rural dwellers and poorer members of society. The VCP's goal was to create a 'people's army' of guerrilla troops to fight the French. Thus between 1945 and 1954 great changes were set in motion which affected every stratum of society in northern Vietnam. In terms of gender relations the combined effects of socialism and war were mooted ideologically in the Constitution of 1946 and the Marriage and Family Law of 1959.

Vietnamese traditions of stoicism in war for both males and females, coupled with the socialist promise of greater access to land and food, education and health facilities, led to a change in perceptions of gender as well as to significant changes in class relations. Socialism brought state-mandated rights for women and changes in the family organisation of agricultural labour. War, on the other hand, drew millions of men into active service and left large numbers of positions to be filled by women. Indeed, the most striking change in the situation of women since the mid-1960s has been their movement into the Vietnamese labour force outside the household.

State-mandated changes undoubtedly benefited women as well. A number of rights were proclaimed, including the stipulation in the Constitution of 1946 that 'women have the same political, economic, cultural, social and family rights as men. For equal work, they have the right to equal pay. The State protects the rights of mothers and children. The State protects marriage and the family' (Mai and Le 1976, pp. 149–50). In 1959 the first 'Law on Marriage and the Family' was promulgated. At the time, the president of the Democratic Republic of Vietnam, Ho Chi Minh, termed this law 'a revolution, an integral part of the socialist revolution' (Mai and Le 1976, p. 220). The law gave women the right to choose their own marriage partners, gave widows the right to remarry (contravening Confucian dictum and peasant custom), and guaranteed widows' rights to their children and property. Most significantly, Article 29 affirmed that 'housework is considered equivalent to productive labour.' Flying further in the face of custom, the law protected 'the rights of children born out of wedlock, their mothers, natural children and unmarried mothers, who were outcasts in the old society' (Mai and Le 1976, p. 221).

The USA's escalation of the war in Vietnam between 1965 and 1973 expanded the opportunities for women beyond the roles they had previously been accustomed to fill. For a short time from 1965 to 1972 women were swept into positions of responsibility at the same time as they moved to occupy the majority of jobs at the lower end of the occupational scale. With full wartime mobilisation in 1965, the government declared the 'three responsibilities' movement. This pushed women into positions of authority for the first time. The Vietnam Women's Union (the mass organisation representing women in the north) launched the movement in March 1965. It aimed to replace men with women in production and administrative activities, to run family affairs by way of encouraging men to join the army, and to support the front and the fighting (Mai and Le 1976, p. 258). Unlike many other countries involved in wartime mobilisation (e.g. Australia and USA during World War Two), gains made by Vietnamese women in wartime employment, particularly at the low end of the occupational scale, have continued until now. Research from the 1970s on this question, with regard to women in agriculture, concluded that socialist relations of production instituted in the 1950s outweighed wartime necessity as a factor promoting a change in women's status (Werner 1981, pp. 183–84).

As an illustration of the rapid changes that occurred after 1965, one of the principal rice-growing provinces of the north, Hai Duong, experienced a jump in the numbers of chairwomen of agricultural cooperatives—from five in 1965 to 73 in 1966 (Mai and Le 1976, p. 277). When women began to take over traditional male tasks, they came under the derisive regard of older fellow villagers. Nonetheless, women ploughed and harrowed, formerly male preserves, as well as continuing the traditional female occupations of cultivating, weeding and transplanting. As some women replaced men as village heads, they were seen as challenging the customary social order—like 'frogs jumping on the altar' (Mai and Le 1976, pp. 261–62; Eisen 1984, p. 242). In early 1967, to speed the pace of replacing absent men with women managers, the government issued a directive stipulating quotas for the hiring of women managers in direct proportion to the number of women employees in any given agricultural or industrial enterprise (Eisen 1984, pp. 247, 155–57). Between 1965 and 1967 these measures brought large numbers of women into assistant managerial positions.

Women occupied more positions of responsibility in those sectors of the workforce traditionally seen as women's domains—education, particularly in primary and lower middle schools, and health services. (Women cadres held 28 per cent of the leading posts in education and 8 per cent of those in health services) (Mai and Le 1976, pp. 279–80). The number of women workers in industry rose, according to official estimates, from 170 000 in 1965 to 500 000 in 1969, and the Women's Union rhapsodised, 'no profession—worker, teacher, engineer or physician—was closed' to women (Mai and Le 1976, p. 265). Taken overall, women's participation in the workforce between 1965 and 1973 was limited to low-level jobs, albeit over a much wider range of the employment spectrum. This was true also in the military sector, where there was a long tradition of the whole population heeding the call to arms when the country was threatened. According to Women's Union figures, women's militia and self-defence forces accounted for 41 per cent of the total forces. The militia and self-defence forces assumed responsibility for civil defence, maintaining security in the rear and repairing damage caused in bombing raids (Mai and Le 1976, p. 269).

The 1973–86 period: peace and socialism

In early 1973, however, the Paris peace talks led to a negotiated settlement that resulted in the withdrawal of USA and their allied forces from southern Vietnam. The end of the threat of aerial bombing, coupled with the withdrawal of foreign forces in the south, eased greatly the military pressure on the north. In 1975 the war ended and the re-unification of the country began. In terms of gender roles peace signalled an end to the drive to assign women to responsible positions by means of quotas. Rather, men began to return from the military in great numbers to take up the civilian jobs they had left behind. So while both men and women were freed of the previous fear of wartime death and destruction, the attention of the state and society as a whole turned toward rebuilding shattered lives and restoring infrastructure at every level. While men returned to old jobs, women did not move out of their place at the base of the economy. In fact, women's occupation of lower-level jobs remained relatively constant throughout the period, and through 1986 women formed 70–80 per cent of agricultural labour and over 46 per cent of industrial labour in state enterprises ('Woman Workforce in Vietnam' 1987, p. 5).

Did their increased prominence in the economy lead to greater involvement in management and leadership? It appears that during the period 1965–1972 when the socialist government was most committed to pushing women into management positions, women's political participation was greatest. After peaking in the early 1970s women's participation in positions of responsibility dropped markedly although this was at a level higher than the years prior to 1965. At the same time their occupation of lower-level jobs remained relatively constant in the agricultural sector while falling somewhat in state enterprises.

Political participation

To assess this situation from another perspective, it is worth looking at the political participation of women in terms of their representation in state and party bodies over the period from the late 1960s to the early 1990s. Turning first to women's representation on representative government bodies (Tables 14.1–14.4), one notes that the percentage of women in the National Assembly peaked at over 30 per cent in 1972 and 1975 after a low of 11.6 per cent in 1961. After 1975 women's representation fell below 20 per cent in 1986 where it has remained since. Overall, where figures are available, the high point of Vietnamese women's representation in government from district down to commune level was 1967. Thus, the number of women on District People's Councils doubled between 1965 and 1967 and at the commune level almost tripled. By 1986 women's representation had fallen dramatically in People's Committees at the commune and district levels—from 32.7 per cent to 8.35 per cent and 26.48 per cent to 4.9 per cent respectively.

Table 14.1:   Women in government, national level—% (number)

National	1961	1972	1975	1982	1986	1992
National Assembly deputies	11.6 (53)	30 (125–9)	32 (137)	21.7	17.7	18.4

Table 14.2:   Women in government, provincial level—% (number)

Province	1965	1972	1982	1986
Provincial Assembly deputies	22.8	34.7	22.5 (1024)	28.8 (1014)

Table 14.3:   Women in government, district level—% (number)

District	1965	1967	1972	1975	1982	1986
People's Council	20.7	44.7 (5862)	40	36.6 (4693)	23.1 (6528)	19.6 (5211)
People's Committee	—	26.5 (891)	—	13.6 (405)	5.6 (336)	4.9 (230)

Table 14.4:   Women in government, local level—% (number)

Commune	1965	1967	1972	1975	1982	1986
People's Council	16.5	46.5 (73 705)	40.87	37 (56 356)	23.6 (70 098)	19.5 (59 283)
People's Committee	—	32.7 (14 234)	—	18.5 (6012)	7.7 (1662)	8.3 (4619)

Sources: Mai Thi Tu (1976, pp. 291–92); Ha Thi Que (1978, p. 41); Werner (1981, p. 173); Thayer (1988, p. 28)

Statistics for women heads and deputy heads of ministries and offices with ministerial standing, as well as other offices, institutes and national enterprises (Table 14.5), the statistics are more difficult to compare for a number of reasons. First, for 1965 and 1972 no percentages are given. The reunification of north and south in 1976 increased the size of the government bureaucracy. The number of ministries, offices, institutes and enterprises has expanded since that time. But, it is apparent from Table 14.5 that in the decade from 1965 to 1976 the number of women in state positions jumped rapidly. This is particularly noticeable for deputy heads of various state bodies.

Table 14.5:   **Women in state leadership positions—% (number)**

	1965	1976	1982	1986
Heads of ministries and equivalent	—	—	8.1 (5)	4.8 (3)
Heads and deputy heads of ministries	(6)	(19)	—	—
Deputy heads of ministries and equiv.	—	—	4.1 (12)	4.4 (13)
Heads of government bureaux, divisions and institutes	5	37	2.9 (24)	4.2 (43)
Deputy heads of government bureaux, divisions and institutes	16	82	3.9 (97)	6.1 (154)
Directors and deputy directors of national enterprises	8	44	—	—
Directors of national enterprises	—	—	2.6 (21)	3.2 (39)
Deputy directors of national enterprises	—	—	4.8 (66)	3.5 (94)

Note: 1965 and 1976 figures for northern Vietnam only
Sources: Ha Thi Que (1978, p. 41); 'Women's Participation in State Administration and Economic Management' (1987, p. 27)

From 1982 to 1986 the number of women with the rank of minister declined from 8 per cent to just under 5 per cent. Figures for female deputy heads of state offices rose from about 4 per cent to 6 per cent in this period as did directors of national enterprises while the number of deputy directors fell from about 5 per cent to 3.5 per cent.

There is also a striking increase in women's participation in the VCP between 1965 and 1967. In 1965, the percentage of women in the party was 5.4 per cent. After the 1967 resolution urging the recruitment of women, the number rose to 25 per cent in 1973 (Eisen 1984, p. 282). However, despite the fact that the number of party members grew from one million in 1975 to 1.6 million in 1982, over 80 per cent of VCP membership was male in 1983 and the actual percentage of women in the Party had not increased (Eisen 1984, p. 252). Indeed, figures for the period 1982–86, provided by the Women's Union, give the percentage of women in the VCP as 16.47 per cent in 1982 and 16.69 per cent in 1986 (Vietnam Women's Union 1987, p. 54). On a regional level, the political reports of the Sixth Party Congress of December 1986 cited the disproportionate lack of overall party membership in the south. Yet, at the same time a number of leaders (including the female general, Nguyen Thi Dinh, and the current president and a vice-president) in the Women's Union hail from the southern part of the country. For VCP positions from 1982 to 1986 more extensive figures are available (see Table 14.6). These show a pattern of slight gains for this period.

Table 14.6: Women in Communist Party positions at the national, provincial and local levels—% (number)

	1982	1986
National level		
Central committee members	4.3 (5)	5.5 (7)
Alternates	3 (8.3)	12.2 (6)
Province level		
Members at provincial party headquarters	8.7 (143)	11 (231)
Assistant secretaries	1	1
Standing committee members	3 (14)	6.1 (33)
District level		
District party committee members	10.5 (1473)	13.4 (2534)
District party secretaries	3.3 (15)	2.9 (13)
Part standing committee members	5.1 (219)	6.8 (331)
Commune level		
Committee members	12.5 (4920)	13.3 (6075)
Secretaries	2.92 (126)	3.8 (163)
Standing committee members	4.9 (512)	4.9 (541)

Note: Sevefjord's figures (p. 20) for 1983: provincial level, 8.8%; district level, 9.6%; commune level, 11.8%

Source: 'Women's Participation in State Administration and Economic Management' (1987, p. 54.)

To give some indication of women's participation in the VCP in 1992, *Youth* magazine, the official organ of the Vietnam Youth Union, reported that 15 per cent of the delegates to its National Congress in 1992 were women out of a total of 800 official delegates. ('Doan TNCS Ho Chi Minh' 1992, p. 3) Since the Youth Union is an important channel of recruitment to the VCP, the 15 per cent figure for female representation is comparable to the 18 per cent figure for women's representation in the 1992 National Assembly.

Employment

As has been seen above, the period after 1975 witnessed a reversal in the gains made by women during the war in terms of political and administrative roles. Nevertheless, their wartime employment did stake a greater claim for female participation in more diversified occupations and at higher positions than had been the case prior to 1965. The new constitution of the Socialist Republic of Vietnam (SRV), promulgated in 1980, reiterated the principle of equality between men and women but did not erase the fact that opportunities for women were severely curtailed after 1975 (Ngo 1983, p. 2). This situation was replicated in agriculture where, following their period of greatest advancement from the mid-1960s to the mid-1970s, women's public status decreased, particularly at the commune and district levels. At the same time, their contribution to the agricultural economy remained high. According to the official statistics of the Women's Union, 'women peasants had little power over the distribution of crops' (Mai and Le 1976, p. 279). Measured by figures showing the percentage of women at commune level in the countryside, women's political status was in decline. Rates of female participation in management dropped. In the late 1960s chairwomen of co-operatives numbered 3.3 per cent, women members of managing committees numbered 18.3 per cent, while female heads of work brigades accounted for 9.65 per cent of the total (Mai and Le 1976, p. 279). Between 1976 and 1986 women presidents and vice-presidents of people's committees decreased dramatically at the commune level. Figures for co-operative heads show that in 1976 there were 1401 women heads and deputy heads while in 1984 the number had fallen to 788; on a provincial level they had increased from 6 in 1976 to 9 in 1984 (Sevefjord 1985, p. 19). Whereas in 1966 3 per cent of co-operative heads were women (in the north alone), twenty years later in 1981 for the whole country north and south, 5.1 per cent were women while 18.3 per cent were listed as deputy co-operative heads (Eisen 1984, p. 248).

A number of factors have affected women's contribution to this critical area of the economy. These include the skewing of the gender ratio by conditions of war and full military mobilisation before 1973 as well as socialist ideology giving support to greater gender equality. Official figures list women as comprising 'over 60 per cent' of the (state) agricultural workforce and as 46.5 per cent of the industrial workforce ('Woman Workforce in Vietnam' 1987, p. 5). Independent researchers working on the agricultural sector, however, put the percentage in that area significantly higher (White 1984a, p. 91). Figures released in 1980 show the agricultural workforce in the north to be 80 per cent female and for the country as a whole, 70 per cent female (*Tap chi cong san* 1980). These official figures only consider women's production in the state sector of the economy. When one includes their contribution through labour in the private sector, the results are even more striking. Official statistics by the early 1980s credit women with the 'main role in boosting household animal husbandry' (Sevefjord 1985, p. 61; Nguyen 1987, p. 1). Government figures for this period show over 90 per cent of all the vegetables and meat (poultry and pigs) for domestic consumption produced in private family plots. As in state sector agriculture, female labour accounts for the majority of cultivators.

In the period from 1981 to 1985, agriculture and forestry accounted for approximately 59.6 per cent of the national income. By 1983 approximately 73 per cent of the total population worked in these two areas. Huge numbers of able-bodied men (numbering over one million including reserves and paramilitary groups) were drawn into the army. During this period, the whole female population of working age was involved in production. The effects of this situation on family and village social structures have not been comprehensively studied but are undoubtedly profound, as is revealed by the plight of single mothers, women forestry workers and female heads-of-household (see below).

The organisation of agricultural labour from the early 1960s was based on the formation of large-scale co-operatives, combining a number of villages into communes. This was similar to Chinese rural structures under Mao but in Vietnam the co-operative system was smaller and less draconian. By the early 1970s the state sought to apply the principle of 'the scientific organisation of labour' where women, children and older persons were assigned specific repetitive tasks in kind of assembly line process for rice cultivation. This method did not raise productivity, however (Nguyen 1983). By 1979 a combination of crises in international relations and a decline in domestic production led to a series of reforms, including a system of two-way contracts which allowed peasants to sell their surplus over and above the quota due to the state. By the early 1980s the government feared a loss of control over the economy and withdrew the reforms. This situation remained in force until the VCP's sixth congress in late 1986 where, as will be described below, decentralisation of agriculture became official policy again. These changes have led, in agriculture, to renewed emphasis on the 'family farm' as the key unit of production (de Vylder and Fforde 1988; Beresford 1988).

On a theoretical level, the economic reforms since 1979 have blurred the earlier socialist division between production for the state sector and domestic production on private family plots. European and American theorists of gender issues fear that the reforms devalue the individual contribution that women's work makes to the family budget. Socialist feminist writers argue that the previously universal co-operative system favoured women more than the present system because women's labour in the co-operative was paid separately according to a system of work points. This procedure made it very clear how much a wife or mother contributed to the household budget from state sector production. The introduction of family sub-contracting, and then the newer policy of the household as the main unit of agricultural production may, by contrast, have led to changes in the economic system that devalue women's work. These writers argue that such reform measures aim to strengthen the family as the basic unit of production and will commercialise the products of family labour. Writers on gender relations further point to the potential of the new system for re-subordinating women's labour inside the family and withdrawing the separate work status women enjoyed under the system of collective farming (White 1986, pp. 143–50). With regard to women's social status these arguments assume a direct correlation between women's measurable economic value and their social value. In light of recent work on the attitudes of families and women towards family planning and other family issues, this correlation is by no means certain. In rural areas a woman's status today is governed far more by whether she is married and has a child (preferably a son), than by her economic value to the family unit. Meanwhile, the traditional practices of patrilocal residence for daughters-in-law and no inheritance of housing property for married women continued as before. As the head of the Women's Union and central committee member of the VCP, Truong My Hoa, had stated 'A woman's reproductive function is still seen as a national asset' (Truong 1994a, p. 11).

While the effects of these reforms await systematic documentation, studies to measure the status of women in the family have begun to emerge in the form of surveys on family decision-making. While these are as yet inconclusive, the changes made in the 1979 to 1982 period do not seem to have qualitatively affected the *types* of labour that women perform. Women are confined to manual labour in agriculture, forestry and industry, whereas their male counterparts are given preference in technical training and operating machinery (Eisen 1984, p. 156; Larsson and Birgegard 1985, p. 72).

Family responsibilities and women's status

Presumably in response to this situation and in preparation for the Fifth Party Congress in 1982, the Vietnam Women's Union held a seminar in 1981 on how women viewed their status. The comments of participants drew attention to major obstacles to improving women's status. These included: traditional attitudes, health (including pregnancy, high birth rate, lack of family planning, childcare), women's workload (earning a livelihood and growing food for family use) (White 1984b).

As far as attitudinal obstacles are concerned, a monograph on women in Vietnam published by the Women's Union (Mai and Le 1976) identifies several problems that arose from the 'three responsibilities' movement that began in 1965. They noted that while women's contributions could not be ignored, the reluctance to accept women's participation in the leadership and economic management of the state revealed itself in subtle ways. The first group of female chairwomen and deputy chairwomen were nicknamed '"slug commanders of snail soldiers", implying thereby that women were slow, weak and incapable' (Mai and Le 1976, p. 280). While some cadres may have shown some understanding of Party directives, when it came to actually appointing women to office, 'they proved reticent. "You have to be imaginative and resourceful to lead. That woman already has her hands full with her kids. Who would look after them?"' (Mai 1976, pp. 280–81). So went one respondent. Other cadres were too mechanical in carrying out selections and thereby discriminated against new women candidates. The director of the Women's Union cadre-training school (established in 1960), for example, expressed concern over the need to have more women cadres 'because women understand each other more clearly' (Le Thu cited in Eisen 1984, p. 241). The practice that was most deleterious to the promotion of new women's cadres and managers was the appointment of women merely to fill the quotas without any rational process of selection by male cadres. In this way, those promoted were left without help or support, often 'to handle new tasks beyond their capacity' without the benefit of additional training (Mai and Le 1976, p. 282). The latter practice, particularly, explained the swift demotion of a number of women cadres at the end of the war as well as the increasing demand by women's groups since the beginning of the 1980s for additional training for women.

In 1975 the government initiated the campaign for a 'new culture family', indicating a return to the official emphasis on the responsibilities of motherhood. This campaign called for 'equality between husband and wife, family harmony, obedient children and family planning' (Quinn-Judge 1983, p. 6). The program sent ambivalent signals, however. It raised the problems of delinquent youth and identified the cause as lack of parental supervision. This inspired the 1982 Women's Union campaign to promote better mothering and maternal education. Women were exhorted to devote more time to family life (Quinn-Judge 1983, p. 5). Although the agenda for the 'new culture family' urged men to take on more responsibility for childcare and domestic chores, implementation of the policy seemed to fall to the Women's Union, thereby implying that it remained primarily a women's issue. In the media, the policy was translated in the official women's magazine, by depicting women in softer, maternal imagery where before 1975 emphasis rested on their wartime contributions. The rhetoric of the 'new culture family' has been powerless to stem another social problem. The rising divorce rate among young couples in urban areas today causes the authorities grave concern and remains symptomatic of the economic and social malaise in the country ('Some Problems in Present-day Family Life' 1988, p. 27). The rising divorce rate adds to the number of single-parent families, many of whom are headed by women (Ungar 1994, pp. 71–72).

Problems relating to health (including the high birth rate, lack of family planning and the responsibilities of childcare) are another major area in which women are disadvantaged in comparison with their male counterparts (Allen 1993, pp. 13–17). The 1980 Constitution gave a commitment to raising the standards of women's lives and developing maternity homes, crèches and other amenities to improve their living conditions (Ngo 1983, pp. 2–3). According to the 1979 census the birth rate in Vietnam was estimated at between 2.6 and 2.8 per cent (Lam 1987, p. 325, 332). The high birth rate translated into large families. In the decade from 1965 to 1975 the average family throughout the country had six children. This rate fell to five children per family by the end of 1983 (Lam 1987, p. 329). Among rural women in particular, gendered attitudes of son-preference still provoke anxiety. The folk saying that 'ten daughters are not as good as one son' places real social pressure on married women to produce a son, however many daughters the family may already have. Another 'truism' makes the point even more strongly: 'One hundred women are not worth one testicle' (Eisen 1984, p. 19).

As economic pressures worsened in the late 1970s and early 1980s other forms of birth control such as condoms and the Pill were either unavailable or too expensive for ordinary people. Accordingly, abortion was officially sanctioned. The government further promoted programs penalising, with a reduction of rations, those families having more than two children and offered cash incentives for sterilisation. These programs have tended to be most effective in urban areas (Lam 1987, p. 326, 329). According to 1981 figures, however, 81 per cent of the population was rural while only 19 per cent was urban. As a result, the policy of limiting the birth rate had little impact in rural areas away from the major administrative centres until the early 1990s.

Use of the IUD was also encouraged as part of the government's efforts in family planning. Since hygiene is minimal due to the lack of soap, not to mention antiseptics, the frequency of complications and infection with the IUD was quite high (Lam 1987, p. 333; Sevefjord 1985, p. 17, 46). In 1985 a Swedish study on the health of female workers in a model pulp and paper mill project in Vinh Phu province in the north of the country listed pregnancy, breast feeding and sick children as key factors affecting the productivity of women workers. According to the study, 'women in general are overworked and the health starts deteriorating rapidly once they have children' (Sevefjord 1985, p. 63). Of 186 women surveyed, women with small children or pregnant women were in the poorest health, with 20 per cent of these women weighing less than 40 kgs (Sevefjord 1985, p. 46). Productivity in the factory also suffered. Absentee rates for female workers surveyed over three months in 1984 showed: 16 per cent were absent 10 days out of three months due to illness; 18.5 per cent were absent nine days on average due to sick children; and 7 per cent were off 49 days on average due to pregnancy or childbirth (Sevefjord 1985, pp. 85–86). (During this period no male workers were reported absent to take care of sick children). On this work-site the Swedish aid agency (SIDA) provided additional food rations to the workers. However, factory management policy provided extra rations only to those reporting for work each day. Therefore, any woman staying home to care for a sick child, for example, lost her food bonus. The researcher concluded that women at this site received 'additional food to a much less extent than men...due to her biological functions and responsibilities towards children' (Sevefjord 1985, p. 66). Calling attention to this general situation, Mai Thi Tu, a senior member of the Vietnam Women's Union, told an interviewer in 1981 'In factories where women are managers, the working conditions are better than when the management is all men' (Eisen 1984, p. 155). This observation appears to hold for the SIDA-supported Bai Bang project where the factory's higher echelons contained no women (Sevefjord 1985, pp. 54–56). Childcare facilities were reported to be numerous but foreign residents noted that the centres lacked equipment and food for the children (Sevefjord 1985, pp. 12–14; Larsson and Birgegard 1985, p. 25; Mai 1983, p. 66).

Women were described, and described themselves, as overworked. In a survey on 'How Much Time Is Devoted to Household Chores by Women State Employees' in 1983, the following results were noted. An average Hanoi woman working for the government, Party or a mass organisation, spent a total of 87 hours per week on office work, a supplementary income job and on household chores, of which 26.2 hours were spent on housekeeping and 6.5 hours per week on marketing. Of the sample surveyed, 'only 10 per cent of the women could take time out to study and 18.7 per cent to look after their children's schoolwork' (Eisen 1984, p. 161). A survey of factory workers in the Vinh Phu pulp and paper mill showed that women took responsibility for approximately three-quarters of the cooking, cleaning, shopping, and laundry, 50 per cent of the childcare (in addition to 16 per cent of children in crèches), almost 50 per cent raising domestic animals, and 37 per cent on family (private) food plots. In their study of a rural commune in 1979 and 1980, Belgian and Vietnamese surveyors found that women under 30 worked 12 hours per day for direct economic ends (8 hours in the co-operative and 3 hours in the garden) in addition to three or more hours in other domestic chores and childcare (Houtart et al. 1984, pp. 105–107). As mentioned above, official statistics nationally demonstrated that women played the principal role in boosting animal husbandry and cultivating vegetables on private household plots (at this time limited to 5 per cent of the household's allocation).

The heavy workload carried by women further limits the time and energy they have available to devote to leadership activities. Women who want to increase their political participation need the time to be active in various organisations, state and party. The Women's Union, the official mass organisation representing women's interests, is subordinated to the Trade Union Federation (unlike the Youth Organisation). (In each factory and state enterprise, a Women's Commission exists within the trade union governing that enterprise, and all women employees are automatically considered members) (Eisen 1984, p. 88; Sevefjord 1985, p. 51). Yet, ultimately, the work demands placed on women militate against greater political participation.

Not only do high birth-rates and workloads affect women's health, but the mortality rate also skews the population ratio and thereby places more demands on women. In the 1980s conditions of war and mobilisation, which returned after a brief hiatus of peace from 1975 to 1979, continued to affect the imbalance in the demographic structure of the population. While mortality rates were not released, official statistics in 1982 calculated the percentage of females in the total population as 51.5 per cent and the number of males at 48.5 per cent. In 1982, among those in the 25–35 age-group, 56.8 per cent were female and 43.2 per cent were male. This means that many widowed and unmarried women fell into that population cohort. Many of them had children to care for without having the added support of another working adult in the family. Considering the critical percentage of women in the agricultural and industrial workforce, it is not surprising that the government began to re-orient various policies towards women. The expanded provisions of the 1980 constitution and renewed expressions of official support for single parents appeared in 1981. Reports of the Women's Union in 1982, the Fifth Party Congress, and a new resolution on the development of women's roles in 'socialist construction and national defence' in 1984 demonstrated this new government position. *Nhan Dan* (The People's Daily) reported in 1982 that hundreds of thousands of women were single parents, and it urged those with 'feudalistic prejudices' towards unmarried mothers and their children to adopt an official attitude of 'humaneness' (cited in Sevefjord 1985, pp. 78–81). These statistics further gloss over the estimated 1.4 million disabled persons and half million orphans for whom the state lacks the resources to provide adequate care (*Los Angeles Times* October 11 1987). This burden further falls on the backs of the majority of agricultural producers in the country—women.

The period since 1986: economic liberalisation

The late 1980s marked a watershed for Vietnam in terms of socialism and the economy. The sixth VCP congress of 1986 marked the divide in Vietnamese history between the 'old' socialism and the 'new'. Previously, Vietnamese socialism, like its counterparts in the former Soviet world, relied on a centralised, command economy where private enterprise at every level was declared illegal and the state was the source of all resources for industry and development. From late 1986 with the declaration of the policy of 'renovation' (*doi moi*), however, Vietnamese socialism altered dramatically. The state introduced changes that mirrored the Open Door policy introduced in the People's Republic of China in 1978. Central to these was the development of the economy through the opening of markets to domestic and international investment. Private enterprise was encouraged in a consistent way and the state looked to growth in the agricultural and handicraft sectors to generate resources for investment and export. These policy changes led to a jump in rice production that made Vietnam a net exporter of grain for the first time in over four decades. The shift in economic policy and incentives for family production and private sale of foodstuffs led to a vastly expanded food supply for the population as a whole. Encouragement of labour-intensive light industry took precedence over the development of heavy industry (Norlund 1995), and the state looked for ways to cut administrative costs as a further boost to production.

Did these changes interrupt the trends of the early 1980s with regard to gender? As we have seen, from the late 1970s to the early 1980s women lost gains made in earlier times—for example in occupying political and administrative posts. Educated women benefited from increasing openness in social attitudes to women's roles but rural women had their opportunities narrowed as encouragement for women to remain on the farm increased. There they worked for lower wages while their men-folk began to seek work in the cities where the pay was higher. In terms of workload the burden for women was increasing as the demands for private production and the desire to increase income pushed peasants into producing new or extra crops, as well as new types of handicraft items for sale in the markets. As to health, by the late 1980s the reduction in state funding for medical services caused a decline in state-funded health services available in rural areas while better facilities became available in urban areas for patients able to pay. Standards of education have also been affected. The identification of the household as the primary unit of agricultural production, combined with the 'user pays' principle at various points in the education cycle, have reduced the education opportunities for girls in rural areas in particular. Overall, in the countryside the renewed emphasis on household production has tended to heighten the importance of the traditional family structure as a vehicle for concentrating economic benefits. At the same time the socio-economic status of rural women has declined with the falling status of agricultural labourers while the economic status of males, who could more freely go to the cities to find higher paid work, has risen. Thus, the benefits of the new economic policy have become increasingly gendered in rural areas and among industrial workers because male waged labour is more highly valued than female waged labour.

Renovating the family

As a prelude to the 'renovation' changes, the state sought to guarantee stability for women in the family. In 1986 after extensive consultation within the government, Party and the Women's Union, the government issued the 1986 Marriage and Family Law. It reiterates the principles of the 1959 law on the equal rights of spouses, the legality of only one wife, and adds that large transactions (in relations to property, for example) require the consent of both spouses. It further stipulates that children have the same rights and duties in the family—in other words daughters have equal rights with sons to inherit from their parents (Ungar 1997, p. 288). These last two rights were not mandated in earlier periods. The Women's Union has continued the push, with mixed results, to consolidate the positions held by women in the early 1980s and to broaden their role in government. In late 1988, however, assiduous efforts by the Women's Union prompted the Council of Ministers to issue Decision 163 ruling that the Women's Union representatives, from national to local levels, had to be consulted and given the opportunity to comment on draft policies and laws relating to women and children. The Women's Union welcomed this as a great victory in their efforts to aid women in the new era of renovation.

The Women's Union has argued for further commitments by government to women cadres and industrial workers. Decision 04 of July 1993 issued by the Party's Political Bureau answered calls for increases in the percentage of women cadres in government agencies, and improvements in the training of women in state bodies and mass organisations. It also noted the need for increases in the number of women cadres in state enterprises, especially those that have a significant proportion of female workers, and encouragement for gifted female scientists and managers. Moreover, it pointed out that where necessary the retirement age for such talented women could be raised to sixty (the same as for male cadres) (Vuong 1995, p. 7). More recently, the president of the Women's Union has called for between 20 and 30 per cent of all National Assembly members to women with a similar target for a number of state and party bodies (Truong 1995, p. 5).

The role of the Women's Union is itself undergoing change due to the 1986 policy of renovation. As a mass organisation in the new market-orientated era, its budget has been cut as have those of all government departments and mass organisations. These organisations have been strongly encouraged to become partially self-supporting and to seek outside funding for projects. At the same time, the 1986 change in policy direction has made more intricate the relations between the mass organisations and the state and between the mass organisations and their members. The lines of authority for the mass organisations seem to be less clear than they were under the 'old' socialist regime. These conditions make advocacy of women's issues more complicated than in the past.

The government's Open Door policy has encouraged organised action in response to important issues raised by international organisations like the United Nations. These responses have aided the Women's Union and related groups to bring into the public domain discussion of pressing matters including violence against women and children and awareness and prevention of HIV/AIDS. One outgrowth of this international contact was the National Committee for the Advancement of Women in Vietnam, with an executive board headed by the president of the Women's Union together with vice-ministers and representatives from the Ministries of Foreign Affairs, Education, Finance and others. The Women's Union, with its focus on furthering government policy on women's issues, has been joined by other state organisations having primarily a research function. State organisations, particularly professional research groups attached to the National Centre for Social Sciences, to universities, and to ministries have answered the call by government agencies as well as by foreign aid donors for new social science studies on the changing situation of women and families. Most prominent among these research groups is the Centre for Women and Family Studies based in Hanoi with a branch in Ho Chi Minh City.

In the decade since the 1986 renovation policy began, has the occupational structure changed markedly for women? According to the 1989 census, out of a total of over sixty-four million people, 75 per cent of the population live in the rural areas. Seventy to 80 per cent of all women living in rural areas are involved in agriculture or a combination of agriculture and child-rearing. In addition they are primarily involved in unskilled and un-mechanised agricultural work. The total agricultural workforce amounted to 21 102 000 people in 1988. Of these 55.4 per cent (11 692 000) were female and 44.6 per cent (9 405 500) were male. Moreover, the census figures show that the females in the highest child-bearing age bracket (ages 20–34) carry a greater share of the agricultural workload than males in the same age bracket who are involved in agricultural work.

As a result of long years of war, there is a marked gender imbalance (with more women than men) in the cohort of the population born before 1950. Large numbers of women lost their husbands during the war (see Table 14.7). Mogadham notes that this low sex ratio, with only 95 males to every 100 females, is exacerbated by male out-migration (Mogadham 1994). For the generation born after the war the gender imbalance is minimal, but the burdens continue to be heavy for their mothers and grandmothers.

The average household size, 4–5 persons per households nationally, is lower than it was in the 1960s while the average birth rate is above 2 per cent, higher than the government's target. As to family size, women, particularly in the rural areas, are still caught between the social necessity to produce a son and the often-expressed desire to limit family size to reduce the burden of childcare. In the late 1980s, for a brief period after the government declared the policy of the household as the key unit of production, many farm families sought to produce more children in order to collect the extra land. Co-operatives were allocating land for each child in the family. With the end of the land re-allocation rounds in the early 1990s the government's family planning policy, urging two-child families and IUD use for women, seems to have had a greater impact in the countryside. A definite increase in the use of contraceptives was reported for the 1992 to 1993 period—these included primarily the IUD, the Pill, and condoms. In addition abortion/menstrual regulation are widespread (UNICEF 1994, p. 32).

Table 14.7:   Widowed males and females by age cohort in 1989 (%)

Age bracket	Widowed males	Widowed females
40–44	0.9	5.7
45–49	0.7	9.0
50–54	2.9	21

Renovating the workplace

Working conditions have also altered with the drives to make state enterprises more accountable and to encourage private enterprises. State enterprises have retrenched workers and private enterprises are not following the labour policies mandated by the state for women workers. Between 1990 and 1991 about 553 000 women state workers were laid off (UNICEF 1994, p. 32). Estimates place the percentage of women state workers retrenched at 60 per cent. Many of these women have turned to the private sector for new work (Tran and Allen 1992, p. 6). Previously, women working in state enterprises had won conditions involving six months paid leave at childbirth. Because of the competitive nature of private enterprise, however, these conditions have been eroded. In response to this situation the Women's Union urged its branches to provide input into the formulation of the 1994 Labour Code, and a separate chapter of the Code was devoted to female workers (Vuong 1995, p. 7; 'Documents: 1994 Labour Code' 1995, pp. 144–48). The Labour Code regulates working conditions for women with special attention to pregnant women and mothers of infant children. These regulations extend to both state and private industry and respond to the criticism that formerly female state employees (comprising 14 per cent of the female workforce) were the principal focus of government regulation (Le 1995, p. 213). All the same, doubt about the extent of the implementation of these provisions remains. In rural industries, such as forestry, where mechanisation has increased the number of women workers has declined since the mid-1980s as mechanised labour with its higher status has tended to remain the preserve of male workers.

While the economy has improved overall, in 1995 Vietnam only had an annual per capita income of US$240. Despite this low income, health practices showed success in improving life expectancy and reducing infant mortality. Nonetheless, poverty and malnutrition remain endemic. In 1994 approximately 45 per cent of Vietnam's 14.5 million households were below the poverty level and in 1990 malnutrition was estimated at 41.8 per cent among children under five years (UNICEF 1994, p. 17, 69). These areas became further targets for the Women's Union policy

Table 14.8:   School attendance by sex for children age 10 and above in 1989 (%)

Educational level	Proportion males	Proportion females
Never attended school	7.8	16.7
Primary school	80.4	74.4
Secondary school and above	11.8	8.9

as part of a strategy by the government and international aid donors to increase income generation for women and families.

In the area of education the new farm policies giving households principal responsibility for production, coupled with the low status of daughters, has led a greater number of families keeping daughters rather than sons away from school (see Table 14.8). Thus, in 1989, according to the census, the percentage of illiterate girls was increasing and was about double that of boys. Desai (1995) notes that during the lower secondary years girls' enrolments drop by 30 per cent while those of boys drop by only 14 per cent. Given the state's commitment to rural education in the past, this trend gives real cause for concern.

Conclusion

The state policy under the 'old' socialist system was developed in a situation where the majority of the people worked in the rural sector as a stable self-sufficient farm population. The urban areas were envisioned in almost Confucian political terms as little more than state administrative centres. Nowadays, however, market changes under the new socialist policy of renovation have stimulated the growth of urban regions and created new social classes. The resultant migration to the cities, mainly by young men in search of work, has sharpened the division between rural and urban areas. Changes in land law after 1988 have intensified this gap as it is incumbent on female members of the household to stay on the farm and work the land (as well as care for the children); since land left fallow for twelve months reverts to the commune. Where husbands were once away at war, rural males now join the urban labour market for as long as possible. Clues to government views of the link between the economy and gender issues can be gleaned from state propaganda posters showing rural women in a series representing the key economic groups: peasant woman, male industrial worker, military man, and bespectacled male intellectual. The other guises in which 'woman' appears most frequently in official poster art comprise equally traditional roles—as wives in a nuclear family, in a family planning tryptich or as nurses, health-care workers or as part of anti-AIDS campaigns.

More prosperous urban women have the means to create their own modern image to some degree (Ungar 1994). Well-educated women have a wider range of occupational choices than before the late 1960s. They benefit from socialism's commitment to the work ethic for males and females alike and take full advantage of influences sweeping in from the capitalist East and West including 'open door' China and the states of the former Soviet Union. Whether these influences are totally beneficial is a point of great contention for both feminist researchers and the state. In the cities western fashions, beauty contests and pop music accompany economic prosperity, as do social problems like the growth in prostitution and drug use (a problem in some rural areas as well).

Do cosmetics and high heels signal the subversive aspect of youth culture or a protest against the poverty and the de-feminised image of the war years? Is the new image of urban 'mod' femininity an assertion of female selfhood? Or, as an older generation of socialist cadres and western feminists see it, a triumph of self-centred, bourgeois values of woman as sex object? Viewed from a Western context, is the new feminisation a backward step, an invocation of 'fifties' values? Or is it a softening of woman's image consonant with a retreat from the martial values of the wartime era and a desire to taste the fruits of peace and increased prosperity nineties style?

In the four decades since independence women in Vietnam have made great strides. Despite the strength of traditional social attitudes towards women, educated urban women have managed to retain and expand their peacetime roles in professional occupations in a society that is still 'Confucianised'. Female participation in politics, for example in the National Assembly, rivals that of their sisters in a number of Western countries. The challenge for the future lies not only in addressing the status of the new socialist 'middle class' but in improving the position of women in other sectors including urban female workers at the low end of the wage scale and the majority of their sisters down on the farm. A measure of the state's socialist commitment to advancing the status of women in the future will be whether the gains of the past are maintained in the face of the market pressures of the twenty-first century.

The author is indebted to: Drs David Marr and Terry Hull, Australian National University; Dr Christine Pelzer (White); Diana Darlington; Prof Carlyle Thayer, Asia-Pacific Centre for Security Studies (Hawaii); Professor Le Thi, Director ret., Centre For Women and Family Studies, Hanoi; and Vietnam Women's Union.

References and recommended readings

Allen, Suki 1993 'Women and health in Vietnam,' *Development Bulletin*, vol. 26, no. 1, pp. 13–17.

Australian International Development Assistance Bureau 1992 *Vietnam: A Country in Transition: Health Sector Background Study*, Australian International Development Assistance Bureau, Canberra.

Beresford, M. 1988 *Vietnam: Politics, Economics, Society*, Pinter, London.

Barry, Kathleen ed. 1996 *Vietnam's Women in Transition*, Macmillan, Houndsmill.

Dan So Viet Nam:1–10–1979 (The Vietnamese Population) 1983 Socialist Republic of Vietnam General Population Census Central Committee, Hanoi.

de Vylder, Stefan and Fforde, Adam 1988 *Vietnam—An Economy in Transition*, Swedish International Development Authority, Stockholm.

Desai, J. 1995 *Viet Nam through the lens of gender*, UNDP, Hanoi.

'Doan TNCS Ho Chi Minh-tu dai hoi V den dai hoi VI' (The Ho Chi Minh Youth Union: from the Fifth to the Sixth Congress) 1992 *Thanh nien* (Youth), vol. 11–10 to 18–10, p. 3.

'Documents: 1994 Labour Code of the Socialist Republic of Vietnam (Excerpts)' 1995 *Vietnam Social Sciences*, vol. 1, no. 45, pp. 144–48.

Eisen, A. 1984 *Women and Revolution in Vietnam*, Zed, London.

Fahey, Stephanie 1998 'Vietnam's women in the renovation era,' *Gender and Power in Affluent Asia*, eds K. Sen and M. Stivens, Routledge, London.

Goodkind, Daniel 1995 'Rising gender inequality in Vietnam since reunification,' *Pacific Affairs*, vol. 68, no. 1 (Fall), pp. 342–59.

Grace, Paul ed. 1974 *Vietnamese Women in Society and Revolution*, trans. by Ngo Vinh Long, Vietnam Resource Center, Cambridge.

Ha Thi Que 1978 'Khac phuc cac quan diem sai trai, day manh cong tac can bo nu' [To overcome incorrect viewpoints and promote the work of women cadres], *Tap chi cong san*, vol. 11, pp. 36–46.

Houtart, F. and G. Lemercinier 1984 *Hai Van: Life in a Vietnamese Commune*, Zed, London.

Kleinen, John 1999 *Facing the Future, Reviving the Past: A Study of Social Change in a North Vietnamese Village*, Institute of Southeast Asian Studies, Singapore.

Lam Thanh Liem 1987 'La planification familiale au Viet-Nam,' *Population* (Paris), vol. 42, no. 2, pp. 321–36.

Larsson, K. and L. E. Birgegard 1985 *Socio-Economic Study of Factors Influencing Labour Productivity in the Forestry Component of the Vinh Phu Pulp and Paper Mill Project in Vietnam*, Swedish International Development Authority (SIDA), Stockholm.

Le Thi 1995 'Women's labour and socio-economic status in a market-oriented economy,' *Vietnam in a Changing World*, eds I. Norlund, C. Gates et al., Curzon Press, Richmond.

Mai Thi Tu and Le Thi Nham Tuyet 1976 *Women in Vietnam*, Foreign Languages Publishing House, Hanoi.

Mai Thu Van 1983 *Vietnam: un peuple, des voix*, Pierre Horay, Paris.

Marr, D. G. 1988 'Tertiary education, research, and the information sciences in Vietnam,' *Postwar Vietnam: Dilemmas in Socialist Development*, eds D.G. Marr and C. P. White, Cornell University Southeast Asia Program, Ithaca.

Ngo Ba Thanh 1983 'The equality of Vietnamese women in fact and law,' *Women of Vietnam*, vol. 2, pp. 2–3.

Ngo Vinh Long (ed. and trans.) 1973 *Before the Revolution: Vietnamese Peasants Under the French*, Massachusetts Institute of Technology, Cambridge.

Nguyen Du [1766–1820] 1973 *Tale of Kieu*, trans. and annotated by Huynh Sanh Thong, Vintage, New York.

Nguyen Duc Nhuan 1983 'The contradictions of the rationalisation of agricultural space and work in Vietnam,' *International Journal of Urban and Regional Research*, vol. 7, pp. 363–79.

Nguyen Thi Dinh 1987 'Five years of activities of the woman (sic) movement and the Vietnam Women's Union, *Women of Vietnam*, vol. 2, p. 1.

Norlund, Irene 1995 'Vietnamese industry in transition: changes in the textile sector,' *Vietnam in a Changing World*, eds I. Norlund, C. Gates et al., Curzon Press, Richmond.

Pham Thi Mai Chi 1988 'General information on early childhood development in Vietnam.' Paper presented at the Australian Early Childhood Association Conference in Canberra, 5–8 September.

Quinn-Judge, S. 1983 'Vietnamese women: neglected promises,' *Indochina Issues*, no. 12, p. 42.

Sevefjord, B. 1985 *Women in Vietnam—Women in Bai Bang: An Evaluation of the Effects of the Bai Bang Project on the Lives of Female Workers*, Swedish International Development Authority (SIDA), Stockholm.

'Some problems in present-day family life,' 1988 *Vietnam Courier*, vol. 1, p. 27.

Tap chi cong san [Review of Communism] 1980 October.

Taylor, Sandra 1999 *Vietnamese Women at War: Fighting for Ho Chi Minh and the Revolution*, University of Kansas Press, Lawrence.

Thayer, C.A. 1988 'The state in Vietnam,' draft chapter.

Tran Thi Que and Suki Allen 1992 *Vietnam: Country Gender Analysis*, Swedish International Development Authority (SIDA), Stockholm.

Truong My Hoa 1994a 'A woman's reproductive function is still seen as a national asset,' *Far Eastern Economic Review*, September 8, p. 11.

—— 1994b 'Building on the Vietnamese women's tradition of building and defending the country in the present renovation,' *Women of Vietnam*, vol. 4, pp. 2–3.

—— 1995 'Strategy for the advancement of women,' *Women of Vietnam*, September, pp. 4–5.

Tuong Lai ed. 1991 *Sociological Studies on the Vietnamese Family*, Social Sciences Publishing House, Hanoi.

Ungar, E.S. 1994 'Gender, land and household in Vietnam,' *Asian Studies Association of Australia Review*, vol. 17, no. 3, pp. 61–72.

—— 1997 'Gender and real property in Vietnamese law and practice: commune, household and individual,' *Asian Laws Through Australian Eyes*, ed. Veronica Taylor, Law Book Company, Sydney.

UNICEF 1994 *Situation Analysis of Women and Children in Vietnam*, UNICEF, Hanoi.

'Vietnam: directive on woman cadre-related work issued,' 1994 *BBC Summary of World Broadcasts, Asia-Pacific*, 6/6.

Viet Nam Intercensal Demographic Survey 1994 *Major Findings*, Statistical Publishing House, Hanoi.

Vietnam Social Sciences: Bimonthly Review, 1995 (Special Issue on Vietnamese Women), vol. 1, no. 45.

Vietnam Women's Union 1987 *Bao cao dai hoi phu nu Viet Nam lan thu 6* (Report of the 6th national congress of the Vietnam women's union), Vietnam Women's Union, Hanoi.

Moghadam, V.M. 1994 *Market Reforms and Women Workers in Vietnam: A Case Study of Hanoi and Ho Chi Minh City*, UNU/WIDER Working Papers no. 116, UNU/WIDER, Helsinki.

Nordic Institute of Asian Studies 1999a *The Vietnamese Family in Change: the Case of the Red River Delta*, Curzon, London.

—— 1999b *Women's Bodies, Women's Worries: Health and Family Planning in a Vietnamese Rural Commune*, Curzon, London.

Viet Trang 1988 'Healthcare for children in rural areas,' *Women of Vietnam*, vol. 2, p. 2.

Visvanathan, Nalini, Lynn Duggan et al. eds. 1997 *Women, Gender and Development Reader*, Zed, London.

Vuong Thi Hanh 1995 'Activities for women's equality and development by Vietnam's Women's Union,' *Women of Vietnam*, September, pp. 5–7.

Wiegersma, Nancy 1988 *Vietnam—peasant land, peasant revolution: patriarchy and collectivity in the rural economy*, St Martin's Press, New York.

Werner, J. 1981 'Women, socialism and the economy of wartime North Vietnam 1960–1975,' *Studies In Comparative Communism*, vol. 14, nos 2–3, pp. 165–90.

White, C. P. 1982 'Socialist transformation of agriculture and gender relations: the Vietnamese case,' *Institute of Development Studies [IDS] Bulletin*, vol. 13, no. 4, pp. 44–51.

—— 1984a *The Role of Collective Agriculture in Rural Development: The Vietnamese Case*, Research Report, ODA, ESCOR Research Scheme 3592, Institute of Development Studies at the University of Sussex, Sussex, December.

—— 1984b 'Women, employment and the family: report on a colloquium comparing the women's movement and government legislation for gender equality in Britain and Vietnam,' *IDS Bulletin*, vol. 15, no. 1, pp. 57–61.

—— 1986 'Deux Modeles pour la transformation socialiste de l'agriculture: leurs consequences sur les relations entre sexes,' (Two models for the socialist transformation of agriculture: the consequences for gender relations), *Revue Tiers Monde*, vol. 27, no. 105, pp. 143–50.

'Women's participation in state administration and economic management,' 1987 *Women of Vietnam*, no. 4, p. 27.

'Woman workforce in Vietnam,' 1987 *Women of Vietnam*, no. 2, p. 5.

Index

Abdurachman Wahid, 156
abortion, 174, 220, 232, 254, 257, 280, 310
Aceh, 161
agriculture and women's labour, 10, 20, 28–30, 70, 91–3, 153–4, 256, 268, 274, 291–2, 295, 296, 300, 307, 308, 310, 312
All Burma Students' Democratic Front, 285
All China Women's Federation, 5, 64–8, 76, 79–80
All Women's Affairs Committee, 285
Amein Rais, 156
androgyny, 5, 81
Anti Fascist People's Freedom League (AFPFL), 283
Anwar Ibrahim, 3, 16
Asia-Pacific Economic Cooperation (APEC), 3, 7
Aquino, Benigno, 118, 122
Aquino, Corazon, 10, 118–19
Arenas, Rosemarie, 117
Asian values, 4, 18, 46
Association for the Advancement of Feminism, 197, 202, 204
Association for the Promotion of the Status of Women, 252
Association for Southeast Asian Nations (ASEAN), 278
Association of Women for Action and Research, 52–3
Aung San, 271, 272, 277, 283
Aung San Suu Kyi, 10, 13, 266, 276–7, 283, 284, 285
Awakening Society, 239–40

Ba Maw Chain, 272
Balabagan, Sara, 130
Bali, 143, 150, 156, 224
beauty contests, 67–8, 120, 285, 313
Beijing conference, see Fourth conference on women

bigamy, see also polygyny, polygamy, 260
birth control, see contraception, population, demographic changes
Brahman vs Subaltern, 88–9, 94
bride price, see also dowry, 94, 250

caste system, 88–90, 98, 101–2
Convention on the Elimination of Discrimination against Women (CEDAW), 3, 6–7, 66, 151, 159, 200, 203, 215
Central Women's Committee, 243
Centre for Women's Development Studies, 91
Centre for Women and Family Studies, 310
Chen Muhua, 68
Chiang, Claire, 40
childcare, 133, 210, 238
    responsibilities for women, 27, 195, 304, 305
    leave from work, 50, 305
children,
    as prestige for women, 302
    delinquency and, 303, 313
    protection laws, 308
Chipko movement, 92
Cho Cho Kyaw Nyein, 283
citizenship rights and gender, 49–50, 61, 141, 159, 162
civil society, see also human rights, 63, 67, 163
class status, 20–24, 85, 89–90, 101–2, 163, 251
    occupation and, 21
clothing, see also Mao suit, veil, 164, 313
Coalition of Indonesian Women for Justice and Democracy, 140, 161, 163
colonial legacies, 20, 86, 90, 91, 98, 103, 189, 270–1, 291–3

'comfort' women, 183
communes, agricultural, 301
communism, communist, 5, 59–60, 64–8, 91, 121, 291, 293
   women in Chinese Communist Party, 68–70
   women in Vietnam Communist Party, 298–9
Confucianism, 8, 9, 171, 173–4, 189, 230, 231, 249, 250, 292–3, 294, 313
Congressional Spouses Foundation, 117
conjugal dictatorship, 115–16
constitutions, 49–50, 61, 80–1, 86, 91, 98, 104, 132, 148, 151, 154, 159, 211, 239, 248, 252, 270–1, 293–4, 304
consumers, women as, 81, 154, 164, 221–2
Contemplacíon, Flor, 10, 11, 129–30
contraception, see also population, abortion, demographic changes, 8, 73–7, 149, 156, 173–4, 213, 253, 304–5, 310
Council of Women in Burma, 272
Cultural Revolution, 59, 65, 67, 77
Cyborg women, 224

de Venecia, Gina, 117
Declaration on the Elimination of Violence against Women (DEVAW), 3, 6–7,
Democratic Progressive Party (DPP), 241
demographic changes, see also population, 26–7, 40, 88, 190–1, 304, 310
Deng Yingchao, 68
development,
   as gendered, 1–4, 18, 19–20, 64
   narrative, use of by women, 2, 230
Dharma Wanita, 14, 142, 148, 162, 163
diaspora, Filipino, 113–14, 128–9
divorce, 26, 61, 133, 146–7, 175, 190–1, 251, 259–60, 304
doi moi, 307, 308, 310, 312
Doi Takako, 219

domestic violence, see violence against women, rape
domestic labour, 70, 81, 176–7, 249, 294, 305–6
   maids, 20, 28–9, 114, 124–5, 201, 238
   professional housewives, 209–10, 238
double-burden, 27–8, 47, 81, 134, 217, 238, 302, 303, 305–6
dowry, see also bride price, 93–4

economic crisis 1997, 17, 18, 105, 150, 152, 157–8, 178–9, 258
economic growth, 18, 62, 105, 148, 150, 164, 176, 229, 248, 266, 274, 277
education, 24–5, 40–1, 47, 52, 76–8, 125, 191–2, 211, 261, 270, 273, 279, 312
   gender and course of study, 24–5, 41, 192, 212, 232–5
   gender and enrolment rates, 24, 78, 149, 150, 179–80, 192, 211–12, 232–3, 255–6, 308
   of children as mothers' role, 211
   to increase status, 8, 171, 179–81
employment, see labour
Enrile, Juan Ponce, 118
environmentalism, 92–3
Equal Opportunity Laws (EOL/EEO), 8, 45, 49, 63–4, 66–7, 86, 148, 154, 170, 176, 179, 200, 203, 208, 214–6, 221, 237
ethnicity, ethnic minorities, 18, 21–22, 26, 85, 140, 164, 266, 267, 281, 282, 284, 285–6

factory work and women, 19, 20, 23, 71, 127, 150–1, 176–9, 193–4, 235, 257–8, 300
family, 25–8, 171–2, 302, 303, 308
   'Asian family', 11, 25–6
   nation as family, 141–2, 145, 162
   'new culture' family, 304
female infanticide, 7, 74–6, 86–7, 107
feminism, see also women's studies, womanism, 31–2, 52–4, 79–81, 239–40

and class differences, 90, 101–2
as globalisation, 3, 116–7, 164
Western vs Asian, 3–5, 14, 79–80,
    120, 123–4, 182–3, 200–1,
    220–1, 240–1, 285
footbinding, 189
'four self's movement', 67
Fourth world conference on women,
    Beijing, 6, 63, 154, 203
Free Movement of New Women
    (MAKIBAKA), 120–1

GABRIELA, 123
Gender Development Research
    Institute, 253
gender narratives, 2–3, 5, 59–60
Goh Chok Tong, 39, 47, 48
Graduate Mother Scheme, 14
Great Leap Forward, 61, 70
Great Marriage Debate, 14, 47, 51–2
Green Revolution, 152–3

Habibie, B.J., 161, 162
health, infant, see also maternal health
    149, 273–4, 279, 311
HIV/AIDs, 73, 157, 252, 255, 258–9,
    280–1, 309, 313
Ho Chi-minh, 293, 294
Hong Kong Council of Women, 201
Hong Kong Women's Christian
    Council, 202–3
Hong Kong Women Workers
    Association, 203
Hpoun (nobility of manhood), 269
Hu, Richard, 48
human rights, see also civil society, 3,
    7, 121, 162, 163, 253, 278, 283,
    285

International Labour Organisation
    (ILO), 151, 164
International Monetary Fund, 179
International Women's Year/Decade,
    6, 201, 220–1, 241, 252
Internet, 13, 31, 68
Islamic Law, 26, 30, 31, 33, 34, 44

Japayukis, 123, 124, 129–31
Java, 143, 146, 150

Jiang Qing, 68

KaPaPa, 122–3
Khin Kyi, 272
Kinship, see also family
    patterns, 26, 142–6, 250–1, 308
    and politics, 113, 115–20
Kim Mo-im, 181
Korean Women's Associations United,
    (KWAU), 184
Korean Women's Development
    Institute, 181
Korean Women's Hotline, 184–5
Kuo-min-tang (KMT/GMD), see also
    Nationalist Party, 240, 242

labour, see also agriculture, factories,
    managers, work conditions,
    labour force participation rates
        (LFPR), 20–4, 41–4, 46–7, 72,
        87–8, 124–6, 153–4, 159, 176–
        9, 192–3, 235–7, 256–7, 274,
        299–302, 310–12
    labour rights and activism, 14, 71,
        93, 151–2, 179, 306
    married women and, 177–8, 193,
        208, 215, 235
    part-time, full-time, 216–7
land rights, see property rights
language and gender, 159–60, 293
Lee Kuan Yew, 13–14, 47, 49, 51
Lee, Jennifer, 40
Lee In-ho, 181
legal cases, 92, 95–7, 132
Legarda, Loren, 119
Li Xiaojiang, 79, 80
Lim Hwee Hua, 40
Lin Biao, 68
literacy rates, 77, 87, 255, 293
Liu Hsiu-lien, 240

M-Curve, 177, 215, 217
Macapagal, Gloria, 119
Mahathir Mohamad, 3, 4, 16, 17
Mahila Mangal Dal, 92
'mail-order brides', 114, 124, 131–2,
    135
managers, women as, 126–7, 237, 295,
    296, 298, 300

Mathura, 96–7
Mao suit, 68, 81
Mao Zedong, 62, 68, 116, 301
Marcos, Imelda, 10, 113, 115–16, 119, 122, 132
Marriage, see also labour and married women, 93–4, 134, 146–8, 172–3, 211, 250–1
  age at marriage, 173, 190, 213, 260
  free choice vs arranged, 26, 158, 172
  marriage laws, 61, 146, 259–60, 293, 294, 308
  polygyny, polygamy, concubinage, see also bigamy, 27, 44, 45, 52, 148, 201, 308
  secular vs religious, 146–7
Marsinah, 14, 151–2
Marxism, 60–1, 79–81
masculinity, men, 244, 265–6, 271
maternal health, 74, 149, 150, 254, 279, 302, 305, 306, 308, 311
maternity leave, 50, 61, 237
matrilineality, matrilocality, 142–4, 250
medical benefits, gender discrimination, 48–9
Megawati Sukarnoputri, 10, 155
middle class, rise of, 18, 141, 154, 163
military, women's participation in, see also Tatmadaw, 272, 274, 293, 295
Minangkabau, 143
Ministry of Women's Affairs, 159–60, 162, 163
modernity,
  non-Western, 3, 12
  vs tradition, problematic nature, 19
moral power of women, 113, 122
mothering/motherhood, 8, 113–14, 124–5, 132, 171, 176–7, 243, 303
Muslim Women's Bill, 101
Mya Sein, 271
Myanmar, 276
Myanmar Maternal and Child Welfare Association (MMCWA), 285
Myanmar Women's Entrepreneurial Association, 278

Nairobi Conference on Women, 159

National Commission for Women's Affairs (NCWA), 248, 252, 254, 257, 260
National Committee for the Advancement of Women in Vietnam, 309
National Council of Women, 251
National Council of Women's Organisations, 31
National Council on the Integration of Women in Development, 24
National League for Democracy (NLD), 276–7, 283
Nationalist Party, see also Kuo-min-tang, 60
nationalism, 51–2, 270–1, 284
  national identity and women, 4, 91, 99, 103, 120, 142, 182
  women's paid work as national duty, 70, 177, 215
Ne Win, 272, 275, 276, 277, 278, 279, 284
Neo, Lily, 40
New Economic Policy, 18, 105–6
New Order, 14, 139–41, 146, 148–9, 151, 152, 160, 162, 164
Nguyen Thi Dinh, 298
nuns, see also thilashin, 121–22

One Child Family policy, 73–6
Open Door policy, 62, 69, 266, 277, 278, 307, 309, 313
Overseas Contract Workers, see also domestic labour, Japayukis, sex work, 127–8, 152, 161–2, 258

Palma, Cecilia Muñoz, 119
Panchaya, 92, 104–5
patrilineal, patrilocality, 142–4, 302
peasant-women, see agriculture
Pibul Songgram, 251
Planas, Carmen, 115
political power and women, 40, 68–70, 104–5, 115–20, 154–6, 181–2, 196–7, 203, 217–21, 239, 258, 269–71, 275, 283, 295, 296–8, 309
  electoral support, 218
  quotas for women, 104–5, 239, 303

unofficial power, 11, 15, 113–20, 123–4, 145, 269–70
polluting effects of women, 268
pornography, *manga*, 224
population, see also contraception, birth control, demographic change, government plans, 73–6, 147, 149, 156, 173, 231, 253–4
growth rates, 73–4, 172, 190, 213, 230–1, 253–4, 267
Presidential Commission on Women's Affairs, 181
prestige and femininity, 145
property rights, 20, 30, 42, 61, 94, 132–3, 175, 189, 203, 250, 267–8, 294, 302, 308
prostitution, see sex work

Ramos, Fidel, 113, 117, 118
Ratna Sarumpaet, 151
rape, 4, 6, 60, 90, 96–8, 133, 140, 151, 161, 184–5, 199–200, 260, 281, 282
reformasi,
Indonesia, 14, 139, 141
Malaysia, 3, 16, 31
refugees, 282
religion, and women, 30–32, 86
Buddhism, 13, 249–50, 265, 269, 282, 284
Christianity, 89, 202–3, 272
communal tensions, Hindu–Muslim, 5, 98–102
fundamentalism, 98, 103
Hinduism, 88–9, 268
Islam, 16, 30, 31, 89, 155–6, 164
Renana Jhabvala, 93
'renovation' see *doi moi*
Research Centre for Women's Studies, 91
Roop Kanwar, 101–2
rural women, see agriculture

San San Win, 282
Sanda Win, 278
Sanskritisation, 89
Santiago, Miriam Defensor, 113
Sati, 101–2
Saya Kin, 269

Self Employed Women's Association (SEWA), 93
sex-ratios at birth, see also son-preference, 75–6, 86–7, 107, 175
sex work, 123, 129–31, 156–8, 184, 189, 201, 208, 224–5, 258, 279, 280–1, 313
sex tourism, 123, 127–8, 224–5
sexual harassment, 90, 133, 199
sexuality and personal freedom, 156, 174, 183–4
sexually transmitted diseases (STDs), see also HIV/AIDS, 157, 254–5
Shah Bano, 99–101
Shahani, Leticia, 120
Shin Nakyun, 181
Shin Saw Pyu, Queen, 268
single-parent families, 172, 175–6, 211, 258, 260–1, 294, 301, 306–7
Sisters of Islam, 31
Siti Hardianti Rukmana, Tutut, 155
Social Democratic Party of Japan, 219
socialism and women, 63, 291, 292, 300, 301–2, 307, 313
Soin, Kanwaljit, 53
son-preference, 8, 74–5, 173–5, 189, 231–2, 248, 302, 304
spiritual power vs economic power, 145
State Law and Order Restoration Council (SLORC), 13, 276, 277, 278, 279, 282
State Peace and Development Council (SPDC), 278
structural adjustment programs, 105–6
Suharto, Mrs, 10
Suharto, President, 139, 155, 160, 161, 162, 163, 164
Sulawesi, 142–4, 157
Sumatra, 143–4

Tale of Kieu, 293
Tan, Sr Christine, 122
Tatmadaw (armed forces), 265, 266, 272, 276, 277, 282, 285, 286
Thanpuying La-iad, 251
thilashins (nuns), 269, 275
Three Responsibilities Movement, 302–3

Timor, 150, 161
Tin U, 278
Trade Union Federation, 306
'traditional' woman, 19, 267
  challenged by 'modernity', 2, 170–
    1, 197–8, 204
trafficking in women and girls, 7, 76,
    133, 157, 225, 258–9, 279, 280
Trung sisters, 293
Truong My Hoa, 302

unemployment, 78, 178–9, 193
United Nations, 3, 6–7, 45, 62, 66, 116,
    159, 164, 201, 221, 229, 241̓, 252,
    282

veil, 3, 5, 12, 19, 31
Vietnam Women's Union, 294, 300,
    302, 303, 306, 308, 309, 311–2
Violence against Women (VAW), see
    also rape, 4, 26, 60, 90, 98, 114,
    122–3, 129–32, 133, 152, 157,
    160–1, 163, 183, 184–6, 198–200,
    239, 260

wage differentials and gender, 42–3,
    72, 125–6, 176, 195, 257
Wan Azizah Wan Ismail, 3, 10, 11, 16
war, 13, 120, 220, 281
  expanding roles for women in,
    291–3, 294, 301
War-on-Rape Campaign, 199–200
We Burmans Society (*Dobama Asi-
    ayone*), 271
welfare, 272, 275
  Mother–Child Welfare Act, 175–6
  Working Women's Welfare Law,
    215
widows, 175, 272, 294, 306, 310
womanism, see also feminism, 14, 31,
    79–80, 200–1, 218–9, 239–41
Women for the Mother Country, 115
Women for the Ouster of Marcos
    (WOMB), 122
Women Lawyers Association of
    Thailand (WLAT), 252
Women's Charter, 44–6
Women's Culture Club, 251

Women's Development Plan, 252
Women's Law, 66, 69
Women's Studies, 66, 79–81, 241–2,
    309–10
Women's Solidarity for Human Rights,
    152, 161
Wong, Aline 40
work and employment, see labour
work conditions, 71, 178, 257, 311
World Wide Web, see internet

Ye Qun, 68
Yee Shoon, Yu-Foo, 40
youth activism, 139
Youth Union, 299, 306

Zhou Enlai, 68

Resources on the World Wide Web

Visit the *Women in Asia: Tradition, Modernity and Globalisation* web-page for direct links to the sites listed below. This web-page is regularly monitored to update links.

http://www.mcauley.acu.edu.au/womenasia/index.html

Asia general

Global List of Women's Organisations—
    http://www.euronet.nl/~fullmoon/womlist/womlist.html#c
ISIS International—http://www.isiswomen.org
Southeast Asia Women Studies Bibliography—
    http://www.lib.berkeley.edu/SSEAL/SoutheastAsia/seatabl.html
Women Connect Asia—
    http://www.WOMEN-CONNECT-ASIA.com/hotlinks.htm
UNESCAP Discussion Paper on Women in Asia 1998—
    http://www.unescap.org/theme/part2v.htm

International organisations

Asia-Pacific Economic Co-operation (APEC)—
    http://www.apecsec.org.sg/workgroup/gender.html
International Labour Organisation—
    http://www.ilo.org/public/english/140femme/index.htm
Statistics and Indicators on the World's Women—
    http://www.un.org/Depts/unsd/gender/intro.htm
United Nations— http://www.un.org/womenwatch/
    UNIFEM—http://www.unifem-eseasia.org/
    UNDP—http://www.undp.org/gender/
World Bank GenderNet—http://www.worldbank.org/html/prmge/index.htm

Burma

Burma Project of the Open Society—http://www.soros.org/burma.html
Burma Women's Studies Bibliography—
    http://www.lib.berkeley.edu/SSEAL/SoutheastAsia/seaburm.html

China

New Women in China—http://sun.ihep.ac.cn/women/cwomen.html
World Bank China Country Gender Profile—
　　http://www.worldbank.org/html/prmge/info/china.htm
Women's Organisations in China—
　　http://www.euronet.nl/~fullmoon/womlist/countries/china.html

Hong Kong

Gender Research Program—http://www.cuhk.edu.hk/hkiaps/GENDER/gen.htm
Equal Opportunity Commission—http://www.eoc.org.hk/
　　(in Chinese and English)
Women Services Resource Page—http://women.socialnet.org.hk
　　(in Chinese and English)

India

Government of India—http://india.indiagov.org/social/menu.htm
South Asia Women's Network—
　　http://www.umiacs.umd.edu/users/sawweb/sawnet/internet.html
World Bank India Country Gender Profile—
　　http://www.worldbank.org/html/prmge/info/india.htm

Indonesia

Badan Pusat Statistik, Republik Indonesia (Statistics Indonesia)—
　　http://www.bps.go.id/index.html
Clearinghouse for Women and Development—http://www.pdii.lipi.go.id
　　(Indonesian)
World Bank Indonesia Country Gender Profile—
　　http://www.worldbank.org/html/prmge/info/indone.htm

Japan

Chronology 1945-1995 by Yoshino Yuko—
　　http://www.jca.ax.apc.org/~yuko_y/chron.html (Japanese)
Gender Information Site, Office of the Prime Minister—
　　http://www.sorifu.go.jp/danjyo/index2.html
National Women's Education Centre—

http://www.nwec.go.jp/Kaikan/center/center.html (Japanese)
Voice of Women Wide Web, Women's Studies Society—
    http://www.jca.ax.apc.org/wssj/ (Japanese)
Women's Studies, Nara Women's University—
    http://www.lib.nara-wu.ac.jp/josepage.htm (Japanese)
Women's Studies Page—
    http://www.yahoo.co.jp/text/Social_Science/Women_s_Studies/ (Japanese)

Korea

Ewha Woman's University—http://ews.ewha.ac.kr:8081/ews/eng/index.html
Korean Women's Association United—http://www.women21.or.kr
    (Korean and English)
Korean Women Workers Association United—
    http://www.kwwnet.org (Korean and English)
Korean Council for Women Drafted for Military Sexual Slavery by Japan—
    http://witness.peacenet.or.kr (Korean and English)
Women's Hotline—http://hotline.peacenet.or.kr (Korean and English)

Malaysia

FemiNet Malaysia—http://ideal.upm.edu.my/~gansl/FemiNet/main.html
HAWA Bahagian Hah Ehwal Wanita—http://www.kempadu.gov.my/hawa
    (Malay and English)
Women's Institute of Management (WIM)—http://www.jaring.my/wimnet/
Women & Human Resource Studies Unit, Universiti Sains Malaysia—
    http://www.usm.my/women/
World Bank Malaysia Country Gender Profile—
    http://www.worldbank.org/html/prmge/info/malays.htm

Philippines

GABRIELA: National alliance of women's organisations—
    http://members.tripod.com/~gabriela_p/
National Council of Women of the Philippines—
    http://www.kababaihan.org/wewatch98/agenda/ncwp.htm
Philippines Women's Studies Bibliography—
    http://www.lib.berkeley.edu/SSEAL/SoutheastAsia/seaphil.html
Philippines Women's Organisations—
    http://www.euronet.nl/~fullmoon/womlist/countries/philippines.html

World Bank Philippines Country Gender Profile—
      http://www.worldbank.org/html/prmge/info/philip.htm

Singapore

Association for Women's Action and Research—http://www.aware.org.sg/
Centre for Environment, Gender and Development—http://www.engender.org.sg/
Singapore, The National Web-site—http://www.sg/

Taiwan

Statistics on Social & Political Participation of Women—
      http://www.taipei.org/info/98html/s-women.htm
Women's Research Program, Population & Gender Studies, NTU—
      http://www-ms.cc.ntu.edu.tw/~wrp/

Thailand

Mahidol University, Instit for Population & Social Research—
      http://www.mahidol.ac.th/mahidol/pr/pr.html
Ministry of Public Health—http://www.moph.go.th/ (Thai and English)
National Statistical Office—http://www.nso.go.th/ (Thai and English)
Office of National Economic and Social Development Board—
      http://www.nesdb.go.th/ (Thai and English)
World Bank Thailand Country Gender Profile—
      http://www.worldbank.org/html/prmge/info/thaila.htm

Vietnam

Vietnam Women's Studies Bibliography—
      http://www.lib.berkeley.edu/SSEAL/SoutheastAsia/seaviet.html
Women's Organisations in Vietnam—
      http://www.euronet.nl/~fullmoon/womlist/countries/vietnam.html
World Bank Vietnam Country Gender Profile—
      http://www.worldbank.org/html/prmge/info/vietna.htm

For Product Safety Concerns and Information please contact our EU
representative GPSR@taylorandfrancis.com Taylor & Francis Verlag GmbH,
Kaufingerstraße 24, 80331 München, Germany

Printed and bound by CPI Group (UK) Ltd, Croydon, CR0 4YY
14/04/2025
01844622-0001